High School Basketball on Maryland's Eastern Shore: *A Shore Hoops History*

MITCHELL NORTHAM

Copyright © 2022 Mitchell Northam

All rights reserved.

No part of this publication may be reproduced, stored or transmitted in any form or by any means, electronic, mechanical, photocopying, recording, scanning, or otherwise without written permission from the publisher. It is illegal to copy this book, post it to a website, or distribute it by any other means without permission.

Mitchell Northam asserts the moral right to be identified as the author of this work.

FIRST EDITION

ISBN: 979-8-9856254-0-0

For Mom and Dad.

For the 754.

And for anyone who has ever played, coached, watched or loved high school basketball on the Eastern Shore of Maryland.

CONTENTS

3 - Introduction

8 - Beginnings, with May Brooks and Ed Walter

18 - Bad Luck for the Boys

21 - Dick Dehart and the Tourist Town Squad

29 - The Shore's Overlooked Black High Schools

42 - Lambert's Seahawks

46 - Colonel, Pocomoke and the 1976 All-Shore Final

64 - Brenda Jones, A Modern-Era Winner at Snow Hill

75 - A Gem, a Star and a Warrior: Gail Tatterson Gladding

90 - The Lessons of Greg Bozman

102 - Mills, Miller and the Perfect Eagles

116 - Sherron Mills: One of the GOATs

123 - More Than a Coach: Allen Miller

129 - Tia and Barb

153 - Kelley Gibson: A Real Role Model for Easton

171 - The Man, Shooter Collins, And Triple Overtime

190 - Grayson Hurley: A Big Man with a Big Heart

201 - Rams on Parade

212 - Carlton Dotson: The Fallen Star

231 - Andre Collins: The Kid from Crisfield

245 - Winning, the Butch Waller Way

275 - An Oral History of Perfection: The 2002 Wi-Hi Indians

301 - 2003 Bennett, The Unlikely Champions

310 - David Byrd's Title Town

332 - Coaching Angry

340 - Pocomoke Flow

349 - Keve Aluma: From the Soccer Pitch to Blacksburg

370 - Best of the Rest

382 - Acknowledgements

384 - Sources

"Basketball is my love and passion. As long as I can remember – they got pictures of me when I was 3, shooting hoops." – Jamaal King Jr.

"I just think there's a special excitement around it. In the early days, it was covered more. It was what was going on here, on the Eastern Shore, in the winter. It was in every newspaper, on every TV station." – David Byrd

"Sports are co-curricular. The basketball court is a classroom. There's so much stuff there that you learn about life. And that's what kids remember." – Butch Waller

"Basketball reaches our Black males. It steers them in a different direction." – Nick Purnell

"I always did love basketball." – Hanee Camper

"There's some history here that we don't want to lose. We want to keep it so that future generations will know some of the great players that came up… Basketball on the Eastern Shore has been amazing." – Paul Butler

---

"I just wanted to see something new every day, and write a story with it." – Gus Haynes

FOREWORD

BY: PAUL BUTLER

You probably have fond memories of the first basketball game you went to as a kid, whether it was high school, college or the pros.

As an Eastern Shore of Maryland native, I certainly remember my initial experience at a Wicomico High basketball game.

The year was 1973. I remember being bundled up in a huge coat on that chilly January night as my dad, mom, brother Brian and sister Monica entered the Wi-Hi gym. My brother and I were already making a name for ourselves as basketball players at the local Salvation Army Boys Club. I was 11-years-old at the time, Brian was 8 and we were so excited to see the "big boys" play.

If I were to tell you that the gymnasium was packed, that would certainly be an understatement. That night, Wi-Hi and their "Big 3" of Harris Strozier, Marion Ennis and a budding superstar named Ed Lashley, were facing off against cross-town rival James M. Bennett. It wasn't just packed in the gym that night, it was standing-room-only. I remember watching Coach Butch Waller's Indians running the fast break, Lashley stopping and knocking down jump shots from the top of the key, and the home fans going wild.

Why was this so exciting to me? I loved basketball, played every day, lived in a Wi-Hi district, and couldn't wait until I would attend in a few years and play on that floor and in that exciting atmosphere.

My name is Paul Butler, a Wi-Hi graduate that would later go on to coach at my alma mater as an assistant to the legendary Butch Waller before embarking on a 24-year career in television as a sportscaster and news anchor. I even returned to Delmarva and spent a few years reporting on the local high school and college sports scene. And covering Bayside Conference basketball was my favorite season because of the long, rich history of hoops on the Eastern Shore. During my time in television, I met a budding young reporter named Mitchell Northam who was working for the local Salisbury newspaper, The Daily Times.

Mitchell, like me, was captivated by basketball on Delmarva, but especially the Bayside Conference. The coaching legends, the Division I talent produced from small towns like Crisfield, Snow Hill, Mardela, American Corner and Centerville – just to name a few.

I think it's the coaches that make the conference so special. So many great basketball minds and unique personalities, cooking up quirky offenses and defense to beat their opponents. Northam developed a great relationship with some of those coaches, and with so many good stories about local athletes – and also a few tragic ones – the former Daily Times reporter wanted to write about and preserve the history of basketball on the Shore.

If you are a basketball junkie, or just a casual fan, this is a great read.

As a former sportscaster, I thought I knew a lot about basketball – boys and girls – in the Bayside Conference. Ha! Mitchell Northam laid that notion to rest. From learning that Cambridge High School was the first basketball power on the Shore and actually played for the high school national championship in 1930, to finding out that perennial power Wi-Hi was winning conference championships as early as 1925, to discovering that the Easton Warriors won the first girls state title for an Eastern Shore team in 1943 as they completed an undefeated season. And who do you think won the first boys state title for a Shore school? It was 1952, and that team belonged to the now-closed Ocean City High School.

But more than the schools, Northam explores the great talent that the Eastern Shore has produced. Names like Walt Hazzard from the all-Black Moton High School in Easton, Somerset High School scoring machine Levi Fontaine, Worcester's Talvin Skinner and Mardela's Tia Jackson... Kelly Gibson, Sherron Mills, Albert Mouring, Andre Collins, Bubby Brown, and on and on and on.

But the real personalities are the coaches. You learn what makes them tick and what made them so good. Bill Cain at Crisfield, Grayson Hurley of Cambridge, Snow Hill's Brenda Jones and Allen Miller, Merrill Morgan at Colonel Richardson, Barbara McCool at Mardela, Pocomoke's David Byrd and Gail Gladding – and not to mention, my mentor and coach Butch Waller, who at the time of this writing was entering his 54th season as the head coach at Wi-Hi.

Northam does exactly what he set out to do: taking a deep look at, documenting and exploring why Eastern Shore basketball is so special. It may not get the notoriety or respect as basketball schools on the other side of the Chesapeake Bay, but in the Bayside Conference, basketball always has been -- and always will be -- king when it comes to high school sports in our piece of the world between the Atlantic Ocean and the Bay Bridge.

In an enjoyable read, Northam captured something that was long overdue.

Paul Butler is the Director of Communications for Wicomico County Public Schools. A graduate of Wicomico High School and Salisbury University, he was formerly a news anchor and the sports director at WBOC-16 for several years.

INTRODUCTION

Whenever I think about high school basketball on the Eastern Shore, I think about Butch Waller's office and the first time I stepped into it.

Before a Jan. 14, 2013 boys game between Wicomico High School and city rival James M. Bennett, I had only been in what is often referred to as the "Waller Dome" once or twice. Before it was renovated a few years back, you could feel how old Wi-Hi's gymnasium was when you walked into it. On weeknights in the winter, the lights bounced off the worn-out hardwood and gave the gym this infectious yellow glow. You could feel the history there; every ball that had been bounced, every dunk thrown down, every charge that had been taken and every game that had been played on that old wooden court.

And if you couldn't feel it, all you had to do was look over at Butch. He'd either be pacing the sidelines in front of Wi-Hi's bench, talking tactics with his longtime trusted understudy Doug King, scribbling on a clipboard, or he'd be sitting quietly – studying the game unfolding in front of him, feeling it out, like an overeager kid digging through a cookie jar.

After the game, if you waited around just long enough, Butch would invite you into his office. There might be some leftover pizza from the concession stand, or a few Gatorades waiting in the mini-fridge. He'd offer those to you, but that's not why you were there.

Waller's office, which is nestled just off-center court, in a hallway behind the scorer's table, is like walking into a museum of Bayside basketball history. Most of the paint was peeling back then, but you couldn't tell because the walls were covered by newspaper clippings, photos, posters and other memories from a lifetime in the sport.

There's a framed photo of Bubby Brown, playing in the game in which he scored his 1,000[th] point while wearing Waller's snug black shoes. There are articles from the 70s, 80s, 90s, aughts and teens. There's a large photo of Waller's greatest team, the undefeated 2002 Wi-Hi squad. There's a story about him retiring – one of several which proved to be untrue. There's a letter Waller received from North Carolina Tar Heels' legend Dean Smith. There are photos by Todd Dudek, Joey Gardner and Justin Odendhal – some of the awesome photographers that have worked for the Daily Times newspaper in Salisbury. And there's even a few stories written by me.

Again, you didn't stay at Wi-Hi for hours after a game for a drink and a snack. You stayed to get an education on the sport. You stayed to hear Waller's stories. You stayed to hear King and Bill Weber talk about some of the greatest games they had seen. You stayed to watch Waller meticulously fill out that night's Bayside scoreboard.

The first time I got the opportunity to do this was after that Wi-Hi and Bennett game, which ended in a narrow two-point victory for Waller's Indians. Bennett's star player at the time, Kory Holden – who'd go on to be a solid Division I player – had a chance to tie the game up for the Clippers with the last shot. He got to the rim, but he did not score. As he was guarded by Thomas Brown, Holden's lay-up bounced off the glass and into the hands of the victorious Indians.

I was at that game as a half-fan, half-reporter. I was a 20-year-old community college student who was trying to create an entry for myself into a career of sports journalism. For the most part, I had no idea what I was doing. Aside from a brief gig as a reporter for a weekly paper in Salisbury – that started and folded in the span of, oh, three months – I had little experience. When that paper shut down, the Star Democrat of Easton – the newspaper my grandparents read when I was a kid – gave me an opportunity to be a stringer. I was still a bit ticked off the paper didn't mention the greatest athletic achievement of my high school career – catching an interception for the Colonel Richardson Colonels in a 21-18 football loss to Easton in 2009 – but I didn't hold a grudge. And I needed cash, and I wanted to write. The Star Democrat had plenty of work for me in the fall, and I learned a ton from David Insley and Bill Haufe about covering sports, but the work they had for me sort of dried up in the winter. So, even though I wasn't getting paid and wouldn't be published in the paper, I still went to games and wrote about them on a little blog I had.

The victory that day for Wi-Hi wound up being the 700th in Waller's career. When the game ended, he held court with a few media members behind the scorer's table, and Weber – the longtime scoreboard operator at Wi-Hi – urged me to join in on the scrum. To Waller, it was like I had been covering his games for years. He treated me the same as the reporters from WBOC and the Daily Times.

One of us asked Waller what his 700th win meant to him. And he said what he's uttered every time he's hit a milestone. He chuckled and said, "It means I'm old. I've been here a long time, but I've been very lucky to have really dedicated players that play really hard."

For the next four years – for DMVelite and then the Salisbury Daily Times – I was very lucky to be able to cover high school basketball in the Bayside Conference, where the stories and unique personalities were endless. I was lucky to have had an audience with Gail Gladding, to see her coach and to hear about her playing days in the WBL. I was lucky to watch Dayona Godwin score more than 2,000 points for Stephen Decatur. I was lucky to cover Kory Holden, Jorden Duffy, Keve Aluma and Manny Camper as they blossomed into Division I prospects. I was lucky to see Kesha Cook's Mardela teams run opponents out of the gym. I was lucky to witness Nick

Purnell coach an unlikely Washington team to its first state tournament appearance in nearly 40 years. I was lucky to step into gyms like Kent County's, which rocked during the playoffs. I was lucky to see how Crisfield's Graveyard intimidated opponents. I was lucky to chronicle Derrick Fooks, Tyler Nixon and Pocomoke's run to a state championship in 2016. I was lucky to write about Andre Collins' return to the Shore as a coach. And I was lucky to hang out with Butch Waller, in his office, on bus rides and at games, and hear him talk about basketball, a sport that is nearly a religion on the Eastern Shore.

But not everyone is as lucky as me. Not everyone has talked to all of these coaches and players. Not everyone has heard the stories of the 1952 Ocean City High boys team, Levi Fontaine, Talvin Skinner, the 1979 Snow Hill girls team, of Sherron Mills, of Barbara McCool and Tia Jackson, of Albert Mouring, of David Byrd, Allen Miller and Phil Rayfield. Not everyone has had the chance to walk into Waller's office, or share a beer with Byrd at a Buffalo Wild Wings, and hear stories of the best teams, the most talented players, the iconic coaches and the greatest games of high school basketball on the Eastern Shore.

***

My goal in writing this book is to make those stories accessible to everyone who wants to learn about them. I hope that opening this and turning to any page will be like walking into a museum, where you can hear the sound of squeaky shoes and balls bouncing, and the smell wafting through the air has hints of Old Bay. If there was an Eastern Shore basketball museum, that's what I would expect it to be like, and I'd expect it contain artifacts from some of the stories I've strived to tell here. I'd also expect this fantasy museum to sell scrapple sandwiches, but that might be asking for too much.

This book won't be a complete history of high school basketball on the Eastern Shore. To chronicle every season, every team and every player, this book would have to be at least seven-times thicker. Instead, with extensive research, dozens of original interviews and countless hours of work, I have attempted to write about the teams, people and games that were essential in molding the history of the sport on the Shore and creating the culture around it. There are many ways in which a book on the history of high school basketball on the Eastern Shore can be written. This one is my contribution. And I hope one day, another journalist or historian with a love for the game and the region comes along and fills in everything I missed.

But this book is mine. And it's for anyone who has ever played or coached in a basketball game on the Eastern Shore. It's for anyone who has ever felt joy or heartache after a Bayside Conference contest. It's for anyone who has been impacted by the sport on Maryland's slice of the Delmarva Peninsula. It's for those local legends – like Kelley Gibson and Merrill Morgan – who helped mold the history. And it's for anyone who has ever called the Eastern Shore home.

ESPN's Wright Thompson once wrote: "The homogenization of America has left people wandering the land in search of a place to belong. We are a tribeless nation hungry for tribes."

A lot of folks on the Eastern Shore find those tribes on the Chesapeake Bay as fishermen and crabbers, near the ocean as surfers and beachgoers and enthusiasts of Thrasher's fries, as farmers in the flat and spread-out land of places like Caroline County. Or on sports fields, aligning their identities with football, field hockey or lacrosse.

Many others, like the countless people whose stories are told in this book, find their tribes in gyms, with a ball and two hoops.

***

After almost a decade in journalism – or at least, writing and getting paid for it – I am not an expert on one thing.

The only thing I really know, that I can talk about with some sort of authority, is home.

I know the Choptank River, and the chicken houses that line the back roads of southern Caroline County. I know where the best scrapple sandwiches are, from Mary's Country Store in Harmony to Johnny's Sub Shop in Salisbury. I know where to get a pile of old Daily Times or Star Democrat newspapers for a backyard crab feast. I know that, if you turn by the Wal-Mart in Cambridge and just keep on going, you'll eventually hit Hoopers Islands, which feels like the end of the world, but there's a great seafood buffet there at Old Salty's. I know about the movies filmed in Berlin and St. Michaels. I know how RAR's unique and tasty beers revived downtown Cambridge. I know that the South starts just below turn four at the racetrack in Dover. I know where Patty Cannon's house is, unfortunately. I know the hell that Hurricane Sandy brought to Crisfield. I know that the removal of the Talbot Boys monument was long overdue. I know that there's nothing really like seeing pumpkins fired out of cannons during the first weekend of November in Bridgeville. I know that Rise Up has the best coffee, but the most delicious donuts on the peninsula are down in Onancock at Corner Bakery. I know all of the myths and legends about Suicide Bridge. I know where you should and shouldn't speed between Mardela Springs and Federalsburg. I know that, if it's late and you need WiFi in Pocomoke, you go to McDonald's.

And I know the power, magic and history of Bayside Conference basketball.

One more thing…

People have asked – and I'm sure will continue to ask – why I wrote this book. It was, I assure you, not for the money. The answer can be summed up in a line from Rick Bragg, the fantastic southern storyteller:

"I write about home so I can be certain that someone will. It is not much more complicated than that."

BEGINNINGS,
WITH MAY BROOKS AND ED WALTER

"Back then, a couple of them weren't allowed to go down to the other end of the floor." – Vic Burns

In everything, someone has to be first. Chris Ford of the Boston Celtics drained the first three-pointer in NBA history. Cynthia Cooper was the first MVP of the WNBA Finals. Big Boi and Andre 3000 were the first rappers from the South to win at the Source Awards. Dale Earnhardt was the first NASCAR driver who was cooler than a polar bear's toenails. And Virginia Gov. Ralph Northam – no relation – claims to be the first man to dunk a basketball on Tangier Island.

But when it comes to high school basketball on the Eastern Shore of Maryland, it is difficult to decipher exactly when, where and who played in the earliest game.

In 1891, Dr. James Naismith – a Canadian-American physical education teacher at the International YMCA Training School in Springfield, Massachusetts – invented a game with teams of nine men and two peach baskets that could be played indoors during the winter while the popular sports of football and baseball were on hiatus. Initially, it was two words: "basket ball." A man by the name of Maurice Joyce met with Naismith and in 1892 brought the game to Washington, D.C., teaching it while he was the physical education director at the Carroll Institute. Joyce, according to John McNamara's book "The Capital of Basketball," later reduced the number of players on each team from nine to five, a change adopted by the national rules committee in 1897. The Evening Star newspaper of Washington, D.C. first wrote of a local high school basketball game on Jan. 6, 1900.

The first college basketball game – most historians believe – was played a few years earlier, on Feb. 9, 1895, when the Minnesota School of Agriculture beat Hamline University 9-3 on a makeshift court in the basement of Hamline's Hall of Science. A year later, the University of Chicago beat Iowa 15-12 in the first college game that used modern five-man lineups. Basketball became an Olympic sport by 1936, and the National Basketball Association was formed in 1946. The wild and crazy ABA changed the game forever when it introduced the three-point line in 1967. Decades later, an average audience of 20.5 million people in the U.S. and Canada watched the Toronto Raptors beat the Golden State Warriors the 2019 NBA Finals, in which 148 beyond-the-arc shots were flushed across six games. In the 1990s and 2000s

– when Michael Jordan, Kobe Bryant and hulking centers and forwards owned the sport – all high school players wanted to do was dunk. By the time 2020 rolled around, all they desired to do was swish half-court threes like Steph Curry and Klay Thompson.

According to Jason Rhodes' 2012 book on Somerset County, organized sports started gaining popularity on the Eastern Shore in the late 1800s. That's when some of the first semi-professional baseball teams started up in the region.

While writing and researching this book during the awful and inconvenient COVID-19 pandemic, I heavily relied on the deep archives of Newspapers.com. Based on my findings, Snow Hill's Democratic Messenger was the first Eastern Shore newspaper to mention the game of basketball in its pages on July 7, 1906. But that's all it was, a mere mention. The newspaper ran an excerpt of a short fictional story which referenced basketball, buried on page seven. In 1913, the Denton Journal ran a brief explaining the game and its history.

A year later, on Oct. 31, 1914, the Journal briefly reported: "The basketball team of Greensboro High School is scheduled to play here with Denton today." It's unclear if the newspaper had a sports reporter or a sports editor, or if anyone actually covered the game. There was no follow-up, no game recap. The outcome remains a mystery. But among the historical artifacts available, this little game played between two schools in northern Caroline County that no longer exist may have well been the first high school hoops contest on Maryland's Eastern Shore. Today, the youth of Denton, Greensboro, Ridgely, Goldsboro and other surrounding communities all go to North Caroline High School.

On April 15, 1916, the Daily Banner in Cambridge deemed it important enough to report on a basketball injury in Federalsburg, a small town in southern Caroline County. 14-year-old Claudell Galloway, the son of a local doctor, apparently fractured his right arm while playing for Federalsburg High School. "He was running with the ball when another member of the team crashed into him, throwing him heavily on the ground," the report read. It's unknown if young Galloway ever recovered, or ever got the chance to attempt an Iverson-esque crossover.

By then, basketball was being played by several teams at the high school level across the Shore. Down south toward the beach in Worcester County, a county championship tournament was organized between the teams at schools in Snow Hill, Pocomoke and Berlin. Schools from the small communities of Girdletree and Stockton were added the next season.

Girls were playing basketball too, and getting the proper recognition for their talents. The front page of the May 20, 1916, Democratic Messenger featured the headline: "Snow Hill Girls Win the Basket Ball League Cup."

Below the headline was a photo of the nine-member Snow Hill squad, each wearing white shoes, white shirts with dark sashes and dark pantaloons; a far cry from the sleeveless jersey, lightweight shorts, leg sleeves and flashy Nikes sported by Delaware native Elena Delle Donne as she led the Washington Mystics to a 2019 WNBA Championship.

As expected, the language used to describe the style of play in the early 20th century was at a simple level. No one was dropping dimes or throwing down thunderous dunks, no one came off screens to knock down silky jumpers, and post moves were either nonexistent or not mentioned. A sampling from the Democratic Messenger, describing a Snow Hill girls' win over Girdletree on April 21, 1917: "The jumping centre Sarah Hayward needed only a little more training to put the ball in the basket… Esther White and Nellie Trader showed what they could do. Lillian Riley made some wonderful throws and she had a good co-worker in Addie Bevans."

Uh-huh. Indeed.

Prose and descriptive adjectives be damned, Snow Hill rolled to a win in their next game too, taking down Princess Anne, 30-12. On May 25, 1917, Snow Hill won its second straight county title for girls basketball, topping Pocomoke 19-17. The Democratic Messenger again put the story on the front page of the next day's paper with the headline: "Snow Hillers Trim Pocomoke." The story was just below a notice to the young men of Worcester County to register for the draft. It had been a little over a month since the U.S. entered the first World War. Even back then, high school basketball was worthy enough for front-page coverage on the Shore.

Play would resume after the Great War, and one of the Eastern Shore's first boys basketball powers would emerge in Cambridge, a northern Dorchester County town squished between marshland, the Choptank River and the Chesapeake Bay, known for being a prominent stop along the Underground Railroad for famed abolitionist Harriet Tubman. Cambridge High School began their 1922-23 season by beating Seaford High of Delaware, 30-15. Clyde Hynson scored 18 points for Cambridge and the Daily Banner referred to him as a "husky centre" who "ran rampant about the armory court like a Greek fleeing from Smyrna" (this was not a weird nod to Smyrna, Delaware, but rather a timely reference to the destruction of the Greek city Smyrna, destroyed in a fire near the end of the Greco-Turkish War in 1922). Hynson was a fullback for the football team too, and he scored 14 points in Cambridge's next win, a 35-10 victory over Easton.

Just as Cambridge was rising, a team on the Lower Shore was too at Wicomico High School – known then and now as simply, Wi-Hi – led then by coach Bill Duffy. The two squads met on the court on Feb. 9, 1924, at the First Regiment Armory in Cambridge and the Wi-Hi Indians came away with a 15-14 victory for their seventh straight win of the season. Wi-Hi leaned on its stout defense and, according to a Salisbury Daily Times game story, Wi-Hi didn't allow Cambridge to score against them "within the 17-foot line."

If you're asking yourself why these early scores are so low, it's because the shot clock didn't exist yet. Possessions could last forever. The NBA introduced a 24-second shot clock in 1954 and high school leagues and the college game soon followed.

Except in Maryland.

Scores would increase over time and sitting on the ball was universally frowned upon, but the Old Line State didn't implement a shot clock for public school boys basketball until the 2017-18 season, much to the chagrin of a handful of Shore coaches.

In 1925, organizers of the sport in the region put together a postseason tournament to determine the Eastern Shore Champions. Duffy's Wi-Hi team steamrolled its way into the final game by taking down Cecilton 66-14 in the semifinals. In the final on March 16 at Washington College, Wi-Hi edged out Chestertown 27-23 for the Eastern Shore crown. Jimmy Chapman led the way with 10 points. Washington College sent the winners a silver cup with team members' names inscribed on it.

Two years later, the Wi-Hi boys found themselves playing for the Eastern Shore Championship again, but more was on the line this time. The winner of the Eastern Shore would advance to the semifinals of the state-wide high school basketball tournament put on by the Playground Athletic League of Maryland. Wi-Hi easily bested Elkton in Centreville on March 18 for the Shore crown and set their sights on Hyattsville, a squad from Prince George's County who had just trounced Bel Air 53-24. On a Friday night at Washington College, Wi-Hi was outmatched, losing 49-25. Just like that, the Eastern Shore's first chance at state-wide bragging rights for basketball were gone. Allegany would beat Hyattsville six days later for what is regarded as the first state championship in Maryland high school basketball history. Beginning in 1927, Allegany won eight state titles in a span of 11 seasons.

Also in 1927, Wicomico County would hold its first county championship for girls basketball and Wi-Hi took that title home too, with Dora Taylor and Hilda Heath leading Wi-Hi to a 32-8 win over Hebron. The following season, the Wi-Hi girls ran into some unexpected trouble in Crisfield and found themselves on the wrong end of a record book entry. Crisfield star Ideila Horsey was, apparently, unguardable on Feb. 7, 1928, and scored every single point for her team in a 54-10 victory. The Salisbury Daily Times wrote it was "believed to be" a Delmarva Peninsula record. Nowadays, a performance like that would've gone viral, but this era was still a long way away from iPhones and Instagram.

The Eastern Shore got some nationwide recognition for basketball in 1930 when Cambridge's boys team traveled to Chicago, Illinois, to play for the national high school basketball championship. They would fall to a team from Nevada early in the tournament, 29-22.

Cambridge would be the first Eastern Shore team to advance to a state championship final in 1936, but again, Bill Bowers' Allegany team awaited. A 23-0 scoring run in the second quarter powered Allegany to another championship, beating Cambridge by a final score of 38-16. The Baltimore Sun wrote the Cambridge squad put up a "plucky battle," but the Shoremen wanted to be so much more. They were tired of finishing in second to those people from the Western Shore (to Eastern Shore folk, everything west of the Chesapeake Bay is the Western Shore, by the way). They wanted to show the state there was basketball talent here and that they could play with anyone.

The Eastern Shore would have to wait several years to prove it. And even after it did, the region's teams have always felt like underdogs when they traveled across the Bay Bridge to the state final four.

After Bobby Cavanaugh's Fort Hill teams won back-to-back state titles in 1938 and 1939, Maryland's high school basketball tournament was put on the shelf while the country went to war again.

***

During World War II, the Eastern Shore was home to several POW camps that put German and Italian soldiers – mostly captured in North Africa – to work at lumber mills, farms, orchards, canneries and chicken houses in Berlin, Cambridge, Church Hill, Easton, Hurlock and Westover for about eight cents a day. While some of those captured soldiers played soccer on nearby fields in their spare time, local high schoolers didn't get the chance to compete for the state's basketball crown from 1940 through 1946.

However, a photo from the Feb. 4, 1940, edition of the Baltimore Sun crowns "the Blue Belles of Cambridge High School" as the state champions for girls basketball. A caption underneath a photo of the team, coached by Ed Walter, says they won 61 straight games. It's unclear if Cambridge simply claimed the title because they won so much or if they captured the title in a tournament. If it's the latter, who sanctioned the tournament remains ambiguous. Nonetheless, the team – led by sisters Caroline and Jane Gordy – were one of the first truly dominant teams on the Shore. Newspapers around this time often mistakenly referred to the team's head coach, Walter, as "Walters." There wasn't an S at the end of the man's name.

At least one boys team during that time might've had a decent shot at winning a state title too, as Sudlersville won 20 straight games over the span of two seasons.

But on Jan. 4, 1946, Sudlersville's run came to an end as they lost 35-33 to Cambridge in front of an announced crowd of 574 fans inside the victor's gym, despite Bill Stevens' 19 points. Cyril Pritchett scored 11 points for

Cambridge, including the game-winning bucket. Cambridge followed the triumph up by beating a team above their level, taking down the men's team from Salisbury State Teachers College 53-18 on Jan. 19, 1946, powered by Johnny Ransome's 21 points.

While the on-court accomplishments of Eastern Shore teams were impressive, the most important thing to happen in 1946 was the formation of what is now known as the Maryland Public Secondary Schools Athletic Association (MPSSAA), which is essentially the governing body of public high school sports in the state. Initially named the "Health and Physical Education Association of Maryland Schools" – HPEAMS just doesn't have the same ring to it – the organization decided at a meeting on Jan. 26, 1946, that they would hold a statewide high school boys basketball tournament at Washington College and the University of Maryland beginning in 1947. The organization's first president was William Brish, an assistant superintendent in Prince George's County, and Mardela High School Principal W.E. Twilley served as the District 5 representative. The group began using the MPSSAA name around 1951.

Ed Walter coached football, and boys and girls basketball at Cambridge in the late 1940s. In 1948, his Cambridge girls team won a state championship. From Richard Woolfolk.

In lieu of a proper state tournament in 1946, Salisbury State hosted a tournament for boys and girls teams on the five lower Eastern Shore counties: Caroline, Dorchester, Wicomico, Somerset and Worcester. The other Shore counties competed in a tournament at Washington College. On the Lower Shore, Wi-Hi claimed the boys' title and Hurlock captured the girls' trophy in front of a crowd of about 1,000 people. Elkton won the boys' title of the mid and upper Shore schools, but refused to play Wi-Hi for an overall Shore Championship. Guy Johnson, the principal at Elkton, responded to Benn Maggs' invitation via telegram saying, "Sorry, unable to accept your offer." Ed Nichols of the Salisbury Daily Times took Elkton – and the newly formed state athletic association for not intervening – to task in a column: "What help the state board exhibited, you can jot down on your fingernail."

When the state tournament did get underway a year later, the field was loaded with Eastern Shore talent by the time the semifinals rolled around. All public schools in Maryland were split into four classes based on enrollment, and the Eastern Shore had a representative in three of the four boys' championship games. Cambridge advanced to the Class B title game against Westminster by beating Wi-Hi, Easton topped Denton to earn a spot in the Class C bout, and tiny Vienna edged out Sudlersville 28-27 – led by Elwood Davenport's 14 points – to put them in the Class D final vs. Mt. Ranier.

In 1947, the odds finally seemed to be in the Shore's favor. They would have three chances to take home the first boys' state title for the region.

***

Vienna is a near-microscopic community of less than 300 people in eastern Dorchester County, situated on the Nanticoke River. In colonial days, it thrived on shipbuilding and tobacco farming and was raided by British troops during the War of 1812. In 1946 though, the town had a hoops squad that packed a big punch. Coached by Emerson Hurley, Vienna lost just two games all season, both to Cambridge. Still, Vienna was no match for Mt. Rainier, who thumped the Shoremen 34-16 at the University of Maryland. Jimmy Moyer led the way with seven points and Vienna led 14-12 at halftime, but they couldn't hold on to the lead.

The boys from Cambridge and Easton didn't have much better luck on the big stage. Cambridge fell 39-24 to Westminster and Easton lost 42-29 to Greenbelt. Luck for the Eastern Shore boys had run out.

However, hope for basketball bragging rights for Eastern Shore folk still lived on with the girls teams. There was indeed a girls state high school basketball tournament in 1947, and Hurlock, Cambridge and Easton would each advance to their respective finals as Eastern Shore representatives.

Hurlock's path to the championship was a strange one. After playing Federalsburg to a 16-16 tie after regulation and one overtime, state officials opted to not play another period of overtime in the Class D semifinals. Instead, the winner would be decided by free throws – a finish akin to penalty kicks in soccer. Eloise Covey sank both of her attempts for Hurlock while the Federalsburg shooter missed. Violet Weller's Hurlock team was outmatched in the state final though, getting beat 28-10 by Gwynn Park.

In the Class C semifinals, Betty Whitaker's 11 points led Easton past Denton, 23-11. On March 29, May Brooks' undefeated Easton girls team entered the state final with a chance to make history for the Eastern Shore. Hurlock had lost, but Easton and Cambridge still had a chance to bring gold back home. For Easton, the weight of historic pressure was heavy: not only did they have the chance to finish the season 20-0 and without a loss, but they also had the opportunity to become the first basketball team from the Shore – boys or girls – to win it all. After a closely contested match with Greenbelt in College Park, the Warriors prevailed, winning 16-15 and bringing back a trophy to Easton and the Shore. Ann Jump scored six points, including the game-sealing basket in the final minute of play.

May Brooks guided the Easton High School girls basketball team to its second state title in 1949, when the game was still played using now-defunct six-on-six rules. *Courtesy of the Talbot Historical Society, Easton, Maryland.*

Later that day, the Cambridge girls would triumph too. In a game that tipped off at 7:30 p.m. at Western Maryland College, the girls coached by Ed Walter beat Westminster 21-20. The ending of the game was thrilling, as Westminster led by a point with less than 30 seconds to play. But on Cambridge's final possession, Helen Lord was fouled as she was heading to the basket. She sank two free throws, taking the lead and sealing the win. It was the first loss of the season for Westminster and the second state title of the day for the Eastern Shore.

Vic Burns grew up in Cambridge and attended Cambridge High School. He would go on to coach North Dorchester to the state championship in boys basketball in 1999. His mother was a 1947 graduate of Cambridge and still somewhat remembers the dominant girls squad.

"She didn't really recognize some of them because a lot of the players on that team were underclassmen," Burns said. "Back then, a couple of them weren't allowed to go down to the other end of the floor."

Indeed. In those days, almost all girls high school basketball across the country was played with six-on-six rules. Each team had three guards and three forwards, and the forwards were the only players allowed to shoot at the basket and they had to remain in the front court. Beginning in 1958, some states began to phase out the six-on-six game.

Still, regardless of whether the game was played with six players or five, a state championship is a state championship. And Walter and Brooks were the first coaches to win them for the Eastern Shore.

Walter also coached football and boys basketball at Cambridge, and led the Blue Belles to state finals in 1948 and 1949. In July 1949, at the age of 37, he quit coaching to become the postmaster in Cambridge after receiving the nomination from President Harry Truman. He later became the President of the Maryland chapter of the Postmasters Association and also served as a District Chairman in the MPSSAA.

"He was a very prominent coach," Burns said of Walter. "I know he was big in sports."

An obituary for Walter couldn't be located, but a story in an Oct. 30, 1967, edition of the Salisbury Daily Times said he was recovering from a surgery at Johns Hopkins Hospital. Then, 11 days later, the same newspaper ran a column about his death from cancer, with editor Dick Moore writing, "Ed was one of those leaders who somehow found the time to do a lot more than just his job... He had a great sense of responsibility and devotion to his country, his state and his community." The U.S. military veteran was just 55 years old.

Later, a baseball field on Linden Avenue in Cambridge was renamed J. Edward Walter Park. It was once home to the Cambridge Dodgers, a minor league affiliate for the major league club then-based in Brooklyn, New York. Branch Rickey oversaw the construction of the park in 1946 and committed $60,000 to build it. With a 91-34 record, the Cambridge Dodgers won the Eastern Shore League pennant in 1947. Don Zimmer, the 1989 National League Manager of the Year, played for Cambridge as a Dodgers farmhand in 1949. Cambridge High School later played its football games at the park.

Brooks led Easton to another state title in 1949, beating Richard Montgomery 36-22. She coached and taught at Easton from the early 1930s through 1969 and would become a staple in the Talbot County sports community for decades, coaching basketball, volleyball, tennis, track and golf. Brooks is also credited with helping introduce and popularize the sport of field hockey on the Shore. She died in Denton in 1999 at the age of 92. In her obituary, which ran on the front page of the Easton Star Democrat, her cousin Ruth Wales said, "They all say she was tough and hard, but she was good. She was very well respected and loved."

Stories of the triumphs by the Easton and Cambridge girls ran in newspapers across the region, capturing headlines in the Hanover Evening Star, the Baltimore Sun, the Easton Star Democrat and the Salisbury Daily Times. Walter and Brooks aren't mentioned often nowadays, but the pair will always be the first two coaches that brought the Shore its first state basketball championships.

BAD LUCK FOR THE BOYS

"Those games will live with me a lifetime." – Sam Seidel

As a new decade began, the Eastern Shore was still searching for its first state title in boys basketball. By the start of the 1950-51 season, girls' teams had won a trio, with Easton claiming two Class C titles and Cambridge winning one in Class B. All the boys had done was go across the Bay Bridge and return empty-handed.

Between the 1946-47 season and the 1949-50 season, 16 boys teams from the Eastern Shore advanced to at least the semifinals of the state tournament. 11 of them advanced to the final. None of them won it all. Cambridge advanced to the Class B final three straight seasons and lost by double-digits each time. Sam Seidel guided Wicomico High School to the Class A final in each of his first three seasons on the job between 1948 and 1950, but the Indians fell short each time. Charles Dondero had taken Ocean City High to the Class D final in 1948 and 1949, but lost to Williamsport and Damascus.

Entering the 1950-51 season, Seidel's Wi-Hi Indians and Dondero's Ocean City Vikings had the best chances of breaking the Shore's run of unluck in the state tournament, largely because they were armed with two of the region's tallest and most talented players.

Wi-Hi had Marvin Long, who football coach Charlie Berry called "a boy with big hands who sure can snag those forward passes." A lanky forward, Long was about 6-foot-2, but tough and skilled around the basket. He often played through pain and illnesses too, as newspapers from the time mention him having battles with grippe (an old term for the flu) and injuries to his feet.

Ed Athey, then the athletic director at Washington College, told Ed Nichols of the Salisbury Daily Times in 1951 that Long was the best player on the Shore. "His ball-handling and general floor play was far ahead of the other players I saw," Athey said. "He moves about with a lot of poise and savvy. He handles the ball with a lot of finesse. Another asset is his shooting on the move. I'd say he's college material."

Indeed, Long would go on to briefly play for the University of Maryland Terrapins. He was a standout starter on the Terps' freshman team, but was cut from the varsity squad as a junior just before the start of the 1954-55 season. Another Wi-Hi player, Bob Hardiman, featured in 43 games for the Terps under head coach Bud Millikan between 1954 and 1957.

"I have yet to see anyone compare with Long," said Athey, who must've had the misfortune of not seeing Ocean City High play in the 1950-51 campaign.

Because while Seidel had Long at Wi-Hi, Ocean City had senior center Steve Gulyas, who stood around 6-foot-5 and was built like a tank, armed with broad, bruising shoulders and hands as big as catcher's mitts. He could palm a basketball in each hand at the same time, jump as high as anyone on the floor and run like a gazelle. In his first game as a freshman on Jan. 22, 1948, he scored 25 points in an 81-23 Ocean City victory over Mardela. Later that season, in the 1948 Class D state final – which was played in Ocean City in front of a record crowd – he was the Vikings' leading scorer with 16 points in a 49-33 loss to Williamsport. A year later, Gulyas poured in 23 points in the 1949 Class D state final, a 63-54 loss to Damascus in Rockville.

But Ocean City was also armed with Albert Willis, a fellow senior who was a smooth operator with the ball in his hands, also armed with a precise set-shot.

Long and Gulyas clashed on the court on Jan. 9, 1951, in Ocean City. And despite Long playing on a bruised foot, he outmuscled Gulyas and guided the Indians to a 33-29 triumph down by the sea. Gulyas had scored a total of 74 points across his last three games, but contributed just two foul shots and zero points from the floor in the loss for Ocean City. Long had eight points and dominated on the glass.

Gulyas got back on track a few games later, dumping 28 points on Snow Hill in a win. He might have been motivated by his standing in the race for the Eastern Shore's scoring title. Mardela's Tommy Bounds had a lead in late January, averaging 19 points per-game. A week later, Gulyas took the lead in the race after scoring 31 points in a dominant win for Ocean City over Berlin's Buckingham High School. Dondero continued to run the Vikings' offense through Gulyas, who finished January by scoring 38 points in another win over Worcester County rival Snow Hill.

But Gulyas still couldn't get the best of Long. In the final on-court meeting of their respective high school careers – the 1951 regular season finale – Long outscored Gulyas 17-12 in a tight 41-39 win for Wi-Hi. Luckily, Ocean City's path to get back to the state final didn't have to go through Salisbury.

While Gulyas and Long received most of the attention from the local newspapers as the top two players on the Shore, there was one boy who was better, according to the numbers. Herbert Janney was a senior in 1951 and averaged 29.4 points per-game for Salisbury High School, one of the Eastern Shore's Black high schools. He went on to play for Vernon "Skip" McCain down at Maryland State College in Princess Anne.

By the 1950-51 season, Maryland had moved to a three-class system for sports based on school size. Ocean City moved up to Class C. As the playoffs wound down, the only team standing between Ocean City and the state semifinals was Sudlersville, a small town in the northeastern corner of Queen Anne's County that is best known as the birthplace of Baseball Hall of Famer Jimmie Foxx. Sudlersville's top two players were Dick Anthony and Vernon Pinder, a pair of farm-raised boys who combined to average 30.6 points per-game that season. But in the battle for the Class C Eastern Shore title, which was played in Federalsburg, Sudlersville was no match as Ocean City prevailed with a 57-41 victory. Gulyas had 18 points, but the reliable Albert Willis led the way with 20 in front of a capacity crowd.

Ocean City got to play the state semifinal game on its home court and breezed by Clarksville with a 52-41 victory. Willis had 19 points, Gulyas added 13, and Charles Dondero's boys were in the state final for the third time in his five years on the job. But waiting for the Shoremen in College Park were the defending champions, Barton High School.

The Braves were coached by Johnny Thomas and hailed from a small coal-mining town in Allegany County, situated just north of the West Virginia border along Georges Creek. Barton had stormed its way through the playoffs by thumping Friendsville, Hancock and Sherwood high schools.

Ocean City was in trouble from the jump on March 17, 1951, as Barton had built a 22-5 lead by the end of the first quarter. But Dondero's squad rallied, and trailed by just three points with about two minutes to play. Barton turned to its star in the frontcourt, 6-foot-2 Andrew Tichnell, who outclassed Gulyas on the final two possessions. The Cumberland Times described it this way: "Tichnell, however, faked his bigger opponent out of position both times and dribbled around him for lay-ups." Ocean City couldn't muster a response and Barton won 52-45, led by Tichnell's 24 points. Gulyas, in his final game in a Vikings' jersey, had just 12 points. More than 250 Ocean City fans had traveled to College Park for the game, just to see their home team lose again.

Wi-Hi managed to get to the Class A final in 1951 too, but suffered a narrow defeat at the hands of Hagerstown, 28-27. It was the second straight year they had lost the title game by a single point.

"I thought we had the better ball club both years," Indians' head coach Sam Seidel told the Salisbury Daily Times years later, in 1968. "Those games will live with me a lifetime."

The 1950-51 season proved to be just another year of unfulfilled high hopes for boys basketball teams on the Eastern Shore. Again, they were defeated by teams from the western part of the state. Again, they felt disrespected. Again, they couldn't win on the big stage.

All of that was about to change. One of those mountain boys from Allegany County was on his way to a resort town to teach some basketball.

DICK DEHART AND THE TOURIST TOWN SQUAD

"I've just got a good group of boys, that's all." – Dick DeHart

Two things changed for the Ocean City High School boys basketball team in the early summer of 1951.

First, the star player the Vikings leaned on so much, Steve Gulyas, had graduated. The son of an Ocean City boat builder, he entered the military and served the Navy aboard the USS Apache, working on communications. Instead of swishing shots and gobbling up rebounds in gymnasiums along the Shore, he was repairing radios in the Pacific Ocean.

And head coach Charles Dondero resigned, leaving his post as the Vikings' head basketball coach on May 10. A native of Closter, New Jersey, Dondero came to Ocean City in 1945 after being discharged from the military. He had served the Army in World War II as a member of the 88th Infantry Division in Italy and earned a Bronze Star. Dondero was a graduate of East Stroudsburg Teachers College where he lettered in baseball and soccer, but at Ocean City he found his greatest success on the hardwood. In boys basketball, he guided the tiny high school in the resort town to four Worcester County titles, three Eastern Shore Class D championships and three appearances in the state final.

But at the end of the 1950-51 season, he needed a change of scenery. He and his wife went to Florida, and he told the Salisbury Daily Times he didn't plan to coach again for at least a year.

"I'm a man of leisure right now," Dondero said. "Truthfully, I enjoyed my five years of coaching the youth at Ocean City High. They're a great group of kids."

So, suddenly, Ocean City had an opening. It needed a new boys basketball coach.

The school had recently hired Richard "Dick" DeHart to teach health and physical education. And he just happened to have an impressive resume as an athlete in a region of Maryland that had beat up on Eastern Shore basketball teams pretty good over the years.

DeHart was a 1945 graduate of Allegany High School where he lettered in football and basketball, and was the captain of the baseball team. He was known in those parts – wedged between West Virginia and Pennsylvania – as a stout defender on the court, and a tough-as-nails football halfback that weighed about 144 pounds soaking wet.

Between 1927 and 1950, Allegany – under the tutelage of head coach Bill Bowers – won 10 state titles. Other teams from western Maryland, such as Fort Hill, Barton, Hagerstown, Williamsport, Bruce and Beall, had also collected championships in boys basketball before 1952. And they typically bested teams from the Shore to win them.

After graduating from Allegany, DeHart briefly served in the Navy as a hospital apprentice during the closing months of World War II and then went on to attend West Virginia University, where he ran cross country. After graduating from WVU, he taught one year at Achilles High School in Virginia, just north of Newport News. In 1951, he crossed the Chesapeake Bay and landed a job at Ocean City High. On Halloween, the announcement of DeHart's hiring ran in the Salisbury Daily Times, with a photo of him wearing a dark suit, white shirt, a patterned tie and a clean haircut.

***

While Ocean City had a new coach and had to figure out how to play without big Steve Gulyas, Sam Seidel was back on the sidelines for Wicomico High School and Marvin Long was still patrolling the paint. Seidel returned to the Indians' bench after coaching a U.S. All-Star Basketball Team during a tour of South America. Meanwhile, Long had a growth spurt, shooting up two inches to 6-foot-4. The year before, he had averaged 13.7 points per-game. With the added height, many expected that scoring total to increase.

"He's the best high school player I've seen in quite some while either in Wilmington or on the Eastern Shore," veteran referee Tom McMenamin told the Salisbury Daily Times of Long.

Wi-Hi had another student that year who might've been a better basketball player than Long. During one girls' game during the 1951-52 season, Margaret Ann Pusey hung 51 points on Snow Hill. She also had performances of 48 points at Pittsville and 31 points at Pocomoke. "Don't know how I do it," she told the Daily Times. "I just take aim at the basket and shoot. Then hope it goes in." Indeed. It was that simple for her.

Elsewhere on the Shore, Cambridge High School was expected to have a strong team too. Like Ocean City, they were coached by another West Virginia University graduate in Ed Sidaris. Difference was, he actually played for the Mountaineers on the court in the 1948-49 season. And the first-year team at Stevensville High School was coached by Ben Scharnus, who was drafted by the Boston Celtics after playing at Seton Hall.

With Gulyas gone – and with the chance to implement his own tactics and philosophies – DeHart had to figure out how Ocean City was going to win games. Ben Lewis and Bunky Bradford were returning starters at the forward spots. Bert Raughley would fill in at center for Gulyas. Billy Brown subbed in for Albert Willis, who had also graduated, and Lionel Massey paired with Brown in the backcourt. George Hurley proved to be a versatile sixth man.

In their opening game, the Vikings leaned on what had worked in previous years: give the ball to the big man. While Raughley played center, he was not as towering as his predecessor, checking in at about 6-foot-1. Still, Raughley proved to be skilled near the basket and scored 17 points as DeHart won his head coaching debut 49-35 over Crisfield at home on Dec. 11.

While feeding Raughley worked against the Crabbers, DeHart wanted to get other players involved. And the Vikings' next game was no easy task, as they'd have to play Wi-Hi on the road. The rookie head coach's squad would prevail, with Lewis scoring 10 points and four other Vikings adding eight points each as Ocean City topped the Indians 45-44 in front of a crowd of about 500 fans. Marvin Long got his points – 18 of them – but Ocean City left with the win and DeHart called the victory a "team success."

After an 87-57 win over Pocomoke on Jan. 16 – in which they were powered by Bunky Bradford's 21 points – DeHart's squad was 6-0. After improving to 7-0 after a victory over Mardela – in which five Vikings scored in double digits – the opposition's principal, Bill Twilley, called Ocean City one of the best teams he had ever seen.

"There's more overall scoring balance," Twilley told the Daily Times. "Every player on the starting five is a good shot. I know it's a better ball club without the tall Steve Gulyas. Last season the opposing team designed its defense to stop Gulyas and one other player. It's a different story now. You have the problem of stopping the whole crew. All of 'em can ring the hoop."

DeHart had a team that wasn't short on offensive talent, but on the other end he opted to use a zone defense frequently. And the Vikings executed it well. Around this time in college basketball, some coaches were griping loudly about this new defensive strategy and a few, including a handful in the Big Ten, wanted it banned.

"We use the zone as a change of pace," DeHart said that season. "It puts the pressure on the opposition especially if it has limited scoring punch on set shots."

In some ways, Ocean City almost had to use the zone defense. Athleticism was not in abundance and the team was short on height. Aside from Raughley, no other player was above 5-foot-11. They used that zone and they used their speed, running at a breakneck pace – faster than a prairie fire with a tail wind – when they came up with a turnover. Seven members of this Vikings' team also ran cross country.

"Ocean City has the most beautiful fast break of any I've seen on the Eastern Shore," Dick Smith, who was then the coach at Lord Baltimore High School in Ocean View, Delaware, told the Daily Times.

Behind that stout defense and a versatile, selfless scoring attack, Ocean City was 12-0 by Feb. 9. Fresh off a 58-30 win over Pocomoke – where Bradford and Raughley combined for 41 points – DeHart still wasn't satisfied with the level of play he was seeing from his Vikings. He told Ed Nichols of the Salisbury Daily Times, "We're not playing good ball. Our passing game has been below par the last couple of weeks."

Few teams were capable of exposing Ocean City's mistakes, but Wi-Hi was one of them. They handed the Vikings a 50-37 loss in the regular season finale in front of more than 615 fans, who were packed into the armory in Salisbury (the facility only comfortably sat 150 people) like sardines in a can.

Seidel defended Ocean City man-for-man in that game. Marvin Long poured in 22 points, and even a full court press deployed by DeHart in the third quarter couldn't close the gap for the Vikings. They finished the regular season 15-2, also losing a game to the Red Shield Boys Club.

Both Wi-Hi and Ocean City would – as expected – win Eastern Shore titles in their respective classes. For the Class A crown, the Indians beat Cambridge 37-30 to improve to 17-2 on the year. In the Class C title game on the Shore, Ocean City beat Hurlock 78-38, also raising its record to 17-2 on the season.

"Guess you could attribute the success of the team to accurate shot-making and good ball-handling," DeHart told the Daily Times. "Of course, the teamwork by everyone greases the hub and makes the wheel spin faster."

At this point, Raughley and Bradford had established themselves as the Vikings' go-to scorers. A lanky, spring-heeled center, Raughley averaged 14.9 points per-game while Bradford – a speedy, smooth dribbler on offense and an annoying gnat on defense – was clipping 12.3 points per-game. While he was listed as a forward, Bradford typically ran the offense and was usually yo-yo-ing the ball on the fast break. Still, against Hurlock, it was Ben Lewis who led the scoring charge with 20 points.

For a bid to the state final, Ocean City was pitted against Federalsburg High School, which was also 17-2 on the season. Situated in southern Caroline County, Federalsburg is a small town that has the Marshyhope Creek running through it. The team in 1952 was coached by Roger Ewing, an Appalachian State University graduate, and led on the court by Charley Ruf and his 11.2 points per-game.

But the boys from blue-collar Federalsburg proved to be no match for the lads from the resort town. Ocean City won handily at the Salisbury State Teachers College, 52-33. Federalsburg actually jumped out to a 10-8 lead, but Ocean City pulled away with an 18-0 run in the second quarter. Ruf led the Feds with nine points, but Bradford and Lewis each had 13 for the Vikings.

With the win, Ocean City was again bound for College Park.

Joining them as representatives from the Shore were Wi-Hi in Class A and Easton High School in Class B.

It was the opinion of at least one man that Eastern Shore teams were finally ready to compete – and beat – the opposition from west of the Chesapeake Bay for state supremacy. Crisfield High principal George F. Carrington told Ed Nichols at the Salisbury Daily Times: "We've finally caught up with the western teams of the state. Our boys play a good brand of ball now." Carrington also predicted a victory for the Vikings, adding: "There's nothing in Allegany County to stop Ocean City."

Heading into the state semifinals, Wi-Hi was going to be down two starters as sharpshooter Bobby Hardiman had a back injury and steady guard Jack Barnett had a torn leg muscle. Hardiman wound up toughing it out and playing, scoring nine points, but his efforts – nor Marvin Long's 29 points – were enough for Wi-Hi to beat Montgomery Blair. Seidel's side bowed out of the semifinals with a 60-44 defeat as Ocean City and Easton advanced. It was the fifth straight year that Wi-Hi had lost at the state tournament.

Easton High boys coach Emerson Smith reviews a play with his team during a practice in 1952. The two players in the back are Sammy Lister and Bill Beauchamp, while the players in the front are Roy Hicks, Roland Dobson and Powell Wrightson. Courtesy of the Talbot Historical Society, Easton, Maryland.

The Vikings got by Barton – the reigning two-time Class C champs – with a 70-60 victory. Ocean City built a fat 65-27 lead heading into the fourth quarter, but then had four starters foul out. Barton outscored DeHart's team 33-5 in the final period, but the hole Barton was in was simply too deep.

Raughley anchored the Vikings in the win, dominating the paint with 13 points and 13 rebounds. Lewis and Bradford each had 14 points.

In the championship games on March 22, Easton was bested in the Class B game by Lonaconing, a school in another small mountain town in Allegany County. The Eastern Shore's hopes and Carrington's bold declaration now resided with Ocean City, which was playing New Windsor of Carroll County for the Class C title.

This was the fourth time since 1948 that boys from the resort town had made it to the state final. This time, they would not be denied. This time, they played their best basketball. This time, they won the first state boys basketball championship for the Eastern Shore.

By halftime, Ocean City had built a 45-26 lead and cruised in the second half to a historic win for a region long-starved for recognition in the game of basketball. Ben Lewis and Bunky Bradford each scored 17 points, Raughley added 15 and George Hurley notched 14 points – shooting a perfect 6-of-6 from the floor along with two made free throws. The final score was 70-55. And while Easton lost, their fans and cheerleaders stuck around to root for Ocean City. It really was a championship for the Shore as a whole, and Raughley – who was also the President of the Student Government at the school – penned a letter of thanks to Easton afterwards.

DeHart was somewhat speechless after the win. He told the Daily Times, "I've just got a good group of boys, that's all. Wonderful team spirit was exhibited all season. We had no individual stars. All the boys were standouts."

***

The Vikings graduated eight players from that 1952 championship team – including Lewis, Bradford, Raughley and Hurley – and were unable to qualify for the state tournament in 1953. That summer, Dick DeHart left Ocean City for a better job and a bigger challenge more inland, succeeding Sam Seidel at Wi-Hi.

Although Seidel's tenure at Wi-Hi was a short one, he was very successful, innovative and introduced tactics to the Shore that were, at the time, groundbreaking. Seidel was one of the first coaches on the Delmarva Peninsula to utilize a zone press defense. And he was one of the first to implore his players to shoot from distance, using a one-handed jump shot. Wi-Hi went on deep postseason runs in each of his six seasons on the job, making the state final four times and also appearing in the state semifinals twice.

Seidel would find success in other parts of life too. The year before he left his post at Wi-Hi, he founded an insurance company – the Sam Seidel Agency. In 1960, he founded the Peninsula Insurance Co. and in 1978, he formed the largest privately owned insurance operation in Maryland. Before coaching and teaching at Wi-Hi, Seidel served in the Navy during World War II aboard the USS Leon in the Pacific Theater. He had risen to the rank of lieutenant by the time he was discharged in 1946. Seidel also coached soccer at Wi-Hi.

Later, Seidel would become a member of the Salisbury City Council, and served on President Jimmy Carter's White House Council on Small Business. At Salisbury University, the school of education and professional studies is named after him and his wife, Marilyn. Seidel died in 2001 at the age of 78.

Paul Sarbanes was one of Seidel's players who found success on and off the court. After helping Wi-Hi make the state final in 1950, where they lost by a single point to Allegany, Sarbanes went on to play basketball at Princeton University. Sarbanes became a Rhodes Scholar, got a law degree from Harvard and then turned to politics. A Democrat, he represented Maryland's 3rd and 4th Congressional Districts before becoming a U.S. senator, an office he held from 1977 to 2007. Sarbanes told the Salisbury Daily Times that Seidel would take his Wi-Hi teams to the University of Maryland Eastern Shore – an HBCU, then known as Maryland State College – to scrimmage with the Black players. It was an exercise that was more than just basketball practice.

"Sam imparted values, values which still guide me in my professional and personal life," Sarbanes told reporters around the time of Seidel's death. "My fondest memory is his pulling us all together and holding us to a standard of excellence not just in terms of playing basketball, but how we conducted ourselves on and off the court. That was important to him."

***

Dick DeHart's tenure at Wi-Hi would prove to be shorter and less successful than Seidel's. He was announced as the school's newest history teacher, varsity boys basketball coach and JV football coach that August at just 25 years old.

By July 1954, DeHart was gone and on to his next gig, becoming the head men's basketball and football coach at Division II Davis & Elkins College in West Virginia. He had led Wi-Hi in the 1953-54 season to an 11-4 regular season mark, a Class A Eastern Shore championship and a state semifinals appearance. Ed Nichols of the Salisbury Daily Times wrote that DeHart was "a swell fellow" and unlike other come-heres. He didn't complain about the Eastern Shore folk or weather or government or newspapers; he just coached basketball and was mostly friendly as he went about his business. Taking over for DeHart at Wi-Hi was Denver Knapp, who also coached football.

DeHart jumped jobs again in 1956, becoming the head men's basketball coach at Millersville State Teachers College in south central Pennsylvania, which was then an NAIA school. DeHart also taught health, physical education and biology at the school, which he made his long-term home. DeHart coached at Millersville for 26 seasons, piling up a 321-298 record, a resume that included six NAIA district championships. He is the school's all-time winningest coach and was inducted into its athletics hall of fame.

The first coach to ever bring the Eastern Shore a state title in boys basketball, DeHart died in 2015 at the age of 87 in Lakeland, Florida.

***

While Ocean City High School enjoyed its greatest success on the basketball court in 1952, a new high school was being built just nine miles inland along Route 50 in Berlin. Stephen Decatur High School opened in 1954 and the next year, Ocean City's students were bused there. The school in the resort town closed and the building on Maryland 528 and Third Street was transformed into the town hall.

Decatur is now the largest high school on the Eastern Shore, according to enrollment figures in 2021. It is the only high school gym on the Eastern Shore to host a U.S. President, as Donald Trump held a rally there on April 20, 2016, in the lead-up to his unlikely and polarizing election victory. As Trump spoke and riled up the capacity-crowd, U.S. and Maryland flags were behind him, and a basketball hoop hung above him.

The Decatur Seahawks have continued on Ocean City's legacy of excellence in basketball, capturing a state championship in 1970. Between 2016 and 2018, the school won a Bayside Conference title and made three straight trips to the state final four.

THE SHORE'S OVERLOOKED BLACK HIGH SCHOOLS

"Truthfully, I didn't see anyone in the tournament who could out-shoot Levi Fontaine." – Joe Robinson

One of the true Eastern Shore basketball legends that folks don't talk about nearly enough is Levi Fontaine.

There are two reasons for this. First, Fontaine played in the 1960s, an era that has largely been forgotten by hoop heads on the Eastern Shore. People can talk for days about the '80s and '90s and 2000s, but the '60s get glossed over. We don't have film or an abundance of articles from those days, and the folks who remember the era best are fading. In the decade, Jack Morgan coached Crisfield to a pair of Class C state crowns in 1961 and 1964, and Easton captured a Class B title in 1968 under the direction of Gary Shaffer.

But the second and probably more important reason that folks don't mention Fontaine often is this: He played during the era of segregation and starred at the all-Black Somerset High School in Princess Anne. Fontaine rarely played against the Wi-Hi's, Crisfield's and Easton's. Instead, he was gliding past defenders and finger-rolling his way to the rim against Salisbury, Woodson and Mace's Lane – other Black high schools in the region during that time.

If Fontaine was white, or at least played at a predominately white school, he likely would've garnered more media attention than just a smattering of short below-the-fold briefs in the Salisbury Daily Times.

Alas, his talent was too impressive to ignore. Coaches around the Shore saw it quickly, and then-Pocomoke High School head coach Phil Slacum was incredibly relieved that he didn't have to devise a scheme to contain Fontaine on a regular basis.

"To tell you the truth, I don't know how we'd defend against Levi Fontaine," Slacum told the Daily Times. "That boy can shoot from either hand, off either foot from anywhere. He's the best shooter I've ever seen on this Eastern Shore."

***

Levi Fontaine burst onto the scene as a sophomore in the 1963-64 campaign. Fontaine stood about 6-foot-3, with a short and neat afro, a thin mustache and chiseled arms. He was armed with a silky jumper and a knack for putting back offensive rebounds. He was coached at Somerset by Joe Robinson, a 26-year-old former Maryland State College football and basketball player. He unleashed Fontaine and a press on opponents up and down the Shore. The Somerset Dragons were 15-1 at the end of its regular season, powered by Fontaine's 24.8 points per-game average. There was just one game all season in which he didn't score more than 20 points, notching 17 in a late season win in Denton over Lockerman High.

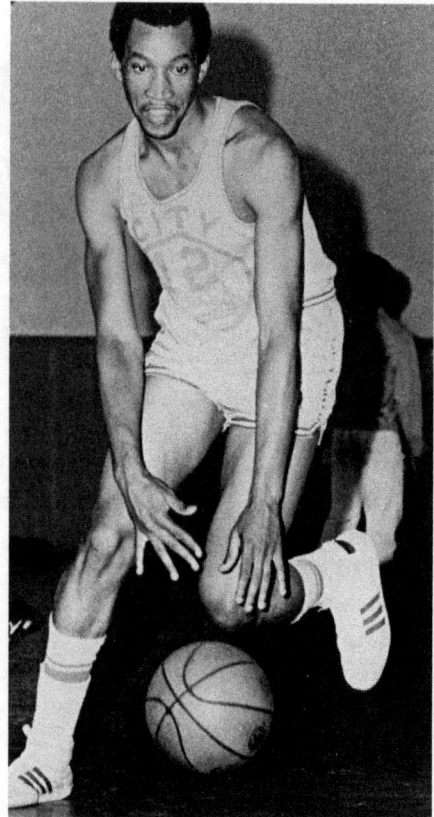

Levi Fontaine led Somerset High School to back-to-back state championships in 1965 and 1966. Maryland Eastern Shore Athletics.

In the state playoffs, Fontaine got a chance to shine in front of everyone. Once the tournament reached the District Finals stage, white schools and Black schools could be matched up against each other. In March of 1964, two Black high schools captured District 5 titles on the Shore. Mace's Lane bested Easton 54-52 in a tight Class A bout and Fontaine's Somerset squad easily dispatched North Dorchester, 64-39, in the Class B contest. More than 1,800 people packed inside the old Wicomico Youth & Civic Center to see the twin bill.

"Levi Fontaine was one of the better players at that time," said Vic Burns, who grew up in Cambridge and years later coached North Dorchester to a state title. "I saw him play a couple of times and he always was one of the players who stuck out in my mind as being one of the better players to ever come off the Shore."

Both Mace's Lane and Somerset won in the next round, too, punching their tickets to College Park and the state semifinals. The Cambridge-based Mace's Lane was led by Earl Mack's 20 points in a 59-47 win over North Caroline High while Fontaine and Arnold Ballard combined for 27 points to push Somerset over Chestertown, 60-51.

At the University of Maryland, neither squad could prevail. Fontaine was held to 16 points and Somerset lost to Walkersville by eight. Fontaine connected on a 25-foot jumper with about three minutes to play to cut the lead to four, but the Dragons couldn't quite close the gap and Fontaine fouled out before the final buzzer. In the Class A semifinal, Mace's Lane fell to Beall in a disappointing fashion.

Fontaine grew an inch over the offseason and played with a purpose his junior year. Somerset began the season on a long winning streak, and each victory was highlighted by an impressive performance from the Dragons' star. It wasn't until Jan. 30, 1965 – after he scored a season-high 43 points in a drubbing of Worcester – that his picture appeared in the Daily Times for the first time.

A bit ahead of his time, Fontaine began to rely on shooting from the corners. Nowadays, that's one of the most efficient shots a player can take, as it's worth three points and typically more likely to go in than from other spots along the arc. As a two-pointer – as it was in the days Fontaine played, long before the three-point shot existed – it wasn't as valuable. Still, he became a bit of an expert at catching and shooting from those corners. Like Marlo in HBO's television series "The Wire," he owned those corners.

"'Give the ball to Levi and Shoot! Shoot!' was the cheer, I believe, according to those who witnessed his incredible range," says Greg Bozman, who is now the athletic director for public schools in Somerset County.

Fontaine also had some help on the 1964-65 Somerset team, as Thomas Stewart averaged more than 20 points and 12 rebounds per-game. Fontaine finished the regular season averaging 25.4 points per-game. The duo carried the offense, while Robinson's 3-1-1 press drove the defense.

"Run, run, run the opposition into their own mistakes," Robinson once told the Daily Times of his scheme, which often suffocated teams.

Robinson would also say of the team, decades later to the same newspaper: "And the speed that we played with was different. We played from one end to the other. And we practiced at that speed, and that's how you come out with championships."

Again, Somerset bulldozed its way through the early rounds of the playoffs. And this time, it made its way to the Class B title game. Waiting for them was Bill Talley's Walkersville squad, who had bested the Dragons the year before. But this time, Fontaine would not be contained.

The game was essentially Fontaine versus Gordon Smith, Walkersville's 6-foot-2 All-American. Fontaine scored 24 points in the first half, giving the

Levi Fontaine was the first native of the Eastern Shore of Maryland to be drafted into the NBA, selected by the Warriors in 1970. Maryland Eastern Shore Athletics.

Somerset Dragons a four-point lead at the break. In the third quarter, Somerset jumped out to a 13-point lead, and that's when Smith flipped his switch. With his left thigh bandaged up, he hit a driving lay-up to close out the third quarter, and would score 14 points in the final period. Walkersville briefly retook the lead at 73-72, but Fontaine responded with a turnaround jumper. A free throw from Ernest Leatherbury gave Somerset a two-point cushion at 75-73, however Smith still had the hot hand and enough time for a shot. As three Dragons closed in on him, he fired up an attempt that bounced off the rim. Players fought over the rebound and it rolled out of bounds. A jump ball was called, Fontaine won it, and Somerset ran out the clock and captured the Class B state title.

Fontaine finished with 36 points while Smith – who would go on to be the captain at Cincinnati and be drafted by the Boston Celtics – ended up with 39 points. The two performances still rank in the top 15 of the highest single-game scoring totals in the history of the state tournament. After the game, Walkersville retired Smith's No. 14 jersey.

Capping off a 21-1 campaign, Somerset was the sixth Eastern Shore school to win a state championship in boys basketball, but the first from Somerset County and the first Black high school to do so.

The next season, the 1965-66 campaign, Fontaine and Robinson led the Somerset Dragons on a repeat run. During the regular season, Somerset played a rare game at Crisfield and did not disappoint. In front of a standing-room-only crowd in the gym by the bay, Fontaine dropped 30 points in an impressive 98-53 victory. After the loss, two-time state champion head coach Jack Morgan did not mince words.

"This is the best team I've ever seen on the Eastern Shore," Morgan told the Daily Times. "I'm not sure, but it is doubtful if anyone in the state of any classification could beat this Somerset team. We don't feel humiliated when losing to an opponent like this."

Indeed, Somerset was 16-0 by March 1966, scoring 97.4 points per-game while allowing just a hair under 61. Fontaine averaged 27.6 points per-game and was garnering the attention of colleges. The Dragons thumped Pocomoke by 47 points in the opening round of the playoffs, and nearly doubled-up Mardela – 125-64 – in the next game. Somerset was moved to Class C for the 1966 playoffs, but rolled through it just the same. In the state semifinals, Fontaine had 27 points and a career-high 29 rebounds in a 77-47 win over Mt. Savage of Allegany County.

"When you played Somerset it was end-to-end, four quarters, all night long," Warren White – who played in those days at Salisbury High, then at James M. Bennett – told the Daily Times. "100 points was nothing."

Fontaine was magnificent again in the state final. In his last game wearing No. 41 for Somerset, he tallied 32 points and 23 rebounds in an 88-71 win over Poolesville. With the victory, Joe Robinson's Somerset team became the first Eastern Shore school to win back-to-back state titles in boys basketball.

"Truthfully, I didn't see anyone in the tournament who could out-shoot Levi Fontaine," Robinson told the Daily Times after his 28th straight win, a streak spanning two seasons.

Three years after Fontaine powered Somerset to back-to-back state titles, the school closed and its students were integrated into Washington High School. Decades later, in 2022, players from those Somerset teams gathered in Washington's gym to see a trio of banners raised in their honor: one for the 1965 title, one for 1966 and one for their five regional championships.

***

After Fontaine graduated from Somerset High, he didn't go far. Together, he and Joe Robinson – and Thomas Stewart – went across town to Maryland State College, Robinson as the new head coach and Fontaine as the new star player of the Hawks.

"He was such an outstanding role model, outstanding coach, and knowledgeable coach," Kirkland Hall told the Daily Times. Hall played for Robinson at Somerset, and years later was the head basketball coach of the Hawks from 1976 to 1984. "He taught us a lot about basketball, but also about life. I think that is the most important thing. He taught us respect, respect for the game, for each other, for our families, for our communities. And you can see the comments from other people that that was the way he was. Hard taskmaster, but he loved us and did everything he could to make us who we were."

The Hawks went 77-25 over their next four seasons. In 1970, Fontaine's senior campaign, Maryland State went 20-0 in the regular season and 29-2 overall, captured the NAIA District 19 title and earned a No. 1 ranking in the AP's Small College Poll. The following academic year, the historically Black college changed its name to The University of Maryland-Eastern Shore. Fontaine finished his college career with 1,538 points and was inducted into the UMES Athletics Hall of Fame in 1984.

Fontaine was one of two Hawks, along with Jake Ford, to be drafted into the NBA in 1970. Fontaine was selected with the second pick in the fifth round by the San Francisco Warriors while Ford was taken with the third pick in the second round by the Seattle Supersonics.

Warriors chief scout George Lee told the Oakland Tribune that Fontaine was "a good shooter and ball-handler," which might've been underselling the Princess Anne native just a bit, considering he shot better than 50% from the floor in his senior college season. Warriors player-coach Al Attles told the San Francisco Examiner, "Fontaine's a flashy shooter. He's got a lot to learn, but he looks like a kid who can learn quickly."

Problem was, the Warriors were deep at both guard spots during Fontaine's rookie season. He played in just 36 games, and saw more than 10 minutes of action in just six contests. His best performance came on February 17, 1971, at home against the Boston Celtics when he scored 16 points on eight shots in eight minutes. In a loss to Seattle the following month, Fontaine had 11 points and four rebounds while Ford, his former college teammate, had eight points and three assists.

Fontaine was ejected from the final NBA game he ever played in, a 136-86 playoff loss to the Milwaukee Bucks, for throwing a punch at Dick Cunningham. He was released by the Warriors prior to the start of the 1971-72 season. He tried making his way in the flailing and fun ABA, but was unceremoniously waived by the Pittsburgh Condors.

While Fontaine's NBA career might've been short and somewhat unadorned, his mark on Eastern Shore basketball should be remembered. He is one of a small handful of men to make it from the courts of the Delmarva Peninsula all the way to the game's highest stage. He was a scoring machine that no local coach could figure out how to slow down. He steered tiny Somerset High to two straight state titles, and was a key part of a golden era for hoops at the Shore's lone Division I institution.

***

Before and after Levi Fontaine torched nets in Somerset County, there were other teams and players from Black high schools on the Eastern Shore that represented the region well, but didn't always get the same amount of media coverage as their white counterparts.

Back in the 1950s, Maryland's state high school basketball tournament was segregated, too. At that time, Black high school teams were not permitted to mix with white teams in state tournament play. So, the Black high schools started their own tournament.

It's unclear, exactly, what year the "State Negro Basketball Tournament" – as it was dubbed in newspapers in the 1950s – started, but the first team from the Eastern Shore to win it all was Mace's Lane of Cambridge in 1953. Behind the play of Leroy Kane, Mace's Lane made its way into the Class B championship by besting Greenwood of Princess Anne and Salisbury High School in the earlier rounds of the playoffs. The title game was held at Morgan State College in Baltimore, and Mace's Lane beat Sollers Point of Dundalk, 62-54, led by Kane's 22 points. A Daily Times story from March 16, 1953 notes that it was the first "Class B colored title ever brought back on the Eastern Shore."

The Easton Colored School opened in 1870. In 1937, it was renamed as the Robert Russa Moton Junior and Senior High School and continued to serve as the all-Black school in Easton until 1967 when Talbot County schools were fully integrated. Shown here is the girls basketball team at Moton in 1959. Courtesy of the Talbot Historical Society, Easton, Maryland.

A few years later, it was Moton High School in Easton that was the true powerhouse among Black high school teams on the Eastern Shore. The school originally opened in 1870 on Port Street and was the first Black public school in Talbot County. In 1937, it was renamed after Robert Russa Moton, an author and educator from Virginia. In 1953, the school was moved to Glenwood Avenue. A year later, following the ruling in the landmark Brown v. Board of Education case, Talbot County granted its Black students the choice as to which school they wanted to attend. But few Black students strayed from Moton. And athletics at the school flourished.

In boys basketball, the Moton Tigers won five state titles and nine district championships between 1953 and 1967. The first state title team was coached by Marion J. Waller, but he resigned after the 1955 season with a record of 121-27 – an 81.7% winning percentage. Roger Bryan succeeded Waller, and coached the Tigers to five more state championships.

Bryan's best team might've been his 1957 squad. By February 15 of that year, Moton had won its 40th consecutive game, beating Garnett High of Chestertown 113-56 behind 34 points from the high-flying Richard Milbourne.

Milbourne was a talented scorer, no question. He once scored 51 points in a single game and finished his career at Moton with more than 1,000. Milbourne went on to play at Bowie State and professionally, briefly. But in 1957, he wasn't the best player on his team. That title belonged to the freshman point guard, Walter Hazzard, who learned how to play basketball on a wooden backboard near the corner of Graham's Alley and Dover Street in Easton. Hazzard was a skinny and slender guard with a buzz cut. Bryan, then the head coach, requested that the cafeteria workers at Moton give him extra biscuits at lunch to fatten him up. Despite his beanpole-like frame, Hazzard was a real wizard with the basketball.

In the Class C semifinal that year, Hazzard dazzled with 25 points and 11 assists in a 110-49 win over Harriett Tubman of Ellicott City. In the final, Moton swamped Lincoln High of Frederick, 85-46 behind 43 combined points from Hazzard and Milbourne. It was Moton's third straight state title. Salisbury High won the Class B Negro title that season too, beating Sollers Point, 62-56.

Moton would win the Class C Negro state title again in 1958, its fourth straight – and run its winning streak to 71 games – but did so without Hazzard. Midway through his sophomore year at Moton, Hazzard's family moved to Overbrook, Pennsylvania, a neighborhood northwest of Philadelphia. His father was a Methodist minister and was accepted a new job at a church there.

Hazzard became an exceptional college and professional basketball player. The 6-foot-2 guard went to UCLA to play for the legendary John Wooden and was part of the first Bruins team to make a Final Four in 1962 and the first to win a national championship in 1964. After totaling 30 points, 17 assists and 10 rebounds at the Final Four, Hazzard was the NCAA Tournament's Most Outstanding Player in 1964. He was also named the USBWA Player of the Year and was tabbed as a consensus All-American.

At UCLA, Moton High School product Walt Hazzard was the Final Four's Most Outstanding Player in 1964. He went on to play a decade in the NBA and later coached UCLA in the 1980s. UCLA Athletics.

After averaging 16.1 points and 5.5 rebounds per-game in his career for the Bruins, Hazzard was drafted by the Los Angeles Lakers. That summer, he helped the U.S. National Team win the gold medal at the Olympics in Tokyo.

Across 10 seasons in the NBA, Hazzard averaged 12.6 points, 4.9 assists and 3.1 rebounds per game. He was an All-Star in 1968 with the Seattle Supersonics. Hazzard later became the head coach at UCLA, guiding the Bruins from 1984 to 1988. UCLA won the NIT under his watch in 1985, and then won the Pac-10 Conference and made the NCAA Tournament in 1987 - a season in which he was also named as the conference's Coach of the Year. Hazzard later worked for the Lakers as a scout. He died in 2011 at the age of 69 following complications from heart surgery.

Moton ceased being the all-Black high school in Easton in 1967 when Talbot County Schools were fully integrated. By then, the historically Black high school teams that did remain on the Eastern Shore were playing against the white teams, even in state tournament competitions.

***

A year after Somerset's second state title, Mace's Lane of Cambridge carried the torch for Black high schools on the Shore behind the play of Larry Farrare.

His 31.5 points per-game was the second-best mark among all players in the state in the 1966-67 season, and he powered Mace's Lane to the Class B state final. Despite putting up an incredible 37 points, Farrare's squad fell to Frederick Sasscer High from Prince George's County, 94-79.

Mace's Lane made four trips to the state tournament between 1964 and 1969. It later became a middle school in the Dorchester County system.

"Just about every town had a Black high school before 1969," said Vic Burns, a 1970 Cambridge High School graduate. "Cambridge played Mace's Lane two times a year in basketball. Those were some of the best games that there were. The football games were heated up too. Those kids all played with each other anyway on playgrounds. There were some good Mace's Lane teams."

Farrare was a marvelous athlete at 6-foot-4, with lanky arms and strong long legs. He won the state's long jump and high jump titles in 1966 and 1967, and ran the anchor on the state championship 4x400 relay team in 1967. Farrare was also a member of the Maryland Junior Olympic team. Burns recalled that Farrare was once invited to a camp with the Philadelphia Phillies of Major League Baseball.

"He could dunk, he could handle the ball, behind the back stuff, he could just do everything," Burns said. "To me, he was like, the first, what I would call – the athletic prototype of basketball players of today. He was that type of player. The Farrare's of Cambridge were very well-known, athletically."

Warren White, who coached Parkside's girls team to a state championship in 1999, said Farrare was "one of the best pure shooters from the Shore."

Farrare wound up playing college basketball, but not until nearly 14 years after his high school career ended. After working for eight years as a supervisor for a tuna company, Farrare wound up playing at UMES for three seasons, from 1981 to 1984. Through 55 appearances with the Hawks, he averaged 7.8 points and 2.7 rebounds per-game while shooting 49.7% from the floor. In the April 9, 1984 edition of Sports Illustrated, he was featured in the "Faces in the Crowd" section for being "the country's oldest major-college basketball player."

After his playing days were over, Farrare went on to referee countless of Bayside Conference high school games on the Eastern Shore.

***

Three years after Levi Fontaine led the Somerset High School Dragons to their second straight state championship, the school closed. In 1969 – 15 years after Brown vs. Board of Education – all schools in Somerset County were desegregated. Washington High in Princess Anne was big enough to absorb all of Somerset's students, so the school building was no longer needed. Mace's Lane in Cambridge and Carter G. Woodson in Crisfield also closed that year.

The last remaining all-Black high school on the Eastern Shore was Worcester High in Newark, a tiny community situated along Route 113, sandwiched between Berlin and Snow Hill. Worcester was home to the boys basketball team that handed Somerset its lone loss en route to its 1965 title, and Worcester High would produce Talvin Skinner, who would follow Fontaine as the next Eastern Shore product to play in the NBA.

"At Worcester High School, we had a bunch of guys that lacked any real basketball fundamentals and then there was me," Skinner told the Dispatch of Ocean City in 2018. "The coach would tell them 'Just give Talvin the ball,' so it was often me against everybody else."

Al 'Hondo' Handy, who starred on Stephen Decatur's 1970 state championship team said of Skinner: "He was a dominant player."

After starring on the greatest Maryland Eastern Shore team of all-time in 1974 – in which the Hawks went 27-2, won the MEAC and became the first HBCU to play in and win a game in the NIT – Skinner was drafted by the Seattle SuperSonics with the eighth pick in the third round. As a senior for John Bates' dominant Hawks' squad, Skinner – while sporting a big afro, calf-high striped socks, Converses and the No. 41 jersey – averaged 16.3 points and 12.3 points per-game while shooting 50.7% from the floor. Also on that UMES squad was Granville Cannon, a star for Somerset High who scored 40 points in the Class C semifinal in 1968.

"I played against Granville Cannon in the mid-80s," said former Crisfield player Greg Bozman, a frequent player in local men's leagues. "If he had been 6-foot-3, he also would've been in the NBA."

Years later, Bates told the Daily Times that Skinner was the "heart and soul" of that Hawks' team and "the best all-around player" Bates ever coached. A wing who was a fearless rebounder and could score inside and out, the Berlin native was valued for his versatility. Skinner played two seasons for the Bill Russell-coached Sonics, averaging 4.6 points, 4.2 rebounds and 1.1 assists per-game across 145 professional appearances.

Skinner notched eight double-doubles in his NBA tenure, and arguably his best performance came on March 24, 1976, where he tallied 26 points, 13 rebounds and three assists, leading the Sonics to a 25-point victory over Bob Dandridge and the Milwaukee Bucks. During his rookie season, he once held hall-of-famer John Havlicek to 5-of-16 shooting in a game that ended in a seven-point win for the Sonics in Boston. Russell told the Boston Globe that Skinner was "the key man" for Seattle that day.

Russell's affinity for Skinner didn't last, as "Mr. 11 Rings" waived the

Eastern Shoreman before the start of the 1976-77 season.

Skinner stayed in Seattle when his playing days were over and had a long career working in the airline business for Boeing. He returned to basketball eventually, working as an assistant coach specializing in player development and rehab with the WNBA's Seattle Storm. He was a member of the staff that helped guide the Storm to a championship in 2004, the first for the franchise.

"He coaches us on the bench," then-Seattle forward Adia Barnes told the Spokane Spokesman-Review of Skinner. "Sometimes you get caught up in games, you get disgusted on the court, but he's always behind us saying, 'Slow down and do this,' and when you cool down the little things he sees gives us a different perspective. And that really helps us."

A native of Philadelphia, Rubin Collins played at Washington High School and then at the University of Maryland Eastern Shore where he starred on the Hawks' team that made the 1974 NIT. Maryland Eastern Shore Athletics.

A two-time All-MEAC selection, Skinner was inducted into the MEAC Hall of Fame in 2002 and the UMES Athletics Hall of Fame in 2004. As of 2021, Skinner is still the most recent former UMES player to be drafted into and play in the NBA.

"Skinner was the best 6-foot-6 rebounder that I've ever seen," said longtime Pocomoke head coach David Byrd, who played against the Supersonic in high school. "He was very quick off the floor, slender, could jump out of the gym, (and had) long arms. He was a really, really great rebounder. He was on a heck of a team at UMES. He'd come back and work out in our gyms when he was in the NBA."

A Maryland Eastern Shore teammate of Skinner's, Rubin Collins – a graduate of Princess Anne's Washington High – was also drafted into the NBA, in 1974 by the Portland Trailblazers, but he never played a minute for them. As a high schooler, Collins broke Fontaine's single-game scoring record for a Somerset County player with a 45-point outing against Pocomoke in 1971.

"He was the best basketball player I had seen," said Clarence Johnson, Washington High's principal at the time. "Rubin Collins could change the complexion of a game quicker than anybody. Rubin was something else. And John Bates was one hell of a coach."

***

Decades after Somerset High School closed, Greg Bozman made sure the teams led by Levi Fontaine and coached by Joe Robinson got their proper recognition. Bozman was the athletic director for Somerset County Schools by 2022, and had banners commemorating the Dragons' pair of state championships made up and hung in Washington's gym.

After Fontaine won his second state title with Somerset in March 1966, the beginning of the Associated Press story that was picked up in newspapers across the Old-Line State read: "Remember the name Levi Fontaine. Spectators at the Maryland High School Basketball Tournament will remember it. And Poolesville can't forget it."

Amen. We mustn't let Fontaine, Talvin Skinner, Larry Farrare, Walter Hazzard and the great players, teams, coaches and stories from the Eastern Shore's Black high schools slip from our memories.

Player	Team	G	MP	FG%	FT%	TRB	AST	PTS
Fontaine	71-72 Warriors	35	6.0	.366	.757	0.4	0.6	3.8
Skinner	74-75 Sonics	73	21.6	.409	.649	4.7	1.2	4.8
Skinner	75-76 Sonics	72	17.0	.463	.613	3.7	0.9	4.3

LAMBERT'S SEAHAWKS

"Our press was really devastating." – Al 'Hondo' Handy

Al Handy – known to his friends as Hondo – was one of the first six Black students to attend Stephen Decatur High School, enrolling there as an eighth grader in 1965.

Worcester County was the last county in Maryland – and among the final 25 districts in the U.S. – to desegregate its schools. Worcester High was the final historically Black school on the Eastern Shore to close, shutting its doors prior to the start of the 1970-71 academic year. The building is still standing as of this writing, serving as offices for the Worcester County Board of Education.

Handy grew up in the tiny Worcester County town of Newark, and in those days, the Black folk in town attended nearby Worcester High.

But one day in middle school, Handy was sent home with a letter. It was the county school board informing parents that, eventually, over the next few years, all the schools in Worcester County would be desegregated. The letter also came with an opportunity: Decatur was going to admit a handful of African-American students, right away, kickstarting integration in the school.

A few of the boys that were part of that first group of Black students to integrate Stephen Decatur became the core for one of the Eastern Shore's best high school basketball teams ever. Coached by Ward Lambert, steered on the court by Oliver Purnell, and powered by a tough defense and a breakneck pace, the Seahawks sprinted through the local competition on its way to a state championship in 1970, Handy's senior year. He too was a starter on that team and an integral part to the Seahawks' success.

Lambert, who played at the University of Virginia, motivated the Seahawks with a simple math equation at the beginning of the 1969-70 season. To become state champs, Decatur would have to play – including the playoffs – 24 games. So, after each win, Lambert would post how many games the Seahawks had left until they were raising a trophy. After their season-opening victory, his sign read "One And Oh, And 23 To Go." After the second win, "Two And Oh, And 22 To Go." And so forth.

"We just won the game last night, and we come in and admire the bulletin board, go to practice and prepare for the next game," Handy said.

That year, Decatur looked good and played well. The Seahawks were a sharp-dressed team, with dark blue warm-ups and white popped collars. During games, each player sported thick white wristbands and striped socks that went midway up the calf. All players wore white shoes, but a few of them sported Adidas, with the brand's trademark three stripes sticking out in team photos. Under Lambert, Decatur was a team that liked to look good and play good. The Seahawks scored quickly on offense and suffocated teams on defense.

Stephen Decatur players celebrate their state championship in College Park after beating Frederick 64-63 in 1970. Stephen Decatur yearbooks.

"They'd press the living daylights out of you and ran the floor," said David Byrd, a player for Pocomoke that season. "Probably one of the first teams on the Eastern Shore to do that. They were well-coached. Lambert was calculated. They ran a very good fast break and they had an eraser in there with Sherwood Purnell and super quick guards."

Lambert's Seahawks often deployed a 3-1-1 press on defense, with Oliver Purnell in the middle of the zone, like the defensive quarterback. Sherwood Purnell roamed the back of the press, and Ron Dixon, Handy and Milton Purnell were at the front. With that scheme, Decatur relied on turning defense into offense.

"The press was designed to allow a team to throw the ball in. Then we had to be perfectionists at trapping the ball. As the ball is being thrown in, we're running as fast as we can to trap the person receiving the ball. And then the third person is running directly to the inbounder," Handy said. "Our press was really devastating."

And on the offensive end, all season long, Oliver Purnell dazzled opponents with his superb ball-handling skills.

"He went to a camp that summer and had this behind-the-back move. Back then, nobody had heard of behind-the-back," Handy said of Purnell. "He was just a good leader, especially on our defensive press."

Like Handy, Dixon and the trio of Purnells were among the first group of Black students to attend Decatur. This kinship – combined with their relationship on the basketball court – made the young men uniquely close.

"Some of my friends in my community didn't like us going to (Decatur)," Handy said. It probably didn't help that Handy and his Seahawks thrashed Worcester High handily, twice: 93-52 and 99-59. Worcester was armed with future NBA player Talvin Skinner, but Sherwood Purnell was a bad matchup for him, size and skillset wise.

The Seahawks lost just once in the 1969-70 regular season, with their only defeat coming to Washington by just two points at the Wicomico Civic Center. With their heads hanging after their first loss of the year, Lambert came into the locker room and the players thought he was going to rip into them. Instead, he told them, "Fellas, this loss has just made us state champions." The players, bemused, turned to themselves and said, "How the hell does he know that?"

Recalls Handy: "It was just another motivation."

The Seahawks breezed through the playoffs, beating Easton, Cambridge, North Caroline and Havre de Grace by an average margin of 27.5 points per-game

In the final, the Seahawks just squeaked past Frederick, 64-63, for the lone state basketball title in the school's history.

"My mother was their No. 1 fan," said Derrick Fooks, a 1983 Decatur graduate. "After she retired, she just started going to all the basketball games."

Coached by Ward Lambert, the 1969-70 Stephen Decatur boys basketball team went 23-1 and won the school's first state championship. Stephen Decatur yearbooks.

Sherwood Purnell went on to play at the University of Delaware, where he averaged 5.3 points per-game. A younger Purnell, Gerald – who, as an eighth grader, was a team manager for the 1970 Decatur squad – played college basketball at Bucknell for Jim Valvano. He averaged 15.7 points per-game across 75 collegiate contests.

Oliver Purnell played at Old Dominion and later became a collegiate head coach after assisting Lefty Driesell at Maryland for a bit. Oliver led teams at Radford, Old Dominion, Dayton, Clemson and DePaul, winning 448 games and taking six trips to the NCAA Tournament. Oliver was also an assistant on the 2004 U.S. Olympic basketball team that won bronze.

Lambert went on to coach at Salisbury State College – which later became Salisbury University – in the fall of 1970. He coached the Sea Gulls through the 2000 season, retired with 433 wins and took Salisbury to the NCAA Tournament five times. Handy was one of Lambert's first Salisbury recruits. Doug King, who played his high school ball at Wi-Hi, was one of his last.

"That was the best time. We were good. Even the 6 a.m. practices were fun. He's a good man," said Doug King, who played for Lambert in his final season. "He was mean as hell, but he knew what he was doing."

And the members of the 1970 Seahawks would agree. Lambert's tactics that led Decatur to the state championship became influential on the Shore.

COLONEL, POCOMOKE AND THE 1976 ALL-SHORE FINAL

"They'll never let anybody do this again." – Merrill Morgan

Beginning with the tourist town boys from Ocean City High School in 1952, teams from the Eastern Shore have claimed 31 Maryland Public Secondary Schools Athletic Association (MPSSAA) state championships in boys basketball through 2021. Most of the time, those titles were won over opposing squads from Baltimore, western Maryland, Prince George's County, or someplace where the people didn't know the difference between Worcester County and Worcestershire sauce. Teams from the Shore always felt like they had to prove themselves when they crossed the Chesapeake Bay. Coaches and players typically felt slighted by western shore folks.

But in 1976, the Class C Championship would be decided by two teams that called the Delmarva Peninsula home. For the first time ever – and the only time in the history of boys basketball in the state – two teams from the Bayside Conference met in a state final for all the marbles.

In the semifinals, Carey Reece's Pocomoke Warriors beat Bruce High School of Westernport 71-69, and Merrill Morgan's Colonel Richardson Colonels topped Walkersville of Frederick County, 60-55. The state final at Cole Field House was the first appearance for CR and the third for Pocomoke, which claimed the 1971 title under the guidance of Ronnie Ross.

This is something that could not happen for many years, because both Colonel and Pocomoke were bracketed in the 1A East Region for state basketball tournaments. And each region winner – North, South, East and West – made up the four semifinalists for the state final four. But back in the 1970s, there were several districts for each of the four classifications, not the four regions. In 1976, Colonel was a member of District 7 and Pocomoke was a member of District 8.

Clarence Johnson was born and raised in Princess Anne and still lives there as of this writing. He was the principal at Washington High School from 1971 to 1983 and has served in various leadership roles with the MPSSAA and the Bayside Conference, most recently as the conference's executive director. "It had to be because in those days there weren't regions. There were districts. And it had to be somebody got an automatic bye," Johnson said, trying to dig several decades back through his memory.

Recently, the MPSSAA went back to the eight-region playoff system. In

2020, Colonel Richardson and Kent County were placed Region I of the 1A East with schools from Cecil and Harford Counties, and all other 1A East Bayside teams were placed in Region II. Once the eight region champs are decided, they are then reseeded for the state quarterfinals based off of regular season winning percentage.

So, an All-Shore final is once again possible, but as of this writing, it hasn't happened since 1976 in boys basketball.

Coached by Carey Reece, the 1975-76 Pocomoke boys team went 22-2. Pocomoke yearbooks.

***

Pocomoke and Colonel Richardson are separated by just 72 miles. To reach Colonel from Pocomoke, you just turn left on Route 13 from Old Virginia Road, hop on Route 50 in Salisbury and ride that to Mardela, then wind your way through Sharptown and Eldorado until you reach the town limits of Federalsburg. Then you hang a left on Reliance Road, a left onto Federalsburg Highway, then a left on Three Bridges Road and pass all the chicken houses until you reach American Corner Road. Then take a right, then a left onto Richardson Road, and just when you think you've reached the middle of nowhere, you'll come upon a complex of a middle school, a high school, a bunch of solar panels and athletic fields.

Full disclosure: I'm a graduate of Colonel Richardson High School. And so is my sister, my father, both of my grandparents, and a few aunts and uncles.

So, the stretch of that drive between Salisbury and Federalsburg is one that I've driven probably hundreds of times. If God were to ever take my eyesight away from me, I'm confident that I could still make that trip without a scratch. It's the route my Dad drove every other Friday and Sunday for several years, picking up my sister and I for the weekend from Federalsburg to take us to the house in Mardela he shared with my step-mom. And when I turned 16, I powered my Pappy's 1985 El Camino down that path countless times. On Black Friday in 2010, I got my first speeding ticket making this drive, coming out of Eldorado after working a shift at the Salisbury mall, a bit too eager to get home for leftover turkey sandwiches after an all-nighter. And I've driven to Colonel Richardson so many times, I can tell you that you get from 319 Maple Avenue in Federalsburg to the high school in eight minutes and 11 seconds. But if the roads are wet, slow down on the turns on Laurel Grove Road, or else you might hydroplane and obliterate a wooden fence with an old blue Chevy.

Alas, the journey to the 1976 All-Shore state final didn't begin in Pocomoke, or on the shores of Cherry Beach in Sharptown, or at the Tastee-Freez in Federalsburg.

No, it begins in 1956, when a young man from Montclair, New Jersey went down to Durham, North Carolina to take his education – and his expertise in basketball – to a higher level.

The 1975-76 Colonel Richardson Colonels. Coached by Merrill Morgan, the Colonels went 18-6. Colonel Richardson yearbooks.

***

Long before Mark Alarie or Christian Laettner put on a Duke Blue Devils' jersey with the number 32 on it, Merrill Morgan wore it. "It's hung from the rafters," he recalls, with a laugh.

"I had wanted to go to Duke for a long time," Morgan says. "I had a copy of Sport Magazine that I read and there was an article in there about Dick Groat, who was an All-American in two sports (baseball and basketball) there. He talked about how he was impressed by their baseball program. Well, I was impressed by their basketball program. That was one of the reasons why I picked Duke."

Listed as a 6-foot-2, 185-pound guard, Morgan was a decent player his rookie year at Duke on the freshman team for the 1956-57 season. His first heroic moment for the Blue Devils came in Winston-Salem on December 1 that season, as he sank four free throws in the final minute to seal a Duke win over Wake Forest. Morgan had 12 points in the 76-74 victory. "Morgan can hit well from outside and is probably the best set shot we have," Duke assistant coach Joe Belmont told the Raleigh News & Observer in January 1957. A month later, Duke freshman team head coach Whitt Cobb told Morgan's hometown paper, the Montclair Times, that Morgan was "offensively, the best we got" and a "terrific shooter, both inside and outside... And he is the hardest worker on the team. He means business when he goes out on the court."

Indeed, if the three-point shot had existed in those days, Morgan might've knocked down a whole bunch of them for Duke. Morgan made his varsity debut on December 19, 1958, but played just four minutes of scoreless action against Penn. The next day, Morgan shined, scoring 20 points in a seven-point road loss to Villanova, and he scored most of those buckets on set shots from outside the paint, according to a News & Observer game story. Later that season, Morgan had 10 points and five rebounds in a 59-60 home loss to N.C. State, leading Duke in scoring in front of some 7,500 fans.

Morgan played sparingly his next two seasons in Durham. Vic Bubas arrived as the head coach for the 1959-60 season. But while Morgan's playing time decreased, he was part of some important Duke teams. In 1960, the Blue Devils won the ACC tournament for the first time since 1946 and made their second-ever appearance in the NCAA Tournament. Morgan totaled eight points and three boards during Duke's tourney run. Duke was decent the next season too, going 22-6, but the most memorable thing they did was get involved in a brawl with Tobacco Road nemesis UNC, an incident that some credit for intensifying the bitter rivalry between the two blue bloods.

A member of the Kappa Sigma fraternity, Morgan graduated from Duke in June of 1961 and then soon married a North Carolina girl, Alice E. Sims, whom he met at Duke. They settled down in East Orange, New Jersey, and Morgan joined the Army reserves. He was assigned to D Company of the Second Training Regiment in Fort Dix for basic training.

But basketball called him back to the court, and he wanted to be a coach. A friend he had met at Fort Dix recommended he should take over the boys program at Woodbury High School, which had a reputation as one of the worst teams in the state. He soon became a history teacher and the head coach there in south Jersey. After his fourth season, in which the team went 10-12, Morgan was unceremoniously fired in March 1967. And unjustly so, according to the 11 students – including a handful of his players – who picketed outside of the school after word spread. While Morgan won just 10 games in his fourth season at the helm, it was the most wins for the team since 1953 and Woodbury was eligible for the state tournament for the first time in eight years. But Morgan had some language in his contract that said he had to achieve a record above .500 by his fourth season.

By then, Morgan had completed his master's degree for counseling, and he wanted to find a place where he could coach basketball and be a guidance counselor. He cast a wide net, spanning his search as far north as New Jersey and as far south as the Carolinas.

"There were a lot of states that would not let you be a coach and a counselor at the same time," Merrill's wife Alice says. "For whatever reason. North Carolina was like that then; they wouldn't let you have that combination."

Months later, he found the right match in a small community on the Delmarva Peninsula.

***

In the spring of 1960, the construction of South Caroline High School began near American Corner, a backroads community of mostly farms smack dab between routes 16 and 313, which run through the small towns of Preston and Federalsburg, respectively. The school was originally proposed in the late 1950s – around the same time North Caroline High School was built – and the idea was to consolidate the students from Preston and Federalsburg and put them in one school in a central location. Caroline is the only county on the Eastern Shore that doesn't belly-up against the Chesapeake Bay or Atlantic Ocean, and the only county that doesn't have routes 50 or 13 running through it. It's pressed up against the Delaware border, far away from city folk in Salisbury, tourists in Ocean City and watermen of Cambridge and Crisfield. And the high school in southern Caroline County isn't really near much of anything besides flat fields, chicken houses, fleets of John Deere tractors and the old A. Curtis Andrew auction barn.

A few months before the new school was set to open, the historical society in Federalsburg made a recommendation: the school should be named for Col. William Richardson, considered by many to be a patriot of the American Revolution. In 1774, he introduced the bill in the Maryland Assembly that formed Caroline County and later served as Colonel of the 5th

Maryland Regiment, leading troops in the Battle of Harlem Heights and the Battle of Camden. According to a book on the history of Caroline County published by J.W. Stowell in 1920, Richardson was commissioned in 1777, "to remove the continental treasury to Baltimore" when the British attacked Philadelphia. This was a collection of notes the Continental Congress had and needed to keep safe. In 1778, he was a member of the convention to ratify the Constitution of the United States. And from 1789 to 1793 he was a Presidential elector in the electoral college. He died in 1825 and is buried at Gilpin Point along the Choptank River.

The Caroline County Board of Education ultimately agreed with the historical society on the name change. "South Caroline" is a bit boring anyways, no? Who needs another directional school?

Students from Preston and Federalsburg high schools officially became students of Colonel Richardson High School on January 2, 1962. G.B. Hastings served as the first principal. The boys basketball teams from Preston and Federalsburg had already been practicing together as a unit since November in Federalsburg. In their first official game as the Colonels, they bested Stevensville 44-39.

Still, even with the formation of Colonel, southern Caroline County was not known for its excellence in high school sports. Federalsburg made the state semifinals once in boys basketball, in 1954, and won state titles in boys soccer (1922) and girls field ball (1946). Varsity sports teams from Preston never sniffed the state final four in any sport. Colonel produced just two winning records in its first six seasons of boys basketball, and in that span they never beat rival North Caroline.

Cliff Mister was a member of that first basketball team at Colonel in 1962, and on October 22, 1967, he – then as the sports editor for the Salisbury Daily Times – broke the news of Merrill Morgan's hiring as the new head boys basketball coach in his column, "Say Mister!"

"They had the right combination. They were ready for a change in coaching," Morgan said. "And I could be a guidance counselor."

The school was desegregated by the time Morgan was brought in and his first basketball team in the 1967-68 season featured the likes of Clint Cephas, Dennis Brummell, Glen Fluharty, Joe Duncan and George Batson; surnames that would continue to pop-up on Morgan's rosters over the next few decades. When Morgan's coaching tenure at Colonel began, tiny towns like Pittsville and Deal Island still had high schools and fielded teams.

"They always had a Fletcher or a Batson or a Bolden on the team," said David Insley, who covered the latter part of Morgan's career for the Dorchester Banner and Star Democrat.

Mister described Morgan in a December 8, 1967 story as "soft spoken" and "congenial," but called Colonel a "mammoth rebuilding job." Although

Morgan lost in his coaching debut – a second-half collapse on the road against Queen Anne's – and finished his first season at American Corner with an 8-12 record, he ultimately proved to be up for the task of building up Colonel's basketball program. Colonel finally beat North Caroline that season – 51-49 behind Fluharty's 11 points and 25 rebounds – breaking a 12-game losing streak to their county rival. And in the playoffs, they bested the Bulldogs again, 74-72 in double overtime behind 25 points from Fluharty and 17 from Cephas. Morgan's shot was still superb too, as he scored 24 points in a student vs. faculty game that spring.

"We played hard and we had a lot of quick players," Morgan said of his inaugural team.

By 1972, Morgan had the Colonels competing for Bayside titles. They lost the conference championship that year and in 1975 to Washington. The loss to Washington that season was the first for CR that year, as they completed an 18-0 regular season behind the play of all-state selection Carlton Cannon, 6-foot-8 Melvin Baltimore, and sharp-shooting All-Bayside selection Mark Messick. Cannon had six games that season with 30 points or more. The Colonels made it to the regional finals, but fell to Gwynn Park, 66-64. Still, the following year still looked strong for them. Messick would be back, and Washington might not be quite as tough.

But another team in the Bayside South had state title dreams too.

Pocomoke's Anky Tull goes for a lay-up against James M. Bennett during the 1975-76 season. Pocomoke yearbooks.

***

Anky Tull is basketball royalty in Pocomoke. In each of the Warriors' four state championship wins, Tull has some sort of connection to them. His older brother, Mitchell Tull, was a starter on the 1971 state title team and his son was the point guard on the 2002 team. Tull was Derrick Fooks' lead assistant on the 2016 team, and – as a senior forward – he was a starter for the 1975-76 Warriors, coached by Carey Reece. Tull, one of six children, was born and raised in Pocomoke. He came to the game of basketball by playing with his two older brothers and with the kids in his tightly-knit neighborhood.

Reece had some pretty good teams during his run at Pocomoke. He took the job over from Ronnie Ross in the fall of 1971 and had accumulated an 83-21 record entering the 1975-76 season, but a state championship had eluded him. Reece was previously the head coach at Stephen Decatur before Ward Lambert took over. His coaching debut at Pocomoke in 1971 was an 85-60 home win over Wicomico High, in which the Warriors forced the Indians into 38 turnovers. As he chewed tobacco on the sidelines and spit it in a can next to his spot on the bench, Reece made it clear from the start that defense would be an emphasis for Pocomoke under his watch. Minus the tobacco, that fiery defensive identity and tradition has stayed with the program to present day.

In the 1974-75 season, Reece had a talented squad that went 18-4. But each of those losses were to Washington High – a team that went 27-0 and won the state championship.

"One of the toughest players I ever played against was Vincent Cottman. He was a heck of a long ball shooter. Really quick." Tull said of Washington's 1975 team. "With Washington beating us and winning it all in 1975, that gave us more inspiration and motivation to win it as seniors. Plus, we were a good team."

Entering the 1975-76 season, Reece had three senior starters returning in 6-foot-5 dominant center Jeff Ballard, a 5-foot-9 dependable guard in Gary Holden, and Tull – a versatile 6-foot forward who could shoot and rebound- averaging 11.7 points and 8.1 boards per-game as a junior. Around them were John Norris, Jon "Putt" Johnson, Morris Dickerson, and Gary's younger brother Bruce.

"If we can stay out of foul trouble, we should be awfully tough," Reece, then 35 years old, told the Daily Times. "Our game (will be) tough, aggressive defense (and) will revolve around Ballard. He'll have to be aggressive and yet smart, because we have no one with that kind of height to replace him."

"We were a defensive team," Tull said. "We had really good guards in the Holden brothers. We had Jeff Ballard, a four-year starter, and John Norris was a pretty big, rough guy. Putt Johnson was our sixth man. We all played football together. We were all close. We had a bunch of athletes that worked hard… I played the small forward, basically. I was the shooter."

That school year, Tull and those Pocomoke boys guided the Warriors to their first and only state semifinal appearance in football in the fall. In the spring, they were on the baseball team that made it to the state final as well. For sure, these Warriors were some talented all-around athletes, but their skills may have been best suited for the hardwood.

***

Colonel Richardson started the 1975-76 campaign off with a bang, blowing out Cambridge-South Dorchester 100-43 on the road. Kendall Cannon led the way with 16 points and seven boards. Merrill Morgan's side put an emphasis on defense, too, and the squad led the conference in fewest points allowed per-game with a 58.4 mark that season. On offense, the Colonels were a run-and-shoot club, led by Mark Messick, Gary Corsey, Mike Brown and Cannon.

"Mark Messick could play. Golly, he could play," Gary's older brother, Tom, says.

Down south, Pocomoke got off to a 6-1 start and notched their seventh win by beating Stephen Decatur 69-57 at the Wicomico Civic Center on Jan. 14 behind Jeff Ballard's 28 points and 22 rebounds. Colonel remained unbeaten that same night, improving to 8-0 with a one-point road victory at Queen Anne's. Mike Brown connected on a lay-up with two seconds left to seal the 60-59 win.

By mid-February, Colonel had been beaten a few times, but still managed to lock-in the second-best spot in the north Bayside standings with a 63-60 win over North Caroline. Mark Messick had 24 points and 12 rebounds for the 13-4 Colonels in Ridgely.

Meanwhile, Pocomoke kept winning, and improved to 16-1 with a 70-42 home win over Mardela. Ballard was celebrated for becoming the fourth Warrior in school history to hit the 1,000-point mark, but John Norris led the way with 18 points and eight rebounds. Pocomoke finished the regular season with a 16-2 record, losing only to James M. Bennett and North Caroline along the way.

Back in the 1970s, the Bayside Conference held its own mini-playoffs to decide a conference champion before the state tournament took place. The north champion would play the south runner-up, and the south champion would play the north runner-up. So, in 1976, the semifinal matchups were Queen Anne's vs. Washington and Pocomoke vs. Colonel Richardson.

On February 25, 1976, on a neutral court at Parkside High School, the Colonels and Warriors met for the first time that season. The result wasn't close. Pocomoke bested CR 73-55 to advance to the Bayside Championship game, which they would win over Queen Anne's, 64-60. A 23-9 second quarter run from the Warriors separated them from the Colonels. Ballard had 20 points and 18 rebounds with ease, imposing his large frame against the undersized Colonels.

In the state playoffs, Pocomoke faced St. Michaels in the regional semifinals. The Saints don't have much history of winning basketball, but they were pretty talented in 1976 because of a baseball player's skills on the hardwood. Harold Baines terrorized Shore teams on the diamond and gave opposing pitchers nightmares. He batted .532 as a senior in 1977, was named an All-American, and was plucked out of high school by the Chicago White Sox in the amateur draft. Baines made six MLB All-Star teams, led the majors in slugging percentage in 1984, won a Silver Slugger award in 1989, and ranks in the top 50 of all-time career hits, RBIs, games played and sac flies in MLB history. He won a World Series as an assistant coach in 2005 and was elected to the Baseball Hall of Fame by the veterans' committee in 2019.

Before he was a Hall of Fame professional baseball player, Harold Baines was a standout basketball player in St. Michaels too. He's pictured here, second from left, at the Easton YMCA in the early 1970s. Courtesy of the Talbot Historical Society, Easton, Maryland.

But in March of 1976, he was the best basketball player St. Michaels had. He scored 35 points in the Saints' regular season finale win over Parkside. And his double-double of 22 points and 11 rebounds led the Saints to a 62-43 win over Snow Hill at the Wicomico Civic Center, setting up a duel in the District 8 semifinals with Pocomoke.

"He was a good basketball player," Tull says of Baines. "He was an all-around athlete, period. He was a tough player."

It was Tull who was assigned to defend Baines in the regional semifinals, and he held the future baseball Hall of Fame inductee to just 10 points- less than half of his scoring average that season. Tull had 13 points, Ballard had 25 points and 10 rebounds, and Pocomoke won handily, 66-46. Reece was well-dressed for that match-up – he's pictured in the Daily Times wearing shiny black shoes, bell-bottom corduroy pants, a jacket with a popped collar and his dark hair combed over.

The region final between Pocomoke and Washington required some late-game heroics. Tull hit a lay-up with 11 seconds left to punch the Warriors' ticket to College Park. While Ballard was bottled up, Tull had 25 points to lead Pocomoke to a 54-52 win.

Colonel needed some luck to win its regional, too. In Chesapeake City, Colonel trailed Bohemia Manor by seven points at halftime, then stormed all the way back to lead by 11. But the game flipped once more and was tied 55-55 in its waning moments. Mark Messick scored on a close-range shot and Kendall Cannon sank a free throw, giving the Colonels a final edge of 58-57. Merrill Morgan credited his pressing defense for the win, while Cannon finished with 20 points.

Leading up to the state final four at Cole Field House, Daily Times sports editor Rick Cullen knew what was at stake and pondered on what an All-Shore Class C final might be like in his column on March 11. He noted Colonel lacked height, but Morgan had turned the program into one of the Shore's most-respected. "The Colonels can jump and run and run and run. A quick pressing defense turns many games around. The Colonels have probably generated more excitement and frustration this season than any team in recent years," Cullen wrote. "(Colonel) manages to jump out to huge leads, only to lose them, and drive their fans crazy overcoming the deficit." Of Reece's side, Cullen simply wrote: "Pocomoke is Pocomoke."

Colonel bested Walkersville and Pocomoke squeaked by Bruce to set up the Bayside clash in College Park. Gary Holden's 30-foot buzzer-beater was the difference between the Warriors and the Bulldogs from western Maryland.

From Tull's point of view, there was one thing about Colonel that made them formidable: "They brought Mark Messick to the floor." Messick was a two-time All-Bayside selection and the conference's Player of the Year as a senior in 1976. That season, he had nine games of at least 20 points and 10 rebounds. "Mark Messick was their everything," Tull said. "He lived up to the hype. You couldn't stop Mark Messick."

Looking back, Tull is honest about how Pocomoke had viewed Colonel in the moments leading up to the game: "We had kind of taken them for granted because we had beaten them before, convincingly, in Bayside's."

But since that loss in the conference playoffs, Morgan had adjusted his defense. Instead of playing Pocomoke straight-up, man-for-man, he was going to press. Colonel got Pocomoke's best weapon, Jeff Ballard, into foul trouble early on in the state final. With the big man on the bench, Colonel's lineup – which had an average height of 5-foot-8 – could do what they did best: run. Ballard finished the first half with just two points and Colonel forced 15 first-half turnovers and sprinted out to a 13-point halftime lead. Tull had seven of those first-half turnovers.

Pocomoke's Jeff Ballard (44) shoots over Colonel Richardson's Mark Messick (33) in the 1976 Class C state title game. Pocomoke yearbooks.

"I remember thinking at the time – when we were getting blown out by Pocomoke (in Bayside's) that this was a really good team and we just weren't going to win that one," Morgan said. "So, I tried a new defense. They were confused by the press."

The Pocomoke locker room was not a pleasant place to be at intermission at Cole Field House. The tobacco was flying from Carey Reece's lips like bullets firing from a machine gun. Reece was angry, like his emotions had been marinating in ghost peppers and kerosene.

"At halftime, Mr. Reece... He cussed us out. He fired us up," Tull recalls. "And when we came out in that third quarter, we knew what we had to do. We came prepared. Mark was still getting his. But we just concentrated on what we needed to do. At that point we just felt like we weren't going to be denied by Colonel. They were smaller than we were and they didn't have an answer for our bigs."

Colonel came out firing on all cylinders again, and Messick sprinted towards the rim for a score on the first possession of the third quarter, but he rushed his shot and it clanked off the rim. Morgan considered calling a timeout to calm his team down. Instead, he let the boys play on. It's a moment of indecision that he still thinks about. "In the second half, we wanted to try and hold the ball and slow it down. Mark Messick was particularly active," Morgan said. "That's where I made my mistake. We were quicker than they were, but we couldn't settle down."

By the end of the third quarter, the game was tied at 49-49. And then, Pocomoke put the game on ice by outscoring Colonel 31-17 in the final period. The final was 80-66 as the Warriors captured the state crown.

"It worked well in the first half, but the half-court press disintegrated in the second half," Morgan told the Hanover Evening Sun after the game. The difference in the second half was that Ballard and Tull played smarter, more aggressively and more focused. At halftime, Ballard had two points and Tull had one. At the end, they combined for 31 points and 23 rebounds. Gary Holden had 18 points as well.

Pocomoke celebrates its 80-66 state final win over Colonel Richardson. 1976 was the only time two Bayside teams played each other for a state title in basketball. Pocomoke yearbooks.

For Colonel, Messick padded his stats, finishing with 33 points and 13 rebounds, but Cannon was the only other Colonel to score in double-digits, winding up with 13 points. Reece complimented Colonel after the game, telling the Associated Press, "They played exceptionally well. They're a hustling crowd; by far the most aggressive team we played all year. They go after you and never let up."

Pocomoke's win marked the fourth time in the previous six years that the Class C title was won by a team from the Lower Shore – Pocomoke in 1971, Crisfield in 1973 and Washington in 1975 preceded Reece's side as champs. Over the next six seasons, Bill Cain would guide Crisfield to three more Class C titles. Pocomoke would have to wait nearly three decades before celebrating in College Park again.

Reece went out on top, stepping down as head coach that offseason. He handed the reins of the program over to Chip MacDonald, stayed around Pocomoke one more year, and then became the principal at Ocean City Elementary in 1977. He returned to the sidelines with Cain a few times, helping coach teams in the Bayside All-Star games.

The Shore put on a show in the Class C final in 1976 that no one should forget. The only time since that it has come close to happening again was in 1989, when North Caroline and Snow Hill both made the Class C final four, but the Bulldogs lost in the semifinals.

Said Morgan: "I said after they changed divisions around, 'They'll never let anybody do this again,' to have two teams from the Eastern Shore in the final. That was the first and last time."

Head coach Merrill Morgan receives the runner-up trophy for Colonel Richardson after they fell in the 1976 state title game to Pocomoke in College Park. Colonel Richardson yearbooks.

***

Reminiscing about his 1976 team, Merrill Morgan said, "That was a particularly tough loss... It was difficult. That was the only time we played for a state championship."

Morgan would continue coaching basketball at Colonel Richardson through 2005. He would reach the state final four just three more times in his long tenure as the lead basketball guru in southern Caroline County, in 1977, 1990 and 1995. Previously, he led the Colonels to the state semifinals in 1973, too.

Throughout his career in basketball, from the time that he was playing in youth leagues at the age of eight, through his high school days, through Duke, through coaching in New Jersey and at Colonel, Morgan only missed one game, ever. In December of 2003, his wife's mother died, so Morgan skipped Colonel's Christmas tournament game to be with family in North Carolina. Colonel lost by a single point in double-overtime to Stephen Decatur at the convention center in Ocean City as Aaron Wyatt exploded for 44 points for the Seahawks.

Still, Morgan's streak was incredible. And so was his resume. Ahead of the 2004-05 season, he was within reach of 500 wins. As he climbed in age, people – including administrators at Colonel Richardson High School – wondered aloud when he might step away from basketball. Morgan never really had concrete plans to put away his whistle though.

"People would ask me when I was going to retire," Morgan says. "I was in no hurry."

Morgan's last team was arguably one of his best ever. Led by Wayne Batson, Tony Howe, Joey Fletcher, Rodney Griffith, Brandon Caldwell and Robert Jackson, the Colonels went 20-4 in 2004-05 and went all the way to the regional semifinals. That year, if you wanted to have a seat for the varsity game that tipped off at 7:30 p.m., you needed to be at the JV game. Even if your mother was the head cheerleading coach, that didn't reserve you a spot in the bleachers to see the high-flying Colonels in Morgan's final season.

"They were a good team. I had enough talent where I could've had two successful teams. We were a pressing team, and we could run because of the depth," Morgan says. "Wayne was the point guard, and a very good one, especially on defense. They were all very good defensively. Joey could play anywhere, either way. He had size and was long. Those two got a lot of playing time."

David Insley, who covered the Colonels that season as sports scribe for the Dorchester Banner, says: "Joey could cut through anything. Wayne could slap the ball out of anybody's hands. It was the Joey and Wayne show, but they had depth."

Much of the players on that team had risen up together through the JV ranks. Under Morgan, CR had a solid feeder program. By the time players got to varsity, they had chemistry with each other and understood Morgan's system. For a long time, the JV squad at Colonel was shepherded by Tom Corsey, a 1972 Colonel Richardson graduate and a Caroline County native. After earning a degree from St. Paul's College – a private historically Black institution in Virginia – Corsey returned to his alma mater in 1979 to coach football, track and basketball. In more than two decades of working together on and off the court, Morgan and Corsey developed a close friendship.

"Mr. Morgan put a lot of work in with not just kids here, but with kids all over the place," Corsey said. "People don't know half of what we've been through together, us two."

When Corsey's son Desmond was born, he weighed only a pound and had a collapsed lung. Desmond stayed for a whole year in a children's hospital and, at the time, Corsey didn't own a car. So, Morgan drove him back and forth across the Bay Bridge, often multiple times a week, to go see his son in Baltimore. Morgan is the boy's godfather. "Mr. Morgan won, a lot, with just Preston and Federalsburg kids," Corsey said. "We had the best coach."

The Colonels were 5-0 after beating Crisfield 75-55 on Dec. 29, 2004 behind 15 points, six assists and five steals from Batson.

Tom Corsey has been an assistant boys basketball coach at Colonel Richardson under both Merrill Morgan and Brad Plutschak. Photo by Mitchell Northam.

"They were as talented as those teams with Albert Mouring, they just didn't have Albert. They were hard-nosed basketball players," Corsey said. "And Wayne was one of the best against the press."

Another highlight win along the way was an 84-82 overtime triumph at Wicomico High School on Jan. 22, in which Batson tallied 16 points, six boards and four assists. After the game, Wi-Hi head coach Butch Waller simply said: "That's a good team."

"I had a tough time beating Merrill," Waller said. "We're sort of cut out of the same mold. We both did our homework."

A month later, in Centreville, Morgan won his 500th game with a 76-46 victory over Queen Anne's. At that time, he and Waller were the only two coaches in the Bayside with that many W's.

In Morgan's final regular season home game, Fletcher netted 31 points – punctuated with a thunderous dunk – in a 76-52 win over James M. Bennett to give the longtime head coach a proper send-off. Before the game, Morgan received plaques and messages from several prominent folks, including then-Maryland Gov. Bob Ehrlich, Duke coach Mike Krzyzewski and his first Colonels' team from 1967-68. Vick Corsey, a member of Morgan's 1975 team, told the Star Democrat, "Duke has Krzyzewski... but we're blessed to have Merrill Morgan. It's been a good run and no better person deserves it."

Morgan won his 505th and final game in the second round of the playoffs over Crisfield, a dominant 77-27 home victory spearheaded by Batson's 16 points, five assists and seven steals. Morgan and the players cut down the nets after the game, knowing it was his last time coaching in that gym. In the regional semifinals at the University of Maryland Eastern Shore in Princess Anne, the Colonels ran into their old county rival, the North Caroline Bulldogs. Ron Ringgold spoiled the storybook season, scoring 10 of his 23 points in the fourth quarter as North High pulled away for a 58-42 win. Colonel turned the ball over 20 times and missed eight free throws. Still, they were just the fourth Colonel team – ever – to win 20 games or more.

"By the end of the season, you could kind of see this resolution in Merrill's face," Insley said. "He had reconciled himself to it."

Morgan stepped away from Colonel Richardson's sidelines after the 2004-05 season. The school later named its gym after Morgan and retired the No. 32 jersey, the number he wore at Duke decades ago. In 2017, Federalsburg dedicated its new basketball courts at the marina to him.

"We're going to miss him," Batson told the Star Democrat after the 2005 Bayside Senior All-Star Game. "It was a good season for us. I wish I could stay another year, but he's retiring. I just hope the next coach does what Coach Morgan has done for Colonel."

At the end of the season, Morgan let it be known to the brass at Colonel Richardson that he wanted his successor to be either Tom Corsey or Brad Plutschak. Corsey had been Morgan's assistant for 26 years at that point, and is widely respected in youth sports circles in southern Caroline County. Plutschak, then a guidance counselor at the school, had been Morgan's JV coach and varsity assistant for the few seasons leading up to his departure. "They were the only candidates, in my mind," Morgan said. "They were my recommendations."

Still, Morgan knew that who would be selected to replace him was ultimately not his decision. Principal Christine Handy heard Morgan's endorsements, but rejected them. "It kind of hurt me, because I thought I was next in line," Corsey said. "I had been there my whole life. It took me a lot to get myself together… I had to let it go."

Instead, Handy tapped Reuben Collins – a North Caroline graduate with little experience – to be Morgan's replacement. And Collins lasted short of two seasons. "Christine Handy was his buddy," Insley said. "And then Collins bolted in a season and-a-half."

Darnell Lake finished out the latter portion of the 2006-07 season as Colonel's coach, and then Plutschak took the reins of the program. As of this writing, he is still the head coach. The 2022-23 season will be his 16th.

Initially angry with how the interview process to replace his good friend went, Corsey left Colonel at the end of the spring of 2005 and went north, joining Steve Perry's staff on the North Caroline boys team. But wearing blue and white never felt right to Corsey. Black and red always suited him better. When Plutschak got the top job, Corsey returned to southern Caroline County and has been there ever since. "I had to come back home. I just wasn't a North Caroline boy," Corsey said.

The 2021-22 school year was Corsey's 42nd straight year of coaching year-round. At CR, he has guided teams in football, boys and girls basketball, and track and field. That's 126 consecutive seasons of coaching young folks in Caroline County.

"In the end, it worked out," Morgan said. "Brad and Tom have been excellent."

Along the way, through nearly four decades of coaching in the Bayside Conference, you'd be hard-pressed to find someone who had a remotely bad word to say about Morgan.

"He's one of the most respected men in basketball on the Eastern Shore," said David Byrd, the head coach at Pocomoke from 1977 through 2003. "He was quiet – and a Dukie – but he's a great guy and had good players. He always remained calm. The place could blow up next door and Merrill would still be calm."

Said Insley: "Merrill was the eye of any storm. He was like a Zen Garden."

"I love Merrill. There's not much not to like about him," said former North Dorchester coach Vic Burns. "He was always a gentleman and we had some real battles."

Through 38 years of mentoring young men at American Corner, of coaching countless games against rivals, and of taking an uncountable number of bus rides up and down the Shore and across the Bay Bridge, Morgan always had the respect of his players and the admiration of his peers. Some would argue that is more valuable than any championship.

BRENDA JONES,
A MODERN-ERA WINNER AT SNOW HILL

"Brenda was a tough coach. There was no mediocre – you either did it right or you didn't do it." – Gail Tatterson Gladding

Women have been playing basketball for nearly as long as men have. According to the 2005 book "Shattering the Glass" by Pamela Grundy and Susan Shackelford, which details the history of women's hoops, women at Smith College in Northampton, Massachusetts, were playing Naismith's game as early as the fall of 1892. Those games were organized by one of the game's earliest advocates, Senda Berenson. By 1895, the women were playing basketball as far south as New Orleans. And on April 4, 1896, Stanford beat Cal 2-1 in the first women's intercollegiate basketball game.

For the decades that followed, everyone sort of put their own spin on rules and regulations in women's and girls' basketball. For some asinine reason, girls were rarely permitted to play by the same rules as the boys. Berenson would oversee games featuring five to 10 players on each side, while some places elsewhere were playing games with six or nine players on each team. In 1934, most states and schools adopted new rules. In hindsight, they look unnecessary and obnoxious. Instead of five players to each team, the women would play with six. There was a line drawn at center court. A team's three forwards would be on the offensive end, tasked with scoring buckets, and then their three guards would be on the defensive end to guard the basket. The guards and forwards could not cross the halfcourt line.

Sounds weird, right?

It sounds more like lacrosse than basketball.

Additionally, players were allowed just two dribbles and then had to either shoot or pass. Tie-ups were not allowed outside of the lane. After made baskets, a referee would bring the ball to midcourt and inbound it to a forward on the other side. On top of that, there was the built-in sexism, so many games played by girls and women were relegated to courts deemed unsuitable for boys and men; courts that often weren't regulation size. Many states lacked organization in their leagues, and rules could still differ depending on which part of the country you saw a game. But the norm in most places was a divided court with the players playing a version of six-on-six.

The Easton High School women's basketball team for the 1933-34 school year. From left to right: Geometry teacher Edith Reese, players Rose Mayer, Mildred Dunham, Frances Haley, Patricia Haley, Shirley Morton Miller, Eleanor "Topsy" Tarbutton and Mary Buffet. Courtesy of the Talbot Historical Society, Easton, Maryland.

This is how girls high school basketball was played for decades in many states across the country. Rules changed slightly over time, and some states allowed two roving players who could cross midcourt. Longtime Pocomoke head coach Gail Gladding said she learned to play the game with two forwards, two guards and two roving players. "The rovers could run across half-court, but the others could only go to half-court," she said.

By the beginning of winter in 1969 in the state of Maryland, things were changing in girls basketball. The Salisbury Daily Times reported on Dec. 2: "Adopted nationally has been an experimentation set of rules similar to the play of the boys."

Wow, what a bold and crazy idea.

The Times went on: "Each team will be comprised of five players – same as the boys. Play will be over the entire court – same as the boys. In the past, powder-puff scholastic basketball has been looked upon as an uninteresting ho-hum sport."

Huh… And did playing with the same rules as the boys spark more interest in the sport?

Indeed, it did.

Coaches on the Eastern Shore were excited about the rule change ahead of the 1969-70 season, including Wicomico High School's Gretchen Byrd. She told the Daily Times, "I'm sure it'll make girls basketball much more interesting, not only for the players, but the spectators… The game will require more skill and better ball handling. I'm not criticizing game officials, but I hope they hold their whistles a lot more and permit the girls to play."

Maryland was slightly ahead of the curve on changing rules for girls high school basketball. And by 1972 – the year Title IX was signed into law by President Nixon on June 23 – most high schools in most states were playing a version of five-on-five with rules resembling the boys game. New Jersey adopted the rule change in 1975 and Texas in 1978. The last holdouts were Iowa and Oklahoma, which were playing by the old six-on-six rules until 1993 and 1995, respectively.

But Title IX, as Grundy and Shackelford write in their book, sparked "an athletic revolution" and "would open doors to women throughout educational institutions – including those in gymnasiums." Simply put, Title IX barred educational institutions from discriminating based on gender. It sought to level the playing field and equalize opportunities for girls and women across schools and the sports they sponsored. The legislation would have an incredible impact on college sports and passed with little opposition.

When the girls high school basketball rules changed in Maryland, Byrd and other coaches around the Shore began advocating for a district tournament. Ahead of the 1971-72 season, the Bayside Conference announced it would hold a conference championship game between the end of the regular season and the start of the state playoffs for girls and boys basketball. Cambridge beat North Caroline 42-30 for the inaugural girls Bayside crown and the game has been held nearly every year since – save for the years where inclement weather forced organizers to scrap the game, 1989 and 2003, and the year where it was canceled due to COVID-19, 2021.

By 1973, the state of Maryland had restarted its state tournament for women's basketball, which had lain dormant since 1949. Less than a decade later, the first professional basketball league for women launched in the U.S. under the banner of "the WBL," short for: Women's Professional Basketball League. The WBL would eventually fold, but it laid the groundwork for the WNBA, which launched in 1996. In 2020, viewership for the WNBA Finals spiked by 34% from the previous season, drawing an average of 570,000 viewers. On April 4, 2021, 4.1 million people watched Stanford beat Arizona in the NCAA Division I women's basketball national championship, marking the third title for legendary coach Tara VanDerveer. In 2022, when South Carolina beat UConn for the national championship in Minneapolis, Minnesota, 4.85 million people watched on ESPN – the most in 18 years.

It was unclear why the Maryland Public Secondary Schools Athletic Association had shelved the girls high school basketball tournament from 1950 through 1972, but on March 14, 1993, former Wi-Hi girls coach Mary Morling Troy told Salisbury Daily Times sports editor Rick Cullen: "The reasons given were spending too much time away from school and it was too costly." Troy said she and Easton's May Brooks "raised ol' Harry" with state officials over the absence of a girls tournament.

When the state tournament for girls basketball returned in 1973, the MPSSAA opted to narrow the field for the championship. Instead of crowning a champion in each of the four school-size classifications – as it did for boys – the girls tournament would be a combined one. This made getting to the final four – let alone winning the championship – much more difficult, especially for smaller schools. The girls tournament was played this way for three seasons, and then each classification got its own tournament and its own champion – just like the boys – in 1976.

But one tiny school on the Eastern Shore had the right coach and just enough talent to compete for state titles right away, no matter the competition.

***

Snow Hill is a small town in the middle of Worcester County pressed between the Pocomoke River and Route 113. The Pocomoke Forest is to its west, and the Chincoteague Bay is to its east. It's surrounded by even smaller communities like Newark, Cedartown and Girdletree. Snow Hill was founded by English settlers sometime around 1686 and some folks claim its name comes from a neighborhood in London – which makes some sense, considering there aren't many particularly large hills there, and the Eastern Shore rarely gets much snow; just enough to make a fuss over, typically. In 1742, Worcester County made the town its county seat. With its location on the Pocomoke River, Snow Hill thrived as a port town, and despite two major fires, it is still home to several buildings built in the 1700s and the 1800s.

In 2019, the population in Snow Hill was less than 1,700 people, and the snug community isn't known for much. A few scenes from the 1999 film starring Julia Roberts, "Runaway Bride," were filmed there. If Snow Hill has a claim to fame, it is being the native home of a handful of exceptional athletes: Negro League World Series champ and 1975 Baseball Hall of Fame inductee Judy Johnson, 1993 NBA Draft pick Sherron Mills, and Ben Tate – who owns a handful of high school rushing records in Maryland, was one of the SEC's top rushing leaders in 2009 at Auburn, and played in the NFL for five seasons.

And then there's Gail Gladding.

Back in 1973, long before she was married, her last name was Tatterson. And that season, she might've been the best girls basketball player in the state. At 6-foot-2, Tatterson could score at the rim and out-rebound smaller players with ease, and she was armed with the toughness of leather and steel, which made her a difficult assignment for opponents her size, too.

With Tatterson leading the way on the hardwood, and with the teachings of Brenda Jones, Snow Hill High School's girls basketball team could hang with – and beat – just about anyone.

Before 1968, Jones had never seen the ocean. The daughter of a railroad worker, she grew up in what she called "the heart" of West Virginia, "like the Hatfield's and McCoy's – right next to Kentucky." And that's not hyperbole. Jones' hometown of Williamston borders Kentucky and is the home of the Hatfield McCoy Country Museum. After studying and playing college basketball at Marshall, Jones found her way to Snow Hill through a placement office. She had a job offer from a junior high school in Baltimore, but an untimely death created an opening at Snow Hill High School for a gym teacher. Jones hopped on a train and started at Snow Hill in the fall of 1968, teaching physical education and health, and coaching basketball, softball and field hockey. "I had never seen a hockey game in my life," Jones recalls. She came to Snow Hill without a car, and would teach at the high school until her retirement in 2000.

Jones had been through the change from six-on-six to five-on-five in girls basketball, she'd seen the arrival of the Bayside Championship for her sport, and she'd seen the return of the state tournament. Jones called the six-on-six version of the game "boring." Thankfully for her, she only had to coach it for one season.

"The transition, I loved," Jones said. "My early teams – it took me about three years. They were ahead of their time. They were just good. It wasn't a hard transition for me to coach them."

From game one in the 1972-73 season, it was clear the Eagles had the talent to compete. Behind 23 points from Tatterson and some stellar defense from Carolyn Trader and Nadine Bishop, Snow Hill waxed county rival Stephen Decatur in the season opener on September 15, 76-37.

While Snow Hill's players might've been ahead of their time in talent, Jones was innovative in her preparation. It's common now for women's college basketball teams, but back in the early 1970s, it was unheard of for a girls high school basketball team to use boys as practice players. Except for at Snow Hill.

"I used boys in my practices. I treated them like they were on my team," Jones said. "They kept all my stats for me (during games) and I practiced with them, and I did not let them cut (the girls) any slack. So, we looked like girls, but played like guys... The only way you can get better is to play against better. I held them accountable. They had to make good grades. And when they came to practice, they didn't play around."

By January 28, 1973, Snow Hill was still undefeated with a perfect 7-0 record after walloping another Worcester County foe, Pocomoke, 62-32. Tatterson again led the way in scoring with 20 points, and again, Bishop was the lead stopper on the defensive end. A month later, Snow Hill beat North East High School 41-28 for its first Bayside Championship – in any sport. Back then, schools in Cecil County – where North East is located – played in the Bayside Conference. That changed near the end of the 1970s.

On March 3, Snow Hill punched its ticket to the state semifinals by winning the District 10 championship over Cambridge at Wi-Hi, 48-40. Tatterson and Teresa Waters combined for 31 points and gave the Eagles their 18th win of the season.

"They just played like guys. And we had a bout five different types of presses," Jones said. "I ran them. If they could tolerate me, they could tolerate anything... They didn't care who scored, as long as they won."

The first final four for girls high school basketball in the state of Maryland in the modern era was held at Catonsville Community College, just southwest of Baltimore City. The four qualifying teams were Middletown, Parkville, Sherwood and Snow Hill. Parkville is in northeast Baltimore, Middletown is northwest of Frederick, and Sherwood is in Montgomery County. All things considered, the field was diverse in that it represented different parts of the state.

Behind 30 points and 29 rebounds for Tatterson, Snow Hill easily bested Middletown in the semifinals, 67-47.

"She was a very talented all-around athlete," Jones said of Tatterson. "Which, for her height, usually they're very awkward. She was a good hockey player, softball player and basketball player. Usually a tall girl is very awkward, but she was very talented. No question about it."

Against Parkville in the final, the Eagles wouldn't be as lucky. Tatterson and defensive stalwart Bishop fouled out in the fourth quarter and Parkville was able to pull ahead just a bit before the final buzzer sounded. Parkville won the first modern-era girls high school basketball championship in the Old Line State, topping Snow Hill 49-44 behind Jane Menzies' 21 points. Tatterson and Waters each finished with 14.

Years later, in 1987, Jones would tell the Salisbury Daily Times her 1972-73 team was arguably her most talented. The Eagles finished 19-2, and Tatterson went on to play at Salisbury University, where she became a Hall of Fame inductee in 1990, and then starred in the short-lived WBL for the New Jersey Gems and the New York Stars. Waters played at the University of Maryland Eastern Shore, Carolyn Trader and Regina Brittingham landed at UMBC, and Bishop played at Salisbury too.

"We did pretty good for our tiny school," Gladding told me in 2016.

But Jones wanted more than just "pretty good." She wanted to win the whole thing. She wanted to bring the gold home to Snow Hill. The following season, in 1974, Waters averaged 24.2 points per-game, and Snow Hill again won the Bayside Championship and again made the state final, but lost by two points to Sherwood. In all, seven points separated Jones and the Eagles from back-to-back state championships.

***

Snow Hill consistently stayed in the hunt for Bayside and state championships under Brenda Jones' guidance throughout the 1970s. Again in 1975, they made the state final four, but bowed out in the semifinals. Jones took a one-year sabbatical away from coaching in the 1977-78 season to recover from an illness – and the Eagles went 11-6 without her – but she was back on the Eagles' bench by December 1978.

"I had seven seniors coming back," Jones said. "I decided I was going to coach. I didn't care what anybody said."

The Eagles weren't just experienced, sharp and talented, they were deep. Jones told the Salisbury Daily Times on December 8, 1978: "We will be strong if everyone can live up to their capabilities… I have a team composed mainly of seniors who are hungry and want to put it together and go all the way." And indeed, in the first game of the season, Snow Hill showed how formidable they could be, thrashing Crisfield 78-17. The Eagles led 42-7 at halftime, five players scored in double figures and they shot 75% from the field. It seemed like, even if they were blindfolded, Jones' side couldn't miss against the Crabbers.

Facing Pocomoke on January 30, 1979, a win wouldn't come as easy for the Eagles. But Jones deployed an effective full-court press against the Warriors to capture a 54-42 home victory. Dessie Bratten tallied 15 points and 14 rebounds for Snow Hill, while sophomore Toni Bishop grabbed 13 boards. The Eagles had a 9-2 record and were owning teams on the glass.

But the one squad that gave Snow Hill fits was Mardela, the second real power in girls basketball to rise up on the Eastern Shore. "It was always between Barbara McCool and myself," Jones said. "She had great teams too. She really did."

That season was McCool's 13th on the job, and she had one of her most skilled teams ever. Pam Hopkins and Kim Horsey led the Warriors of Mardela, and in the previous season, they had powered McCool's side to a 19-3 record, a Bayside title and an appearance in the Class C state final. Both Hopkins and Horsey would play Division I college basketball – at Morgan State and UT-Chattanooga, respectively – and were often the best players on the court in nearly every game they played in during high school.

Carolyn Hutson, Kim Horsey and Pam Hopkins were the stars for Mardela in 1977-78, leading the team to a 19-3 record, a Bayside Championship and an appearance in the state final. Mardela yearbooks.

By February 23, 1979, Mardela was 13-1 and responsible for handing Snow Hill two of its three losses on the season. The Warriors defended their Bayside title by beating Kent County 63-55, with Hopkins and Horsey combining for 52 points and 34 rebounds. McCool's side then geared up to make another run for the state semifinals, but Snow Hill stood in their way.

"The hardest game was against Mardela, to get off the Shore," Jones said.

The Eagles and Warriors met for the third time in the 1978-79 season for the Region IV title and the chance to go back to states on March 3 at Tawes Gym at Salisbury State College. Horsey was coming off a game against Colonel Richardson in which she racked up 33 points and 21 boards in a 77-27 playoff victory. Snow Hill's Bratten had 16 points and 13 rebounds in the Eagles' win over Pocomoke. But against Mardela, Bratten was going to have to play even better.

Or, she'd need her teammates to step up.

That proved to be the winning formula. The Eagles put in a total team effort, erased a 10-point halftime deficit and upset Mardela 48-45 for a bid to the Class C state final four. The Eagles outscored the Warriors 18-8 in the final quarter, and Mary Taylor swished a shot from the top of the key to give Snow Hill a one-point lead with just a few seconds remaining.

"Barbara was calling timeouts and she couldn't slow us down," Jones said. And in the waning moments of the game, after Taylor hit the go-ahead shot, McCool called a timeout that she didn't have, sending Snow Hill to the free throw line with the lead. The veteran-laden Eagles were emotional on the bench. Victory was within reach, but Jones demanded that they compose themselves. She told her players, "You can't understand what I'm saying to you if you're crying. Straighten up. We can win."

The Eagle who would take the decisive free throws thanks to McCool's gaffe would be Donna Smith. And, while Smith was a superb ball-handler, she was far from being the team's top shooter.

"She was a really good point guard, but she couldn't shoot worth a darn," Jones said. "So, during the timeout, I told her to take her time. They handed her the ball and it was like it was on fire. But she hit both of them."

Smith's swishes put the game on ice for the Eagles. Hopkins and Horsey were each held under 15 points, while Taylor scored 19 for Snow Hill. Bratten chipped in 12 points and sophomore Toni Bishop – playing with a dislocated thumb – pulled down 11 boards. "The girls really kept their cool and hustled to turn the game around," Jones told the Daily Times after the win.

Jones would later tell the same newspaper, "As far as I'm concerned, that game against Mardela was the state championship. The two best teams in the state were on the court that night. It was not my best team as far as individual talent goes, but each kid contributed in one way or another. They gave more than they had."

It was likely easy for Jones to say that with some hindsight, considering her two games in Catonsville were a breeze for the Eagles compared to the regional final against Mardela. Snow Hill beat Mount Savage in the semifinals, 50-42, and then bested Smithfield 58-49 for the Class C state title. It was the first state championship ever won by a Snow Hill team and the first for a girls basketball team from the Eastern Shore in the modern-era.

"The key was our defense," Jones told the Daily Times after the triumphant victory. "It was just a total team effort."

Indeed, Jones again used a full-court press to give her unit an advantage, and the Eagles jumped out to a 24-14 lead. Snow Hill was up by 12 points at halftime, largely thanks to Lounell Coleman scoring 10 of her game-high 20 points in the two minutes before intermission. Coleman made most of her shots against Smithfield from the corners. She told the Baltimore Sun after the game, "I seemed to be more relaxed. They weren't really coming out on me, and when I make my shots, I get my confidence back. If I didn't, I just get disgusted."

There was little reason for any Eagle to be disgusted after the win. They all played well. Taylor finished the game with 14 points, and Bishop had eight points and an astounding 27 rebounds. And Bratten chipped in eight points and 16 boards. After the game, the Eagles' bus received a police escort back into town, and more than 150 people were there to greet them when they arrived home.

"It has been a long time coming," Jones told the Sun. She later told Diane Turner of the Daily Times, "This is a special group of players… It was amazing to watch the team peak during the state finals."

Jones was named Bayside Coach of the Year, and Coleman and Taylor landed on the All-Bayside First Team, alongside Mardela's Hopkins and Horsey and James M. Bennett's Suzanne Hastings. Taylor finished the year averaging 6.2 steals and 7.4 assists per-game, while Coleman averaged 12.5 points per-game, despite missing several contests near the end of the regular season when she was hospitalized with viral meningitis. Healthy in the state final, Coleman put her talents on full display. Watching from the stands, Stephen Decatur head coach Sue Brinsfield told the Daily Times, "Coleman couldn't miss." Remembering the team's triumphs recently, Jones opted to give another player a bit more credit: "Mary Taylor was the key to it all. She really was."

***

Brenda Jones continued to shepherd Snow Hill's program through the next decade and she piled up a ton of wins along the way. Under Jones, the Eagles had established a tradition of winning and they were the first real power in girls basketball on the Eastern Shore. "We have developed a true team atmosphere," Jones told the Daily Times in February 1983, amidst another undefeated start. The next season, she had a team start 20-0 before sputtering out in the postseason.

Jones even got calls from college teams wanting her to come be their coach. She turned down an offer from a small school in North Carolina, and from Delaware State. At the time, Delaware State's athletic director was Nelson Townsend, a former Worcester County vice principal.

"I'm so thankful I didn't do that," Jones says. "The fun thing for me was to take raw talent and ambition, and see what happened from the ninth grade to the 12th grade. I liked to mold kids and see the process."

Ahead of the 1987-88 season, Jones called it quits after 18 years of coaching. She stepped away from the sidelines with a record of 266 wins and just 51 losses, an extraordinary winning percentage of 83.9%. Under her watch, Snow Hill won seven Bayside Championships, had five undefeated regular seasons and went to the state final four nine times. Between 1981 and 1984, she guided the Eagles to 80 straight regular-season victories. In all, she had just two losing seasons.

"I lost the fire," Jones says. "I was done. I was ready. I loved it. I truly did love it. And I loved it for the players. It's the biggest thing that's ever happened to little girls from Snow Hill."

Jones briefly returned to the sidelines to coach the South teams in a few Bayside Senior All-Star games in the late 1990s.

While speaking with a Daily Times reporter in 1987, Jones said: "I don't think I'm a superior coach. We won because I convinced the kids that if they wanted to go on to school, they could find a way to go. What I'd like to be remembered for is teaching my girls how to win and how to succeed in life. I cared about them, not for the games they won, but for them as individuals. Basketball was a way for them to go on and better their education."

Two of Jones' former players – Gail Tatterson Gladding and Teresa Waters – would also become championship-winning high school basketball coaches in Maryland. After coaching a few years at Salisbury University, Gladding led Pocomoke to a 1A state championship in 2008, and Waters coached Oakland Mills to a state title in 1998, and River Hill to the crown in 2006 and 2019. Waters has more than 500 wins and Gladding retired with more than 400.

"Brenda was a tough coach," Gladding told the Daily Times in 1987. "There was no mediocre – you either did it right or you didn't do it. She deserves a lot of the credit for my career. She taught me everything I know and I don't know anyone who knows more about the game than she does. I've never met anybody who could pull out a game the way she could."

Hearing that quote from Gladding recently, Jones said, "Yea, she's right."

Jones added: "I was a tough coach. Caring, but tough… I didn't care who you were or who you belonged to; you did it my way or the highway. I wanted you to be humble. If you lose, you walk off the floor like ladies and accept the loss… You had to succeed in the classroom. I made sure that if you were capable of college, I wanted you in that direction. I didn't want you slacking. I held you accountable for everything. I think that's important. When we went to the state tournament, we were probably one of the best-dressed teams there – and I had poor kids. Back then, you had to present yourself well. I didn't dress slouchy, so I didn't want them to either. And if they didn't have it, I made sure they got it. I never had a kid get in a fight. I never had a kid embarrass me."

In an interview with 695Hoops.com, Waters once said of Jones: "She was tough as nails and her coaching style reflected it. She taught me mental and physical toughness."

While Jones was appreciated by her former players, she also held in high-esteem by her rivals. Barbara McCool told the Daily Times: "I thought she had a well-disciplined team that knew the game. She had some good players, but I think she was the reason they were good. I have a lot of respect for her."

Reflecting on all her teams accomplished, Jones said, "The thing about being in Snow Hill, once we got started, they all just worked hard… I can honestly say, I have great memories."

A GEM, A STAR AND A WARRIOR: GAIL TATTERSON GLADDING

"Pocomoke doesn't complain. They just beat people."
— David Insley

It was the spring of 1978, and Gail Tatterson had just completed her first season on the job as a graduate assistant coach under Shirley Duncan for the women's basketball team at Eastern Kentucky University. She had also earned her master's degree in physical education. When Tatterson was hired at EKU, Duncan told the student newspaper, the Eastern Progress, that Tatterson would "be a welcomed addition and will contribute a lot of character to the team."

A year prior, when Tatterson ended her decorated career in college basketball at Salisbury State College, she figured her playing days on the hardwood were over. There was no professional basketball league for women in the United States in 1977 and going overseas to pursue a career in hoops in a foreign land didn't really seem like an option for the 6-foot-2 girl who grew up on a 300-acre family farm in Snow Hill on Maryland's Eastern Shore. Tatterson's father had died in 1975 so she felt a sort of responsibility to provide for her mother and siblings. She estimated a teaching salary could do that, and she also thought that coaching could keep her close to the game she loved so much.

Tatterson was a supremely talented basketball player. She led Snow Hill High School to an appearance in the state final in 1973, and then became one of the best players ever at Salisbury State. She was molded by Brenda Jones, Snow Hill's no-nonsense coach who recognized Tatterson's talents quickly and aimed to toughen her up.

"Gail was so tall. I put boys on her at practice and she would complain about people being all over her," Jones says. "I said to her, 'If you can't take it, sit down and just shut up.' If you're a great player and somebody can get into your head, it messes your game up."

After that moment, few ever rattled the 6-foot-2 forward. As a member of the She Gulls (yes, the Salisbury women's basketball team went by that nickname back then in a blatantly sexist way) Tatterson was often unstoppable. Newspaper reports at the time cited her as having a vertical jump of 24 inches and she was the first women's basketball player at Salisbury to score more than 1,000 points in her career. She averaged about 14 points per-game, and with her on the team, the Gulls proved to be a difficult out even when facing opponents from the big-time college ranks. On Feb. 3, 1976, Tatterson poured in 32 points and 17 rebounds in a one-point loss to the Maryland Terrapins. "Gail played a beautiful game," Salisbury head coach Mariuna Morrison told the Salisbury Daily Times after the game.

Terps' head coach Chris Weller was well-prepared for Salisbury the next season, taking a 78-41 victory, but Tatterson still finished with 18 points and nine boards. Weeks later, on Feb. 13, 1977, Tatterson led the Gulls to a 63-47 win over Villanova with 30 points, 17 rebounds, three blocks and three assists. She wasn't widely known then, but Tatterson was often the top player on any court she stepped on, no matter the opponent. As a senior at Salisbury, she averaged 20.7 points and 16.2 rebounds per-game while shooting 57.7% from the floor.

Gail Gladding, then Tatterson, was a standout player for Salisbury State in the 1970s. She's still sixth all-time in scoring with 1,168 points. Salisbury University Athletics.

But something happened near the end of Tatterson's year as a graduate assistant at Eastern Kentucky that got her attention.

A man from Ohio, Bill Bryne, had a crazy idea: he was going to start a women's professional basketball league. And he would call it just that: The WPBL – before later dropping the P for a short, sweet and simple WBL acronym. According to Karra Porter's informative book on the short-lived league, "Mad Seasons," Byrne was a man who had gone from operating a sporting goods store in Columbus, Ohio, to being the director of player personnel for the Chicago Fire of the gone-in-a-flash World Football League, to being the founder of the American Professional Slo-Pitch League. What made him qualified to start and run a league for women's basketball, the first of its kind? Nothing, really. He was just the first with the gumption to try and do it.

When Byrne began laying the groundwork for the WBL, women had been playing full-court five-on-five basketball for less than a decade. And women's basketball had just made its debut at the Olympics a year prior, in 1976 in Montreal. Still, he believed a pro league could work. On Oct. 11, 1977,

Byrne's new venture was incorporated as a non-profit organization in Ohio. Three months later, an advertisement for the league ran in the Wall Street Journal to attract investors and potential team owners. It declared the league would play its first campaign across the 1978-79 season. The cost for a franchise, according to Porter's book, was a $50,000 entry fee and about $250,000 in annual expenses.

Tatterson didn't think much of the WBL – much less pursuing a career in it – when she first heard of it. But a friend of hers from Eastern Kentucky, Rich Bruer, mailed her a copy of the league's first draft class. Tatterson glanced over the list and noticed several familiar names. The players drafted were not only ones she had played against in college, but many that she had bested. "I was approached by a man from New Jersey who was looking for players and he asked me to come and try out, so that's what I did," Tatterson said. "If they could make the draft, I could make it as a walk-on."

Bruer, who lived in Little Silver, New Jersey, put Tatterson in touch with the owner of the state's WBL franchise, the New Jersey Gems. So, Tatterson tried out for the Gems that August – and she impressed their coaching staff. She gave an interview to the Salisbury Daily Times in September and said, "I told them if the money was right, I'd sign. The Gems' management says the money won't be great."

The money wound up being good enough, apparently. On Oct. 31, Tatterson agreed to a one-year deal with the Gems worth $6,000, making her the first woman from the Eastern Shore to sign a professional basketball contract. Tatterson would joke years later that she was "highly paid" making about a grand above the league minimum.

Tatterson and Jo-Ellen Bistromowitz, a Montclair State product who played professionally in Germany and Belgium, were the first two players ever signed by the Gems. The team was coached by Don Kennedy, who had previously coached the men's team at Saint Peter's University to 323 wins and five NIT appearances across 22 seasons. Each WBL team would play a 34-game regular season in its inaugural year, with 17 games at home and 17 games on the road. The Gems played its games at the Thomas Dunn Sports Center in Elizabeth, where single game general admission tickets were as low as $3, and where 1,924 people attended the first ever professional women's basketball game held in New Jersey on Sunday, Dec. 17, 1978. The Gems lost 123-120 to the visiting Chicago Hustle, coached by Doug Bruno. Tatterson had 20 points, nine rebounds and two blocks in her professional debut, and her family made the 254-mile trek north to see it. "I don't want this to sound as if I'm bragging, but Gail's performance was brilliant," her brother Don told Rick Cullen of the Daily Times.

Don was bragging, but it was absolutely warranted. Two months later, Tatterson earned the league's Player of the Week honors after dropping 44 points and 18 rebounds on the Hustle to snap a six-game losing skid for the Gems.

***

The girl from Snow Hill was quickly turning into one of the WBL's top players, and one that scribes would turn to when they wanted a blunt and matter-of-fact assessment of the league. When the Washington Post dispatched Thomas Boswell to write a lengthy feature on the league, he sought out Tatterson to find the answer to the question: What's the goal of the WBL? She replied: "When the New York bookies carry a line on our games, then we've arrived."

The WBL sort of made up its own rules as it went along in its inaugural season. The league used a ball that was made by Wilson, but was two inches smaller than the ones used by the NBA. The lanes on the court were also cut down to 12 feet from 16 feet, and man-to-man defense was mandatory. Where the league did try to emulate its men's counterpart was in time: the WBL debuted with a 24-second shot clock and 12-minute quarters. A story from Michael Farber in the Hackensack Record at the time claimed that portions of the WBL rulebook were simply photocopied over from the NBA's.

And the league didn't exactly provide ideal conditions for its players as far as lodging, travel and arenas went. Salaries per-player that first season ranged from $5,000 to $15,000. That might seem low – it was – but team owners were still trying to pinch pennies and cut corners in every way they could. Often, as reported by Boswell and dozens of other scribes at the time, players often slept three to four players to a motel room, and they dressed for the game at the motel, then jammed themselves and all of their stuff into a pair of rented station wagons to go play games officiated by high school referees in gyms that were often so frigid that players covered up with towels on the bench. "Even after playing four or five minutes, we were still cold," Tatterson once told the Passaic Herald-News.

Byrne told Boswell, "Someday when we're in our rocking chairs and girls are making $100,000 a year, we'll laugh about these struggling times." Nobody was amused then and no one is chuckling now. WBL players often washed their own uniforms and taped their own ankles. When a 15-seat bus full of New York Stars broke down in Chicago in January 1980, players and coaches walked the next five blocks to play a game at DePaul University, according to a New York Times story from Jane Gross. Players received just $16 to $21 per-day for expenses for road games.

Even the league's first all-star game was a bit half-assed. It was announced that it would be played just 12 days before it happened, and Tatterson was one of the selections on the east team. The game was played at Madison

Square Garden's Felt Forum, which is under the main historic arena. "There's a little gym there – The Little Garden – that was attached to it and we played in there," she said, years later.

The Felt Forum has a low 20-foot ceiling, which is not ideal for basketball, but around 3,000 fans attended the thrown-together exhibition which ended with the East winning 112-99, a score that was displayed on a borrowed scoreboard from a high school in Elizabeth, New Jersey. Uniforms for the game arrived just a few hours before tip-off, according to the News of Paterson, New Jersey. At an after-party following the game, players had to buy their own drinks, Tatterson told the Daily Times, but she also said: "I've never had so much fun playing a basketball game. The officiating must've been good, because I don't remember anything about it."

The Gems missed the WBL's first playoffs, but ended their inaugural campaign with a victory, besting the Milwaukee Does 163-161 in triple-overtime behind Tatterson's 32 points. The Gems ended the season with a 9-25 record, but Tatterson was by-far their top player. She led the team in scoring and rebounding with averages of 20.9 points and 10.3 boards per-game. She made the league's All-Pro team, was fifth in the WBL in scoring and seventh in rebounding.

And Tatterson set one mark that season that still stands as a record as of this writing, one that epitomizes the fearlessness and roughness of the farm-raised girl from Snow Hill. In the 1978-79 season, Tatterson committed 179 personal fouls, about five per-game. Since then, only one women's professional basketball player has tied that record: Yolanda Griffith, who fouled just as much while playing for the ABL's Chicago Condors in 1998. The WNBA record is 143, set by Cheryl Ford in 2005.

Tatterson also led the WBL in field goal percentage in 1978-79 with a 64.6% clip. As of this writing, that mark would be seventh-best all-time for a single season record in WNBA history.

Said longtime Wicomico High School boys head coach Butch Waller: "Gail was a heck of a player."

***

Entering her second season in the WBL, Tatterson was well known as a center who was scrappy on defense and skillful on offense. She was a free agent and highly sought-after, and wound-up landing with the New York Stars. The Stars were 19-15 the season before and it seemed like they'd be better in year two. But the San Francisco Pioneers handed the Stars a loss in the season-opener, beating them 97-95 at the Felt Forum. Tatterson had 10 points in her Big Apple debut. "We played a couple of games before the Knicks, and it was cool except we had to be done two hours before their game started, but the TV people wouldn't wait for us," Tatterson recalled, years later. As of this writing, the Felt Forum is known as the Hulu Theater.

In its second season, it was clear that the WBL was unstable, to say the least. According to Gross' story in the New York Times, the owners of the Stars claimed they lost $350,000 in their first season and were losing $25,000 per night playing at Madison Square Garden. It's unclear what exactly the Stars' owners were paying for at MSG, considering the environment was far from extravagant. The New York Daily News noted that the Stars' locker room was "about the size of a subway change booth with one sink... and little else."

One of the things the WBL lacked early on was real star power and names that were recognizable nationwide. Many of the top college players at the time – like Nancy Lieberman, Ann Meyers, Carol Blazejowski and Tara Heiss – didn't enter the league right away because they wanted to preserve their amateur status for the 1980 Olympics. Byrne was also targeting those games, telling Boswell that the league would "take off" after the USA women won gold. Unfortunately, the Americans – along with Canada, Mexico, Puerto Rico, China and Argentina – boycotted the 1980 games held in Moscow. So, there wasn't a team full of Americans for a mass audience to get excited about basketball and all of those players held off entering the league for nothing, forfeiting stardom and paychecks along the way.

Tatterson averaged 13 points and 10 rebounds per-game for the Stars in 1979-80, but the franchise folded after the season. She rejoined the Gems for the 1980-81 season and received more than double what she made her first season in New Jersey, with a salary of $13,000. But three months into the season, Tatterson was waived by the Gems as the league continued to hemorrhage money. By the summer of 1981, the WBL ceased to exist.

"It was difficult for management – and it was shaky – to meet some payrolls. It was only a matter of time before the league would cave in," Tatterson told Cullen of the Daily Times. "It was fun. I have no regrets. Perhaps I'm owed some money."

She later told Eric Magill of the Daily Times: "There was a sadness when it was over, but we didn't expect it to last after the first year... It meant a chance for us to be in the first women's pro league. A lot of the girls said that. We knew there would never be another first like that, and our names were all on that list."

The WBL may have had a short life, but it blazed a trail for what came after it. And Tatterson – from tiny Snow Hill – was part of paving the way for future leagues, like WNBA, which is still running strong since playing its first game in 1997.

"I had a great time in the league," Tatterson – then going by her married name, Gladding – told me in 2016. "We wanted to be the WNBA."

***

When she was cut by the New Jersey Gems and the WBL ended for good, Gail Tatterson came back to the Eastern Shore and put her teaching degree to use, landing a job at Pocomoke High School. She remained close to the game there, assisting with the girls basketball team for a few seasons. In June 1983, she married Edward "Dicky" Gladding and took his last name. And soon, the name Gail Gladding became synonymous with excellence in women's basketball on the Delmarva Peninsula.

Gladding wasn't interested in putting a jersey on again when Bill Byrne's second professional league – the Women's American Basketball Association – started up in 1984. She was content with teaching and coaching at Pocomoke, and she questioned the stability of the new league when its $300,000 salary limits were revealed. Her instincts proved to be right. The WABA lasted less than one season.

In March of 1985, a different basketball opportunity presented itself to Gladding. Her alma mater, Salisbury State College, needed a new head coach. Gladding had experience as a Division I and a high school assistant, and was arguably Salisbury's best women's player ever, still holding 12 school records when she was hired. Eight years after graduating, she took over the reins of the She Gulls (yes, Salisbury unfortunately stuck with this moniker for its women's teams for far too long, finally dropping it in the 1990s) from Deirdre Kane, whose teams went 26-27 across two seasons. Gladding was the fifth head coach in the history of Salisbury women's basketball and quickly took the Gulls to new heights.

The Gulls went 14-11 in Gladding's first season at the helm, then 17-10 in her second season. Her third season was her best – and Salisbury's best ever – as it was capped off with a 91-67 win over Marywood College in the Eastern States Athletic Conference Championship. Salisbury finished the 1987-88 season with a 20-6 record, a 15-game winning streak and a per-game scoring average above 76 points, all three of which were school records. Despite those accomplishments, the team led on the court by Dawn Webb, Sandy Jankevicius and Myra Sturgis was not selected for the Division III NCAA Tournament.

At the end of that season, Gladding planned to take just a year off to spend time with her family and take care of her children. In the interim, Salisbury tapped men's lacrosse coach Jim Berkman to temporarily oversee the program for a season. The 12-time national champion and most winningest coach in the history of NCAA men's lacrosse guided the Sea Gulls to a 16-10 record and a playoff appearance in 1988-89.

But Gladding didn't return to the sidelines the next season and neither did Berkman. Salisbury instead hired Rhonda Warmsley as the full-time head coach. By 1990, when Salisbury inducted Gladding into its hall of fame, she was raising three boys, all under the age of four years old. Her three-year collegiate coaching tenure ended with a 51-27 record and one conference championship. But she still wasn't finished with teaching basketball.

***

David Byrd knew Gail Gladding pretty well.

Moreover, the athletic director at Pocomoke High School knew how knowledgeable the girl from Snow Hill was about the game of basketball. When Gladding was doing her student teaching at Berlin Middle School in the mid-1970s – where Byrd got his start in teaching – the two would play one-on-one. "I won, of course," Byrd said with his tongue in his cheek. "But I knew she knew the game of basketball… I knew her background. A lot of people didn't realize that she played for Brenda Jones and was a great player at Snow Hill, a great player at Salisbury University, and played for Dean Meminger with the New York Stars.

"Plus, her and I got along."

Byrd remained close with Gladding through the 1980s as she taught at Pocomoke High School and coached at Salisbury. And then, in the summer of 1991, Byrd enlisted her husband Dicky to construct his new home.

"Her husband built my house and she was – as you know, a big woman, about 6-foot-2 – helping put plywood on the roof," Byrd recalled. He then thought, you know, I need a basketball coach. Diane Smith had left her post as the Warriors' play-caller at the end of the 1990-91 season. And there was Gladding, with tools in her hands. Byrd instead envisioned her with a playbook in her hands and a whistle around her neck.

So, Byrd began courting the former WBL star to take over the girls team at Pocomoke. The program at that time was solid – they had made a pair of state final four appearances in 1976 and 1987 – but they had never played for a Bayside Conference crown. Byrd believed the program had a higher potential. And he thought Gladding could help the Warriors reach it. Finally, she told Byrd, "Ok. I'll do it. I want to try it."

In the Bayside Conference preview that ran in the Daily Times on Dec. 6, 1991, Gladding is quoted saying, "We have a long way to go."

Gladding patrolled the sidelines at Pocomoke and guided the Warriors to more than 450 wins over the next 25 seasons. Her teams won 11 regional titles, five Bayside Conference crowns and a state championship. Along the way, Gladding became known around the Eastern Shore to fellow coaches, fans, players and reporters for her wit, toughness, dry humor and diplomacy. If there is a Mount Rushmore of girls basketball coaches in the history of the Bayside Conference, Gladding is on it.

"She did a really good job," longtime Wi-Hi head coach Butch Waller said. "Gail was – what you saw is what you got. She was a bigger version of

Barbara McCool. And I think, to some of the younger kids, she probably intimidated them. But they grew to love her because she knew what she was doing. She was very honest and very fair." Gladding could also be blunt. And anytime another school hosted the Bayside All-Star Game, she let them know when it wasn't up to her standards. "She'd say, 'Butch, for God's sake, don't let these other schools have the All-Star Game. They don't know what they're doing.'"

A North Dorchester High School graduate, David Insley chronicled Eastern Shore high school sports for decades for the Dorchester Banner and the Star Democrat. Photo by Mitchell Northam.

Arguably Gladding's best season came in the 2007-08 campaign, which ended with the Pocomoke girls winning their first state title. The season before, Pocomoke made the final, but fell to Southern Garrett. By Jan. 21, 2008, Pocomoke was 13-0, and Shawn Yonker of the Daily Times projected the Warriors to be a squad that could make the final four again. The team was led on the court by Ashley Bishop, Deyonna Parker, Kori Pitts, Brianna Hall, Andrea Dennis, Kiara Bratten, Whitney King and Kiana Sturgis. Pocomoke was by no means carried by just a single player. They weren't like the Tia Jackson-led Mardela teams or the Dayona Godwin-led Stephen Decatur squads. But what they lacked in star power and size, they made up for it in grit – a signature that all Gladding-coached teams had.

"At every game Gail coached I could expect consistency, quality behavior and success," longtime Star Democrat sports scribe David Insley said. "When Gail took the floor, you knew you were in for a tough game and you were up against the classiest coach around... What has impressed me the most is how she creates the room to describe the need to improve, without stepping on toes. She's not just a leader, she's diplomatic. She's the type of person who should be elected to office."

Gladding never got around to running for mayor or the state senate, despite Insley's recommendation. She had ball to coach.

But, like a politician, Gladding did have a bag of recyclable catch-phrases. Her teams embodied her no-nonsense attitude and her players often sounded like her too when being interviewed. After beating North Caroline 56-41 for the Bayside Conference Championship in 2008, Bishop told the Daily Times: "You control the boards, you control the game." It was a line that Gladding, an expert rebounder in her day, had said countless times. In that game, Bishop was all over the boards, grabbing 15 off the glass to go along with 11 points and four assists. Bishop may have not been a clear-cut Division I prospect, but she was the Warriors' leader that season.

In Pocomoke's playoff opener, Bishop racked up 25 points and 11 rebounds in a 61-37 win over Snow Hill. Nick Purnell wasn't Snow Hill's coach for that game, but took over the following season. Still, being handed a playoff loss by Gladding was a feeling he quickly became accustomed to.

"I coached against Gail a few times. I thought I knew my stuff. But Gail really knew her stuff," Purnell said. "She was a little more seasoned than me. Gail kind of put it on me a couple of times. When playoffs would come around – for some reason – in the (regional) semi's, I would always have to face Gail. And it was like, 'Man. Not again.' Gail was one of a kind."

One coach that Gladding faced off with more than a few times was Barbara McCool of Mardela – another woman who would be on that Mount Rushmore of girls basketball coaches on the Eastern Shore. McCool had been coaching the Warriors at Mardela since before Gladding was in high school. When Gladding took the reins at Pocomoke, the two teams became rivals because they faced off so much when the stakes were high. In each season from 2002 through 2011, either Pocomoke or Mardela was the South representative in the Bayside title game for girls basketball. And because Pocomoke and Mardela were both in the South and both in the 1A class, they often met in the playoffs. 2008 was no different. The 1A East Final – and a ticket to the state final four – would be won by either Pocomoke or Mardela.

"I know Pocomoke quite well. We battle for regions almost every year," McCool told the Easton Star Democrat leading up to the playoff bout. "They've got a great team... They're very quick. They get in transition really easily."

Pocomoke was a bit too quick to start the game, and fell behind early against Mardela's 2-3 zone defense. "They were like flashes up and down the floor. The first two timeouts I called was to say slow down," Gladding told the Daily Times. After settling down, Pocomoke topped Mardela 48-30 at the University of Maryland Eastern Shore for the 1A East Region crown. The key was a 58-30 rebounding advantage. "It's our fourth year going over there," Bishop told the Daily Times. "Hopefully, we'll bring back the trophy this time."

Bishop proved to be key again in the state semifinals for Pocomoke at the University of Maryland-Baltimore County. With 10 seconds left against Digital Harbor, she fired an 18-foot jump-shot from her hip that swished the net, securing Pocomoke's 41-39 victory. "Ashely Bishop had the ball around the three-point line, and she was a forward and not an outside shooter, and she started to wind up a shot from way out, and I'm yelling, 'No! No! No!' and swish it went in," Gladding recalled years later. "Man for man, (the 2008 team) probably weren't as talented, but they had the desire, the drive and they worked really hard."

Bishop finished with 19 points and the Warriors survived a game in which they connected on just one field goal in the third quarter, and a game that featured 11 lead changes. "If it hadn't been for Ashely… We would have never beaten Digital Harbor," Gladding told the Daily Times. During the postgame press conference, Gladding was on her cell phone, trying to find someone to tape the other semifinal game between Allegany and Surrattsville.

It's unclear if Gladding ever found someone to capture that contest, but it sure seemed like Pocomoke was prepared in the 1A State Final. Despite a hiccup in the second quarter where the Warriors fell behind by 10 points to Allegany, Pocomoke stormed back to take a 16-point fourth quarter advantage. In the end, Gladding's girls won 66-53, capturing their first and only state title. The key was Pocomoke's depth, as the Warriors' bench outscored Allegany's 27-10. Also, rebounding was again a factor as the Warriors won the battle on the boards 47-31. The crucial run for Pocomoke came in the third quarter, as it outscored Allegany 15-5. "It's been a long time coming," Gladding told the Daily Times. "I knew we could come back. I know we're not going to get tired. In fact, I look forward to the third and fourth quarters."

A few days after the victory, Gladding penned a thankful letter-to-the-editor in the Daily Times, expressing her gratitude to the Pocomoke fans for making the 146-mile trip to Catonsville at an odd time. The girls state final was moved to a weekday because UMBC's men's basketball team wound-up hosting the America East final. Gladding wrote: "When we came out on a Wednesday afternoon at 3 p.m., I didn't expect many people to be there to cheer us on – what a surprise. We came out to loud cheers. It put us at ease and made us feel like we were playing at home."

***

The 2007-08 season might've been Gladding's most successful one as a coach, considering it ended with her lifting up the ultimate trophy, but her most memorable and most impressive campaign came eight years later.

Before the 2015-16 season got underway, Gladding received a troubling diagnosis, the word that no one wants to hear when they talk to a doctor: cancer.

Many thought she would take the season off as she underwent treatments. Everyone knew that Gladding was going to give cancer the hardest punch she could throw, one that Mike Tyson would be intimidated by, but they didn't expect her to keep on coaching during her battle with the disease. However, Gladding decided that nothing was going to keep her away from the game of basketball.

If she was going to stop coaching, it would be on her own terms. And nobody was going to tell her otherwise.

"I was worried about her health at first, but she said she was going to coach and that's what she did," Byrd said. "Not many people could do what she did."

Through her more than two decades of coaching basketball at Pocomoke High School, Gladding tried to instill resilience and a hard-nosed-can't-quit attitude into all of her teams. In the 2015-16 season, she gave her squad an up-close example of what that looked like.

"I just felt like I could do it," Gladding said in 2016. "I didn't feel tired. I had bad days, but I tried to plan my chemo so I didn't have to miss practice or games. There were days when I was uncomfortable or couldn't sleep, but other than that I felt pretty good and I wanted to coach."

Gail Gladding coached the Pocomoke High School girls team through the 2015-16 season while she was receiving treatment for cancer. The Warriors made the state semifinals. Photo by Mitchell Northam.

Gladding's hair faded and she lost some weight, but other than that, not much changed for girls basketball at Pocomoke. The Warriors still deployed a smothering-style of defense, they were still fundamentally sound, Gladding was still yelling instructions from the sidelines and hollering at officials, and the Warriors were still damn good. Pocomoke breezed through the regular season and won the 1A East Region Championship with ease, 62-32 over Cambridge. By then, Gladding looked like most of her assistant coaches and fellow staff at Pocomoke High School as many of them had shaved their heads to show their support for her.

"As far as a class act, Gladding was that," said Greg Bozman, the girls basketball coach and athletic director at Crisfield. "If she had a better team than you, she'd press you in the first half, and then they just worked on things in the second half. She wouldn't run the score up on you, but she was always competitive."

The on-court leader for the Warriors that season was senior Dynaisha Christian, a 5-foot-11 forward who wound-up playing for Division II Bowie State. When her career at Pocomoke ended, she had scored 1,818 points and owned the program rebounding record with 1,105 boards. "She's not really big, but she's not small either. She's very powerful under the basket," Gladding said of Christian. "She's tenacious under the basket. Her ability to continue to go after the ball is better than most, even in the men's game."

At the state semifinals in Towson's SECU Arena, Pocomoke's storybook season was derailed by Southern Garrett despite Christian's best efforts. The Warriors lost 64-54, but the season remained a remarkable one for Pocomoke, as they finished 21-5. Across those 21 wins, the Warriors won by an average margin of 29 points.

"Pocomoke doesn't complain," Insley said. "They just beat people."

And a few months after the season was over, Gladding got a big win off the court too. At 59-years-old, she was cancer-free. By the summer, her gray hair had returned, and in July, she – on her own terms – finally called it quits and hung up her whistle. "I have grandchildren now," she told me in her office at Pocomoke High School that summer. "I'm just ready to be home."

***

Gladding continued to work at Pocomoke High School as the alternative teacher and stayed close to basketball by helping Byrd out with his various athletic director duties and by staying on as the 1A East Regional Girls Basketball Director for the Maryland Public Secondary Schools Athletic Association. Corey Zimmer took over head coaching duties for the girls basketball team, and with former Pocomoke boys' great Eddie Miller assisting him, the Warriors again won the 1A East Region title. Pocomoke's trip to the state final four in 2017 marked its 14th trip there, but it was the third time the Warriors had gone that far without Gladding as their head coach.

"Being around her and getting to pick her brain showed me that she is a really amazing and warm-hearted person," Zimmer said of Gladding.

When Gail Gladding retired from coaching in 2016, she handed the reins of Pocomoke's program over to Corey Zimmer, but stayed close to the game. Photo by Mitchell Northam.

Sadly, Gladding's cancer did not stay in remission. It resurfaced a few years later and she died at the age of 64 on Aug. 5, 2019 at her home in Pocomoke City, just eight months after she had retired from teaching. Her career in basketball soaked up three paragraphs in the middle of her obituary.

"I really, really miss her," David Byrd said of his friend Gail. "She was everywhere and did everything. She was one of the guys. She liked basketball and I liked basketball. It was a good match for us. She was a great girl."

As a basketball player, Gladding should be remembered as a trailblazing pioneer – having played in the first Maryland state final four for girls basketball and the first professional league for women. She was also a tenacious rebounder who had a soft touch around the rim. Rebekkah Brunson would be an apt modern-day comparison.

"Gail was so talented," said her high school coach, Brenda Jones. "They wanted me to speak at her funeral, but I couldn't do it."

For her career as a coach, peers recall Gladding being even-handed, classy, innovative and excellent. As of 2021, she is still just one of four people to lead a girls basketball team from the Eastern Shore to a state title in the modern era. Players and fellow coaches learned a great deal from her.

"I used to watch Gail's practices and just sit and write," said Derrick Fooks, who has been the boys head basketball coach at Pocomoke since

2003. "And I'd tell her, 'Gail, you know I'm going to do that tomorrow.' Inbound plays, stuff like that."

And as a person, Gladding is memorialized as someone who was both the epitome of the word "tough," but also someone who was very caring; someone who uplifted and led other women, and someone who devoted a great deal of her time to lift up girls basketball on the Eastern Shore of Maryland. She did that as a high school player, a college player, a professional, a college coach, a high school coach, a teacher and an administrator. It might seem cliché, but Gladding embodied Pocomoke's mascot; she was a Warrior, on and off the court.

Annette Wallace, Pocomoke High School's former principal, always looked up to Gladding and admired her strength and perseverance. Wallace told me in 2016: "Gail has taught me to be brave in all situations and not to apologize for being a strong woman. I think strong women sometimes get a bad rap – Gail taught me to be myself and don't apologize for it."

No matter her age, role, title or condition, Gail Tatterson Gladding was always herself: a strong and resilient girl raised on a farm in Snow Hill who loved people and basketball. And she gave everything she had to both.

THE LESSONS OF GREG BOZMAN

*"I'm alright with it. I've lived with it...
Except for the Final Four thing. I really would've liked to have
gone to the Final Four." – Greg Bozman*

"You don't belong here."
"Man, you don't either."

This exchange between two former Division I college basketball players happened in the late 1980s, but it didn't come in a park, on a hardwood court, or in a gym. It took place on the campus of the Eastern Correctional Institution, a medium-security men's prison in Westover, Maryland – then the largest of its kind in the state. It opened in 1987 and created many jobs for Eastern Shore natives looking for work; folks like Greg Bozman, who landed a gig there as a corrections officer.

ECI, stationed near the intersection of Route 13 and the Manokin River, has a capacity of 3,400 inmates. In the first few years it was operational, it hosted a former college basketball phenom in Allen H. "Skip" Wise. A high school All-American at Baltimore's basketball cathedral, Dunbar, Wise led the Poets to 47 straight victories between 1973 and 1974. He went on to star at Clemson where he averaged 18.5 points per-game in the 1974-75 season and became the first freshman to make the All-ACC team. A 6-foot-3 combo guard, Wise was a silky-smooth pure shooter, and left school early to pursue a professional career.

Wise signed with his hometown Baltimore Claws of the American Basketball Association on a five-year deal worth a cool $1 million. According to Terry Pluto's definitive book on the ABA, "Loose Balls," Claws' coach Joe Mullaney once found Wise in the locker room, shivering. Mullaney told Pluto: "I guess the Clemson people knew that Wise was on drugs already."

The Baltimore Claws folded before they ever played a game. Wise played in two games with the San Antonio Spurs and then signed with the Golden State Warriors, but – according to a 2005 HoopsHype story – was cut when head coach Al Attles caught him doing drugs in the locker room during the preseason. On Aug. 15, 1985, Wise was sentenced to prison for the second time in his life – six years for selling heroin to a police informant in Baltimore. When ECI opened, Wise was transferred to the Eastern Shore.

So, Wise and Bozman found themselves in the same place at the same time. The circumstances that led them to ECI were different, but they also weren't. They were two men who loved basketball and who played the game at a very high level, but they also never reached their full potential as players.

When Bozman first spotted Wise in the yard at ECI he called out to him: "What's up, Clemson?"

"He looked at me crazy," Bozman says. "But we played against each other every day after that for about three years. We could play the inmates every afternoon from 4 to 6 p.m. Sunday through Saturday, 4 to 6, we were in the jail, playing ball. Skip was unbelievable. He's the best player I've ever played against, no doubt. Good handles still and he just never missed."

The Salisbury Daily Times regularly ran Wise's stats from prison games in the newspaper. He had 39 points in a game on Jan. 5, 1989, and 32 points on April 20, 1989. ECI had two teams – East and West – and they would regularly play games against other prison squads, like Jessup, and against local teams from men's leagues on the Eastern Shore. In the 1988-89 season, Wise averaged 33 points, 12 rebounds and 10 assists per-game for ECI West. But Wise wasn't the only player in those games stuffing stat sheets. In one contest, Bozman drained a league-record 14 three-pointers.

"The best basketball at that time was against the inmates at ECI," said Anky Tull, who played on Pocomoke's 1976 state championship team and later worked as a corrections officer. "Skip was fantastic. The drugs and streets got into him, but he could still play. He was the best player there. Skip could light you up."

Derrick Fooks, now Pocomoke's head coach added: "I played my share of games at ECI too… That's when basketball was basketball."

After one game where Wise really lit it up, Bozman said while walking by him, "You don't belong here."

It was a compliment, sort of, and it was also true. Wise should've been dishing dimes to Rick Barry and swishing shots for the Warriors – not dropping 40 points on prison guards. But game recognizes game. Wise had played against Bozman enough times to figure out that he was a legitimate and talented baller as well. So, why was Bozman working as a guard, and playing in these games? Why wasn't he, at the very least, playing overseas?

Wise barked back: "Man, you don't either."

***

What happened to Greg Bozman has happened to countless kids across the Eastern Shore who didn't maximize their athletic potential. The reasons for why it happens vary. Some get caught up in drugs, alcohol, tough situations and wrong crowds. Some follow poor advice. Some under or overestimate their abilities. Others get hurt and have their sports careers cut short.

For Bozman, it was a mix of disagreements he had with coaches, homesickness, being born into the wrong era of hoops and one poorly-timed injury.

In high school, Bozman was a 6-foot-6 shooter, and a damn sharp one too. He could swish deep shots from the top of the key, the corners and the wings. And his release was so high that he could shoot over most defenders. Had Bozman come along as a prospect in 2017, a smart high school coach would've given him the green light to take as many three's as he wanted. Scholarship offers would've piled up like Jenga blocks as college coaches clamored over him. He's what most coaches want nowadays: a long wing player who can hit shots from behind the arc and defend multiple positions.

Problem is, Bozman came along in the early 80s. The NCAA didn't widely adopt the three-point shot across men's Division I basketball until 1986. Maryland high schools didn't accept it until the 1987-88 season, with a distance of 19-feet and nine inches.

"When I finally got to play in some tournaments in men's leagues with the three-point line, I was in heaven," Bozman said.

Without the arc, most coaches wanted to stick Bozman in the paint. They wanted him to grab rebounds and score from the post. He could do that, but he didn't really want to. He knew those weren't the best qualities of his game.

"My brother was a little better playing with his back to the basket. I hated it. And it came from playing against him," Bozman said. "You get your shot blocked by your 6-foot-6 older brother, and you're still 5-foot-11, you have to develop other ways to score."

So, by the time Greg Bozman grew to his brother Bruce's height, he was armed with a high right-handed release that was nearly unblockable. And more often than not, when he fired up a shot from 18 feet and beyond, it went in. Plus, he had a solid handle, decent vision and a good sense of the game. "I could play guard, if they let me," Bozman said. But, this was 1979, not 2022. And Bozman was playing on the Eastern Shore, not in New York City. His size was – and still is – a rare and valuable commodity in a conference that has long been overpopulated with pint-sized guards. So, Washington head coach Larry Sterling stuck Bozman in the paint.

Sterling was an accomplished coach, leading the Jaguars to a state title in 1975, but he didn't quite realize what he had in Bozman. Then a junior, Bozman was listed as a center in Washington's preview capsule that ran in the Daily Times on Dec. 2, 1979, and Sterling said of him: "Great coordination, could play guard, he's so agile. Has a good shot, but needs to work on his rebounding." So, maybe Sterling did know what he had in Bozman, but played him at center anyways.

Whatever the case was, it didn't sit well with Bozman.

"It did more damage to my confidence back then than anything," Bozman said. "When you're a kid, you look at things differently. I was always placed in positions in high school that weren't suitable for my type of game. I was playing in the post position at Washington quite a bit and I wasn't really comfortable with that. Really, it just didn't feel like I was playing like I could play. And I didn't think things were going to change under Coach Sterling. He was a great guy, a great coach and it was nothing against him. It was just – when you're young like that, you tend to look for something that suits you."

Bozman averaged just over 10 points per-game at Washington as a junior, but he was fed up with his role and lack of freedom. By the end of February, he had left the team. And before his senior year started, he transferred schools, going to Washington's county rival: Crisfield.

"You didn't do that back then," Bozman says. "But Mr. Cain let me face the basket a little bit more which was more suitable for my style of game."

" Mr. Cain" was Bill Cain, one of the most decorated coaches in Bayside Conference history. Entering the 1980-81 season, Cain was coming off winning his third state championship and fourth Bayside title since 1973.

"He was a disciplinarian," Pocomoke head coach David Byrd said of Cain. "He ruled with an iron fist. He had smart point guards. It was old school basketball."

Cain knew his x's and o's, but more than anything, he was a regimented coach who knew how to get the most out of his players.

"He was so structured. When you got to Crisfield, he was making it like a college. Your name was on your locker, and everything was like a step above what I was used to," Bozman said. "In practice we'd run the 'shuffle offense,' he called it. Everybody played their role the way they were supposed to. And that's why he won. He was really good with that structure. He established roles for everyone. A guy might not take 20 shots a game, but there was a role for him – he could set screens or rebound or play defense. His players adapted to that. At Washington, everyone wanted to be the go-to guy… There was something about, when Crisfield and Washington played, Crisfield would win most of the time and I think it was due to (Cain's) coaching ability."

Bozman's role in Cain's offense was to score. And it was a job he flourished in.

In his debut for the Crabbers, Bozman had 19 points and nine rebounds in a 73-58 victory over Wicomico High School while wearing the purple and gold No. 21. "Greg's got an outstanding outside shot and he can handle the ball better than most his size," Cain told Rick Cullen of the Daily Times.

A few weeks later, Bozman had 15 points in a 61-56 win over Washington. A few weeks after that, he and Kenny Evans combined for nearly 40 points in a triumph over Parkside. "Great high school player and he could shoot it," Bozman said of Evans. "It took us a while to gel, but we had plenty of firepower. There were a couple of times when both of us got hot."

With Bozman and Evans leading the way, the Crabbers ended the regular season with a 14-7 record, but extended the Crabbers' home winning streak to 41 games – a run that began in 1977. It can sound overblown to refer to a high school gym as a hostile environment, but Crisfield really was a difficult place to play for opposing teams because of its loud and loyal fanbase. Cain's defenses – usually 1-3-1 or a 2-3 zone – didn't make things easy for opponents either.

"That place was crazy," Bozman said. "First of all, if you didn't get there at the start of the JV game, you didn't get in for varsity. In that era, for a 15- to 18-year-old kid to walk in on that floor as the visiting team, they were down 10 points right from the beginning. Crisfield was definitely a place where I'm sure many kids did not want to go play there."

At one time, there was a mural outside of Crisfield's gym – which was nicknamed "The Graveyard" – and it depicted headstones for each opposing Bayside Conference school, and it also featured a referee hanging from a tree. It was far from politically correct and has since been painted over.

"It was tough going into Crisfield," said Derrick Fooks, a 1983 Stephen Decatur graduate. "We hated going in there. We lost a game there my senior year of high school, and they still threw ice at our bus. Busted a few of Jimmy Purnell's windows out."

In the postseason, Crisfield topped North Caroline 68-61 in the first round of the playoffs with Bozman and Evans combining for 27 points. In the next round, they combined for 23 points to push Crisfield past Snow Hill in a low-scoring 39-33 affair. In the region final, Crisfield was beaten by Pocomoke on a buzzer-beating shot by Jimmy Schoolfield at Salisbury State. 52-50 was the final, and Bozman – who had 12 points and six boards – is still bitter about the way his high school career ended.

"We got cheated by Pocomoke. I don't say that much, I really don't, but that game – we were up with a couple minutes left. People were actually going out into the lobby making their reservations for College Park," Bozman says. "We were dominating. Their center had fouled out. And then, I hate to say it, but some whistles were swallowed. There were two or three blatant, bad fouls. The last play of the game, when the guy hit the shot, one of the referees had called traveling. So, I thought we were going to overtime. The next thing I knew, when I got to the bench, the scorer's table is being thrown on the floor at Salisbury State and the referees ran out. Our fans went nuts. I was devastated."

The following season, without Bozman, Crisfield would advance much further in the playoffs. Behind the play of Kenny Evans, who was named Bayside Player of the Year, the Crabbers won the Class C state championship – the fourth and final title for Cain.

"Kenny Evans – in my career, and I've played in high school, college and in Europe – he was probably a top 10 shooter that I had ever seen," said Brian Butler, who played for Wi-Hi at the time. "Kenny could really shoot the ball. Kenny was legit. He was a Division I player."

***

Greg Bozman had some interest from college coaches his senior season at Crisfield, but only locally. He received calls and letters from Delaware State, the University of Maryland Eastern Shore and Salisbury State. Instead of going to one of those schools, Bozman looked up Fork Union Military Academy – a private, male-only collegiate prep boarding school in Virginia, located south of Charlottesville and west of Richmond. From 1970 through 2012, Fork Union produced more than 200 Division I college basketball players, according to the Richmond Times-Dispatch.

"I was reading Street & Smith's basketball magazine and I kept seeing all of these players from over the years come from Fork Union Military Academy," Bozman says. "And that name, it was just a pretty neat name." Bill Cain wrote Bozman a letter of recommendation to the school and his brother Bruce drove him to a tryout. Bozman impressed and was rewarded by longtime Fork Union coach Fletcher Arritt with a scholarship and a spot on the 12-man team.

Over the next year, Bozman practiced everyday with nine other players who would go on to play Division I basketball. He was challenged in ways that he wasn't at Crisfield and Washington, and he had a structure to his life.

"I needed the basketball for another year, but I needed the classroom too," Bozman said. "I wasn't a bad student, but I didn't take academics as seriously. And I just felt like I was a potential Division I basketball player, and I just knew I was going to get better."

College coaches would often stop by Fork Union – and not just mid-major coaches; the likes of Lefty Driesell and Dean Smith were regulars there, watching practice. And one day, Bozman had an awesome one. The next day, Bozman was standing in formation when his coach approached him. Bozman saluted and Arritt said, "Bozman. When you get done eating, the University of Georgia wants to talk to you."

Bozman did not finish his breakfast. He was ready to listen to the Bulldogs' pitch. "And then when one wants you, they all start watching," Bozman said.

By then, Bozman had grown to 6-foot-8 and his stock was high among college scouts. Some 70 schools contacted him during his year at Fork Union, but the real contenders for his superb shooting services were Wake Forest, Virginia, West Virginia and Georgia. He stuck with the Bulldogs and committed to them, not long after visiting the school during New Years

Weekend in 1982 where he saw the Bulldogs – then led by Dominique Wilkins – face off against a Kentucky team anchored by Sam Bowie. By the summer, Bozman was in Athens and ready to play in the SEC.

***

Unfortunately, Georgia turned out to be an imperfect fit for Greg Bozman. Or rather, he and head coach Hugh Durham didn't exactly mesh.

"Durham was not a coach that was suitable for my style of play. And I didn't know that at the time,," Bozman says. "You're just thinking these guys are giving you a Division I scholarship, you're not looking at, 'Do I fit in? What kind of style do they play?'

"A lot of it was my fault. I went from being a pretty good high school player to a Division I player and my head was about this big," Bozman says with his hands stretched out wide. "Instead of putting in the work that I should've that summer, I go down there and I wasn't in very good shape. And I couldn't really do what I wanted to do."

Bozman suffered from shin splints and, as he says, was "in pain" often. Still, his teammates knew what he was capable of and implored him to shoot the ball more. Problem was, he didn't really get the chance to do so. "Durham wasn't helping matters much," Bozman said. In the Red-and-White game, Bozman had 17 points but didn't attack the glass and gobble up rebounds like Durham wanted. Durham lashed out at Bozman at the next practice. "At 19 years old, I'm not really trying to hear that."

Five games are all Bozman would play for the Georgia Bulldogs. A few weeks into the season, he packed his bags, threw them in his car, and began a long, lonely 11-hour ride back to Princess Anne.

"I didn't think it was going to get any better," Bozman said. "So, I just went home. It was the dumbest thing I ever did. The guys looked at me like I was crazy. And I don't blame (Durham). I just wasn't the smartest 19-year-old kid at the time."

Looking back, Bozman believes that freedom he had at UGA – an atmosphere that was much different from the militarized one he had grown accustomed to at Fork Union – was "no good" for him. "I think if I had gone to VMI or the Citadel or West Point, I would've been fine. I needed that structure," he said. Without him, Georgia did just fine. For the first and only time in school history, the Bulldogs made the Final Four. Bozman watched from afar as UGA beat Michael Jordan's UNC Tar Heels in the Elite Eight.

When Bozman got home, only his mother spoke to him. "My brother and my dad had no words," Bozman said. But finally, his older brother spoke up, and just kept telling Bozman to go back to school. When that didn't work, his brother called Arritt, who said, "Bring him down here to Fork Union."

Bruce Bozman threw Greg in the car. When they arrived, Arritt told

Bozman that West Virginia was still interested and was prepared to offer him a full scholarship. By January, Bozman was enrolled in Morgantown. He practiced with the 1982-83 team, but had to sit out and take a redshirt season due to NCAA transfer rules at the time.

"I knew right away that it was a nice fit for me," Bozman said.

After a short stint at Georgia, Crisfield's Greg Bozman landed at West Virginia. He played in four games for the Mountaineers in 1984. From the collection of Greg Bozman.

But...

"In the midst of all of this, a girl from back home had kind of become part of my life. And truthfully, my mom had some illness at the time and some serious problems," Bozman recalls. "So, you know how when you're away from home, and you feel like if you've got somebody there with you, it's going to be all better? Well, it really wasn't... What really pushed me over the edge was – an assistant coach at West Virginia said: 'What can you do for your mom back home?' And that didn't sit right with me. I took it as: 'You're putting this above my mom.'"

Bozman played 48 minutes for the Mountaineers across four games. And when his girlfriend went back to the Shore, he did too.

When Bozman arrived home, he was sitting in his father's hardware store when West Virginia head Gale Catlett called. He begged Bozman to come back and even promised to start him on the next road trip. Bozman declined. And just like that, his second chance at being a Division I college basketball player was over.

But one more college was still interested in having him on its team: Division III Roanoke. Bozman went, and ahead of the 1984-85 season, he was tabbed as a preseason D-3 All-American.

But then...

"I messed my foot up. And I knew it was broken," said Bozman. But he was determined to play. "So, I started out really good. Then, as the season went on, it became a problem. I ended up breaking both feet. So, then I'm in a wheelchair with two broken metatarsals. And that was pretty much it... I was bout 40% (healthy) all year."

Bozman went home to Somerset County. He played in 16 games at Roanoke, averaging 8.8 points and 5.3 rebounds per-game.

And that was it. Bozman's college basketball playing career was over. Five games at Georgia, four at West Virginia and less than 20 in the Division III ranks.

"It eats at me. I ruined a lot of good things," Bozman said. "And I have nobody to blame but myself. Just poor choices I made. I've often said that, if I had gone to college at like 24 years old, you probably would've read about me playing overseas somewhere. I just wasn't ready then. But I'm alright with it. I've lived with it."

"Except for the Final Four thing. I really would've liked to have gone to the Final Four."

***

Bruce Bozman was a counselor at the Eastern Correctional Institution in 1988. And his younger brother Greg, then 25 years old, needed cash. "I had to grow up and get a real job with benefits," said Bozman. And so, he joined his brother at the prison.

One day, Bruce Bozman looked down on a sheet of paper containing some new names in his caseload. One stuck out: ALLEN H. WISE. That was Skip Wise – the Skip Wise from Dunbar, from Clemson, from the ABA.

Bruce Bozman had been lobbying the ECI warden for the approval to set up daily basketball games and finally got his approval by the summer of 1988. Those games set up the opportunity for Greg Bozman and the former Dunbar Poet to cross paths.

"You could get good runs around here then with the men's leagues, but I would tell them to put my men's leagues games at 9 p.m., because I'm not missing the games in jail," Bozman said.

A reporter at the Salisbury Daily Times caught wind of Bozman and Wise's games in the prison yard, and wanted to write a story about the two of them. A photographer at the newspaper had planned to stage a photograph that showed Wise on one side of a fence and Bozman on the other. The story was going to be about their basketball careers and how they had both ended up at ECI. But the warden at the time squashed it, Bozman says.

After Bozman and Wise had that key interaction – in which they told each other that they shouldn't be at ECI – it made Bozman sort of reexamine his life, his choices and his mistakes. Wise also told him, "With your height, the way you dribble, you could go to Baltimore right now and be a legend."

"I was kind of beating myself up over it," Bozman said. "This is no disrespect to any corrections officer, but it's not really what I wanted to do for a living, being a jail guard. So, then you start looking at how you messed some things up."

Around the same time he was working at ECI, Bozman was also regularly working out and playing pick-up games at his alma mater, Crisfield High School. Occasionally, kids would recognize him and ask for pointers on the game.

"They let me in the gym all the time because I had played college ball," Bozman says. "So, I had been in there helping kids or playing against them or whatever. And the kids listen to you when they see you play and hear, 'Oh, he played at Georgia, he played at West Virginia.' That was my way in. You have some credibility and you use that to get through to kids."

One day in 1990 after playing a game of pick-up ball in the Graveyard, Phil Rayfield caught Bozman in the hallway and pulled him aside. Rayfield had just been tapped to be the new varsity boys head basketball coach at Crisfield after having previously coached the girls team. That day, he asked Bozman, "Would you be interested in helping me coach next year?"

This would be a basketball opportunity that Bozman wouldn't squander. He quickly replied with one word: "Absolutely."

"I was basically there with him all the time, either on the bench or running conditioning. I loved it," Bozman said. "As far as a role model and a good man, you can't find a finer person. (Rayfield) was like a John Wooden guy – he figured if you prepared in practice, it didn't matter what the team you faced was going to come at you with."

Bozman stuck by Rayfield's side for the next decade to get a proper tutoring in coaching. From 1990 through 1998, the Crabbers boys teams Bozman assisted with won more than 120 games, captured two Bayside titles and made a state semifinal in 1997. And then, prior to the start of the 1998-99 season, Bozman got his own team. He was hired as the head coach of the varsity girls team at Crisfield High School.

The start to Bozman's career as a head coach was rough. Of his 11 varsity players, seven of them were freshmen. The Crabbers finished the 1998-99 season 0-23, but Bozman didn't quit and neither did his squad. The team had been sort of passed around over the past decade with a new coach almost every season, but Bozman stuck with it. Crisfield started the 1999-2000 season with five straight losses, but then broke off a three-game winning streak.

By the end of the 2002-03 season, Crisfield was 17-7 and had just appeared in its second straight regional final. Under Bozman, the Crabbers went from Bayside pushovers to real contenders. Bozman coached an All-Bayside selection in Shayla Handy and a 1,000-point scorer in Nicole Brown.

"It was probably the best five years of my coaching career," Bozman said. "I was really happy about that, because Crisfield was usually the weakest girls team in the Bayside. I remember beating Barbara McCool at Crisfield in 2003 and she was furious. And I'll be honest with you, I loved every minute of it."

Bozman left the Crisfield girls program in 2003 to become the athletic director and boys head coach at Washington, a reversal of the move across Somerset County he made in high school. In 2010, then the athletic director at Crisfield, Bozman was hired as the head coach of the boys team at Snow Hill, following the tragic and untimely death of Allen Miller. It was an odd situation – being the AD at one school and coaching at another, and in a different county too – but it was the lone year that Bozman got to coach his son. The team struggled as it returned just one starter from Miller's 2009-10 team that made the state final, but Bozman guided the Eagles to a season-opening 35-point victory over North Dorchester and a playoff win over St. Michaels. Bozman Jr. made the All-Bayside Third Team.

"Nobody can replace a guy like (Miller). He was such a legend on the Eastern Shore," Bozman told Earl Holland's Sports Refuge Podcast. "It was a good year. I can't say I didn't enjoy it... I just didn't feel real comfortable with (being the AD at Crisfield and the head coach at Snow Hill)."

The following year, Bozman Jr. transferred to Crisfield – and he passed the 1,000-point scoring mark with 31 markers in a win over Snow Hill – and the elder Boz relinquished his head coaching duties at Snow Hill.

But Bozman returned to the sideline again in 2012 to lead the Crabbers' girls once more after the team had gone winless eight years in a row. Again, Bozman turned the Crabbers around. They beat Holly Grove 40-19 just a few days into the season for their first win since 2004, powered by Arielle Johnston's 20 points. The Crabbers finished the 2013-14 season with a playoff victory, leading Bozman's peers to vote him Bayside South Coach of the Year. In 2019, the Crisfield girls made the regional semifinals, and Bozman became the 1A East Regional Director for girls basketball for the MPSSAA, following in the footsteps of local legends like Gail Gladding and McCool.

"Boys are fun to coach, but most of them think they know everything. Girls listen and grow, and it's fun to watch," Bozman said. "Sometimes they go from not being able to play at all to becoming pretty good by the time you're done with them, and that's a good feeling. It's more than winning and losing."

Coaching has been Bozman's way of staying close to the game he loves so much and his way to guide the youth of the Eastern Shore away from the mistakes that he made. As of this writing, the bald, tattooed and bearded gentle giant is a behavior specialist and counselor of sorts at his alma mater. And even in his late 50's, he still has a shooting regiment, beginning each morning with 300 shots in Crisfield's gym.

"The Boz" is also now the athletic director for both of Somerset County's public high schools and was named District 8 Athletic Director of the Year in 2021. He often uses his past to relate to kids, showing them his high school report card that wasn't up to par, or telling them about the teams he didn't last with, or the times he left a tough situation when he may have been better off sticking it out.

The walls in Bozman's office at Crisfield are covered with his accomplishments, pictures of friends and family, and memorabilia. But among the collection of relics are also pictures of him in his WVU and UGA uniforms. Those are keepsakes of what-ifs and what-could-have-beens. But, even more, they're reminders for his purpose now as an educator, coach, and mentor.

"The Shore can catch you up in a net," Bozman said. "I'm not the only one. There's others that made mistakes and came home. I'm alright with it now because I get to give back a little bit.

"We've all had bad times in life. It's how you handle it."

MILLS, MILLER AND THE PERFECT EAGLES

"They just had no answer for Sherron." – Jeff Levan

In June of 1988, Cal Ripken Jr. played in his 1,000th consecutive Major League Baseball game, new NBA franchises in Charlotte and Miami were preparing for expansion drafts, the groundbreaking cartoon mystery "Who Framed Roger Rabbit?" made its debut in theaters, Mike Tyson KO'd Michael Spinks in 91 seconds, and the Fresh Prince's "Parents Just Don't Understand" was 32nd on the Billboard Top 100.

But in Worcester County, Maryland, there was a bit of news that mattered much more to the locals.

Then a rising junior at Snow Hill High School, Norman "Nicky" Purnell got a call during one of those hot, sticky and humid days on the Eastern Shore. The message was short and simple: Come to the gym.

When Purnell and his teammates arrived, Allen Miller began to speak. He told them: "Listen. I'll be your coach next year. And I need you guys to start playing, all summer long."

Miller, a West Virginia native and the son of a contractor, had just been tapped to be the new head boys basketball coach at Snow Hill, succeeding Ed Hancock. At that time, the Eagles had achieved great success in other sports – winning state titles in football and girls basketball – but its boys hoops program had largely underachieved. Entering the 1988-89 season, the Eagles had never played for a Bayside Conference Championship and had never appeared in a state final four. Their boys basketball team was fine, but they always seemed to finish second or third behind Pocomoke and Crisfield in talent, success and popularity.

But when Miller was hired, that all began to change – quickly.

Miller had previously been a coaching nomad on the Delmarva Peninsula. He had guided the boys varsity basketball program at Northampton High School in Virginia. He had coached baseball at Pocomoke and he had just coached the JV boys basketball squad at Snow Hill in the 1987-88 season.

Jeff Levan came to the Eastern Shore from Towson in the late 1970s to attend Salisbury State College. He had a "non-distinguished career," he says, playing basketball for the Sea Gulls – then coached by Ward Lambert. Levan worked in sales for the Baltimore Sun in an office they had on the Delmarva Peninsula. An all-around sports fanatic, Levan met Miller during a game of slow-pitch softball. As young professionals, they struck up a friendship and became roommates in Ocean City and Miller would often pick Levan's brain on basketball. When Miller got hired as the Snow Hill JV boys basketball coach ahead of the 1987-88 season, Levan helped out. And when Miller moved up to varsity, Levan did too.

"I think (Hancock) kind of got a little pushed out from Allen. It was very awkward the year we did the JV. He barely spoke to us. We had very little interaction with the guy. It was strange. I think once Allen was in the school system he knew his days were numbered," Levan said. "All I know is, I got the call from Allen that summer. He said, 'I got the job. Do you want to be my assistant?'"

Jeff Levan greets Gary Briddell as he exits the court in the 2017 3A state semifinals. Levan has coached under Allen Miller and B.J. Johnson at Snow Hill and Stephen Decatur. Briddell went on to play at Salisbury University. Photo by Mitchell Northam.

Purnell knew Miller well because he had played on JV as a sophomore. Ahead of the 1988-89 season, they made the jump to varsity together. Purnell was born and raised in Snow Hill and came from a family of point guards. His cousin Kevin was the first 1,000-point scorer in Snow Hill history and accomplished the feat before the introduction of the three-point line.

"We're a point guard family. When we go to family gatherings, all we're doing is talking basketball," Purnell said. "When I could grab the ball, I started playing, and then I watched my cousin play. I'm being biased, but he's one of the greatest Snow Hill players to ever come through. We all followed him. The second generation, we all reached after him."

Purnell, who stands around 6-foot-3, also played quarterback on the football team, which was coached by Moe Barber. At the age of 48, Barber died on the sidelines during a Sept. 16, 1989 game at Easton after collapsing from a massive heart attack in the second quarter. Barber coached Snow Hill to state titles in 1980 and 1982. When he died, he was three victories shy of 100 for his career.

"I always looked at football as my way of staying in shape for basketball, but I feared getting hurt," Purnell said. "I was fortunate enough my senior year to make the Mason-Dixon Second Team. Only reason why I got it was because we ran the option. They'd tackle the fullback and I'd ride it through. I used to hear referees say, 'Damn. We messed up again,' because they'd blow the whistle early."

On the court, Purnell was tall enough to play in the post in the Bayside Conference. But in their lone JV season together, Miller saw his ability to handle the basketball, to make decisions, and to run an offense efficiently. Hancock didn't like it.

"We got into it with (Hancock) because he didn't like big guards," Levan said. "Well, Allen made Nicky the point guard anyway. And then he made a smooth transition to varsity."

In Hancock's final season coaching basketball, Snow Hill made the regional final, but lost to Pocomoke at the University of Maryland Eastern Shore. Purnell was brought up to the varsity for the playoff run. Before the tip-off against Pocomoke, he was sweaty and out of breath. He knew he wasn't going to play in that game, but it was his first time playing in a Division I college gym. So, he went all out in the warm-up, giving 110% worth of effort in the lay-up line.

A season later, Purnell would be much more to Snow Hill than just another body on the bench.

***

When he got the top job at Snow Hill, Allen Miller knew the team had potential to be not just good, but great. To realize their promising capabilities, he wanted his players to play together as often as they could, to build cohesion, chemistry, familiarity, and stamina that would be unmatched by opponents on the Shore and across the Chesapeake Bay.

"The thing about that team was, they won everything in the AAU from the time they were 10-years-old," said Brenda Jones, who had retired from coaching Snow Hill's girls team, but still paid close attention to the local sports scene.

Miller secured his boys a sponsor for the summer leagues – Laws Lumber Company – and the Snow Hill players spent the hot months hooping all over the Lower Shore. They played in an outdoor league ran by Wicomico High School's Butch Waller, and they traveled to outdoor courts on Fourth Street in Ocean City, on Flower Street in Berlin, and all over Salisbury. Back then, the Salisbury Daily Times sponsored its own summer basketball league too and hosted games at the Wicomico Youth & Civic Center.

Every now and then, these leagues would attract scouts and coaches from colleges. One night, on July 25, 1988, former Maryland Terps coach Lefty Driesell – then newly hired at James Madison – came to the Midway Room in Salisbury's Civic Center to see one particular prospect: Sherron Mills.

"Sherron is not a showboat," Miller told the Daily Times of his star player. "He's polite, comes to do the job, a joy to coach... He speaks softly and carries a big stick."

Sherron Mills led Snow Hill to its first state title in boys basketball in 1989. He scored 47 points in the championship game, a record that still stands as of this writing.. VCU Athletics.

Indeed, a 6-foot-9 forward, Mills was sort of Snow Hill's trump card. The Bayside Conference has long been a league dominated by exceptional guards, but sometimes a team will get one really great post player with some real length and height, and that has – typically – been a pathway to dominating the conference. In the summer of 1988, everyone from Waller to Driesell to scouts in North Carolina knew how good Mills was. On the Shore, there was no other player that could match him consistently. And there's really never been another player like him since.

"He was big," Waller said of Mills. "Around here, you don't get big kids. You get someone who is 6-foot-4, and you think you've got a stud. Is it the chicken? The water?"

Nothing stunted Mills' growth. And he – known by his teammates as "Syxx" – was every bit of 6-foot-9. There was no embellishment of his height on the roster. By the age of 13, Mills could touch the rim. By the time he was 15, he was dunking with relative ease. Mills made his varsity debut as a sophomore on Dec. 9, 1986 in Pocomoke City. In an 84-70 loss to the Warriors, he made his presence known, notching 22 points and 10 boards. Nine days later, he went head-to-head with Decatur's Andre Foreman – a future Division III star at Salisbury – and came away with 17 points and six rebounds in a four-point loss, while Foreman had 24 points.

Heading into the 1988-89 season – his senior campaign – Mills had already been named First Team All-Bayside following his junior season, which saw him block 105 shots and average 22.7 points and 13.1 rebounds per-game. As a junior, Mills had also already set Snow Hill's single game rebounding record with 37. He was bound to break Snow Hill's all-time career scoring record, and there was really no individual accolade he coveted. He just wanted to win – big.

The biggest change between Mills' junior and senior seasons was the absence of Lamont Dale. A 6-foot-3 guard, Dale was a stellar scorer for Snow Hill and Mills often deferred to him. Dale graduated from Snow Hill in 1988 and went on to play at Hagerstown Junior College and at Texas Tech, where he averaged 10.9 points, 3.6 rebounds and 2.2 assists in the 1991-92 season for the Red Raiders. Following a lengthy illness, Dale died in 2018 at the age of 48.

"Sherron was an introverted kid who deferred a lot to Lamont. That was Lamont's team and there was a tendency to stand around and watch him," Levan said. "When it became Sherron's team, I think it became a better team. Not anything against Lamont, but Sherron just became a little more extroverted and more dominant."

The night that Driesell saw him play, Mills tallied 23 points, 11 rebounds and four blocks in a 20-point win. Other college coaches were in the building, too, like Radford's Oliver Purnell and Charlotte's Jeff Mullins. But, "when Lefty walked in, they all had this look of defeat in their eyes, because the whole place gravitated to Lefty," Levan said. Snow Hill won the Salisbury summer league and Mills was on the map as a legitimate prospect.

"I'll go where the good players are," Driesell told the Daily Times. "But it makes it nice when I can see good players so close to my beach house."

By the start of the 1988-89 high school season, Mills had committed to Radford along with Tyrone Travis of Cambridge. At that time, the Highlanders were coached by someone the Shore knew even better than Driesell – his former assistant and a Stephen Decatur graduate, Purnell – a starter on the Seahawks' 1970 state title team.

In the season-opener, the Eagles traveled to Cambridge to face the Vikings, and Mills outscored Travis 28-15 en route to an 81-66 win for Snow Hill – Miller's first as the head coach. And in his varsity debut at point guard, Purnell racked up 10 points, four assists and four rebounds.

"Nicky was a different type of guard," Pocomoke's David Byrd said of Purnell. "A big guard. Slender, but big. One of the best on the Bayside that year."

Mills continued to establish his dominance early on in the season, showing that he could be an alpha dog and carry his team with Dale no longer on the roster. On Dec. 16 against Parkside, Mills filled the box score with 33 points,

14 boards and seven blocks. Even when he didn't score a ton, Mills still set the tone of the game. In a Dec. 19 triumph over Stephen Decatur, he had just 12 points. But he owned the paint with 16 rebounds and nine blocks.

"You don't find a 6-foot-9 guy on the Eastern Shore with the touch he had," Byrd said of Mills. "We got lucky to beat him as a junior. Sherron was the man. He just had an unbelievable touch around the basket."

Mills' talents alone might've been enough on most nights to carry Snow Hill to victories, but the Eagles' roster was more loaded than a baked potato at Guy Fieri's house. On any given night, any of six different players could go off for 25 points or so. On Jan. 7, 1989, sharpshooting senior Richard Milbourne – whom Mills called "Top Gun" – torched the nets for 29 points in a 112-55 beatdown of James M. Bennett. On Jan. 28, versatile wing Shawn Johnson dropped 25 points in a win at Parkside to help Snow Hill improve to 15-0. A week later, Nick Purnell had 19 points and eight rebounds in a 106-73 victory at Washington.

"Syxx was the go-to, but Richard Milbourne was the Number 2 guy. But then, if Richard was off, I could go to Shawn," Purnell said. "And then we had another guy, a sleeper that everyone forgot about named George Towsend. He stood at about 5-foot-11, but he played like he was 6-foot-9. So, that year, man… I could pick whoever I wanted to.

"We had one white kid on the team," Purnell continued, "named Mark Ward. And with us being predominantly Black, Mark would come in and everyone forgot about him. I got three to five assists off of him a night, because he would sneak behind the zone and I would thread the needle. This is no lie: he could've started on any other program in the Bayside except ours. He was our sixth man."

Purnell and Johnson had a unique chemistry because they grew up together. They often referred to themselves as Larry Johnson and Stacey Augmon, for the two UNLV Runnin' Rebels stars of the late 80s. "We had a good one-two punch," Purnell said.

The Eagles played a game at rival Pocomoke on Jan. 20 that season, and Byrd switched to a triangle-and-two defense at halftime in an effort to take Mills and Purnell out of the game. Byrd somewhat succeeded in that Pocomoke held Mills to six second half points, but Johnson took over point guard duties and scored 13 points – while Ward had 11 points – to lead the Eagles to an 86-75 road win. It was akin to that scene in The Wire, when D'Angelo goes with Wee-Bey for a pit beef sandwich run and leaves Poot in charge, and Poot stands on the couch in the courtyard like he's the man. With Mills guarded by Pocomoke as tightly as a Peruvian necktie, Johnson was.

"Shawn got it done, just to let people know how versatile we were," Purnell said. "We were like the Dream Team."

"There was more to that team than just Sherron," Levan said. "Shawn

Johnson was just outstanding. For two years, we put him on the other team's top player and he basically eliminated the guy- regardless of position. It didn't matter. And he played at the top of our 1-2-2 press."

Said Byrd: "Miller knew he had a good team and everyone else knew he had a good team. You got to have the horses to pull the wagon. I just think he gave them a little more electricity to push them on. He was extremely competitive."

***

Snow Hill really only had one close call in the regular season, where its perfect record was in danger of being blemished. On Jan. 31, Mills was sick and was held out of the starting lineup in a game at Stephen Decatur. The Eagles trailed the Seahawks by 11 points at halftime. In the third quarter, Mills entered the game and Milbourne scored 13 points amidst a 28-10 Snow Hill run to take the lead back. Mills had 15 points and Milbourne finished with 32 points in the come-from-behind victory.

"It was like in Space Jam, when they go in at halftime and drink the special water. Sherron did something and we hawked them down like gangbusters," Purnell recalled. "It was fun, but we knew we had a purpose."

The Eagles played their next game without Mills too, a Feb. 3 meeting with Washington at home. But Snow Hill got by with ease, taking a 106-73 victory as Milbourne, Johnson, Purnell, Ward and Antonio Henry all scored in double-digits.

Snow Hill was lethal on both ends of the court. Not only did they have multiple elite scorers, but the Eagles were also armed with long, versatile, quick and smart players who could defend multiple positions. In half-court sets, Mills patrolled the paint and blocked damn near any shot that floated by him. But the Eagles could press teams into submission, too.

And Snow Hill didn't play just one defense.

After each made basket, Snow Hill would then launch into one of four defenses, depending on where they scored from. If Mills dunked in the paint, the Eagles would shift into "Iowa" – an aggressive 1-2-2 press for the opponent's next possession. If Milbourne drained a three-pointer, they went into a more passive 2-2-1, which Miller called "Villanova." If Snow Hill didn't score, or if it scored off a free throw, they played man-to-man – known to the players as "Indiana." When the opposing team was inbounding the ball in the half-court on out-of-bounds sets, Snow Hill played a 2-3 zone.

"Miller was a huge, huge Bobby Knight guy. If you asked him, he'd tell you that 'Season on the Brink' was the greatest book ever written," Levan said.

After the Eagles played together all summer long, Miller began implementing the defenses in November. Once the Snow Hill players mastered the different strategies, Miller never introduced anything new. To his players, the assignments were simple. To opposing offenses, it seemed confusing and frightening; a bit helter-skelter-ish.

On Feb. 8, Snow Hill set the school record for wins in a single season and improved to 18-0 after Mills tallied 29 points and 17 boards in a 90-75 home victory over James M. Bennett. On Feb. 17, Mills passed Purnell's cousin, Kevin, as Snow Hill's all-time leading scorer as he notched 32 points in a home triumph over Mardela.

"We are successful because we play great team ball, we pass a lot, we have a 6-9 guy like Sherron, and we have a great bench," Miller told the Daily Times. "We come out and put pressure on you, and as soon as someone gets winded, boom, someone comes off the bench fresh."

By the end of the regular season, Mills was averaging 26 points, 14 rebounds and nine blocks per-game. Each of Snow Hill's other four starters were scoring at least 11 points per-game too. Snow Hill was 22-0 and set to face North Caroline in a highly-anticipated Bayside Conference Championship game – perhaps one of the most hyperbolized Bayside clashes ever.

North Caroline's Jeff Chambers tallied 797 points and 769 rebounds across four seasons for James Madison. In 1992, he led the CAA in blocks and rebounds. JMU Athletics.

"The hype around it wasn't really about us vs. North Caroline. It was about Sherron vs. Jeff Chambers," Purnell said. "The South talked about Sherron, but the North talked about Chambers."

And for good reason, too. While Mills dominated the paint and the glass in every gym south of Sharptown, Chambers owned every rim north of East New Market. While Mills was committed to Radford, Chambers had locked down a free ride to college with Lefty Driesell at James Madison. Mills had two inches on Chambers, but they were both exceptional talents. Chambers was averaging 24 points, 15 rebounds and six assists for the 18-2 Bulldogs.

But the game never happened. On the Friday the championship was going to be played – Feb. 24 – a blanket of snow covered the Eastern Shore with accumulations ranging from seven to eleven inches, and wind gusts up to 25 mph. The game was pushed back to Saturday, but the snow didn't fade away as the Delmarva Peninsula remained frigid. The contest couldn't be played on a Sunday, and the state playoffs began Monday.

Then-Bayside President Doug Fleetwood, who was also the head football coach, principal, and all-around man in-charge at Cambridge-South Dorchester High School, attempted to reschedule the game for Monday, March 6, but state playoffs would've still been ongoing. Snow Hill and North Caroline initially agreed to the date, according to various newspaper reports at the time, but Snow Hill backed out when it learned that it wasn't mandatory for them to play in a conference game past Feb. 25, a statewide cutoff date. And why play in a game that's purely for bragging rights when one slip, one fall, one injury could jeopardize your chance at a state title? Fleetwood was not pleased and estimated that the conference was going to lose more than $2,000 in revenue from lost ticket sales.

"I'm disgusted with the whole mess. What a joke," Fleetwood told the Daily Times. "I'm not happy about it because it would've been fun."

But there was still a chance for Snow Hill and North Caroline to meet each other on the basketball court in 1989 because of how the regions were set up. Back then, the Bulldogs played in Region III with teams like Colonel Richardson, Kent County, Perry Hall, Havre de Grace and Joppatowne. And Snow Hill played in Region IV, which included all the other Class C teams on the Eastern Shore. If Snow Hill and North Caroline both won out through the playoffs, they would meet for the Class C state final.

"All year, everybody talked about North Caroline vs. Snow Hill," Levan said. "And the game never really took place."

***

The playoff format back then saw the top six teams from each region make the field, with the top two teams in each region getting a bye. Because of its pristine record, the Eagles got the first round off. In the regional semifinals, fourth-seeded Mardela awaited them at the University of Maryland Eastern Shore.

Mardela at that time – and still today – was known much more for girls basketball than boys, especially considering that Barbara McCool's side was armed with Tia Jackson then. But in the 1989 playoffs, the Warriors had a talented and well-balanced boys team, too. Ron Wainwright was the head coach and Mardela finished the regular season with 15 wins. His peers voted him as the Bayside South Coach of the Year – considering Wainwright had slowly improved the team from one victory in the 1985-86 season and turned it into a playoff contender. On the court, Mardela was led by Charlie Byrd, who would go on to make the All-Bayside First Team. But Rudell Brown,

Andy Cray and Antonio Lewis were key contributors, too. Each Mardela starter averaged between nine and 13 points per-game. Joe Hayman, the coach at St. Michaels at the time, once likened Cray to Arizona's Sean Elliott for his superb ability to impact the game without touching the ball.

In the first round of the playoffs, the Warriors topped Pocomoke. People were high on Mardela, especially WBOC sports anchor George Evanko, who declared that Mardela would hand Snow Hill its first loss of the season.

In 1988-89, Mardela head a stellar boys team too, coached by Ron Wainwright. He was named Bayside Coach of the Year. Led on the court by Charlie Byrd, the team made the region finals, but lost to Snow Hill. Mardela yearbooks.

"Mardela brought a lot out of us. They were a sleeper," Purnell said. "They gave us all we could handle until the last five or six minutes; until that 6-foot-9 monster turned the switch on. But Mardela gave us fits. All the credit goes to Ron Wainwright. He knew x's and o's, how to hit us, what buttons to push."

With 4:45 remaining in the regional semifinal, Mardela was playing Snow Hill tightly, trailing by just four points. And then, their hopes of a historic upset crumbled like a dry biscuit. After Mardela's Tony Johnson was whistled for an offensive foul, the Eagles embarked on a 14-4 run. In that span, Mills totaled five points, two blocks, and seven rebounds as the Warriors committed six turnovers. Mills finished with 33 points as the Eagles coasted to an 84-74 victory.

"He's just a force," Wainwright said of Mills. "He's so big that he makes people change their shots and do things that they would not normally do. He crushed us inside."

In one season at Maryland Eastern Shore in 1990-91, Easton's Dondre Phoenix averaged 6.9 points, 2.1 rebounds and 1.7 assists per-game, making the All-MEAC Rookie Team. Maryland Eastern Shore Athletics.

Next up for Snow Hill was a third and decisive meeting with Easton, which was coming off a win over Stephen Decatur. Purnell felt like this game, the Region IV final, was really the state championship.

The Eagles had seen Easton twice before, once in the regular season and once in the John H. Coleman Invitational, a holiday basketball tournament that was played in Worcester County. In that tournament, Snow Hill got by thanks to an excellent performance from Mills – 33 points, 13 rebounds, 11 blocks – but the Eagles were still tested by the Warriors in the 92-73 victory. Purnell met his match at point guard and he was outplayed that day by Easton's Dondre Phoenix, who poured in 31 points. After that game, Miller told the Daily Times: "Nobody else in the Bayside Conference can really match-up to us and Easton."

In the second meeting between the Eagles and the Warriors, Snow Hill won again on Feb. 21, 100-87. But again, Phoenix torched the nets and finished as the leading scorer with 30 points.

"I've always said that the best player I've ever played against was Dondre Phoenix," Purnell said. "He was my toughest opponent. In that time, whether it was us or Easton, the state championship was guaranteed to come back. Because Dondre could direct the offense like there was nothing to it. I looked forward to playing against him and watching him play."

By averaging 25.2 points and 7.4 assists per-game in the 1988-89 season,

Phoenix guided Easton to a 19-4 record. The previous year, he was part of the Warriors' team that appeared in the Bayside title game and the state final four. In one season at Maryland Eastern Shore in 1990-91, Phoenix averaged 6.9 points, 2.1 rebounds and 1.7 assists per-game, making the All-MEAC Rookie Team with Snow Hill's Johnson. Then-Hawks' head coach Steve Williams called him a "tremendous shooter." He chose the Hawks over offers from George Mason, Boston, Delaware and Fordham. Phoenix later had a brief stint with the Atlanta Hawks' summer league team.

Easton was also armed with high-scoring forward Wayne Wilson and a skilled center in Wes Cornish who went on to play at Marshall.

The winner of Easton and Snow Hill would go on to Cole Field House in College Park to play in the state final four. But to Miller, that's not what the venue was called. He told his team before the match-up with Easton: "I want to play in Lefty's Place" – a nod to Lefty Driesell, the man who had coached the Maryland Terrapins from 1969 to 1986. Determined to make Maryland the "UCLA of the East," Driesell guided the Terps to an NIT title in 1972, two regular season ACC crowns, and an ACC tournament championship in 1984. He was forced out at Maryland amidst a reckoning in the wake of Len Bias' death from a cocaine overdose. Despite Driesell's unceremonious exit from College Park, he was revered by many coaches on the Eastern Shore.

Miller's trip to Lefty's Place was in jeopardy at the end of the first quarter, as Snow Hill trailed by two points. But the Eagles' offense began to click as Mills opened the second period with a pair of thunderous dunks. Snow Hill led at halftime, then cruised to a 106-90 victory. Phoenix had 29 points, but it didn't matter. For the first time ever, the Snow Hill boys were going to Lefty's Place.

***

In the state semifinals, the Eagles matched up with another team making its first trip to College Park in Boonsboro, a high school in a town of about 3,300 people in Washington County – smackdab between Hagerstown and Frederick.

The Eagles triumphed with little difficulty in the semifinals as Richard Milbourne turned in his best game of the season, scoring 36 points in a 94-75 victory. His performance was punctuated by a trio of fourth quarter dunks. Miller put it simply after the contest: "Milbourne played one hell of a game."

"Richard Milbourne was a shooter," Levan said. "In the conversation of all-time greats, his name gets overlooked. He rebounded; he did a lot of things."

North Caroline made it to the state semifinals too, setting up the potential for a repeat of 1976, when a pair of Eastern Shore teams – then Colonel

Richardson and Pocomoke – played for the Class C final in Cole Field House. But the Bulldogs couldn't get by Milford Mill. Chambers had 24 points and 15 rebounds, but was hobbled by an ankle injury as North Caroline lost by three points. In the final two minutes of the game, North Caroline twice missed the front end of one-and-one free throws.

After the Eagles bested Boonsboro in the semifinals, the players and coaches went back to a hotel in College Park that was the same place nearly everyone from Snow Hill was staying. "It became one big party," Purnell said. "The whole town was in this one hotel." Around 8 p.m. that night, Purnell and his teammates were wondering where Mills – the star player and their leader – was. He should be enjoying this too, they thought.

So, they went to his room. Purnell opens the door and it's dark. In one bed is Mills, under the covers, sound asleep. That night's episodes of Family Matters and Dallas hadn't even started yet. Purnell poked his head in the room: "Sherron, you coming out?"

Mills rolled over, looked at his teammates and said: "Man, y'all better carry your asses to bed. We got work to do."

His teammates did not immediately obey his orders.

"He went to bed and we all still stayed out until about 11:30 p.m. We were like, look, the town is here. We're going to kick it," Purnell said. "Miller had a curfew, and we made it, but then we snuck back out."

Miller checked back in on his players around 1 a.m. – unannounced...

Purnell was asleep by then, but his roommate was not and was instead enjoying the company of a young woman. Miller was furious and took the game jerseys from everyone staying in that room. Nervous that he might not get to play in the state final, Purnell didn't sleep the rest of the night. Eventually, Miller allowed everyone to play, except for the unnamed teammate who snuck a girlfriend into the room.

"We haven't stayed in a hotel in College Park since then," Levan said. "Now, we drive up and drive back. Too many distractions."

***

On Saturday, March 11, 1989, Sherron Mills played like a man who was attempting to change the name of the arena where the Terps played. When he was finished, it was no longer Cole Field House or Lefty's Place. It might as well have been called "Mills' Mansion."

There was nothing and no one who could stop Mills on that day. Wondering if he was going to impact the game was like worrying if the sun was going to come up. He took a wrecking ball to Milford Mill's defense and did whatever he wanted. It was like the Incredible Hulk playing against second graders. Mills started the contest by scoring the first seven points of the game, and he ended it by tallying 10 of Snow Hill's final 12 points. He caught fire like a gas station in a Michael Bay movie.

Mills' final stat line: 19-of-22 shooting from the floor, 9-of-11 from the free throw line, 47 points, 16 rebounds, four blocks, two assists. Nothing shook Mills or got him flustered. He was cooler than Freddie Jackson sipping a milkshake in a snowstorm. Simply put: Mills played a nearly-perfect game of basketball.

"I just had a good day," Mills told the Baltimore Sun. "I just played my game and kept shooting."

Mills broke a 21-year-old state scoring record and Snow Hill won its first state championship in boys basketball, 89-78. As of 2022, Mills still holds the state record for most points scored in a championship game. He set the record on a finger roll in the lane with 25 seconds left.

No matter how many state championships Dunbar, Allegany or Gwynn Park has won, an Eastern Shoreman has owned the scoring record for more than 33 years now. Mills' performance that day continues to be a point of pride for Bayside Conference basketball.

"That dude was on a mission. He bailed us out, because Milford Mill wasn't a bad team. Sherron just went off," Purnell said. "He carried us to that state championship. If he didn't do what he does, we don't win that. Period."

Tom Strickler, a college scout, told the Star Democrat: "He's the best player in Maryland. I haven't seen anybody better."

But Mills' teammates weren't bad either. Hell – Purnell nearly had a triple-double with 10 points, 10 rebounds and nine assists. Snow Hill started to pull away in the second quarter when, up by four, it broke off an 8-2 run thanks to its "Indiana" defense. The Eagles forced three straight turnovers and Purnell finished the fast break twice. By halftime, Snow Hill was up by 19 points. Milbourne added 15 points and 10 boards in his final game for the Eagles.

"They just had no answer for Sherron," Levan said. "They couldn't guard him. I'll put that team against any team I've seen down here ever. We'd kick the ball inside and there was just nothing you could do."

With the state title under their belt, the Eagles finished the year with an immaculate 26-0 record. David Byrd, the longtime Pocomoke athletic director and former boys basketball coach, has been around Bayside basketball for more than five decades. For his money, there have been few squads – if any – better than the 1988-89 Snow Hill Eagles.

"They had all the ingredients," Byrd said. "And I think Miller being all gung-ho put the juice in that squad. If not the best, they're one of the best teams ever on the Eastern Shore."

SHERRON MILLS: ONE OF THE GOATS

"The Minnesota Timberwolves with pick No. 29, the second pick in the second round, select Sherron Mills, Virginia Commonwealth." – Rod Thorn

Even though North Caroline High School's boys basketball team didn't make the state title game in 1989, Bayside Conference fans still got to see Snow Hill's Sherron Mills take on Jeff Chambers of the Bulldogs.

Cambridge hosted the Bayside Senior All-Star Game on March 16, and the two college-bound forwards went at it. Mills finished with 35 points and 15 rebounds, and dunked on Chambers near the end of the first half. In the third quarter, Chambers repaid Mills on a fast-break, taking flight and throwing down a one-handed jam over the Snow Hill star. Chambers tallied 22 points, 18 rebounds and eight assists.

"They were pretty evenly matched, comparable," Snow Hill assistant coach Jeff Levan said. "Chambers was a good player, a physically mature kid. He was a man."

But the real star of the game was another Division I forward, Cambridge's Tyrone Travis. He had just led the Vikings to a Class B championship and showed out one last time on his homecourt, racking up 36 points, eight rebounds, four blocks, four steals and three assists. Travis, Chambers and Easton's Dondre Phoenix led the North to its first win over the South in four years.

Afterwards, all the talk was still about Mills and Chambers. Feeling like he got the upper-hand, Chambers held court with reporters after the game. He told the Daily Times: "I didn't want this game. I wanted Sherron Mills. It's always Sherron Mills this, Sherron Mills that, and I really got tired of hearing all of it... I'm the man around here."

The soft-spoken Mills shrugged it off, saying: "I just went out and played my game."

South coach Carey Reece had a different opinion, telling the Daily Times: "There's no question in my mind that Travis was the best player out there tonight."

All three forwards would go on to have solid careers playing college basketball for mid-major schools in the state of Virginia. Chambers went to James Madison and was a consistent contributor for Lefty Driesell. He started in 93 of the 118 games he played in and averaged 6.8 points, 6.5

rebounds, 2.3 assists and 1.1 blocks per-game across his career with the Dukes. In the 1991-92 season, he led the CAA in total rebounds, blocks and games played. Chambers is still fourth all-time in rebounds at JMU and third all-time in blocks. In 2020, Chambers was named head coach of the men's basketball team at Frederick Community College. His son, Logan Thomas, played quarterback at Virginia Tech and became a tight end in the NFL, catching six touchdowns in 2020 for Washington.

Travis would go on to become one of the best players ever at Radford. As of this writing, he's still 12th on the all-time scoring list with 1,313 points, 10th in rebounds with 718, and first in blocks with 215. In the 1993-94 season, he was an All-Big South First Team selection after averaging 16.4 points and 6.3 rebounds per-game, a season in which he also led the conference in field goal percentage with a 57.3% mark. Travis played professionally in Belgium and Holland. In 2016, he was inducted into Cambridge's athletic Hall of Fame. Travis died on Jan. 3, 2021 at the age of 49 after suffering a stroke just days prior.

Often going by nicknames "Syxx" or "Forty," Sherron Mills stood around 6-foot-9. After a brief stint at Chowan College, Mills landed at VCU where he averaged 11.2 points, 6.6 rebounds and 1.6 blocks per game over three seasons. VCU Athletics.

Mills was a McDonald's All-American nominee after finishing his senior season at Snow Hill with per-game averages of 28.7 points, 14.1 rebounds and 8.3 blocks. He was named Bayside Player of the Year and seemed destined for a starring role next to Travis at Radford.

But Mills never became a Highlander. He didn't meet the NCAA's Proposition 48 requirements, which is a sliding scale combination of standardized test scores and grades in core high school classes. So, Mills went to Murfreesboro, North Carolina and enrolled at Chowan University, a small private Baptist institution that did not compete in NCAA athletics at the time. Mills stayed a semester and got his grades right, but never played in a regular season game for the Braves' basketball team. In the spring, he landed at a Division I school in Virginia, but not at Radford with Travis and not at James Madison with Chambers.

Mills enrolled at Virginia Commonwealth University and was a decent contributor off the bench in his first year with the Rams, who played in the Sun Belt in the 1990-91 season. The following year, VCU moved over to the Metro Conference and Mills began to establish himself as a top player in the league, going up against teams like Louisville, Virginia Tech and Tulane. He averaged 13.3 points and 7.7 rebounds per-game as a junior across 28 starts.

As a senior, Mills' role expanded late in the season when his teammate Kendrick Warren suffered a season-ending leg injury. Mills was asked to do more and, in response, averaged more than 22 points per-game in the final 10 games of the season. On March 5, 1993, he had 19 points and 19 boards in an upset victory over 20th-ranked Tulane. He followed that up with 26 points and 12 boards in a loss to Louisville for the Metro Championship. VCU went 20-10 that season and made the NIT – their season kept alive by Mills' stellar play. In his final game for the Rams, he tallied 24 points and 14 rebounds in a loss to Old Dominion.

Mills' standout performances near the end of the 1993 college basketball season caught the attention of professional scouts, and he was named to the All-Metro Second Team. Mills also had a good showing at the Portsmouth Invitational Camp, a showcase for college seniors.

On July 1, Rod Thorn, the NBA's Executive Vice President of Basketball Operations walked to the podium inside the Palace of Auburn Hills in Michigan to announce the second pick of the second round in the 1993 NBA Draft.

"The Minnesota Timberwolves with pick No. 29, the second pick in the second round, select Sherron Mills, Virginia Commonwealth."

Mills became the first Eastern Shore native to be drafted into the NBA since 1974, when Worcester High School's Talvin Skinner was selected by the Seattle Supersonics. Mills was drafted ahead of guys like Gheorghe Mureşan, Nick Van Exel and Bruce Bowen.

On NBC's draft coverage, Hubie Brown gave some analysis on Mills that the Wolves largely agreed with: "If he's going to play big forward for you, he must bulk up. But he does have inside scoring skills."

A day after the draft, Timberwolves' general manager Jack McCloskey told the Associated Press that he liked Mills' finesse and athleticism but, "He's got to bulk up… He's on the lean side." And, almost immediately, McCloskey couldn't say for certain that Mills would make the team. "He's got a chance. That's all I can say."

Mills started in a summer league game for the Timberwolves that year and played well against the Indiana Pacers. He also had eight points against the Cleveland Cavaliers. "Nobody expected me to be here," Mills told the Minneapolis Star-Tribune. "I just like to play hard so that I can go home and feel good about myself." Mills' laid back and quiet demeanor was the polar opposite of the player Minnesota selected in the first round in UNLV's J.R. Rider, who released a rap album in 1994 and later served jail time for cocaine possession and evading the police.

McCloskey wasn't satisfied with what he saw out of Mills in the summer league and decided he wouldn't make the final roster for the 1993-94 NBA season. The GM told the Star-Tribune: "He needs a year in Europe."

So, Minnesota retained Mills' NBA rights and he went to France, where his team gave him free housing and a car. After a standout 1996 season for Italian side for CX Orologi Siena – where he averaged 16.9 points and a league-leading 11.1 rebounds per-game while shooting 59% from the field – Mills was invited back to Timberwolves camp. In the summer leading up to the 1996-97 season, Mills averaged 5.9 points and 5.5 rebounds per-game in the NBA's summer league.

But again, Mills couldn't crack the final roster. He went back overseas and continued to flourish, playing for teams in Italy, France, Spain and Turkey through the 2000 season. One of Mills' last great games as a professional was on March 21, 1999, when he poured in 26 points, 12 rebounds and seven blocks for Spanish club Bàsquet Manresa. In the 1999-00 season, he played for TAU Ceramica in Spain and averaged 13.5 points, 8.1 rebounds and 1.7 blocks per-game in 33 contests.

"Sherron was a really good guy," former Snow Hill girls basketball coach Brenda Jones said. "He played overseas and would give back to the boys team here; buy them sneakers and stuff like that."

While he played professionally, Mills would always come back to the Shore and play regularly in pick-up games and in men's leagues. It was fun, it kept him in shape, and it gave local basketball fans the chance to see one of the best local players ever in-person. In 2001, he was on a team of Worcester County all-stars and they had a match-up in Crisfield against some former Crabbers, like Andy Collins and Greg Bozman. The men's league they were playing in had been founded by former Crisfield head coach Bill Cain and was shepherded then by Phil Rayfield.

At one point in the contest, Collins drove toward the basket, but received some contact and came down awkwardly, landing on Mills. It was immediately apparent that Mills had broken his left leg in the collision. It was a compound fracture, and the scene was much like the 2014 exhibition the U.S. men's national team played when NBA all-star Paul George fell into the stanchion, or the 2013 Elite Eight when Louisville's Kevin Ware broke his leg attempting to defend a three-pointer. It was gruesome. Play was stopped and Mills was taken away in an ambulance. The players finished the game, but the atmosphere remained ominous and dark. It didn't feel right.

"That was an awful night," Bozman said. "It was a real shame. Andy felt horrible... Sherron was never the same player after that."

"It was a devastating injury and it basically ended his career," said Jeff Levan, the former Snow Hill assistant coach. "He probably had a few more good years of playing and earning in him."

Indeed, Mills' time shooting hoops for lucrative contracts in Europe was over. When he recovered from the injury, he became a commercial truck driver and settled down in Salisbury. He obtained his commercial driver's license and started his own business, SLMM Inc., where he hauled agricultural farm supplies and drove a local route for Perdue Farms. Mills' family says that he loved driving his tractor-trailer, and it reminded him of childhood rides with his father. Mills continued to work out at the YMCA, played pick-up ball every now and then, and was an ultra-competitive player in cards and Scrabble.

In August 2014, the simple joys in Mills' life began to fade away. That year, a doctor gave him a troubling diagnosis – Mills had Amyotrophic Lateral Sclerosis, simply known as ALS and commonly referred to as Lou Gehrig's disease.

"When he got sick, it just happened so quickly," Levan said.

Gehrig was the former owner of baseball's consecutive games played record until Cal Ripken, Jr. broke it. For the New York Yankees, Gehrig was a seven-time all-star, a six-time World Series champion, a two-time MVP and a batting champion. But five years after winning MLB's triple crown, Gehrig was forced into an early retirement at the age of 36. Only this terrible disease was capable of bringing down the Iron Horse. According to the Mayo Clinic, ALS is a progressive nervous system disease that affects and destroys nerve cells in the brain and spinal cord, causing loss of muscle control. Eventually, people with ALS lose control of muscles that are needed to speak, eat, breathe and move. The word "amyotrophic" comes from the Greek language and means "no muscle nourishment."

The incurable disease was relentless and took Mills quickly over the next 18 months. On Jan. 17, 2016, Mills – perhaps the greatest player in the history of high school basketball on the Eastern Shore, a father, a husband, a friend, and a larger-than-life young man armed with an infectious smile – took his last breath at Johns Hopkins Hospital in Baltimore. He was 44 years-old.

"He was one of the greatest, most humble people you would ever want to meet," said Nick Purnell, Mills' high school teammate. "Even though he went on to play professional ball, he was never one to boast about it. When he came home, he was just one of the guys."

Said B.J. Johnson, a young assistant on that 1989 Snow Hill team: "Sherron was the greatest player I've seen with that size on the Eastern Shore. Even more than that, he was a great human being… He never forgot where he came from. He was a phenomenal person."

MORE THAN A COACH: ALLEN MILLER

"I miss him, a lot." – David Byrd

After leading the Snow Hill boys basketball team to a state championship in 1989, Allen Miller joked that he could go from coaching a 26-0 team to an 0-19 one. That spring, Miller returned to Pocomoke for his second season of coaching the Warriors baseball team. For what it's worth, the Warriors finished the 1989 season with five wins in a rebuilding year with Miller as the skipper.

"I always say this about Allen: he might've not known 10% of the game, but he communicated 90% of it. There are some guys who can x-and-o you to death, but they can't communicate. He was a great communicator," said Snow Hill assistant coach Jeff Levan. "Allen could coach anything with a ball and a scoreboard... Those teams would run through a wall. He was great with kids. He wore his heart on his sleeve and he spoke his mind."

While Miller guided several different sports teams over the years, basketball seemed to be the game he knew best, and the sport he had the most success with. With Nick Purnell and Shawn Johnson returning the following season, the Eagles were still a force to be reckoned with in boys basketball. The Eagles started the 1989-90 season with five straight wins, running their consecutive victory streak to 31 games. That came to a halt over the holidays, when Snow Hill played in the Eastern States Invitational in Trenton, New Jersey and lost 60-49 to Essex Catholic.

The Eagles got back on track and won the Bayside South, but fell to Grayson Hurley's Cambridge squad in the conference championship game, 98-63.

"We went up to Cambridge and they kicked our ass," Levan said. "My father came down from Baltimore to watch and we got smoked."

Hurley and Miller would quickly become friends, often piling into Hurley's van – which typically sported bald tires – with David Byrd and other Eastern Shore coaches to attend clinics and to take kids to basketball camps.

"Grayson and Allen Miller were two sides of the same coin: dedicated coaches who have amazing ability to inspire young men to do great things," former Star Democrat and Dorchester Banner sports reporter David Insley said. "I say two sides of the same coin because they accomplished largely the same results, but they had totally different methods of doing it. To call Allen the bad cop sounds a little harsh, but compared to Grayson, he had to be. Grayson was the velvet glove; Allen was the fist inside that glove. Grayson was like the supportive counselor; Allen was the, 'you're going to be an alpha male because you're on my fucking team,' type of coach."

A return to the state final four also eluded Snow Hill in 1990, as the Eagles lost to Colonel Richardson by three points in the Region IV semifinals at the University of Maryland Eastern Shore – largely due to the play of Donnie Bolden and his 24 points. "Donnie Bolden could jump over the rim, I believe," said Derrick Fooks, then an assistant coach at Pocomoke.

Colonel, coached by Merrill Morgan, went on to surprisingly win the region that year, despite their 13-10 regular season mark. While Miller was much younger than Morgan, the elder statesman in the Bayside North always had respect for the Snow Hill coach, later telling the Star Democrat that Miller was "one of a kind."

Snow Hill a consistent contender in the Bayside South under Miller. Often, Region IV – and then the 1A East – was won by either the Eagles, Pocomoke or Crisfield. In 1994, Miller guided the Eagles to another Bayside title game appearance – where they lost again to Cambridge – and a second trip to Lefty's Place in College Park. That team was led by Terrance Palmer, that year's Bayside Player of the Year, who went on to play at Allegany Community College.

***

Allen Miller was happy at Snow Hill, but he always had this itch to coach college basketball. In the summer of 1995, Ward Lambert gave him an opportunity to scratch it. With a 126-45 record in seven seasons, Miller left his coaching post at Snow Hill and joined Lambert's staff at Salisbury State University as an assistant. When Miller left, B.J. Johnson took the reins of the Eagles.

But Miller kept a foot in Bayside Conference sports and continued to pay attention to the high school scene on the Delmarva Peninsula. He was also still teaching in Worcester County schools while he coached at Salisbury University and pursued his master's degree.

In 1999 though, Johnson got the opportunity to return to his alma mater, Stephen Decatur, as the head boys basketball coach. He jumped at the opportunity, and who wouldn't? But it left Snow Hill with a vacancy. Luckily for the Eagles, Miller had a different itch four years later. He was ready to return to high school basketball after a hiatus.

"Snow Hill was Allen's school," Levan said. "There wasn't a lot that went on there without him knowing about it."

In two quick years, Miller again turned the Eagles into championship material. In the 2001 1A East Region Final, he led Snow Hill over Pocomoke and his friend David Byrd, 60-57 behind 30 points from Tony Harmon and a clutch bucket and steal from Jessie Bratten. "Pocomoke was well-prepared," Miller told the Daily Times. "Byrd and I hate to see each other lose."

"They're athletes," Pocomoke guard Eddie Miller said of Tony and Jerrell Harmon, years later. "They love the game and were born to play it. Against them, if you don't come with your A game, you're going to hear it and you're going to feel it."

Once more, Miller was going back to Lefty's Place, and Tony Harmon was a big reason why. In the regional semifinals, he hit a buzzer-beating game-winner over Cambridge-South Dorchester and had turned into one of the Bayside's top players. Harmon had 12 points and 12 rebounds in Snow Hill's state semifinal win over Southern-Garrett, a tightly-played 54-49 result.

In the 2001 state final, Snow Hill faced a talented but inexperienced Oakland Mills team, which carried zero seniors. Miller often prided himself on how smart his teams were, how they minimized mistakes and were excellent at fundamentals. Oakland Mills scored the first bucket of the game, but then Miller turned his press on and Snow Hill broke off a 10-0 run. In the first six minutes of the game, the Eagles forced eight turnovers. Snow Hill never trailed again and won 69-60 for their second state championship in boys basketball under Miller. Tony Harmon had 15 points and nine rebounds, Jerrell Harmon had 16 points, and Buddy Johnson had 19 points and nine boards. After the victory, the 6-foot-5 Johnson scooped up Miller's son and put him on his shoulders, and spun around as the fans chanted: "HILL TOP IS IN THE HOUSE! HILL TOP NEVER STOP!"

For the Eastern Shore, Snow Hill's state title would come amidst a run of championship excellence for the region. Between 1996 and 2003, seven different Bayside Conference teams captured state crowns. The run began with Grayson Hurley's CSD Vikings in 1996 and ended with Bruce Wharton's James M. Bennett Clippers in 2003.

The Harmon's graduated from Snow Hill in 2002 and left with a record of 56-18 in their three varsity seasons. And Miller left the sidelines again in the summer of 2002 also. He remained as a teacher and the athletic director at Snow Hill High School, but handed the reins of the program over to Sean Alvarado, who was formerly the head coach at Delmar and had briefly been Miller's assistant. Alvarado was a Dunbar graduate who played at Kansas, and he brought back some Snow Hill greats to be his assistants, including Nick Purnell.

But Alvarado lasted just two seasons in Snow Hill and suddenly – again – the Eagles had a head coaching vacancy for boys basketball. And again, it was filled by Miller who – again – turned Snow Hill back into a contending team. By the spring of 2007, Snow Hill was in the state final four again. The Eagles left College Park empty-handed that year, but came back in 2008 even stronger.

On the court for the Eagles was Josh Duncan, the lone forward, and four guards in Trevon Johnson, Darryle Dennis, Cedrick Johnson and Keith Jackson – a walking firecracker, an electric athlete, a fearless competitor and, at times, a human highlight reel. Jackson's athleticism and basket-making abilities forced coaches to try some unorthodox tactics.

"We had to throw a junk defense at him," said Wi-Hi assistant coach Doug King. "I don't know where the fuck Waller got this. We put two people on Keith, every time he had the ball, and even when he didn't have the ball. We had to muck the game up."

By Feb. 5, 2008, the Eagles were 17-0 after Miller had notched his 250th career win, via a 76-66 victory over Pocomoke. Snow Hill completed its regular season 22-0 and secured the South's berth in the Bayside Conference Championship. Entering the game, Miller had two state titles on his resume, but he never captured a Bayside title outright. The 1989 game was snowed out, remember, and he lost two other times to Grayson Hurley's Cambridge teams. Awaiting Snow Hill in 2008 was Cambridge, again, but they were now coached by Colvin Camper. Still, the Vikings were talented, led by Tabari Perry, who went on to play at Slippery Rock University and professionally in Germany.

Against Snow Hill, Perry made the case on Feb. 27 that he was the best player on the court in Salisbury University's Maggs Gym. With a bit more than two minutes left, Perry had totaled 20 points and 20 rebounds. But he also had four fouls. And when he went up to block Dennis at the 2:22 mark, the referees whistled Perry for a fifth foul that sent him to the bench. Snow Hill seized the opportunity. They crashed the glass, Dennis scored and CSD missed four free throws in the waning moments of the game. 71-68 was the final score, giving Miller his first Bayside crown.

Snow Hill blew by St. Michaels and North Dorchester in the playoffs, then squeaked by Pocomoke – 76-73 – for the 1A East Region title. Again, Miller was headed to College Park. But this time, it wasn't Lefty's Place; it was the house that Gary Williams built, the Comcast Center.

No matter the venue, Miller and his Eagles had success. In the semifinals, they faced Dunbar, who hadn't missed a state final since 2000. But the Poets hadn't played Snow Hill in that stretch. Dennis, Jackson and Trevon Johnson all scored in double-digits as the Eagles coasted by the mighty Dunbar, 63-54.

In the final, Snow Hill faced a 12-11 Surrattsville team from Prince George's County that was outmatched from the get-go. Sure, they had a guard – Jamahl Brown – who scored 36 points, but only one other Hornet scored more than six points. To beat Snow Hill, Surrattsville needed more balance and more talent. On that day, they simply couldn't match Miller's Eagles. The Hornets jumped out to a 7-2 lead, but the Eagles had a 23-17 advantage at the end of the first quarter, thanks to a falling left-handed floater from Cedrick Johnson at the buzzer. By halftime, Snow Hill led by 13 points and had forced Surrattsville into 12 turnovers.

Miller pulled his starters with 1:24 to play. Duncan and Trevon Johnson got sweaty heartfelt hugs from Miller as they walked to the bench, while Cedrick Johnson got a double high five. With 51 seconds to play, Surrattsville knew they had been beaten. The Hornets advanced the ball and held it while the clock ran out, allowing the Eagles to coast to a 92-75 victory. Snow Hill had six players score in double figures, with Dennis leading the way with 19 points and four assists.

"I don't care where you're playing. When you go 28-0, that's a marvelous season," said Pete Medhurst, who handled play-by-play duties of the state championship broadcast for CN8.

Miller raised both arms and smiled as the final buzzer sounded, then let out a sigh of relief. The man from West Virginia who had become synonymous with Bayside basketball won his third state championship, and had completed his second perfect season. Miller loomed over the sideline that day dressed in a loose white shirt, pressed gray pants, a silver-striped tie, worn brown shoes and his trademark goatee. His son AJ sat behind him, two seats to the right of the scorer's table. He too was dressed sharp in a shirt in and tie, and carried a clipboard as he followed his pops to the locker room.

"Allen Miller was one of the greatest dissectors of the game I've ever seen," said Nick Purnell, an assistant coach on the 2008 Snow Hill team. "He could show us game film and break it down to us where, when we went out, we knew what they were going to do before they did it. When it came to x's and o's – you can never take away what he knew. He disciplined us in a way and knew how to put his foot down. He demanded respect and demanded you to learn what to do and how to do it. His saying was, 'The system is going to be simple but effective.'"

***

Two years later, Keith Jackson was a senior and Snow Hill's true star, and Allen Miller assembled another talented team around him. Snow Hill won 18 games in the regular season and won the South again. For Miller's 300th career win, the Eagles bested North Caroline in the Bayside Championship for the coach's second conference crown. Jackson stuffed the stat sheet with 26 points, six rebounds, three assists, three blocks and four steals. While Jackson could out-play and out-score any other player on the Delmarva Peninsula in 2010, this Snow Hill team was really built around a sound and stout defense. They held North Caroline to just 41 points in the Bayside title game.

"He wasn't a true basketball player," Insley said of Jackson. "He was simply an athlete who could fucking do anything."

Again, Snow Hill blitzed through the playoffs with Jackson leading the way. 29 points in a win over CSD, 24 points in a victory over Kent County and 16 points in a gritty 38-36 triumph over rival Pocomoke. In the state semifinals, Snow Hill fell, but Jackson etched his name in the state record book next to the likes of Sherron Mills and Tia Jackson with an unforgettable performance. Jackson scored 34 points – or, 81% of all of Snow Hill's points – in a 44-42 loss to Owings Mills. He also had 10 rebounds, two assists, two blocks and two steals. As of this writing, Jackson is still one of just 41 boys players ever to score 34 points or more in a Maryland state final four game.

"That boy was a freak of nature," Purnell said of Jackson. "And his sport wasn't really basketball. In football... I saw him at Washington, from the linebacker position, he jetted through, snatched the ball while the quarterback was handing it off, and Keith took it and ran 76 yards. I'll never forget that. He was unreal. I loved watching him play football and basketball."

Jackson was named Player of the Year in the Bayside, and Miller was named Coach of the Year for the third time and final time.

"One of the most interesting guys was Allen Miller," said Paul Butler, who had his second stint as WBOC16's sports director from 2005 to 2008 before becoming a news anchor at the station. "He was a great coach, but also a good guy. He was never shy. Whenever I wanted to do an interview, Allen Miller was always like, 'Come on down.' He had a great personality and a great wit about him. But also, no nonsense when it came to coaching. He didn't take anything from his players, and he demanded a lot of them. I think that's why his teams were always really, really good. He demanded that excellence from them."

***

No one knew it at the time, but Snow Hill's defeat to Owings Mills was the last boys high school basketball game that Allen Miller would ever coach.

On the morning of Friday, Sept. 10, 2010, Miller died at his home after suffering a heart attack. He was just 47 years-old.

"He was one of my best friends and his death was one of the most devastating things I ever went through," said Jeff Levan, Miller's former roommate and longtime assistant coach. "Some of the phone calls I had to make that day were calls you never want to have to make. It was just a real loss for Snow Hill."

The Eastern Shore's sports community was stunned. Miller was so important and meant so much to so many. Not only had he been the off-and-on head basketball coach at Snow Hill since 1988, but he was also a teacher, the athletic director and golf coach at Snow Hill. He was a husband, a brother, a doting father and an awesome friend. He was a man with an exuberant and infectious personality who liked to listen to Jimmy Buffett and talk about basketball. He had a real passion for youth and high school athletics on the Eastern Shore. Miller was really a come-here who became a from-here. He was beloved by many.

"Allen did a great job and he was a great guy," former Snow Hill girls basketball coach Brenda Jones said. "He did a lot for this school, and he was a great father. He raised a lot of those kids."

Miller was also the Bayside Conference President for six years and was influential during his time at the helm of the league. He piloted a transfer policy that the state later adopted, which said that student athletes were not allowed to play for 45 days after switching schools. He pushed the league to adopt an online scheduling system on a nationwide website.

The memorial service for Miller was too big to be held at Snow Hill High School. It had to be moved across Worcester County, to Stephen Decatur in Berlin. Miller's close friend and longtime rival, David Byrd, went out and bought a maroon shirt just for the occasion, to match Snow Hill's colors.

"At (Miller's) funeral, Byrd was Allen Miller. You wouldn't have left dry-eyed; I can tell you that," Pocomoke's Derrick Fooks said. "He had him down to a tee, even the twisting of the tie. I think that's the only time I've seen (Byrd) wear that color. That was priceless."

Byrd told stories about how Miller always put family first, and how he always had his son AJ sitting next to him on the bench. Security in College Park was always tight, but no one was going to stop Miller from having his son on the sidelines.

Miller and Byrd's friendship started in the 1980s, when Miller would just pop in at Pocomoke to watch practice, before he had a team of his own. The two Worcester County coaches became close over the next two decades. They were rivals on the court, but buddies off it. At 7:30 a.m. nearly every morning before school, Miller and Byrd talked on the phone. They talked about a lot of things, but it usually circled back around to the previous night's college basketball slate.

"We miss him. We were really good friends. And we butted heads a few times too, disagreeing on a few things. It was a good relationship," Byrd said. "I miss him, a lot."

Butch Waller was another coach that Allen Miller called a lot. And before cell phones became popular, Miller would call a payphone that was in the lobby outside of the Wicomico High School gym. Someone would grab Waller out of his office regularly telling him, "Mr. Miller is on the phone for you." Miller usually called Waller before his Eagles were about to play a team that Wi-Hi had already faced. They talked players, tendencies, strategies and more.

"And that went on for a couple years, and then he quit calling, because they got good," Waller says. "He did a good job. He was very vociferous. He would take that jacket off and he was like Bob Huggins at West Virginia. He would get after it and yell and scream, but he got the job done."

One year, ahead of a highly anticipated Indians vs. Eagles match-up, Miller went to the art students at Snow Hill and had them make a giant cut-out of Waller's face. Wi-Hi came out of the locker-room, and the bleachers at Snow Hill's gym were covered with fans waving Waller's face. "Everybody stood up and waved in that tiny ass little gym, waving those damn things. I thought it was cool as hell," said Waller, who took one of the cut-outs home as a souvenir.

Some remember vividly how Miller was on the sidelines, as sweat poured off his bald head as he barked assignments with intensity. He always looked sharp at the opening tip, but as games wore on, his shirt would become soaked and untucked, and his tie loosened. As Snow Hill won more than 300 games during his tenure, Miller often became unglued in every contest.

Less than three years after Miller left the Earth, another longtime Eastern Shore coach passed away too. At the age of 57, Dave Monroe died after a battle with cancer on June 5, 2013. Monroe was a 1974 Snow Hill High School graduate who was an Army veteran and held degrees from both the University of Maryland Eastern Shore and Salisbury University. He began coaching the Snow Hill girls basketball team in the 1989-90 season, assisted Vic Burns on the North Dorchester boys team that won a state title in 1999, and then became the head coach of the boys team in Shiloh, a position he held until his death.

David Insley is a North Dorchester High School graduate who covered sports up and down the Eastern Shore for the Dorchester Banner and Star Democrat from 2003 to 2019. He shared beers, meals, conversations and bonds with these coaches over his time covering high school athletics on the Delmarva Peninsula. One memory Insley treasures is the time that he, Dean Sullivan and Miller put away $170 worth of sushi in Salisbury. The day after Monroe died, Insley penned a column and wrote about a basketball contest in heaven, where the Eagles faced the Eagles, with Miller patrolling one sideline and Monroe drawing up plays from the other.

"Too many of our coaches have died way too fucking young," Insley said. "It's a real tragedy.

"And nobody deserves to have the gym at Snow Hill named after them more than Allen Miller. Allen was so much more than just a basketball coach."

TIA AND BARB

"They say that if a coach has one really, really great player in their coaching career, they should consider themselves lucky. I believe I've had the best player in Maryland and probably the best in a lot of states." – Barbara McCool

"Do you play basketball?"

The voice that Tia Jackson heard during one of her walks in the halls of Mardela Middle and High School had a commanding tone, as if the question came from an army general.

Jackson was a freshman that day in 1986. After being born in Baltimore, she had spent a good chunk of her childhood in Delmar – a small town on the Delmarva Peninsula that sits along Route 13 on the Delaware-Maryland line. But Jackson and her family left the region for a few years and lived in Miami, Florida, where she would attend part of elementary and middle school, and follow her three older brothers wherever they went. They returned to the Shore, just in time for Jackson to begin high school.

At the time, Jackson was – as she tells it – tomboyish, tall and awkward, standing around 5-foot-9. Yes, she had played basketball before, but it wasn't organized. Still, her height, toughness and natural athletic abilities gave her an edge.

"I just kind of ran around the court, doing everything that was a violation in basketball, but in middle school they kind of let it go," Jackson said. "I actually didn't start playing basketball or even understanding what it was until middle school."

Jackson looked around that day, then down, and saw who was asking the question – a woman that would change her life.

Barbara McCool was tiny, but intimidating. She demanded respect, and knew a great deal about the game of basketball and how to mold players. And she had a keen eye for talent.

"I knew in my heart that I was supposed to say yes, because she had this kind of presence," Jackson said of her first impression of McCool. "She scared the life out of me."

A bit anxious and unsure of the lady she was staring down at, Jackson was able to utter two words to answer McCool's question: "No, ma'am."

"Well," McCool said. "You do now."

One could easily make the case that Jackson is the greatest – girl or boy, man or woman – to play basketball in the Bayside Conference. In addition to her vast accomplishments as a high school phenom, she went on to play and coach in Final Fours. She was among the first players drafted into the WNBA. She was the head coach of a Pac-12 program, and she's still coaching to this day. When Kara Lawson was hired as the head coach of the Duke women's basketball program in July 2020, one of the first calls she made in assembling in her staff was to Jackson, who is widely regarded as one of the top recruiters in the women's college game today.

"Tia is an outstanding communicator, outstanding teacher, can develop players, does a great job in recruiting," Lawson said. "That lens of having run her own program before, that's something that's very valuable for me as a first-time head coach."

But before Jackson became a coach at the highest level, she was just an awkward kid in a hallway at Mardela Middle and High School, being asked a question by small and demanding white woman. That day in 1986 sparked the basketball career of Tia Jackson, and birthed Mardela's reputation of being a girls hoops powerhouse on the Eastern Shore.

***

Mardela Springs is a small town in northwestern Wicomico County that is smashed between the Delaware border, the mighty Route 50 and Barren Creek, which is connected to the Nanticoke River. Factions of the Nanticoke tribe lived there and they became known locally as the Puckamee Group. English settlers came there sometime in the mid-1600s, when fur traders floated down Barren Creek from the river, and most natives abandoned the area and moved north in the early 1700s. It became known as the "town with three names," as it wasn't really known for one specific trade, export or people. But that changed in the late 1800s when some folks there started bottling mineral water. They didn't want their business to be associated with the word "barren," so they named the town Mardela Springs. Mar for Maryland, Dela for Delaware, and Springs to mostly attract tourism. After the Civil War, it was home to a popular hotel and spa – the Spring House – that attracted visitors from throughout the region. The town enjoyed its most bustling times and greatest economic success in the late 1800s and early 1900s. But by the 1960s, Route 50 had been built up and established as a highway connecting Ocean City to the Chesapeake Bay Bridge. Mardela Springs became an afterthought, bypassed daily by countless drivers. The only reason to stop in Mardela was to fill up one's gas tank.

The town had several one-room or small school houses scattered about, but it wasn't until 1920 when a combination elementary and high school opened near the corner of Delmar Road and Sharptown Road. It was replaced by a larger brick building in 1935. The Mardela Middle and High School that stands on those grounds as of this writing was constructed between 1978 and 1980. While the school's population has increased over the years, it's still one of the smallest high schools on the Eastern Shore. In 2019, it had a sixth through 12th grade enrollment of less than 700 students.

In 1938, Barbara N. McCool was born in Kannapolis, North Carolina to Sara and Wallace McCool. The same town that birthed and raised the Intimidator of NASCAR gave the Eastern Shore one of its most respected basketball coaches, a woman that was as tough as whalebone and hell.

"I was intimidated, but I stood about three extra feet over her," Jackson said of McCool. "She just had this way about her, and that's the command and the demand of a coach. She was very honest. She was not going to give you the fluff."

After graduating from Appalachian State University in 1960, McCool taught in Virginia for a few years before landing at Mardela in 1965, where she immediately began teaching gym and coaching field hockey. Soon, she became the school's head girls basketball coach too, a post she would not leave until her death.

Barbara McCool's first team at Mardela went 9-5 in the 1965-66 season. Mardela yearbooks.

McCool would become synonymous with Mardela. She later became the school's athletic director, and also coached boys soccer, volleyball and track and field for periods of time. While she had tremendous success as a field hockey coach – leading Mardela to a pair of Class C state titles in 1978 and 1982 – she was first and foremost known as a basketball coach. And a damn good one too. McCool is the Bayside Conference's all-time winningest coach in girls hoops, collecting 605 victories across her 44 seasons on the job.

The Warriors teams coached by McCool quickly became known for their feistiness. They may have not always been the biggest, strongest or most talented, but they placed a value on fundamentals, and they weren't going to be out-hustled. McCool was demanding and her instructions could often be accompanied with a bark or a scowl, but she did it all to get the best out of her players. And, more often than not, Barb's teams won, and won big.

"She showed that tough demeanor like us 'big-time' coaches do, but she was a softie. She knew what she wanted to accomplish with those kids and she got her point across, but would bend over backwards to help those kids any way she could," said Wicomico High School's Butch Waller, the state of Maryland's all-time winningest boys basketball coach. "I can tell you that we came from the same stock, we had the same philosophy – some say it was the old school mentality: you just do what you do."

Mardela did not have much of a basketball history before Barbara arrived and flipped the gymnasium into McCool's House of Hoops. The girls team had been to one state final, losing 34-14 in 1948 under the direction of Bill Twilley. The boys squad hadn't been much better. As of 2020, they have only appeared in the state semifinals twice – 1950 and 1955 – and they have never appeared in a Bayside Conference title game.

Under the direction of McCool – and with the help of a few talented players like Tina Wharton, Lenore Morris, Pam Hopkins, Kim Horsey, and later, Laura Wood – the Mardela Warriors began achieving some real success in girls basketball in the 1970s and 1980s. They three-peated as Bayside Champions between 1978 and 1980, beating Easton, Kent County and North Dorchester in consecutive years. A year before Brenda Jones' Snow Hill team became the first girls squad from the Eastern Shore to win a state title in the modern era, McCool directed her Warriors to the Class C state final in 1978. After losing the first two games of the season, Mardela – powered by Hopkins and Horsey – won its next 19 straight games before falling 60-48 to Middletown in the final.

Hopkins and Horsey went on to play Division I college ball at Morgan State and UT-Chattanooga, respectively. Wood later played at UT-Chattanooga too. They're just three of many great players to come through McCool's stellar program.

"When we played against her teams, it was like a war," longtime Pocomoke girls coach Gail Gladding once told the Daily Times. "Barbara just stuck out as an old-school coach. She demanded the best from her kids and I'm sure she instilled the love of the game in many, many, many of her players. She was an icon on the Shore."

But no player before or since has been quite like Tia Jackson, who possessed raw athleticism, unteachable height, an unmatched competitive drive and a willingness to learn.

SHORE HOOPS

***

As a high school freshman, the only people Tia Jackson trusted was her family. To make her into the best basketball player she could be, Barbara McCool needed Jackson to totally buy-in to her methods. The path to that was through Jackson's mother.

"My mom and Coach McCool really hit it off, immediately," Jackson said. "As far as the disciplinary side of things, the demands in the classroom – as long as I took care of business there, my mom was okay with giving Coach McCool the reins to train me."

It was obvious right away that Jackson was talented and could have a real future in basketball. In her debut varsity game as a freshman, she totaled 26 points and 12 rebounds in a dominant 67-22 win over St. Michaels – a school that has never been considered a power in Bayside Conference hoops. Jackson nearly matched that output in her second game, tallying 22 points and 11 rebounds in a 50-44 home win over a tough Stephen Decatur team.

"Coach never let us take an opponent lightly," Jackson said. "You treat every game as if you're David and you're going against Goliath. It didn't matter if it was St. Michaels or Parkside."

When Mardela had Jackson, they were Goliath. And in a Mardela vs. St. Michaels game, well, that was like David vs. Goliath if David was blind and leg-less, while Goliath was jacked up on Mountain Dew and armed with a rocket launcher.

While she was still unpolished as a freshman, Jackson displayed a willingness right away to take the crucial shots. In a mid-season contest against James M. Bennett her freshman year, Jackson swished a 15-footer at the buzzer to send the game into overtime, where Mardela would win by two points. In the first playoff game of her high school career, Jackson racked up 16 points and 15 rebounds and sank a pair of free throws with seven seconds left to give Mardela a 44-43 win over Decatur.

Mardela bowed out of the playoffs in the regional semifinals in Jackson's freshman season, but she led her team in rebounding, averaged about 20 points per-game and was named to the All-Bayside Second Team.

McCool was also Mardela's track and field coach too and thought it could be another sport Jackson could excel at, and another way to keep her in shape. As usual, she was correct. In her first high school track meet, Jackson recorded a long jump of 16-feet, breaking the school record. A few weeks later, she set the Bayside Conference record in the event with a jump of 17 feet and 7 inches.

If basketball hadn't gotten Jackson a college scholarship, track and field might've. She would go on to win nine state titles in the sport – three in long jump, four in triple-jump, one in high jump and one in the 400 meters run.

"Track kept me in shape and helped me appreciate just how important the conditioning and the cardio build-up for an athlete was," Jackson said. "It was a great way to offset being out of basketball season."

Jackson typically listened to every word McCool said, but one of the rare times she defied her was during track season. One of McCool's unbreakable rules for Jackson was to never do any training or any strenuous athletic activity when she wasn't around. One day near the end of Jackson's sophomore year at Mardela, with regionals for track looming, McCool was away from the school for a bit.

"I don't know if she had a doctor's appointment or something in the afternoon – but I had an open gym period," Jackson recalls. "So, I decided I was going to play softball."

With proper practice, Jackson probably would've been a superb softball player too, but she had never played the game in an organized environment before and knew little about the fundamentals. While running out a double, Jackson slid feet first in second base and rolled her right ankle. And it swelled to about the size of a softball.

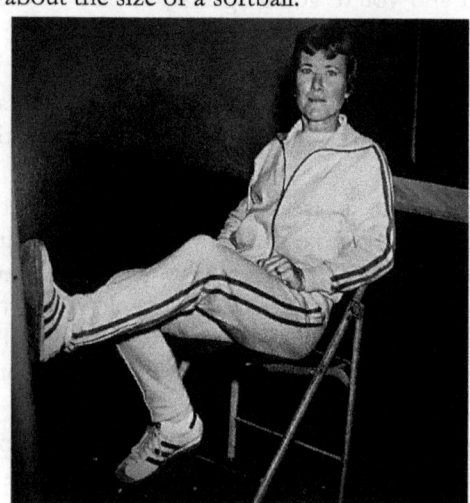

Barbara McCool won 605 girls basketball games across her decades of coaching at Mardela. Mardela yearbooks.

McCool was irate. But she still wanted Jackson to qualify for states and help Mardela win regionals. The 200-meter race was no problem for Jackson and she won it with ease. But jumping was going to be problematic, until McCool got an idea. For the triple-jump, she worked with Jackson to switch up her footing so her final leap would be off her left foot instead of her lame right one. Jackson managed to notch a 13-8 jump, good enough for second place in regionals and a qualifying spot at states.

"She had a gift, man," Jackson says now of McCool. "For her, what looks like a no is always a yes. What seems impossible is always possible. She had a way of getting you to believe that you could jump off a roof and fly. She instilled that in me.

"But, needless to say, I stayed away from softball after that."

When track and field seasons ended, the work wasn't over for Jackson. Nearly every day, she was working out with McCool, honing her skills on the court, improving her knowledge of the game and her athleticism.

"I had to be a willing vessel, but it was all her," Jackson said. "Getting me up in the morning, training me. If I had a summer job, she would train me before and after. She saw something in me that I didn't even know existed. A lot of credit goes to her."

One summer, Jackson took a job at the Milford Pickle Factory and often didn't get home from work until 3 a.m. Still, multiple times a week, she'd wake up at 8 a.m. to work out with McCool.

***

The results of Tia Jackson's work and Barbara McCool's teachings began to surface right away. Heading into the New Year, Mardela was 4-0 and Jackson, then a sophomore, had recorded a double-double in every game. Ahead of a holiday tournament that Mardela hosted that season, Cambridge South-Dorchester head coach Jane Follmer called Jackson "the most dominant player in the area." Follmer threw a Lisa Phillips-led box-and-one defense at Jackson and the Mardela phenom still recorded 26 points and 19 rebounds in a victory.

About a month later, after Jackson racked up 34 points in a 61-23 road win at Wi-Hi, Indians' head coach Debbie Holloway said, "If she isn't the strongest player in the conference, she's certainly one of the strongest. Tia can shoot a jump shot with one or two players on her. It's just very hard to stop her."

January 1988 is when Jackson really began to break out, forcing everyone on the Shore to pay attention. Six times between Jan. 6 and March 5, she notched a stat line of at least 40 points and 13 rebounds. Her run of huge scoring totals was highlighted by a Feb. 20 home game vs. Snow Hill, in which she poured in 51 points and 21 rebounds in a 76-38 victory. That performance broke Mardela's single-game scoring record previously held by Laura Wood and set the season-high scoring mark for boys or girls basketball that season in the conference. Jackson also surpassed the 1,000-point scoring mark for her career that night, becoming the first sophomore to ever accomplish the feat in Bayside Conference history.

"Tia was truly in a class all by herself," said Nick Purnell, who played at Snow Hill in the late 1980s. "That's just one of those names that rings out on the women's side around here. She was a one-woman wrecking crew. You could throw two or three at her and she was still going to do her thing. Nobody could stop her from going to the hole."

Jackson had 42 points and 14 rebounds – and was 20-of-25 from the charity stripe – in a 69-59 regional final win over Decatur, which put Mardela in the state semifinals for the first time since 1978. The Warriors would have to face Brooklyn Park, a small high school just south of Baltimore. In the

Baltimore Sun, a writer who called himself "Prophet Pat" put a spread on the game, making Brooklyn Park three-point favorites. He acknowledged Jackson's talents, but wrote, "One player is not going to beat this well-balanced Bees' quint."

The folks who followed Pat's gambling guidance would've won some cash. Jackson scored 22 points, but it wasn't enough as things didn't go as planned for McCool and co. at Catonsville Community College. The Bees threw a 1-3-1 zone at Mardela and stifled the Warriors' offensive attack. More importantly, Brooklyn Park finished the game with a 36-26 advantage in rebounds. The Bees sent Mardela back across the Bay Bridge empty-handed, winning 76-52.

While Jackson didn't bring the hardware home for Mardela, she finished her sophomore campaign with per-game averages of 31.6 points and 16.3 rebounds, and shared Bayside Player of the Year honors with Parkside's Kristi Lewandowski.

That summer, Jackson was honored at a local awards banquet attended by Muggsy Bogues, a product of Baltimore's Dunbar High School who had just wrapped up his rookie season with the Washington Bullets. But Jackson towered over Bogues, who was perhaps generously listed at 5-foot-3 for the majority of his professional career. Jackson standing between Bogues and McCool – who were about eye-to-eye – made for a funny photo in the June 8, 1988 edition of the Salisbury Daily Times.

"I don't know that I ever grew into myself. I was still awkward," Jackson said. "I still felt like a fish out of water a lot of the time. I was kind of nerdy, but athletic, which was really a weird combination. It was just an odd time for me. I was growing an inch every year and towering over every female in the school. I was just trying to figure out where my footing was going to be. Coach identified the basketball side. I just went in head first."

***

Heading into her junior season, accolades would continue to pile up for Tia Jackson as she continued to be not just the best player on the Eastern Shore, but the most dominant one, and someone who was developing into a legitimate Division I college prospect.

Barbara McCool continued to train Jackson hard and used some unorthodox techniques to get every ounce of athleticism out of her pupil. Often, Jackson would come to school dressed one way and then go throughout the day dressed a very different way, because of McCool. Jackson's coach persuaded her to wear these odd-looking sneakers that had lifts on the balls of the foot. They were supposed to help a player increase the strength in their legs.

"I would train in them, walk around school in them. It didn't bother me because everyone knew it was a Coach McCool thing, and I was already in that awkward phase, so it didn't faze me to be a little bit more awkward," Jackson says of the platform sneakers. "It was like walking on your tippy toes. You couldn't put your heel to the ground. It was really weird."

When she wasn't training Jackson or assisting her with footwear, McCool was still hard at work for her player. Back in those days, long before social media and recruiting networks, a player as talented as Jackson still needed help getting noticed. The Eastern Shore can be an isolated place, and college coaches were more likely to find an autographed picture of King Leonidas than they were to find Mardela on a map.

So, McCool made calls herself on behalf of Jackson, cut up tapes of her highlights and shipped them off. In the offseason, McCool took Jackson to camps full of college coaches and scouts. And when Jackson got the chance to showcase her skills against the very best from around the country, she rarely disappointed.

At a 1987 camp held by University of Maryland coach Chris Weller, Jackson took home MVP honors. In 1988 at the University of Tennessee, she won the camp's one-on-one competition. Near the end of her junior season, she appeared in USA Today.

"Coach was really good at getting me in the right places," Jackson said. "She put me in the right place at the right time and people noticed."

It wasn't until letters from colleges started filling up shoe boxes that Jackson thought she'd be able to play Division I college basketball.

"I didn't know I could play in college until I started getting all of these phone calls," Jackson said. "Coach would always say it, but I'm like, 'You mean I'm going to get my school paid for? No way.' And so, before I knew it, I was being sought after by the likes of Notre Dame, UVA, Iowa, Tennessee, Kentucky…"

The letters, calls and visits from college coaches kept coming in during Jackson's stellar junior season, piling up like hot fries in a bucket from Thrasher's. She started that season off with a bang, notching at least 44 points and 18 rebounds in each of the first six games of the year for Mardela, which were all wins.

Then came Parkside. The team that Mardela hated. The team they always struggled against.

"Parkside, by far," was Mardela's rival back then, Jackson said. "That's it. Parkside was the – (McCool) made us think everyone was Goliath – but we knew Parkside was the one we wanted to get every time."

The Rams were supremely talented in the late 80s and early 90s. By the 1988-89 season, the Rams' best player was Kesha Camper, a 6-foot sophomore forward. But Parkside had two other players over 5-foot-11 in

Buffy Fellenbaum and Dionne Townsend. While Jackson was typically the tallest and most-skilled player on the court in most of the games she played in during her time at Mardela, that just simply wasn't' the case when the Warriors ran up against the Rams.

In Parkside and Mardela's first meeting of the 1988-89 season, the Rams won 66-55 at home behind Camper's 24 points. Jackson had 36 points, but Parkside stalled her just enough. Jackson and Mardela licked their wounds and proceeded to win their next eight games. For Jackson, the run was highlighted by a 58-point outing at Pocomoke.

A few days before, Jackson had wowed the crowd at Colonel Richardson by pouring in 38 points and 23 rebounds. Easton Star Democrat reporter Bill Haufe called her "gracefully elegant." In one sequence he described, Jackson blocked a Colonel shot on one end, sprinted down the court like the track star she was, caught a lead pass, fed it back to her teammate who missed, grabbed the offensive rebound and put it away with ease while being fouled.

McCool told the Star Democrat after that 84-45 win at American Corner: "She can do anything she wants to, athletically."

Except beat Parkside, apparently. The second meeting between the Rams and the Warriors, this one at Mardela, was similar. Yes, Jackson got her stats – tallying 41 points and 15 rebounds – but Parkside's "Triple Towers" of Camper, Fellenbaum and Townsend combined for 47 points. Camper had 14 rebounds on her own in the 61-52 win on Feb. 11, 1989.

Luckily for Jackson, McCool and Mardela, they wouldn't have to see Parkside for the rest of the season or in the playoffs as the Rams were in Class B – now known as the 2A Class – back then. The Warriors rolled through the rest of the regular season without losing a game and Jackson hit a new career-high, getting 60 points and 29 rebounds in a mid-February win at Snow Hill. She passed the 2,000-point mark for her career in the next game.

After discarding Washington in their opening playoff game, the Warriors were back in the regional final. They expected to win and expected to go back across the Bay Bridge for another shot at the state championship. But Stephen Decatur and the Yoder sisters had other ideas.

In what Salisbury Daily Times scribe Pat Henderson called "the biggest upset" of the season, Decatur beat Mardela at the University of Maryland Eastern Shore, 53-42. Alycia and Kelly Yoder combined for 31 points while Jackson was held to 28 as the Seahawks threw a triangle-and-two defense at Mardela's star. No other Warrior had more than six points. Decatur head coach Sue Brinsfield called it the team's "best win ever," and that likely wasn't hyperbole.

"We just hoped we could hang in with Mardela and play good basketball," Brinsfield told the Daily Times. "We put Kelly Yoder on Tia because she was our quickest defender. We worked with Kelly before the game on how to front Tia and how to deny her the ball."

Brinsfield was named Bayside Coach of the Year in 1989 and Jackson took home her second straight Player of the Year award. She also led the entire state in scoring and posted per-game averages of 42.1 points, 21.4 rebounds, 3.5 assists and four steals.

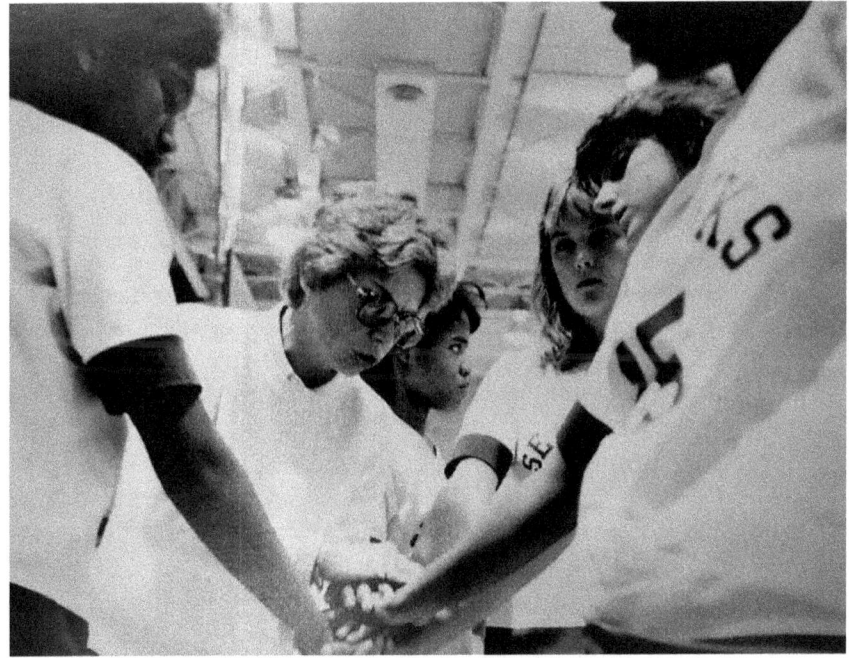

Stephen Decatur girls head coach Sue Brinsfield huddles with her team during a 1984 regular season game in Berlin. Stephen Decatur yearbooks.

***

Entering the summer of 1989, Tia Jackson had piled up scholarship offers from Kentucky, Maryland, Tennessee, Radford, Auburn, N.C. State, Long Beach State and Iowa, among others.

In early May, Jackson was one of 50 high school players invited to the U.S. Olympic trials at Syracuse. There was a total of 157 players at the camp and Iowa's C. Vivian Stringer ran the trials. Wearing No. 55 – instead of her usual No. 11 – Jackson impressed and kept surviving cuts. She made the final 24, but couldn't crack the top 17. Jackson was one of the final seven players cut, but the women who made the team over her – like Virginia's Dawn Staley and Maryland's Carla Holmes – were uber-talented. Jackson proved in the trials that she could hang with the best of the best. Soon after, McCool's phone started ringing. Notre Dame joined the list of offers Jackson already had and more started pouring in. Later that summer, Jackson was named the Most Outstanding Player at a Five-Star camp at Radford. Word spread so much that McCool limited Jackson's recruiting phone calls to Sunday evenings between 6 and 9 p.m.

"What the trials showed us was the level of Tia's ability and potential on the basketball court," McCool told the Daily Times. "We knew what she could do against high school competition, but now we know how she compares against college-level players."

The trials also allowed Jackson to get more face-time with Stringer too. The two had mutual admiration for each other, and Stringer had been courting Jackson. Stringer had seen Jackson play in-person, and soon after the trials, she offered Jackson a scholarship. For Jackson, what really pushed Stringer and Iowa to the front of the pack was when the Hawkeyes' coach visited her at home.

"She wowed the entire family, myself included. It was a no-brainer for me," Jackson said. "I believed in what she was telling me and everything she told me came true, as far as my ability to contribute, compete on a high level, that I was going to get my degree and that it wasn't going to be easy – it wasn't. Whatever it was that I wanted, I could have… Everything about what Iowa was and what Coach Stringer is – it's what I needed."

Jackson narrowed her choices down to five schools: Virginia, Notre Dame, Kentucky, Tennessee and Iowa. And a coach from each school came to Mardela at least once to see her play in-person – even the legendary Pat Summitt visited McCool's House of Hoops.

Before making her decision, Jackson took recruiting trips to Kentucky, Notre Dame, Virginia and Iowa. During her visit to South Bend in the fall of 1989, she got to see a Fighting Irish football game. The No. 1 Irish were playing No. 9 USC, and quarterback Todd Marinovich led the Trojans to a 17-7 lead before the tandem of Tony Rice and Rocket Ismail helped the Irish complete an exhilarating comeback, and Notre Dame won 28-24.

But the Irish's gridiron triumph did not sway Jackson. Ultimately, she picked Iowa over UVA. She signed with Stringer and the Hawkeyes just before the start of her senior season on Nov. 15, 1989. As she put pen to paper, McCool was looking over her shoulder smiling, wearing an Iowa sweatshirt.

Talking to Daily Times sports editor Dave Broughton the next day, Stringer – about to begin her seventh season as the coach of the Hawkeyes – was giddy to be getting a player as talented as Jackson, who also happened to have a 4.1 GPA.

"She has so much natural talent; she has unlimited potential," Stringer said. "She can do basically anything she wants to do; she just needs to go in the direction we want her to."

Mardela's Tia Jackson, surrounded by her parents, signs her national letter of intent to the University of Iowa. Mardela yearbooks.

***

With her college recruitment finished, there were no distractions for Tia Jackson entering her senior season. Named a Pre-Season All-American by Street & Smith's, she opened the year with a 45-point, 23-rebound effort in a win over North Dorchester.

Much like the previous season, Mardela began the year unbeaten, winning seven straight, and then they ran into Parkside. Kesha Camper outscored Jackson this time, 36 points to 33, and the Rams won by nine points at Mardela.

By Jan. 19, 1990, Jackson was averaging 41 points per-game. The second-best scoring average in the conference belonged to a boy, Pocomoke's Mike Roberts, who was scoring 28 a game. That night, Mardela saw Stephen Decatur for the first time since the regional final upset from a season ago. McCool showed no mercy, implementing a full-court press for much of the game. Jackson had 32 points, 21 rebounds and seven assists in a satisfying 67-30 victory.

The Warriors kept winning and Jackson kept stuffing stat sheets. She twice recorded triple-doubles her senior season: 58 points, 15 rebounds and 15 steals in a win at James M. Bennett, and 58 points, 18 rebounds and 12 steals in a home victory over Pocomoke. She was unstoppable.

"I saw Tia dunk a tennis ball once. Barb said she could dunk a softball, which is pretty damn good," said David Insley, who was working as a sports reporter for the Dorchester Banner during the 1989-90 basketball season. "There's absolutely no question, she's the best girls player I ever saw. By a country mile… They'd could've put her out on the floor alone and Mardela still would've won."

Mardela had a few other players this season that contributed to wins too. Pint-sized point guard Melissa Gattis could rack up double-digit assists, and Mardela had an exchange student from Japan in Haruko Shikano who wasn't too shabby on the court.

On Feb. 10, 1990, Jackson got her last crack at Parkside and Kesha Camper, and came up short again. She had 40 points and 20 rebounds, but the Rams won by six points at home. Camper had 24 points and 25 boards in their last on-court meeting in high school.

A few games later, Jackson passed the 3,000-point mark for her career by scoring 37 points in a win over Snow Hill. She was – and still is – one of the most prolific scorers the state of Maryland had seen in high school basketball. Jackson capped off the final regular season of her high school career with 53 points and 19 rebounds in a win over Washington. For the second straight year, Jackson had scored more than 1,000 points in a single season and Mardela finished the regular season with just a pair of losses to Parkside. Jackson and the Warriors set their sights on the playoffs, where the Washington Jaguars were waiting for them in the region semifinals. Jackson whipped them again, tallying 45 points and 15 rebounds in a 69-26 victory, the last game she'd ever play in McCool's House of Hoops.

Finding motivation for the 1A East Region Final in 1990 was not difficult. All Mardela had to do was remember how its 1989 season ended, in a shocking loss to Stephen Decatur. That would've been enough, but in newspaper stories leading up to the big game to be played at the University of Maryland Eastern Shore, the coach of the Warriors' opponent – North Caroline's Jackie Pinckens – doubted Mardela's talent and their ability to play as a complete unit.

"Mardela doesn't have much of a team; they just have one girl that does everything," Pinckens told Easton's Star Democrat.

While this was true some nights for Mardela, it wasn't how every game went down. Melissa Gattis had 10 points and a bunch of assists for the Warriors in their win over Washington. Allyson Ellis and Lori Smith had been playing well too, and for Mardela's press to work effectively, McCool needed every player at their best. Still, Pinckens thought her team was better. Even after the Bulldogs had been thumped by Kesha Camper and Parkside in the Bayside title game, Pinckens didn't seem to have much respect for the schools in the Bayside south.

"Basically, you try to prepare your team for (Jackson)," Pinckens told the Star Democrat. "If we can get Tia frustrated, make her commit some fouls, it would be an asset… Once we get past Tia, we did fine on the inside."

Early on, it seemed like Pinckens' plan might actually work. Jackson picked up two quick first quarter fouls and watched from the bench as North Caroline jumped out to a 15-point lead. But Jackson came back into the game before halftime and sparked Mardela on a 13-point run, contributing nine points and an assist as she sliced up the Bulldogs' defense like a hot knife cutting through a buttered biscuit. Jackson kept pouring it on in the second half and continued to play with an unmatched focus. She finished with 45 points, 19 rebounds, eight steals, six assists and two blocks as the Warriors punched their ticket to the state final four with a 73-63 win over the Bulldogs. Smith and Gattis both scored in the double-digits too.

"There was nothing we could do," North Caroline guard Kelly Carey said. "We'd try to guard (Jackson) and she'd just spin around us."

McCool's team was now bound for the state final four. The Warriors were armed with the top scorer in the state and were just two wins away from bringing home that elusive state title to northwestern Wicomico County. Mardela had been on this platform two years ago and McCool left disappointed with her team's performance. Still, she wasn't going to alter how they prepared. McCool had built this team on speed and stamina. They lived and died with the press, and they leaned on Jackson to lead.

***

Perhaps the greatest single game of basketball that Tia Jackson ever played was her last one wearing the green-and-gold No. 11 for Mardela. It was on the biggest stage of her high school career, and it also happens to be the contest she remembers the least about.

And unfortunately for the Warriors, it was also a game that ended in a loss.

"Sheesh," Jackson replied when she was asked about the game some 30 years after it tipped off. "As people will say often, I was in a zone. So many people reference that game, but sometimes I just play like I blacked out. I just go. That's what I remember about that game. I was in a zone. If it was our game to win, I was going to figure out a way to do it. That was my mindset."

Jackson was simply incredible.

Against Westmar High School – which was located in Lonaconing, Maryland; a place nearly as isolated and obscure as Mardela – she scored 44 points and grabbed 11 rebounds that day at Catonsville Community College. 21 of those points came from the seven three-pointers Jackson swished, and just one point came from the free throw line. The rest were either fast break lay-ups or regular old field goals.

"She did a spin move and finger roll and (the referees) called a walk, only because they had never seen a girl do that before," said Ron Wainwright, who was then the head boys coach at Mardela.

Jackson was indeed a one-woman wrecking crew that day, and did all that while facing a box-and-one defense. It was – and as of 2022 still is – the third-most points scored in a state final four game by a single player. Her day was so impressive that it is still highlighted in the state's record book for girls basketball. Jackson also still holds the state record for most three-pointers made in a state tournament game.

But it all wasn't enough. Jackson scored 44 of the Warriors' 52 points. Westmar scored 57.

And just like that, Tia Jackson's high school basketball career was over.

With averages of 43.2 points and 19.1 rebounds per-game, Jackson claimed a third-straight Bayside Player of the Year award. Two months later, her No. 11 jersey was retired by Mardela

Just before her senior year ended, at one of the final track meets of her career, a North Caroline runner asked Jackson for her autograph. She might not have won a state title for the Warriors, but she shattered records and became a local legend – which wasn't so bad for someone who once told Barbara McCool that she wasn't a basketball player.

And then, Jackson was off to Iowa City, ready to start from scratch again

"They say that if a coach has one really, really great player in their coaching career, they should consider themselves lucky," McCool told the Daily Times. "I believe I've had the best player in Maryland and probably the best in a lot of states."

***

What was somewhat remarkable about Tia Jackson's high school career – maybe even more than the boatloads of points and rebounds she collected – was that she never suffered a significant injury that forced her to miss playing time, despite all the minutes she played and how much McCool's Warriors relied on her.

In her first year at the University of Iowa, the game began to catch up with her. In the second game of her collegiate career, she went up for a routine rebound, but her landing was unexpectedly altered. Her right knee buckled and she was taken out of the game. She had torn some cartilage in it and elected to have surgery to repair it, forcing her to miss the next five games. Jackson was solid in her return, scoring 10 points in 13 minutes against No. 16 Washington, and she ended her injury-shortened freshman campaign averaging 4.5 points and 2.3 rebounds per-game.

On the Eastern Shore, Jackson – standing around 6-feet tall by the time she graduated – was often the tallest player on the court. In the Big Ten, that simply wasn't the case. In addition to wearing a new jersey, living in a new place and adjusting to a new role, Jackson also had to learn a new position. She spent the summer between her freshman and sophomore seasons improving her defense and ball-handling, and adding bulk to her lanky frame.

By her junior year, Jackson had settled in quite comfortably to her role as a wing player, typically playing either the two or the three in C. Vivian Stringer's offense. She had also become the team's go-to stopper, transforming herself into somewhat of a lockdown defender.

In the previous season, after winning the Big Ten, Iowa had been upset in the second round of the NCAA Tournament by Missouri State. Still, a lot of folks had high hopes for the 1992-93 Hawkeyes. Stringer's husband Bill thought they could make history.

"Bill thought (the 1992-93 team was) something special," Stringer told the Gazette of Cedar Rapids. "He thought they could go to the Final Four."

Bill Stringer wasn't just the head coach's husband. He was also the team's strength and conditioning coach. Jackson called him "the team dad" and "our sports psychologist."

On Thanksgiving morning in 1992, the Hawkeyes' world was shaken when tragedy struck. Jackson was preparing to go to her head coach's house for lunch when an assistant coach called. Bill had suffered a heart attack. He died later that day.

Stringer took a leave of absence from the team to grieve over the unexpected death of her husband. While she was gone, all Jackson and the Hawkeyes did was play some of the best basketball of their lives. They were inspired and determined.

"Not that we weren't already motivated, but it was another nudge to say, 'We're going to do this for Coach Stringer.' We played out of our minds all year," Jackson said. "Nothing was going to stop us."

Under assistant coach Marianna Freeman, Iowa started the season 5-0, beating Pitt, No. 4 Maryland, West Virginia, Charlotte and Drake. In that game against the Terps in College Park, Jackson had 10 points, eight rebounds and an assist against Maryland and her old high school rival, Kesha Camper, who was held scoreless in four minutes of action.

Stringer returned to the bench and – aside from a slip-up vs. No. 10 Colorado – the Hawkeyes kept winning. And they kept playing through personal losses too. In January of that season, Chris Street – a star player on Iowa's men's team – was killed in a car accident when his vehicle collided with a snow plow. With Bill Stringer and Street on their minds, the Hawkeyes won 17 games in a row before a pair of back-to-back losses to Penn State and Ohio State in early March. Iowa bounced back, beating Minnesota in its regular season finale to claim a share of the Big Ten title.

Iowa was a No. 2 seed in the 1993 NCAA Tournament and was supposed to host games for the earlier rounds, but their home arena – the Carver – had booked a Guns N' Roses concert. So, the Hawkeyes had to hit the road.

No matter. Iowa thumped host Old Dominion in Norfolk, Virginia, 82-56, then beat Auburn by 13 points for a spot in the Elite Eight, which would be played back home in Iowa City, now that Axl Rose and his buddies' rock show was over. Waiting for the Hawkeyes was Pat Summitt and the Tennessee Volunteers. Entering the game, Summitt had 499 career victories. Tennessee players wore wrist bands commemorating her expected 500th win. The Hawkeyes noticed. And they took it personally.

In a 72-56 victory, Jackson led all scorers with 21 points and six rebounds as Iowa punched its first-ever ticket to the Final Four. The Hawkeyes danced and celebrated in the locker room until they lost their voices.

Making the Final Four with Iowa and Stringer is a special memory for Jackson, but even more vivid for her is what happened in the next game – at the Final Four in Atlanta, against a familiar foe in Ohio State.

The Hawkeyes led by two points late in the game. Then, with 11 seconds to go, a Buckeye freshman sliced by Jackson for the game-tying lay-up.

"It was Katie Smith," Jackson says, the play still itching at her to this day. "I'll never forget it."

In overtime, Jackson scored a on a lay-up with 54 seconds to play to tie the game up. Ohio State knocked down a free throw moments later to take the lead, and the Hawkeyes mishandled their final possession. The Buckeyes won, 73-72. Again, Jackson led all scorers with 22 points.

"I think if you're competitive, you remember the loss. And I was guarding the player who scored the bucket (to send it to overtime). I thought she had used her dribble already and she obviously didn't, and got away with going around me and scoring," Jackson said. "And we had handled Ohio State (earlier in the year). So, they weren't even an issue. In our minds, we'll be in the championship game. Didn't work."

Jackson started every game her junior year at Iowa except for the season opener. She averaged 13.2 points, 5.8 rebounds and 1.9 steals per-game, playing about 28 minutes a night. She was named Honorable Mention All-Big Ten and to the Mideast Regional All-Tournament team. Jackson had established herself as a player who could perform on big stages, and as one of the conference's top defenders.

Iowa began the next season with a 5-0 start and were ranked No. 2 in the AP Poll. But after a Dec. 19 victory against James Madison, Jackson – who was averaging 16.8 points per-game – was done for the year. It was her right knee again. This time, she had torn her ACL. Without Jackson, Iowa lost in the second round of the 1994 NCAA Tournament to Alabama.

After hobbling through a fifth season at Iowa, Jackson was again named All-Big Ten Honorable Mention again and graduated with a bachelor's degree in media studies and film. She left the school ranking in the top 10 all-time in rebounds and steals. As of 2021, Iowa has only made the Elite Eight one other time – doing so in 2019 with a squad led by the stellar post play of Megan Gustafson. The Hawkeyes haven't appeared in a Final Four since 1993.

***

Tia Jackson was at a crossroads when she left Iowa. She assumed her basketball playing days were over as the WNBA did not exist yet. The way she saw it, she had two options: Pursue a career in media and take a job at ESPN, or turn to coaching.

Before the second knee injury of her collegiate career, Jackson had never really considered the latter to be a path for her. But while sitting on the bench and rehabbing her knee, she discovered a new perspective.

"Being sidelined from an injury just gave me an appreciation for coaching. I started to see the game from a different lens. I fell in love with it," Jackson said. "I wanted to play until my legs fell off – which, somewhat happened – but I wanted to coach too."

Jackson started making calls and received two assistant coaching offers, one from Auburn and one from David Glass at Virginia Commonwealth University. Glass had recruited Jackson to Notre Dame when he was an assistant there and VCU was closer to home. Plus, word had spread that the WNBA was coming in 1997 and Glass gave her some time off to rehab from her injuries and train for the new league.

After spending the 1996-97 season on VCU's sidelines, Jackson was invited to a pre-draft camp for the WNBA.

"It was basically, may the best woman win," Jackson said. "And I wound up getting drafted. So, that was pretty cool."

The former Mardela Warrior was the ninth overall pick, selected by the Phoenix Mercury who were then coached by women's basketball legend Cheryl Miller. She was giddy about landing Jackson. "She can not only be our defensive stopper, but can light it up," Miller told the Arizona Republic. "She can put pressure on the defense with her offense."

But Miller wasn't getting the Tia Jackson of 1993 that had shined in the NCAA Tournament. She was getting one who, at that point, had underwent four knee surgeries. Jackson made a promise to herself before the season began: if she needed to go under the knife again, her playing days were finished.

"I wanted to play, but I kind of vowed to myself that if I had to have another surgery – and in my mind, I'm thinking my knees – then I was going to be done," Jackson said. "And then I ended up tearing my shoulder. My body couldn't take anymore. I just walked away."

Jackson wound up playing in 27 games for the Mercury, who appeared in the Western Conference Finals. In her last season of playing basketball, she averaged 2.8 points and 2.2 rebounds per-game – a long way from those 40-point clips at Mardela. Her best game that year came in a July 31, 1997 loss to the Cleveland Rockers, as she piled up 11 points, eight rebounds, two steals and a block in 16 minutes of action.

With her playing career in her rearview, Jackson began climbing the coaching ladder. After spending the 1998-99 season at VCU, she went to the west coast where she was an assistant coach at Stanford and then at UCLA. In 2005, she came back to the east coast when she was offered a job on Gail Goestenkors' staff at Duke, where she helped the Blue Devils reach tremendous heights and began to make a name for herself as one of the top recruiters in the game.

Jackson got back to the Final Four in her first season at Duke, but the Blue Devils – led by Alison Bales, Monique Currie and Lindsey Harding – lost in the national championship game. The next year, they captured an ACC regular season title and appeared in the Sweet 16.

Goestenkors left Duke that offseason to become the head coach at Texas and Jackson departed too, becoming the head coach at Washington in the Pac-12. In her four seasons there, she consistently recruited well – bringing in a top 10 class in 2008 – but the Huskies just couldn't piece together a ton of wins under Jackson. The Huskies took a trip to the WBI quarterfinals in 2010, but missed the postseason in Jackson's other three seasons on the job. After going 45-75 over four seasons, Jackson resigned.

"The bottom line is: win some games. And that didn't happen," Jackson told the Seattle Times. "So, it was best for them to go in a different direction and I don't think there's anything wrong with that… It was definitely a mutual discussion. I can tell you nobody wanted to win more than me."

Jackson went home to Maryland and hung out with her family. After the Washington situation turned sour, she considered taking the year off. But then her phone rang. It was C. Vivian Stringer, who was now the head coach at Rutgers. Carlene Mitchell was leaving her staff to go to UC Santa Barbara, and Stringer wanted Jackson to fill the void on her bench. Jackson obliged. In four years at Rutgers, she helped bring a top five recruiting class twice and helped guide the Scarlet Knights to three postseason appearances.

Jackson's next stop was Miami, as she joined Katie Meier's staff in 2015 and returned to a place where she spent part of her childhood. The Hurricanes made four NCAA Tournaments and Jackson helped mold a pair of WNBA Draft picks in Adrienne Motley and Beatrice Mompremier.

And then, in the summer of 2020, Duke called again.

Jackson wasn't looking to leave her post with the Hurricanes, but – just like she couldn't say no to Barbara McCool on that day in 1986 at Mardela – she couldn't turn down an offer from Kara Lawson, who was tapped to succeed Joanne P. McCallie in Durham, N.C. Jackson hopped from one ACC program to another and is now charged with rebuilding the Blue Devils.

"Duke has always had a pretty special place in my heart, from my first time here. I've always had an affinity for the school and the people here," Jackson said. "And then you insert Kara, and it just takes it to a whole 'nother level... I can definitely sell this woman. In addition to all of her accolades, she's an even better person. That makes what I do the most enjoyable thing ever. I work with someone who wants to impact the lives of young women and do it at the highest level. She's done more than walk the walk. She's done it all."

Coaching for Duke in January 2022, Tia Jackson calls out to her players inside Cameron Indoor Stadium. Photo by Mitchell Northam.

Duke cut its 2020-21 season short due to the COVID-19 pandemic, finishing 3-1. In the 2021 offseason, Lawson, Jackson and the staff combed through the transfer portal to assemble a talented team. Duke started the 2021-22 season strong, beginning it with a nine-game winning streak that included an upset over No. 9 Iowa. The Blue Devils also beat a ranked Notre Dame team, and were ranked as high as 15th in the AP Top 25 Poll. But the final stretch of the season didn't go their way. Duke was swept by rivals UNC and N.C. State, lost five of its last six regular season games and were ousted from the ACC tournament in the second round. When the NCAA Tournament bracket was released, Duke was left on the outside of the field.

But Jackson has helped Lawson assemble an impressive incoming recruiting class, and they'll likely dig through the transfer portal again. It won't be long before Jackson is on the sidelines of a NCAA Tournament game again.

***

As she coaches at the highest level of college basketball today, Tia Jackson thinks of her first basketball mentor often. Barbara McCool did so much for Jackson, from training her in early hours of summer mornings, to making her wear funny shoes that would build up her legs, to driving her to prospect camps from Knoxville to Syracuse.

McCool was the girls basketball coach at Mardela from the fall of 1965 until her death in 2009, a total of 44 years. In that time McCool touched thousands of lives and won hundreds of games. She went 5-0 in Bayside Conference Championships for girls basketball and guided her Warriors to six state final four appearances. She coached scoring machines like Rasheedah Akram, phenoms like Jackson and a host of other talented players, from Pam Hopkins to Casey Morton.

She was small, but McCool was a larger-than-life figure on the Eastern Shore with a fiery spirit and an unmatched enthusiasm for high school athletics. As a coach, she could be tough; as hard as an Augusta brick. But if you played for her, if she cared for you, she'd do anything for you.

"She required a lot out of her athletes, but she'd look after them," said Pocomoke's David Byrd. "She was another one, where, if you were getting ready to play Mardela, you're in for a scrap. She was a fireplug."

"I miss her. We were pretty close."

One time, Byrd and McCool were at a meeting with every athletic director in the Bayside Conference. McCool had her cell phone placed in front of her on the table during the meeting. Then it buzzed. Then a tune played…

> *'Cause I'm a redneck woman*
> *I ain't no high-class broad*
> *I'm just a product of my raisin'*
> *I say "hey, y'all" and "yee-haw"*

McCool let it ring and she kept on talking. She eventually turned her phone off, but not before Byrd and the other athletic directors had a good laugh. "We never let her live that down," Byrd said. "That was so typical. She didn't even blink. Just kept right on talking."

Byrd and McCool often rode together to those MPSSAA meetings, talking about basketball and whatever else came up. Byrd's daughter got her first teaching job under McCool at Mardela.

When Paul Butler returned to WBOC16 in 2005 as the sports director after a tour through the southeastern part of the country, he wanted to add a new wrinkle to the local sportscast. Since leaving WBOC in 1995, the 1980 Wi-Hi graduate had worked in Mobile, Shreveport and Charlotte, and was also an NFL on FOX sideline reporter at his final stop before returning to his hometown. When he got back to WBOC, he wanted to do live reports every Friday night during basketball season, talking with a head coach just before the tip-off of a big game.

But when Butler went to Mardela, McCool wasn't all that interested in taking up the limelight. Often, she'd pull over a player or an assistant coach to talk to Butler instead.

"She'd rather have you interview her players," Butler said of McCool. "She didn't want the focus to be on her. She wanted it to be on the people on the court.

"She didn't care about the interviews or being on camera or anything like that. She was more concerned about her student athletes. She wanted them to be great people, get their education and prepare for the next level. That was her main thing. And then, yes, she wanted them to be good basketball players. She did a great job coaching them. Mardela was always one of the top teams, always vying for a chance to go to the state final four... When she passed away, Wicomico County certainly lost a legend."

McCool began a battle with lymphoma in 2008 that called for six rounds of chemotherapy. She continued to coach through it and missed just one game – the first of her 44-season career.

Butch Waller and McCool had a friendly and professional relationship. For decades, he was the most seasoned and most-winningest boys basketball coach in Wicomico County and she was the same on the girls side. "Barb was hard to get close to," Waller said. "She was all business."

When McCool was in the hospital, basically on her deathbed, Waller went to pay her a visit. Waller didn't know how bad off she was at the time, and McCool wasn't supposed to have any visitors that day that weren't immediate family members. But Waller knew the nurses and talked his way in to see his friend. But McCool was asleep and hooked up to some machines. Instead of disturbing her, Waller wrote her a note:

"Barbara, you've beat a lot of things. Come on, you can beat this. I'm thinking of you. – Butch Waller"

McCool died just weeks later on Oct. 21, 2009, at the age of 71.

In 2015, Wicomico County named two trophies after McCool and Waller, awarded each season to the county's most outstanding basketball players. The boy gets the Waller Trophy and the girl gets the McCool Trophy.

"She epitomizes what coaching is all about at any level, at any sport," Waller told Justin Odendhal of the Daily Times. "If my name is going to be beside somebody, I'd like mine to be beside hers."

Every time Tia Jackson goes back home to the Eastern Shore, she drives – whether it's her car or a rental – to Mardela Middle and High School and pulls into the same spot that McCool parked in every day. And she thinks of that little woman who stopped her in the hallway and asked her a question that changed her life.

"And I'll just sit there. Every time I went home, I would stop at Mardela to see her. That's my way to kind of still have my memory of her and just everything that we've done at Mardela and what Mardela has done for me," Jackson said. "For such a tiny lady, she always packed a powerful punch. I don't say that in a negative way, but how impactful she was in the lives of students that she came across. I'm just one of hundreds. I marvel at what she's done and how she's done it, and I try my best to make her proud showing some examples of that in what I do.

"There wasn't a certain phrase she used, but remaining humble was a big thing with her. It resonated with me just, you know, never forgetting where you come from."

Mardela renamed its basketball court for its longtime girls head coach, Barbara McCool. Photo by Mitchell Northam.

KELLEY GIBSON:
A REAL ROLE MODEL FOR EASTON

"I'm an example that it can happen." – Kelley Gibson

In high school basketball on the Eastern Shore, dynasties are mega rare, akin to acquiring a proper crab cake outside of the Chesapeake Bay watershed or finding someone who struck out Harold Baines while he was smashing baseballs in St. Michaels. In field hockey, Susan Pusey's Pocomoke Warriors had separate runs of eight and five consecutive state championship wins. In football, John Usilton's James M. Bennett teams won three titles in four seasons, between 1982 and 1985.

But in basketball? It has proven to be extremely difficult. On the boys' side, only Somerset High School ever won back-to-back state titles, in 1965 and 1966, and that was before all public schools in Maryland were desegregated. And Somerset dropped down from Class B to C for their second crown. Bill Cain guided Crisfield to five Bayside championships and four state titles between 1973 and 1983, but never won consecutively at the state level.

Perhaps the only team that can truly stake its claim as a dynasty in the modern-era of Shore hoops are the Easton girls teams coached by Tom Callahan. They won three straight Bayside Championships and captured back-to-back state titles in the early 1990s. As of this writing, the group of gals are the only basketball teams from the Shore – boys or girls – to win consecutive state crowns in the same classification.

Easton was difficult to beat for a few reasons: Callahan was a master motivator, Kelley Gibson was arguably the best player in Maryland at that time, and there wasn't a team on the Delmarva Peninsula or in the state who could consistently contain her and Tamara Coursey at the same time.

"Kelley's skill level was out of this world. She was destined for the WNBA," said Tom Corsey, a longtime assistant coach at Colonel Richardson High School. "She had something you can't take away, something you can't teach: her drive. She knew she was going to the WNBA and she let it be known."

Unlike the now-removed shrine to the Talbot Boys – which stood on the courthouse lawn in Easton as the final sanctuary of the last public testament to the Lost Cause in Maryland – Gibson's legacy is one of countless victories.

Gibson won at every level she played at. First for Easton, then at Maryland, then in the WNBA as a member of the Houston Comets, and then finally as a longtime college assistant coach, helping guide several teams toward NCAA Tournament berths.

She is someone that all people of Easton can – and should be – proud of.

***

Kelley Gibson led Easton to back-to-back state titles in 1993 and 1994. University of Maryland Athletics.

Kelley Gibson was born in Easton Hospital and has lived in Talbot County for most of her life. Her father, a Navy veteran, had the family living in Norfolk for a few years when Gibson was a child and when he was stationed there. When the Gibsons moved back to Easton, they settled in a neighborhood along Graham's Alley in the center of town, a place everyone called "The Hill."

The Hill is a historically majority Black community in Easton that is one of the oldest of its kind in the country. It was founded in 1788 by freedmen. In Talbot County, many African-Americans were free from slavery before the Civil War ended. They lived in Easton alongside white folks, working as merchants, carpenters, nurses and farmers, but this little pocket of a neighborhood in Easton was theirs.

As a child, Gibson was, as she says, "a tomboy." If Gibson wasn't at home, she was outside, at a park or on a street, playing some sort of game. She played everything with her brother and her cousins and kids from the neighborhood, from football to baseball to kickball.

"I was outside, just playing, playing, playing," Gibson said. "But basketball was the sport I fell in love with. For me, basketball was just in my family. Everyone from my uncles to my dad to my brother to my cousins. It was always a sport that was just in my family."

Gibson and her group found creative ways to play basketball too. Sometimes, milk crates were available and they could nail those up and shoot through those. Other times, they had to improvise.

"We would take a tire and beat the spokes out and create that circle and hang that up on the tree," Gibson said. "So, then you have a hole and you have a ball. We just played. We figured out ways to create courts… I was just an active kid. I just wanted to play."

The world was Gibson's playground.

As she got older, Gibson began to look up to the boys basketball teams at Easton High School. Led by her cousin Deon Gibson, the squad also featured Wes Cornish, Wayne Wilson, Duane Cephus and Dondre Phoenix. The Warriors went to the Bayside Conference Championship game in 1988 and appeared in the state semifinals. Coached by McKinley "Mac" Hayward, it was the first state final four trip for Easton in 20 years.

"The boys basketball team was everything," Gibson said of her older cousin's squad. "They were one of the best boys teams in the whole Bayside. The high school games were jam-packed. I was trying to be like them."

Meanwhile, the Easton girls team was, frankly, an abomination. In the 1987-88 season, the Warriors girls went 0-19. When they faced rival North Caroline, the Bulldogs absolutely stomped them, 91-2. No team deserved to beaten that badly, but deserve had nothing to do with it. For North Caroline head coach Jackie Pinckens, it was just business.

Gibson didn't know and didn't really care how good or how awful the girls team at Easton was.

"To be straight-up with you, I had no clue what their records were," she said. "The only history of girls basketball that I was aware of during that era was Tia Jackson at Mardela Springs with Barbara McCool."

For her, entering her freshman year at Easton High School, the girls team was the first real opportunity Gibson had to play organized basketball. Her middle school didn't have teams. The closest thing she had to organized ball was playing with the boys at the YMCA, where'd she play in pickup games with her cousin Deon and North Caroline's Jeff Chambers. And even after she joined the Easton girls varsity as a freshman, she still went to the YMCA after practice for runs with the boys.

"All I knew was playing with the boys. Having an opportunity to play with girls, during my era… It was all boys," Gibson said. "It was all about, 'What's Deon doing? What's his team doing?' I went to the games and studied his jump shots. I wanted to shoot like him. I didn't have anyone to look up to from a female's perspective."

***

Working under Lee Hutchison, Tom Callahan was an assistant coach on the Easton team that lost by 89 points to North Caroline in 1988. And he never forgot it.

Callahan started teaching at Easton that year, giving lessons in psychology, sociology and history, and his wife was an art teacher. Callahan was a graduate of Towson University and then received his teaching certification from Washington College in Chestertown. Before teaching at Easton, he was a police administrator and a boat builder. Callahan's father was a teacher too, and his mother was administrator at a school of nursing.

After being hired at Easton, Callahan quickly immersed himself in athletics there, assisting with the JV football team and the varsity girls basketball team.

By the fall of 1990, Callahan was the head girls basketball coach, tasked with rebuilding a program that had two wins in the 1988-89 season, and five victories in the 1989-90 campaign. Luckily for Callahan, that was the same time 5-foot-10 Kelley Gibson was entering high school. Callahan told the Easton Star Democrat of his promising rookie: "She's going to make a lot of noise in the next couple years."

Except, Gibson made a ton of noise right away, like someone popped OutKast's "Stankonia" in a boombox and turned all the way up.

It was immediately discernible that Gibson was – if not a full-fledged phenom – then certainly one of the most talented girls basketball players the Bayside Conference had ever seen. In her varsity debut on Dec. 5, 1990, Gibson – then just 14-years-old – didn't start, but piled up 33 points, 13 rebounds, 10 steals and four blocks in a 60-39 victory over Crisfield. Again: Gibson came off the bench, as a freshman, and dropped a triple-double in her first-ever high school basketball game. Her teammates carried her around the court after the victory, and she would eventually carry them to new heights.

"Coach Callahan was an awesome guy with an awesome personality," Gibson said. "The not starting was something Coach Callahan did out of respect for the upperclassmen. It eventually changed."

Easton massively improved with Callahan as its coach and Gibson as its star. The Warriors finished the 1990-91 season with a 14-8 record and lost to Mardela in the quarterfinals of the 1A Region IV playoffs. Gibson finished that game with 28 points, and concluded her freshman campaign with per-game averages of 21.1 points, 10.8 rebounds, 3.2 steals and 2.8 blocks. The Star Democrat named her as the Mid-Shore Player of the Year. "She can make our team or break the other team," Callahan told the newspaper.

The Warriors lost twice to North Caroline during Gibson's freshman year, but showed the Bulldogs that Easton was no longer a guaranteed victory for them.

"They were our No. 1 rival. Cambridge was the rival for the boys, but for us, it was always North Caroline," Gibson said. "We would get a nice crowd for those games."

Over the next three seasons, Easton went 7-0 against North Caroline as Gibson got better and other talented players emerged for the Warriors.

***

In Easton's first game of the 1991-92 season, Tamara Coursey made it known that Kelley Gibson wasn't the only player opposing teams had to worry about when facing the Warriors. In a season-opening 58-34 win over Crisfield, Coursey had 22 points, six assists and five steals. Gibson also added 20 points and four blocks.

Coursey grew up playing with the boys too, on playgrounds in Denton and at the YMCA in Easton. She played slick and hard, like lipstick on a bathroom mirror. Coursey had quick feet, a smooth shot, and was a persistent defender.

"Tamara was feisty," Gibson said. "She had a nice three-point shot, was a good distributor and a very good defender. We were a very good defensive team. Tamara was kind of the head of the ship and I was the anchor."

With Gibson and Coursey leading the way, Easton finally felt like it had enough talent to beat North Caroline. On Dec. 21, 1991, Coursey had 11 points and five steals, and Gibson poured in 28 points and 17 boards as the Warriors finally got the upper-hand over the Bulldogs, winning 56-51. Easton had a 60-34 advantage on the boards, largely due to Gibson and forwards Jennifer Price and Lee Wildasin, who pulled down 16 and 19 rebounds, respectively.

Wildasin was an athlete that might have not played basketball at Easton in the late 1980s. Softball and field hockey were her sports, so why put the effort in on the basketball court when the team might finish winless? But after Gibson's freshman season, other athletes at the high school wanted to be part of the success too. "A lot of it has to do with one good year," Callahan told the Star Democrat. "Now a lot of other girls are interested and they're coming out."

The victory meant the world to Callahan, Gibson and the Warriors, but it also legitimized Easton as a real contender for girls basketball supremacy on the Eastern Shore.

"We had a nice core," Gibson said. "I felt like we had an opportunity to do some special things."

Gibson had the skills of a guard, but at her height, she was taller than most players in the Bayside Conference and also had a real knack for scoring inside. So, Callahan often played her at center, despite her being just under 6-feet tall. That was largely because, in the paint, on each end of the floor, most teams couldn't stop Gibson from doing whatever she wanted. In a Jan. 17, 1992 victory at Cambridge, Gibson tallied 24 points, 27 rebounds and six blocks, prompting Cambridge coach John Wood to tell the Star Democrat: "When Kelley started going inside, we just didn't have an answer for that. She's super... We can't stop her. I don't know if anybody can."

Easton beat North Caroline again on Jan. 31, 1992, and a grin grew over Callahan's face as his Warriors built a 20-0 lead in the second quarter. North Caroline head coach Jackie Pinckens, who complained about the officials to newspaper reporters after the game, received a technical foul in the fourth quarter. Gibson and Coursey combined for 39 points in a 57-41 win. Callahan told the Star Democrat: "We've come a long way from 91-2."

Weeks later, Gibson and Coursey combined for 53 points in a 74-24 trouncing over North Dorchester to claim the north Bayside division title for the first time since 1978, and just the second time ever. "For a long time, Easton hasn't been a contender for anything," Callahan told the Star Democrat. But with him in the coach's seat and Gibson and Coursey on the court, Easton wasn't just a contender; they were the favorites.

Easton ended the 1991-92 regular season with a 17-3 record and faced Wicomico High School at the Wicomico Youth & Civic Center on Feb. 28 for the Bayside Conference Championship. Behind 26 points from Gibson and 19 points from Coursey, Easton marched to a 51-43 triumph for its first-ever conference crown. Wi-Hi head coach Howard Roberts told the Star Democrat after the game that Gibson looked "the second coming of Tia Jackson." Added Roberts: "Kelley Gibson was magnificent… If she was just a good player, we would have won the ballgame. She's a great player." Gibson also had 12 boards, three steals and three blocks.

Sometimes in tense games, Callahan had a habit of taking his necktie off his shirt and then tying it around his head. In one way, it was his version of the rally cap in baseball – it was time to get serious and kick the game into the next gear. But how serious can you take a man with a tie wrapped around his dome? So, it was also Callahan's way of adding levity to a situation too, and letting his team know that he wanted to win, but he wanted to have a hell of a lot of fun.

"He was a pretty fiery man," Gibson said. "That was definitely his way to amp it up a little bit."

Six days after winning the conference championship, Gibson dropped 43 points and 17 rebounds on Pocomoke to push Easton into the regional final. The next night, Snow Hill used a suffocating 2-2-1 zone press to rattle the Warriors. Despite Gibson's 27 points – which pushed her past the 1,000-point mark for her high school career – Easton fell 58-50 as Snow Hill continued on to the state semifinals.

Callahan was named Coach of the Year, Gibson – after averaging 23.7 points, 14.1 rebounds and 5.3 blocks per-game – was Player of the Year and Coursey made the All-Mid-Shore First Team.

Speaking to the Star Democrat, Snow Hill head coach Bob Mitchell peered into the future: "I think Easton will be back."

***

That summer, Steve Chaney, a new teacher at Easton who later became the head JV boy basketball coach at the school, introduced Kelley Gibson to the AAU circuit across the Chesapeake Bay Bridge.

"Growing up here, the biggest issue is exposure," Gibson said. "I didn't even know what an AAU team was."

She landed on a team called the Maryland Waves that was based out of Annapolis. One of her teammates was Chanel Wright-Greene, who went on to play at North Carolina and then briefly in the WNBA, and another was Kacy Williams, who would leave Georgetown as the Hoyas' all-time leader in assists. The team lost at AAU nationals that summer to a squad called Carolina Flight, which featured future WNBA talents Allison Feaster and Tiffani Johnson.

But Gibson had a good showing at that tournament and throughout the summer, and that's when the offers started flowing in. Halfway through her junior year, she had more than 30 Division I offers. Ultimately, she narrowed her choices down to Virginia and Maryland.

"ACC basketball, for me, that was all I knew. Maryland, Virginia, N.C. State," Gibson said. "It was all about that. That was what I watched and I wanted to be a part of it."

Gibson attended an overnight camp at Maryland that summer and the campus quickly hooked her.

"It gave me like five days to interact with everyone," Gibson said. "I fell in love with everything about the university. Maryland was always in my heart. I felt it in my heart. That was where I wanted to be."

***

Easton again opened with Crisfield to start Kelley Gibson's junior season, and again, she and Tamara Coursey dominated, combining for 53 points in a 70-40 victory.

And again, the duo led Easton past North Caroline on Dec. 20, 1992, as Gibson scored 31 points in a 73-59 win. And again, Easton romped through the regular season, as Gibson drained three-pointers from NBA-range and grabbed the attention of collegiate scouts. After scoring 40 points with little difficulty against Kent County, Gibson told the Star Democrat: "I didn't think it was going to be so easy." After she notched a triple-double in a road win over Pocomoke for Callahan's 50th career win, Pocomoke head coach Gail Gladding told the Salisbury Daily Times: "Gibson has to be one of the consistent outside shooters I've seen."

Easton ended the 1992-93 regular season with just two losses, and then topped Wi-Hi again in the Bayside Conference Championship, 71-64, for the Warriors' second straight conference title. Gibson had 35 points, but Easton had to finish the job without her as she fouled out with 1:32 to play. Coursey added 15 points and Lee Wildasin hit a pair of mega free throws in the closing moments of the game to secure the win and keep Wi-Hi at arms-length.

In the regional final, Gibson showed up big. She had 26 points, 13 rebounds and three blocks on March 5 at Maggs Gym in Salisbury, and Coursey added 23 points, as Easton won the 1A Region IV title with a 63-50 triumph over Pocomoke. In the third quarter of the win, Gibson and Coursey scored all but two of Easton's 24 points. Callahan said after the victory to the Star Democrat: "I've got this great love that's swelling up inside of me for these girls and how hard and how well they played today."

Under Callahan's direction – and with Gibson and Coursey's play on the court – Easton went from 0-19 to region champs in five seasons.

"I loved him to-death. He didn't have a ton of basketball background, but he was a great motivator and he was a competitor. He was in your face, but he instilled a competitive drive in us," Gibson said of Callahan. "You take on the personality of your coach. So, we were pretty competitive and we had every intention to win."

The success didn't stop there. At the state semifinals at the University of Maryland-Baltimore County, Gibson poured on 39 points in a 64-55 win over Milford Mill. The state final was postponed a few days because of an intense storm, but Easton wasn't shaken when it returned to UMBC on Wednesday, March 18, 1993.

Easton forced Williamsport into 19 turnovers, and Gibson had 25 points six rebounds and six blocks as the Warriors won 51-42. Coursey had 10 points and five steals before fouling out. In the modern-era, it was Easton's first-ever state championship in girls basketball. Regardless of if it was five-on-five or old-school six-on-six basketball, it was the first championship for Easton's girls since a May Brooks-coached team last won in 1949.

Callahan, normally animated and loud on the sideline, was battling an illness during the game. Assistant coaches pulled him off the bench to accept the trophy. He handed it off to Gibson, who lofted it up during a celebratory team photo.

"The locker room, you know, it was the first time. It was a surreal feeling. We put Easton the map. And it was great celebrating with your teammates because we were all great friends," Gibson said. "We took a ride back to the Shore, got together at Tamara's house and celebrated and had a great time. It was just an awesome feeling."

Once more, Gibson and Callahan swept Player and Coach of the Year honors. She averaged 26.8 points, 15.9 rebounds, 5.7 steals, 5.2 assists and 3.4 blocks as a junior.

And that April, she signed a letter-of-intent to attend the University of Maryland on a basketball scholarship. Gibson picked the Terps over offers from Virginia, Vanderbilt, Clemson, Duke, Iowa, Temple, Georgetown, Ohio State, USC and several others. That November, longtime Maryland head coach Chris Weller told the Star Democrat: "Kelley is the best high school shooter that I have ever seen."

***

Kelley Gibson had landed her Division I college scholarship, but she still had another season of high school basketball to play. In the fall of 1993 – while she was earning her way onto the All-Mid-Shore volleyball team – Gibson was named as a preseason All-American by the popular basketball publication Street & Smith.

And Gibson lived up to that hype once basketball season got underway. In two of Gibson's first three games of the season – all wins, obviously – she had a pair of triple-doubles. She had 39 points, 22 rebounds and 15 steals in a 102-33 thrashing of Crisfield, and 27 points, 31 rebounds and 23 steals in a 101-20 beat-em-down of North Dorchester. Gibson let everyone in the Bayside Conference know that she planned to continue her dominance.

Until New Year's Day 1994, that is. Gibson and a few others were heading toward Unionville to see another friend that day. Gibson was in the back of the older car, one of those that had hard plastic seats, while her friend drove. "It was back in the deep country. It was a windy road," Gibson said. At some point, the driver lost control of the car and Gibson rocked forward, hitting the interior of the car hard and injuring her clavicle along with some muscles and tendons in her chest. She was sidelined for 25 days, and then returned as if nothing happened with an effort against Stephen Decatur that featured 19 points, seven rebounds, 10 steals and nine blocks on Jan. 26, 1994.

With Gibson back, Easton kept on rolling. In the Bayside Conference Championship in Salisbury, the Warriors snapped Parkside's 12-game win streak while taking a 56-50 victory to claim their third straight conference crown. Gibson had 31 points and was the only Easton player to score in double figures. Parkside had been the only Bayside team Gibson and co. had never beaten, so topping the Rams was like checking off a box on a to-do list for the Warriors.

"We knew we could win the Shore again," Gibson said. "Then it was a matter of getting to states, knowing who the competition was and then getting it done.

In the regional final, Easton got double-doubles from three players as Gibson, Lee Wildasin and German exchange student Kirsten Bergel combined for 56 points and 42 rebounds in a 76-44 win over Pocomoke. In the region final, Gibson and Tamara Coursey – for the last time – handed North Caroline a defeat, combining for 44 points in a 70-40 victory.

After getting past Catoctin, Easton ran up against Joppatowne in the 1A state final. And for one of the few times in her high school career, Gibson wasn't the biggest player on the court. Joppatowne had Brandi Barnes, a 6-foot-4 center who would also go on to play at Maryland.

"She was a legit center. And I played center, but I was really a guard. In high school, if you're the tallest player, you play in the post. So, I had to guard

Brandi," Gibson said. "She had broad shoulders, a center's body, a legit post, the featured player. It was a tough battle for us on the inside. I got beat up in that game."

Gibson powered through in her final game wearing the orange, black and white No. 32 jersey. She had 23 points and Coursey had 27 points in a 66-50 victory. Easton finished the season 25-1 and with back-to-back state titles. The 93-94 Easton girls are still the only girls team from the Eastern Shore to win consecutive state championships. They are also the last north Bayside team to win a state title in girls basketball.

"We knew, on that little area on Route 50 where they put Easton's state championships, we were going to have another out there. We were very prideful," Gibson said. "We had that Warriors' pride. What a way to go out, with a bang."

Gibson was the Mid-Shore Player of the Year again for the fourth time and was selected to the Baltimore Sun's All-Metro team after averaging 28.1 points and 15.6 rebounds per-game. She ended her high school career with 2,278 points, more than 1,000 rebounds and nine triple-doubles. With her leading the way, Easton went 12-2 in postseason play over four seasons. And between December 1992 and March 1994, the Warriors never lost a road game.

"Kelley was a great player," said former WBOC16 sports director Paul Butler. "We don't get a lot of attention for the women's players that we have on the Eastern Shore, but she was one that was just outstanding… She loved talking on the air. Sometimes, you get high school kids, you know, they'll give you one or two-word answers. Kelley would give you complete sentences. I loved interviewing her. She was one of those great players from Easton. She's an outstanding young lady, not only on the court, but off the court as well. Just handled herself well. Very dignified."

On Feb 24, 1997, Callahan won his 100th game. In the offseason, he resigned as the head coach of Easton's girls basketball team.

The Warriors haven't been back to the state final four since 1994. In March 2020, the Warriors were boarding a bus to go there when the state tournament was called off because of the COVID-19 pandemic.

***

The expectations set for Kelley Gibson at the University of Maryland were higher than an elephant's eye.

A few weeks before the season started, Terps' head coach Chris Weller was speaking to a group of reporters in Greensboro, North Carolina when she compared the Easton native to Scottie Pippen, who, at that time, had won three NBA championships, was a four-time NBA All-Star and three-time selection to the NBA's All-Defense team. Pippen was one of the NBA's best players. Gibson hadn't even donned the Maryland uniform yet.

Weller later felt like she had to apologize for the early praise, telling the Baltimore Sun: "I was trying to get people to identify her with someone they knew. Kelley, I'm sorry for putting all this pressure on you. But it's not as if coaches won't figure out how good she is."

During her recruitment, Maryland head coach Chris Weller compared Kelley Gibson's skillset to Scottie Pippen's. University of Maryland Athletics.

Gibson gave opponents a glimpse of her potential right away. In her Maryland debut, she had 12 points and five rebounds in a 68-51 win over Virginia Tech on Nov. 15, 1994. And fellow Eastern Shore native Kesha Camper, of Parkside, had six points in the victory. Camper was a senior and a captain during Gibson's freshman campaign.

"When you look at the history of Maryland, you know, you're trying to live up to the expectation of what was before you," Gibson said. "That was our pressure and it was a privilege. The tradition was unparalleled. Our group was expected to do some big things as a class."

Unfortunately, basketball fans never really got the chance to see if Gibson could become the Scottie Pippen of College Park because of her knees. During a Nov. 30, 1994 game against Howard, Gibson tore the ACL in her right knee. At the time of her injury, Gibson was leading the Terps in scoring through three contests with more than eight points per-game.

"It was first time really experiencing any true adversity," Gibson said. "It was pretty devastating, just going through the whole rehabilitation process and having to sit out. I was all new to that."

Gibson was back on the court the following season, just in time for ACC play. In a narrow 61-60 victory over Georgia Tech in College Park on Jan. 5, 1996, Gibson tallied a career-high 20 points. Her jumper from the foul line with eight seconds left was the go-ahead bucket for the Terps. A month later,

Gibson shined again in an upset over No. 14 Duke, as she had 14 points, seven rebounds and six steals in a 63-52 win over the Blue Devils in College Park. A few days later, Maryland beat another ranked opponent, this time No. 18 Clemson behind Gibson's 28 points, nine rebounds and four assists in a 74-72 victory. Her performances against Duke and Clemson earned Gibson ACC Rookie of the Week honors as a redshirt freshman. She won it for a second straight week after leading Maryland to a win over Wake Forest and scoring 27 points against Florida State.

By the end of the season, Gibson made the ACC All-Rookie Team and finished third in voting for ACC Rookie of the Year. She averaged 14.7 points per-game in conference contests, which led all ACC freshmen.

Gibson continued her steady play as a redshirt sophomore, started 14 of the first 19 games of the season. She notched 16 points in a win over Duke, 18 points in a topping of Iona, and was averaging 9.4 points and 4.2 rebounds per-game.

And then on Jan. 30, 1997, her knees failed her again. With six seconds to play against Florida State, Gibson fell during a baseline drive. It was her ACL, but this time in her left knee. Emotionally, Gibson was ravaged.

"That's when I really started to go, 'Okay. I don't know if I can do this anymore.' The second one really damaged my spirit. I felt like I couldn't go through it again," Gibson said. "But I had the support of my teammates and my family to keep me going."

Gibson's parents were upset too, and her father blamed Weller. He called the Baltimore Sun and vented, which sparked quite a bit of controversy. In a March 19, 1997 story published by Milton Kent of the Sun, Gibson's father claimed that Weller held meal money from Gibson, called her a "bitch" in front of the team, pushed her to play when she had asked to slow down, discouraged her from calling her parents, and "rode her so hard" that Gibson left practice in tears. The Sun noted that six players had issued complaints against Weller. Gibson's father, Greg Richie, told the Sun: "I'm bitter because she's hurt, beaten up and abused mentally and something has to be done."

Maryland officials investigated those complaints and publicly reprimanded Weller at a press conference, but did not ask her to resign. Three of Weller's assistant coaches left, and she said the players would have a say who she hired to replace them. Weller also hired a sports psychologist to the staff.

"I accepted a reprimand for making a few specific comments to a few individuals in the last year that could have been construed as personal attacks and I apologized for that," Weller told the Washington Post. "I'm going to coach the way I coach… I really don't feel bad about the things that I do. I'm not intimidated. I'm going to be me."

Athletic Director Debbie Yow told the Post: "A portion of the complaints were warranted. Part of it was a misunderstanding, a miscommunication."

Gibson could have transferred. Instead, she had a one-on-one meeting with Weller and cleared everything up. Sitting in Weller's office, Gibson told her: "I'm with you. I'm okay. I understand who you are as a coach."

Looking back on the incident with some hindsight, Gibson says: "It was a rocky time with the injuries and parents getting involved. For me, you know, you always have parents that want to protect their children… You have that dynamic – and I've seen it and experienced it now as a coach – where a parent is saying one thing, but this is how the kid truly feels, and you ultimately know that the parent is just trying to protect the child. So, I just had to reassure (Weller) that I was good and we were good."

Gibson and Weller moved on, and the Easton product continued to rehab from her latest knee injury. As a redshirt junior, Gibson played with a brace on one knee and a wrap on the other. Still, when healthy, Gibson played well. In an 84-62 upset that season of No. 7 North Carolina, Gibson contributed 13 points, 12 rebounds and seven assists. By then end of the 1997-98 season, Gibson had led the Terps in assists with 4.3 per-game, and blocked shots with 16.

But then, another knee injury surfaced during the offseason. During a pick-up game with teammates in August 1998, Gibson tore the ACL in her right knee again. This time around, Gibson wasn't frustrated or distraught; she was determined and motivated. This time, there was something more ahead for her than just finishing another season at Maryland.

"At that point I was like – the WNBA was starting and I always wanted to play professional basketball. I have to play. So, the third one was more like, 'I have to do this,'" Gibson said. "And I had some really good athletic trainers who put a different perspective on it. Like, it's just a knee. I remember hearing that. So, I was like, let's get it done. I was chasing a goal, chasing a dream."

By Christmas, Gibson was back in Terps uniform. In her final home game, a 92-79 win over Georgia Tech on Feb. 21, 1999, she had nine points and eight assists. In her last time wearing a Maryland jersey, Gibson had 11 points, four rebounds and four assists in an ACC tournament loss to Wake Forest in Charlotte.

Weller retired as Maryland's head coach in 2002. In her time leading the Terps, she won eight ACC tournament championships, four regular season ACC titles, and took Maryland to a pair of final fours. Despite some of their public differences, Gibson still appreciates her time with Weller.

"Coach Weller was an unbelievable teacher. She's a hall of famer," Gibson said. "You have some pioneers in our game that opened doors and paved the way for women's basketball. And I put her on that Mount Rushmore of pioneers. She's a winner. She was all about being the best you could be. She had high standards and was all about excellence. If you shoot for perfection, you'll reach excellence. And that was just the culture at Maryland. She taught me how to be great."

***

Kelley Gibson went unselected in the 1999 WNBA Draft, but was undeterred in pursuing her goal of joining the new professional women's basketball league.

And making a WNBA roster, it should be noted, is extremely difficult. By comparison, there are 450 roster spots available in the NBA with 15 players on each of the 30 teams. In the WNBA, there are 12 teams with 12 spots, giving us a total of 144 players. Only the best of the best of the best women's basketball players in the world get the chance to compete in the league.

Gibson went to New York in the summer of 1999. She linked up with an agent who landed her a few contracts with semipro leagues in the U.S. and with teams in Russia and Israel. When she wasn't playing, Gibson worked at a temp agency, performing various odd jobs. "I needed to eat. I needed cash flow," Gibson says. At the same time, she wasn't quite 100% recovered from her third knee injury, so the year allowed her to continue to get stronger.

In the summer of 2000, her agent called. Gibson had been invited to the preseason camp for the Houston Comets, winners of the last three WNBA championships. Gibson was elated, but she was also realistic. She looked at the Comets' roster and examined the collection of guards and wings: Jennifer Rizzotti. Tina Thompson. Cynthia Cooper. Sheryl Swoopes.

Some self-doubt creeped in. Gibson idolized Swoopes and had a poster of her in dorm room at Maryland.

Gibson packed a light duffle bag and headed for the airport in Newark, New Jersey. While waiting at the gate, Gibson noticed someone and did a double-take. "Oh shit," she said to herself. "Is that Coop?"

Indeed, it was Cynthia Cooper, the reigning three-time Finals MVP. Gibson – feeling a mix of nervousness, anxiety and excitement – introduced herself. The two then boarded the plane; Cooper took a seat in first class while Gibson trudged toward the economy section. When the plane landed, a limo pulled up. Cooper turned to Gibson and asked, "You want a ride?"

Yes, she did.

Shortly after the limo ride of a lifetime with a player she had long looked up to, Gibson found herself at a Comets practice. There she was, a kid from Graham's Alley in Easton, and across from her was Cooper and Swoopes. Gibson was absolutely starstruck.

Tammy Jackson, a veteran center who played college ball at Florida, pulled her aside and said: "Rookie, let me tell you something. You got a really good chance. You got a lot of potential. But you can't be in awe of Cynthia and Sheryll."

That helped. Gibson shrugged off her nerves. She then just saw Cooper and Swoopes as competitors. They were just two players she had to guard and score against, just like at the Talbot County YMCA, just like at Easton High School, and just like at the University of Maryland.

"That was my position. I had to guard those guys. So, after that moment, it was on," Gibson said. "I took every challenge to defend Cynthia or Sheryl. I mean, it was either one or the other every day. And they respected me because I challenged them. I didn't back down."

Gibson made the team, signing a contract with the Comets on May 2, 2000, largely because she could keep up with Cooper and Swoopes in practice and played hard against them.

Comets' head coach Van Chancellor told the Easton Star Democrat: "Kelley has a great quickness... Her defensive skills are great. You can't teach her athleticism."

And all season long, Gibson had to guard Cooper and Swoopes. Gibson described Comets' practices at that time like "having two Kobe Bryants" on one team. She said Cooper and Swoopes were so competitive that they skipped rest reps. And Cooper often showed up to practice two-and-half-hours before the scheduled start time.

"To be a part of that was unbelievable. It was the most competitive experience ever, those practices," Gibson said. "For me, everyone asks, 'Who's the best player you played against in the WNBA?' For four years, I went against Cynthia and Sherryl every day in practice. It gets no better than that. The level of competition was an all-time high."

Gibson scored her first WNBA bucket on June 15 tallying five points and three rebounds in a 77-53 win over the Miami Sol. Talking to the Baltimore Sun, Cooper said of Gibson: "That girl has stupid, mad, crazy game."

The Comets went on to win the WNBA Championship for a fourth straight time in 2000, sweeping each of their playoff opponents. Gibson played in 17 games that season. She won a title, showed she could play in the best women's basketball league on the planet, and realized a goal.

"Once it started, it was my ultimate dream to play in the WNBA," Gibson said. "And then, to win a title? That's the icing on the cake."

Gibson played three more seasons in Houston. In all, she featured in 100 WNBA games, making eight starts.

Her best game, arguably, came on June 15, 2002, in which she totaled 13 points, four rebounds, two assists and a steal against the Minnesota Lynx. She led the Comets in scoring that night and powered them to a victory.

On May 26, 2004, Gibson was waived by the Comets.

And in 2008, the Comets folded.

"Houston is a great city. The support for the Comets… The crowds were unbelievable. It was a great feeling," Gibson said. "Expansion needs to happen (in the WNBA). It has to happen. Now is a great time for it."

***

Kelley Gibson knew she wouldn't play basketball forever, and she knew what she wanted to do when her playing days ended. When the Houston Comets waived her in the summer of 2004, she told her agent she wanted to be a coach.

Gibson graduated from Maryland with a degree in kinesiology and figured her two career options were being a physical therapist or being a coach.

"After my first injury, being on the sideline, I saw the game from the coaches' lens," Gibson said. "I knew that was what I wanted to do once I finished my playing career. And after three injuries, you become a coach on the floor because you see everything. That's where it started for me."

Gibson's agent called Melissa McFerrin, who had just recently been hired as the head coach at American University. McFerrin had previously been the general manager for the WNBA's Washington Mystics, so the agent had some familiarity with her. At American, McFerrin had an opening for a graduate assistant and Gibson slid right in.

From there, Gibson kept climbing the coaching ladder. Her next stop was at the University of Maryland-Baltimore County where she worked under coach Phil Stern. In 2007, Gibson was part of a staff that helped guide the Retrievers to their first-ever appearance in the NCAA Tournament. To get there, UMBC – a seventh seed in the America East tournament – had to knock off the top three teams in the league standings in Stony Brook, Vermont and Hartford. "We did some special things there," Gibson said.

Gibson then coached at Maine, USC and Syracuse. In 2014, she was part of a staff at Syracuse that oversaw the program's first-ever NCAA Tournament victory. Gibson then spent time at Rutgers working under C. Vivian Stringer. In 2020, when Mardela's Tia Jackson jumped from Miami's staff to Duke, Gibson filled Jackson's vacancy for the Hurricanes.

As of the summer of 2021, Gibson isn't coaching in college. It remains to be seen what the next move is for the Easton product, now 44 years-old. She says she's still open to coaching, and ultimately wants to be a head coach, but doesn't want to go too far away from home with her parents growing in age.

"That's the magical question. I've been working on some side projects. I'm really passionate about bringing exposure here," Gibson says of the Eastern Shore. "In terms of the coaching profession, we'll see."

Gibson looks at the culture around football at North Caroline High

School, where a healthy Pop Warner feeder program has not only made the Bulldogs better, but also produced some big-time college players, like Kendron Wayman at Wake Forest, Ja'Mion Franklin at Duke and David Bailey at Colorado State. Gibson wants that for girls basketball across the Eastern Shore.

"I'm an example that it can happen," Gibson says. "It's just a matter of having hope, having someone lead you."

***

In 2001, Easton renamed a street for Kelley Gibson in the community she grew up in, commonly known as "The Hill." Gibson won a WNBA championship with the Houston Comets in 2000. Photo by Mitchell Northam.

Today, just a about two blocks west of Rise Up Coffee Roasters, a historical marker along Dover Road in Easton lets folks know where the Hill community is. And about 148 feet west of that marker – at what used to be the intersection of Dover Road and Graham's Alley – is something that will forever inform people where Kelley Gibson is from.

In April 2001, shortly after she won a WNBA title, Easton recognized Gibson. The town had a parade for her, the high school retired her No. 32 jersey, and they changed the name of Graham Alley to "Kelley Gibson Street," honoring and celebrating one of the best athletes that has ever called the Talbot County town home. The street renaming became forever official in 2016, when it was unanimously approved by the town council.

"It's surreal," Gibson said of the street sign that bears her name. "That's like, you dream – like, I want to play in the WNBA, I want to win a national championship – that's the ultimate. But for me, getting a street named after you? That's like another level for me. I never dreamed of that."

When Gibson was a child, she didn't have a woman who played basketball to look up to. She didn't know much about the girls program at Easton. Until she was in college, there was no WNBA.

Some folks say that you can't be something until you see it. If that's true, every little girl who dribbles a basketball in Easton can see Kelley Gibson now. They can see her winning championships, going to college, playing professionally and coaching.

And they can see her easily. All they have to do is look up when they're going down Dover Road.

THE MAN, SHOOTER COLLINS, AND TRIPLE OVERTIME

"I've seen a lot of ball players being here with Mr. Morgan. I've seen every one, pretty much. But I've never seen nobody like Albert." – Tom Corsey

The first time Merrill Morgan heard about *The Man* was from his longtime assistant coach, Tom Corsey. A 1972 Colonel Richardson High School graduate who started coaching with Morgan in 1979, Corsey was born and raised in Caroline County, and still lives there as of this writing.

Corsey began delivering reports to Morgan about *The Man* when he was a boy, attending Preston Elementary School. Corsey told Morgan, "You know, there's this kid in Jonestown that plays all the time. I've never seen anyone like him."

When *The Man* was entering the sixth grade, the principal at Preston Elementary told Morgan that he could start for Morgan's team, right then. Intrigued by the idea of there being some sort of uber-talented basketball prodigy in this slice of southern Caroline County, Morgan sought the boy out. To say he was impressed would be a massive understatement.

Morgan told the boy to keep working hard, and maybe, he might just start for the Colonels' varsity squad as a freshman. "You could tell he had all the skills," Morgan told the Baltimore Sun of his first encounter with *The Man*. "He was doing things the other kids couldn't; things some older kids couldn't."

About a year later, the Colonels were on a bus, on their way to play Easton during one of those rare winter days on the Eastern Shore that brings heavy snow. The fastest way to Easton from Colonel Richardson is through the windy backroads of Harmony and Bethlehem, but on a day where snow swept those roads, a bus driver would've likely been inclined to take a path along more main routes. So, the Colonels drove through Jonestown – a modest and historically-majority African-American community situated just outside Preston. The town was established by Jenkins Jones as a community of freedmen during the antebellum years and, according to harriettubmanbyway.org, the town may have assisted famed abolitionist Harriet Tubman in her missions.

As the Colonels plowed through Jonestown on that snowy day in the early 1990s, they passed by its only public park, which has a single small basketball court with one hoop. By the time the bus carrying Colonel Richardson's boys basketball team drove by, *The Man* had shoveled off a few spots on the court, so he could plant his feet safely and shoot.

Indeed, the boy that Morgan had sought out a year ago was out in the snow, working on his game, shooting free throws, unbothered by frigid temperatures. As they passed by the park, Corsey pointed and said, "There's *The Man*."

Albert Mouring would become one of the greatest, most talented and most successful basketball players to ever emerge from the Eastern Shore. After honing his skills by spending countless hours at the park in Jonestown and on a tiny patchy dirt court in his yard, he put Colonel Richardson on the basketball map, and earned Morgan's side invitations to play against teams from Baltimore and Washington D.C., and into tournaments like Slam Dunk to the Beach. A collection of prominent college coaches, including Gary Williams, Jim Calhoun, Leonard Hamilton, Dave Odom and Roy Williams, would come to southern Caroline County to recruit *The Man*.

Jonestown, a historically Black community outside of Preston, has just one public basketball court with one hoop. As a kid, this is where Albert Mouring played before he went on to star at Colonel Richardson High School and UConn. Photo by Mitchell Northam.

"It was hard to dribble on dirt, so it made me focus more on shooting," Mouring wrote in a Facebook post in March 2018. "I wanted to be a scorer and my weapon of choice was the jump shot. As basketball players get older, they lose their athletic ability – the jump shot never goes away. That's how I looked at it as a kid."

Mouring loved the game of basketball so much that he would sometimes be outside shooting well past dark, and long after his bedtime. It was a habit that forced his father – a supervisor at the nearby Pillsbury plant in Federalsburg – to install a light on the pole that held up the basketball hoop in the Mouring family yard.

"What he used to do was crazy," Corsey said. "In Jonestown, the park only has a few parts and pieces out there. One court, one basket and the monkey bars."

Mouring would shoot basketballs through the monkey bars and then chart them – shots missed, shots made – in a notebook he carried with him. When Mouring wasn't shooting the basketball, he was dribbling it. Corsey remembers seeing Mouring walking one day, starting his dribbling near Corsey's mother's home, near the end of Jonestown, and Mouring marched all the way to the town limits of Preston, a distance of about two miles.

"I never seen nothing like that in my life, the work habits that he had," Corsey said. "I've seen a lot of ball players being here with Mr. Morgan. I've seen every one, pretty much. But I've never seen nobody like Albert. His work habits and his desire to be what they named him, '*The Man.*' He wanted to be good."

Mouring would lead Colonel to a state final four appearance as a sophomore. By the time he graduated, he had scored 2,513 career points. Unofficially, the only person in the state of Maryland to score more points than him in boys public high school basketball was Pocomoke's Mike Roberts. In nearly every game he played – no matter the opponent – Mouring was often the best player on the court. And often, the margin between him and the next talented player wasn't particularly close.

And he'd let his opponents know it by doing things that only he could do. Morgan claims that Mouring had a three-point shot blocked only once in high school, by Bruce Green during a game at Kent County. Mouring responded by walking the ball up on the next possession and swishing a pull-up jumper from a deep distance – some say it was a halfcourt shot, others say it was about four feet behind where the NBA three-point line would've been. Either way, it was a hell of a long way away from the basket, and it was a shot that only Mouring could make; and Mouring loved taking those shots, in the way that sharks love blood.

"I don't think anybody ever stopped Albert Mouring," said former North Dorchester coach Vic Burns. "Albert was super. He was one of the better outside shooters we've had around here."

And still – as it always has been with most Eastern Shore prospects – non-believers questioned Mouring's skill level because of the competition he faced. William Wells, then the coach for Baltimore's St. Frances, told the Sun in 1997: "The kid has all the tools. He can shoot. He can go to the basket. The question is whether he could do it against city kids."

Spoiler alert: Mouring could.

At Princeton University's camp in 1996, Mouring won the three-point shooting contest. He dropped 31 points on D.C. powerhouse Gonzaga at the DeMatha Invitational the following season, leading head coach Dick Myers to say, "He even looks good when he misses." In the Charm City Classic in 1997, he scored 23 points. Then 38 against Cape Henlopen and 26 against Hodgson Vo Tech, both of Delaware. He capped his senior year off by scoring 14 points in 12 minutes in the Capital Classic, and Mouring was just the second from Caroline County ever invited to the prestigious all-star game in the DMV, following North Caroline's Jeff Chambers in 1989. In the program for the 1997 Capital Classic, the blurb next to his name read: "If you looked up the word 'offense' in the dictionary, you might find a picture of Mouring."

Indeed, Mouring could play with anyone, anytime, anywhere. He never shied away from the moment, from contact, from big games or monumental shots.

Colonel Richardson's Albert Mouring set the school's scoring record in 1996, dropping 62 points on Queen Anne's. Colonel Richardson yearbooks.

And every now and then, he'd bring the very best out of an opponent, which usually resulted in games that folks on the Shore would talk about for decades. One such contest happened at the Wicomico Youth & Civic Center on a Thursday night in 1996, and much was at stake.

On Feb. 29 that season, Colonel Richardson faced Crisfield in the 1A East regional semifinals. Colonel had Mouring and fellow Division I prospect Kevan Johnson. Crisfield, coached by the great Phil Rayfield, had Andy Collins.

"He was Steph Curry before Steph Curry," Collins' younger brother Andre said of him. "He could pass the ball, but he was more of a two-guard trapped in a small body. He could really, really, really shoot the ball and had a lot of range."

Andre Collins had one of the best seats at the Civic Center that day, just behind the Crisfield bench. As an eighth grader back then, he volunteered as the Crabbers' team manager. Up close, Collins witnessed his older brother mess around and catch a triple-double, and watched Mouring and Johnson combine for 75 points.

The younger Collins would later play four years of varsity basketball for Crisfield and lead the Crabbers to a state title in 2000. About 15 years later, he returned to the Shore as a coach and guided the teams at James M. Bennett and his alma mater. But when people ask him about the best high school game he's ever seen or been a part of on the Delmarva Peninsula, his answer isn't one he has to search long for. He always returns to that 1996 February night in Salisbury, watching his brother and Mouring trade three-point bombs.

"For me, it was the greatest high school basketball game I've ever seen," Collins says. "Just the caliber of players in that game. Just to see both of them pour everything into that game."

And there's a whole bunch of people who agree with him. It's best to let them tell the story.

The people here are identified by what their title or affiliation was in 1996. Unless it is specified otherwise, these quotes are from original interviews conducted by the author.

Colonel Richardson entered the 1995-96 season after making the state semifinals the season prior, finishing Mouring's sophomore campaign with a 22-3 record. Experts again expected the Colonels or Cambridge to emerge from the Bayside Conference's north division. After hitting 94 threes as a sophomore, Mouring was named Mason-Dixon Player of the Year at the end of the 1994-95 season. He shot 52.2% from behind the arc and averaged 24.8 points per-game. And in addition to Mouring, the Colonels returned big man Kevan Johnson too. He blossomed into a Division I prospect as a junior and was an All-Mason-Dixon and All-State selection along with Mouring, averaging 19.6 points and 14.2 boards per-game with his 6-foot-6 frame. The other players on the 1995 All-Mason-Dixon team included Cambridge's Hanee Camper, Laron Profit of Caesar Rodney, and Nandua's Loyal Grimes.

For the first time ever, the Associated Press conducted a weekly poll for boys high school basketball in the state of Maryland at the start of the 1995-96 season. Colonel Richardson was ranked first in 1A. Crisfield didn't receive any votes.

In its season preview on the Bayside Conference's south division, the Daily Times focused on Pocomoke and head coach David Byrd's chase for a state title. The Warriors won the Bayside Conference Championship in 1995 and finished 21-3. They were returning 6-foot-3 forward Mike Dennis and guard David Arnold, the latter of whom went on to play at the University of Delaware.

Crisfield was one of the final teams mentioned. Phil Rayfield was entering his seventh season at the helm of the Crabbers, but coming off his worst season yet, finishing the 1994-95 season with just four wins. In Crisfield's team capsule, 5-foot-7 junior guard Andy Collins was the third returner noted.

DOUG KING, WI-HI GUARD: "Andy was tough. He was probably the toughest one I had to guard, but we played zone a lot. Andy was the man. The first time I ever got ripped in my life was by Andy. I tried to cross him once and – boop – he looked back and started laughing at me."

PHIL RAYFIELD, CRISFIELD HEAD COACH (to the Daily Times): "Andy is top notch. He's come a long way this year in terms of leading the team."

BUTCH WALLER, WI-HI HEAD COACH: "Phil Rayfield was a good coach. And a gentleman. I've seen him get mad, and it's very vivid – I've seen those veins stick out the side of his neck – but he was always suited up and he didn't lose control."

GREG BOZMAN, CRISFIELD ASSISTANT: "I learned a lot about basketball from Coach Rayfield. He was more like a father figure or a philosopher. There would be so many times where, I'd go to work or something would happen, and he'd slip a little piece of paper in my pocket and it would be some quote from some book or some article he had read. But it was just what I needed to hear at the time to get me through the day."

MERRILL MORGAN, COLONEL RICHARDSON HEAD COACH: "Albert was an outstanding player. Probably the best player on the Shore. He had that good combination of being coachable and being the best player but also the hardest worker. He was unselfish too."

WALLER: "Albert was good. Thank God, I only played him once a year."

MORGAN: "Albert made seven or so threes in a game once against St. Michaels, and I was going to take him out as soon as he missed, but I kind of wanted to see if he could keep making them."

BOZMAN: "And Merrill Morgan was one of the greatest coaches ever around here."

RAYFIELD (to the Daily Times): "These were probably the two best teams in the league other than Cambridge."

TOM CORSEY, COLONEL ASSISTANT: "Two outstanding teams. Two outstanding coaches. Crisfield had one of them Collins boys."

The Crabbers started the season 0-3, then went on a tear, winning 15 of their next 17 games. On Feb. 19, Crisfield beat Pocomoke 66-63 on the road, completing a season sweep of the Warriors and setting up a three-way tie for the South's bid to the Bayside Championship game. Ultimately, the nod went to Wi-Hi following a lengthy meeting at Mardela. The Indians were 13-3 in-conference, but Crisfield and Pocomoke were each 12-3 as each Lower Shore school had a game taken away from them due to inclement weather.

"Crisfield appealed and was not happy with the decision," Roger Eareckson, then the Bayside Conference executive secretary, told the Daily Times. A 5-2 vote by county athletic supervisors ruled in favor of Wi-Hi.

"Pocomoke and Crisfield are getting the shaft," Rayfield told the Daily Times. "They've worked so hard, and this will be snatched up from them because of what? A snow game?"

In the north, Cambridge had a slightly better winning percentage than Colonel, which had played more games. The Vikings were 17-1 and the Colonels were 18-3. So, Grayson Hurley's Cambridge team rolled into the Wicomico Youth & Civic Center on Feb. 21 and rolled over Wi-Hi, 86-41. "It was bad," said Indians' guard Doug King. "The best player I played against was probably Hanee Camper. Hanee was the truth. Hanee was a pro." Camper had 17 points and seven rebounds, leading Cambridge to what was then the largest margin of victory in the Bayside title game.

In the playoffs, Crisfield was motivated and the Colonels showed no mercy. Mouring dropped 34 points and Johnson had 20 rebounds against North Dorchester in an 84-57 opening-round victory. The next day, Crisfield whipped St. Michaels, 77-41, behind Collins' 14 points, six assists and six rebounds. In the quarterfinals, the Crabbers beat rival Pocomoke for the third time that season, earning a hard-fought 54-48 victory behind Collins' 14 points, eight rebounds, seven assists and four steals. Meanwhile, Colonel topped Snow Hill 75-58, largely due to Mouring's 35 points.

This set up what would be a game for the history books – or, at least for this history book, anyway.

BILL WEBER, SCOREBOARD OPERATOR: "I was on the clock that night and did not want it to end. It was my third or fourth game that day."

DAVID BYRD, POCOMOKE BOYS HEAD COACH: "I've been at every Bayside game at the Civic Center since 1981. It was a packed house that time. It was a true shootout. I mean, deep shooting, just back and forth."

ANDRE COLLINS, ANDY'S YOUNGER BROTHER: "Albert and Andy were AAU teammates together with the Delaware Sharpshooters, so they had some history together... Unfortunately, I didn't get the chance to play against Albert."

SHAWN TUCKER, FORMER PARKSIDE PLAYER: "It was electric. It was back and forth, back and forth. It was shot after shot."

MORGAN: "It was awesome. It was a great spectator event. We had our two guys and they had the kid Andy Collins."

Crisfield opened the game with a 10-4 run and Mouring started it a bit cold, shooting 1-of-4 from the field in the opening quarter. Still, Colonel Richardson entered the second quarter with a 24-18 lead.

Colonel built a 43-33 lead with 2:40 remaining in the first half, but Crisfield ended the second quarter on an 8-2 run, largely due to Candido Ortiz slipping behind the Colonels' 2-3 defense for easy 10-footers.

Crisfield then seized the game in the third quarter and Collins turned his game up a notch. He flushed a pair of three-point bombs and dished assists to Darnell Turpin for two more deep shots. While Collins was finding the basket and his teammates with ease, the Colonels fell into a shooting slump, making just three of their first 12 shots in the third period. The Crabbers outscored the Colonels 24-13 in the third quarter.

BOZMAN: "Coach Rayfield liked the 1-2-2 (defense). You can't run it against everybody though."

TUCKER: "The Collins boy, he was the original. He could shoot it from anywhere. He was the original Shooter Collins."

BOZMAN: "That was the one game where Andy played like I think he should've played for his entire high school career. He could pass, he could dribble. When Andy turned on that light, you could just tell – he was special."

ANDRE COLLINS: "Andy was more of a sniper. He was stocky and could finish at the rim. But in high school, it wouldn't be nothing for him to dribble to half court and consistently make it from there."

BOZMAN: "Around here, you could get away with being a 5-foot-7 two-guard if you can score."

RAYFIELD (to the Daily Times): "Andy sees the court, finds the open man, has a great handle and can shoot. He has everything a top player could have. I even get him to sell popcorn sometimes for us."

CORSEY: "Albert and the Collins kid going at it… It was unbelievable. When you see two kids go at it like that, matching shot for shot… Both of them had that same desire, to will their teams to the win."

With 4:50 left in regulation, Crisfield led 69-65. And then, Mouring kickstarted a Colonels' run by slashing down the baseline and throwing down an emphatic two-handed jam in Darnell Turpin's grill. Mouring then scored the next 15 points for Colonel. With 11 seconds left in the fourth quarter, and with Turpin hanging all over him, Mouring hit a three-pointer that tied the game at 86-86 and ultimately sent it into overtime.

WEBER: "Albert and the Collins kid were bombing threes. My fingers hurt from pressing the score buttons."

BYRD: "Mouring could play, obviously. The kid could really shoot."

CORSEY: "Albert took the game over in the fourth quarter like I had never seen."

But, nine seconds after his game-tying shot, Mouring was called for his fifth foul while trying to spin around a defender at mid-court. He exited the game with 37 points and 12 rebounds.

RAYFIELD (to the Daily Times): "When Albert fouled out, I thought we had the edge, but they had plenty of players who stepped up."

ANDRE COLLINS: "Colonel had another guy too, Kevan Johnson. To me, he was more of the difference in that game. He was a man amongst boys. He could jump higher than a lot of people I've ever seen on the Bayside. He had a power-type of game. He doesn't get talked about enough, if you ask me."

DERRICK FOOKS, Pocomoke assistant coach: "Kevan Johnson could jump out of the gym."

MORGAN: "Kevan had a bad ankle. He did everything he could to play."

CORSEY: "Kevan was a rebounder and the backbone of the team. Everything went through Kevan. Even though you had Albert, you had to pay special attention to Kevan. He could get the ball off the top of the backboard. We had a real two-headed monster."

KEVAN JOHNSON, COLONEL FORWARD (to the Daily Times): "I told them to just throw the ball in the air high and near the basket."

Johnson exited the game for only 16 seconds during the final two minutes in the fourth quarter. In the first overtime, he scored six of the Colonels' 10 points. To send the game into its second extra session, Tarrell Hammond knocked down a two-pointer, tying the game at 96-96. Hammond had a chance to win it for the Colonels, but was knocked over on his last-ditch leaner.

While Johnson toughed it out and continued playing on a bum foot, the referees banished Andy Collins from the game with 2:19 to play in the second overtime after Darryl Thompson of the Colonels drew a charge on him, resulting in his fifth foul. Collins went to the bench with 37 points, 17 assists and 15 rebounds.

ANDRE COLLINS: "I was actually in pain for my brother."

RAYFIELD (to the Star Democrat): "That certainly hurt us. Probably not as bad as them losing Albert."

Without its two biggest shot-makers and stars – Mouring and Collins – the game continued and was sent into a third overtime when Crisfield's Candido Ortiz pounced on a loose ball and nailed a 24-foot three-pointer with seven seconds left in the second extra period, tying the game at 108-108.

TUCKER: "The place was going crazy. It was like a college atmosphere there. It just came down to the shot at the end. That game was epic for the Shore."

Colonel began the third overtime by shooting 0-of-4 from the field. But a Darryl Thompson lay-up and a bankshot from Kevan Johnson put the Colonels back in the game. With less than two minutes to play in the third overtime, the game was tied again, 113-113.

MORGAN: "The guy who hit the winning shot was a substitute who hadn't seen much action."

At 5-foot-6, David Hubbard was the smallest player on Morgan's roster, but was thrust into action because the players ahead of him on the depth chart had fouled out or were tired.

When the ball landed in his hands with 1:21 to play, he was open, and he let that thing fly. The made-three-pointer was Hubbard's only points of the game and put the Colonels ahead.

DAVID HUBBARD, COLONEL GUARD (to the Star Democrat): "Coach said to get the ball to Kevan, but to let it go if I got it."

RAYFIELD (to the Daily Times): "That three at the end by Hubbard killed us."

MORGAN: "It was wild, as it is anytime you go to three overtimes."

A Darnell Turpin 10-footer and a good free throw from Candido Ortiz tied the game up again for Crisfield, but then Tarrell Hammond drew a foul while driving to the hoop. He hit one-of-two, giving the Colonels a slight advantage with 49 seconds to play.

Crisfield still had a chance to win, but the Crabbers missed four shots in the final 22 seconds of play. When Terrell Jackson misfired on a three-pointer with two seconds left, it ignited a celebration for Colonel Richardson.

ANDRE COLLINS: "It was just an amazing game. Unfortunately, Crisfield came out on the wrong side of that."

MORGAN (to the Star Democrat): "This was just such a great effort. With Kevan hurting and Albert out, this took a lot of heart."

JOHNSON (to the Daily Times): "I said that someone had to step up and that had to be me. I have to play like a senior."

The final score was 117-116 in the Colonels' favor. Kevan Johnson was the leading scorer and rebounder with 38 points and 21 rebounds, but folks don't forget the show that Mouring and Collins put on too.

BOZMAN: "That game was such a battle. It's probably one of the best high school basketball games I've ever seen. It was unbelievable."

CORSEY: "It's the best high school game there has ever been on the Eastern Shore."

ANDRE COLLINS: "Watching (Andy) every day and having to guard him growing up changed my life. He was great at finishing around the basket for his size."

RAYFIELD (to the Daily Times): "You can't ask for anything more than that. When you have two good teams like that it's supposed to go to overtime, right?"

ANDRE COLLINS: "I miss those days. There was so much talent in that game."

MORGAN: "That was probably my best team. But we had to come back and play Cambridge the next night."

In the regional final, Colonel Richardson was bested by the Bayside champs, Cambridge South-Dorchester, 96-77.

Mouring had 33 points, but Johnson's injured ankle continued to restrict him and the big man finished with seven points, 12 boards and three swats.

Neither could successfully contain Hanee Camper, who had 34 points in front of a crowd of more than 1,500 people. The Vikings would go on to win the 1A state title that year.

HANEE CAMPER: "During our time, Albert was the best scorer because he scored without wasting energy. He could shoot the basketball, man... Better than anybody. Two dribbles, pull-up."

Colonel Richardson head coach Merrill Morgan talks to his team during a timeout in the 1994-95 season. The Colonels went 20-3 and made the state semifinals. Colonel Richardson yearbooks.

Merrill Morgan worked diligently to land Albert Mouring and Kevan Johnson college scholarships. He was talking with top Division I coaches on the phone and hosting them in southern Caroline County, often weekly.

"Kevan wasn't a big-time ACC type of player, but could still play Division I," Morgan said. "Albert really was a top prospect."

As a junior, Mouring had a full summer and another season to improve his game and entertain the offer letters that were piling up in his mailbox. But Johnson was set to graduate in 1996 and had to make a decision. A 6-foot-6 forward who was strong, could protect the rim, score and rebound, Johnson was pursued by a plethora of respectable mid-major schools. Two coaches who appeared in Colonel Richardson's gym during the process were Lefty Driesell, then at James Madison, and John Beilein, then at Canisius. Drexel, St. Francis (Pa.) and Hampton recruited Johnson hard too, and he took official visits there. Howard, George Mason, American and UNC-Asheville were also in the mix.

When Driesell first came to Colonel Richardson, assistant coach Tom Corsey thought he was there to recruit Mouring. Driesell told him while the Colonels worked out: "No, I got my eyes on Kevan... There's one thing you can't coach. And Kevan's got it: heart."

College coaches were regularly visiting American Corner between 1995 and 1997. Corsey remembers seeing Miami's Leonard Hamilton, Wake Forest's Dave Odom and St. John's Mike Jarvis. Most were there for Mouring, but some, like Driesell, came for Johnson.

Morgan told the Star Democrat: "This year, more college coaches visited us than in the history of Colonel Richardson put together." Corsey said that Mouring's family installed a separate phone line in the house just for recruiting calls.

Johnson had expressed to Morgan that he wanted to go to a school where the coach wasn't going to up and leave and move onto a bigger and better job. After meeting with Beilein, Morgan seemed sure that he was going to stick around the Buffalo, New York, based school a while, at least during Johnson's four years there.

"Merrill had assured Kevan that, out of all these guys that might be moving on up, he was pretty positive that John Beilein was going to stay," said Merrill's wife Alice. "And then he jumped right away."

Indeed, in 1997, Beilein became the head coach at Richmond. He'd later climb the ladder to West Virginia, Michigan and the Cleveland Cavaliers too, winning an NIT and appearing in a pair of Final Fours along the way.

Driesell unexpectedly came to visit Johnson one day at Colonel, but had his wife Joyce with him. The Driesells had a vacation home in Bethany Beach, Delaware, at the time, so Lefty saw Johnson in-person on a few occasions, stopping at Colonel on his way to views of the Atlantic Ocean. But this time, Kevan wasn't at Colonel when Driesell dropped in. It was after-school hours and Johnson was at home. So, Morgan was going to drive Lefty and Joyce to Johnson's house. But Lefty, at that time – according to Morgan – was very cautious about violating any NCAA recruiting rules, and Lefty was under the impression that there was some sort of rule that forbade coaches' wives from being on recruiting trips. "There was a rule in there," Morgan said. "Something about how your wife can't help recruit." So, before Lefty formally met with Johnson that day, he dropped Joyce off at the Dollar General in Federalsburg so she could kill some time. "So, Lefty Driesell's wife was hanging out at Dollar General while he was out 'crootin," Morgan's wife Alice said. "That's some picture."

But Driesell's persistence and face-to-face meetings stuck with Johnson. "He never let me forget about his school," Johnson told the Star Democrat on May 9, 1996, the day that he inked his letter-of-intent to play for JMU, with his grandmother Virginia Sharp smiling over his shoulder. When

Johnson left Colonel, he was – and still is – one of the few players in school history to finish with more than 1,000 points and 1,000 rebounds. He also blocked a then-school record 422 shots.

Johnson became the second player from Caroline County to play for Driesell at James Madison, following North Caroline's Jeff Chambers. But Johnson would only play just one season for Driesell. The former Maryland coach was fired from JMU at the conclusion of the 1996-97 season, after Driesell had announced that the following season would be his last, and after his Dukes lost in the CAA tournament final to Old Dominion. Driesell would coach again, taking the reins of Georgia State through 2003. He retired with 786 wins and was inducted into the Naismith Basketball Hall of Fame in 2018.

And that's all well and good – but what other member of the hall of fame can say that their wife shopped at the illustrious and exclusive Dollar General in Federalsburg? No one, certainly.

Sherman Dillard was Johnson's head coach for his remaining time at JMU. In four seasons for the Dukes, Johnson played in 81 games, averaging 2.6 points and 2.8 rebounds per-game, shooting 52.5% from the floor. In two seasons, he ranked among the top 20 best shot blockers in the CAA. He graduated with a degree in architecture.

***

On the day he signed to James Madison, Kevan Johnson told the Daily Times that the recruiting process was "a big headache" for him. After watching his teammate go through that stressful time, Albert Mouring didn't want to drag out his recruitment until graduation. Mouring wanted to commit before his senior season began.

Depending on which recruiting service you looked at in the summer of 1996, Mouring was ranked anywhere from the 15th to 29th best recruit in his class. After winning the three-point and free throw contest at the Princeton camp, and putting in a head-turning performance at a Nike camp that put him on the camp's all-star team, it was clear that Mouring was a legitimate major Division I prospect and one of the top marksmen in his class. By August, Mouring had garnered interest from Maryland, St. John's, Clemson, Georgetown, Arizona, Miami, Kansas and several other top programs. Mouring met with Jayhawks coach Roy Williams during an unofficial visit to Lawrence while his AAU team was playing nearby that summer.

"He went big-time at Princeton. From 28 feet out, he would pull up and drain it in your face," a scout who attended the camp, Dan Painter, told the Daily Times. "He's the real deal, and Maryland has got to sign this kid even if it means waiting until the spring."

The college offers for Mouring kept growing. By Sept. 18, he had whittled down his choices to eight teams and would host coaches from those schools for in-home visits in Jonestown. Mouring's eight were: Maryland, Villanova, Wake Forest, Kansas, Miami, Xavier, UMass and UConn. "You don't make those kinds of trips to the Shore if you're not seriously interested. We're not on the fly path, you know," Morgan told the Daily Times.

Maryland was Mouring's first choice for college and the first to pay him an in-home visit. But then-head coach Gary Williams wanted Mouring to commit extra early, Morgan said, and when Mouring declined to do so, a Maryland assistant coach called Morgan the next week to inform him that the Terps were no longer recruiting Mouring. Maryland later signed Juan Dixon.

When the Terps bowed out of the race for Mouring's talents, their former head coach jumped in. Lefty Driesell was still at James Madison and Mouring's friend and teammate Kevan Johnson was just a freshman there, and the feeling of familiarity was appealing to "The Man" from a small town. Mouring's final three choices were Miami, JMU and UConn.

Miami was his first visit and then-head coach Leonard Hamilton tried to win over Mouring with a jet-skiing excursion and a one-on-one meeting with then-Miami Heat center Alonzo Mourning. "I had a lot of fun," Mouring told the Daily Times about his trip to Coral Gables.

And then Mouring went to the other end of the east coast to Storrs, Connecticut, to see Jim Calhoun and his UConn Huskies. Calhoun had been the Huskies' head coach since 1986 and UConn was coming off its fourth Big East tournament title and third straight appearance in the Sweet 16 or better. Instead of bringing in an NBA All-Star or a motorsports toy, Calhoun invited Mouring to watch an intrasquad scrimmage at the Hartford Civic Center. Mouring noticed two things: One, more than 8,000 fans attended the exhibition and they were rabid. It was an atmosphere Mouring hadn't experienced much in high school and he loved it. Two, UConn really needed three-point shooting. Without Ray Allen, UConn fell from fourth in the nation in three-point shooting percentage in 1995-96 to 96th in the nation in 1996-97. Only Rip Hamilton averaged multiple made threes per-game in 1996-97 for the Huskies. Mouring saw a niche he thought he could fill. "They need a shooter... I felt like I could help," Mouring told the Daily Times. "Thinking about playing in front of all those people felt exciting. There's a lot of competition and exposure in the Big East."

Mouring canceled his official visit to James Madison and committed to UConn on Nov. 8, 1996. "I just felt real comfortable at UConn," he told the Hartford Courant.

Although Mouring had signed his national letter of intent to UConn, he still had plenty of noise to make on the Shore in his final season for the Colonels. That fall, the man they called "Ca$h" – according to the 1997 Colonel yearbook – made the homecoming court. His yearbook quote was,

"Why take the two, when you can drain the three?" And more often than not, Albert chose the behind-the-arc attempt. It became his signature, and in his senior year, he further established himself as one of the best shooters the Delmarva Peninsula had ever seen.

Mouring started the year off by pouring in 46 points, 17 rebounds, six assists and four steals in a 94-90 win over Easton. The next game, he scored 51 points in 21 minutes in a blowout 94-62 win over county rival North Caroline. Later in the season, on Jan. 7, he set the school scoring record by scoring 62 points in 31 minutes at Queen Anne's – a stat line notable enough to make the Baltimore Sun. Mouring connected on 11-of-14 three-pointers in the 99-77 victory, bumping up his season average to 43.4 points per-game. Morgan told the Sun: "A lot of people think we only have hicks over here who can't really play. But this is a guy who can play."

Perhaps Mouring's most memorable performance that season was on Dec. 17. It was a lot like his battle with Andy Collins at the Civic Center. Again, a player on the other side nearly matched Mouring, shot for shot.

The game was at Colonel against Butch Waller's Wicomico High School Indians, which were led on the court by Doug King, Damien Johnson, Al Hankerson and Dante Palmer. In the previous season, Palmer hounded Mouring all game long and the Indians were able to hold *"The Man"* to 12 points, but still – the Colonels won 61-58 behind Kevan Johnson's 19 points, 18 rebounds and five blocks.

This Indians team seemed like the one that was going to break Waller's state tournament drought; entering the 1996-97 season, he hadn't guided a team to a final four since 1983. The Indians won the Bayside title in 1997 narrowly over Easton but fell short of reaching College Park.

Still, Wi-Hi was a first-class team. And early on in the season, they didn't want to be target practice for Mouring. But Mouring had a score to settle too. He wasn't about to be held to 12 points again, and certainly not at home.

"The word on Albert was: contact. Teams tried to be physical with him. Easton really tried to be rough with him," Morgan recalls. "Butch said there was no way Albert was going to score 25 points against Wi-Hi that night.

"Well, he didn't. He scored 47."

But Wi-Hi made Mouring work for those points. The UConn-bound guard connected on just two three-pointers. He would need 16 two-pointers and went 9-of-11 from the charity stripe to reach his grand total. But the whole way, Damien Johnson was matching him. Back and forth they went in the fast-paced high scoring affair at American Corner. In the end, Johnson finished with 41 points and Colonel left with a hard-fought 99-92 victory.

"Wasn't a hell of a lot of defense in that game, was there?" Waller says with a laugh.

Doug King doesn't really chuckle when he thinks about that contest.

"We should've won. I had 20 assists. There was like 15 dunks in that game. We were rolling," King says. "We were punishing them."

Wi-Hi had a 39-22 lead at the end of the first quarter and then a 61-47 lead at halftime. Then, Mouring went on his run.

"And then, this little kid off the bench hit a couple three's and cut it to 10," King recalls. He may be thinking of Darryl Thompson or Lamontra Fountain, who combined for 31 points. "Then – I'll never forget it – Albert came down at the end of the third quarter and hit a three from like half-court. The whole gym exploded. They went nuts. And then he just went on a tear. That kind of broke our back. That was a long dark ride home.

"Me and my dad got arguing after the game. He said I should've helped Damien more. I was like, 'Dad. I had 20 assists. What else you want me to do?'"

Damien Johnson was one of the best players Wi-Hi has ever had and still owns some program records. In 1996-97, he scored 600 points while shooting 66% from the floor and averaging 23.1 points per-game, all of which are single season records for Waller's side.

"Damien was the real deal. He could've played Division I basketball. Mike Brey was on him, at Delaware," King says. "He was the best player I had on my team at Wi-Hi. He could jump out the gym; I could just throw it up. When we played at home on Friday's, it was like going to the club. Standing room only."

King continues: "But Albert, yea, that's when you knew he was legit. He showed up. We had more talent than Colonel, but we didn't have Albert Mouring."

Mouring's senior campaign at Colonel ended in the 1A East regional quarterfinals. A three-headed attack of Marty Bailey Jr., Joel Adams and Terry Brooks combined for 79 points to power Easton to a 106-91 playoff win over Colonel Richardson. With 18 seconds left, Mouring made his final shot as a Colonel, slamming down an uncontested right-handed dunk. After flushing five shots from behind the arc and scoring 43 points, Mouring sat on the bench at the Wicomico Youth and Civic Center with a yellow and gray towel draped over his head, reflecting on his high school career and all the playoff battles he had in that arena. "I was thinking about good things," he told the Star Democrat.

At the Bayside Senior All-Star game, Mouring put on one more show for Shore fans, scoring a game-high 32 points. But King scored 26 points and hit eight three-pointers and threw a pair of alley-oops to Damien Johnson. And Crisfield's Andy Collins chipped in 12 points as the South won handily, 123-95. For the third straight year, Mouring was named to the All-State team and named Mason-Dixon Player of the Year. He was joined on the Mason-Dixon team by Delmar's Deric Gaines, Bailey of Easton, Johnson of Wi-Hi and Collins of Crisfield. Collins went on to play at Cecil College, where he was roommates with King and one of the first batch of Shore recruits for head coach Bill Lewit.

***

At UConn, Mouring developed a pregame superstition that kept his family and faith close to him. According to a story from the Middletown Press, Mouring would pray with his family, and then he would open a bottle of oil that was blessed by his grandfather. He'd rub it on his forehead to prevent him from mental mistakes, on his knees to protect him from injuries, and then on the tattoo of praying hands on his shoulder. Mouring also had an affinity for Air Jordans. During a shooting slump in his junior season, he went out and bought a pair of red and black 1's. He wore them the next game and dropped 22 points in a 9-for-13 shooting effort in a win over Pitt.

Colonel Richardson's Albert Mouring played four seasons with UConn, helping the Huskies win a national championship in 1999. UConn Athletics.

Mouring would eventually enjoy a ton of success at UConn, but his freshman season was a bumpy one. Because of his SAT score, Mouring couldn't enroll in college for his first fall semester. Still, he moved to Storrs anyway, got an apartment and worked in a sheet metal factory to support himself when he wasn't studying. "I have a lot of respect for Albert," UConn coach Jim Calhoun told the Star Democrat. "He would go to work at 6 a.m. every morning before joining us at 3:30 (p.m.), all while going to class." Mouring retook the SAT in November and got the score he needed. He enrolled at UConn and joined the team in late December, but featured in just 15 games as the Huskies won the Big East and appeared in the Elite Eight.

But as a sophomore, Mouring found a bigger role on an uber-talented UConn team. The Colonel Richardson product didn't start, but played 18.9 minutes a night in 32 of 36 games that season for Calhoun's side. He was fourth on the team in scoring with 7.1 points per-game and led the Huskies in three-point shooting with a 37.6% mark. In the regular season, Mouring shined in a win over No. 4 Stanford with 15 points, and then tallied 12 points and 10 boards in a win over Georgetown. Mouring was essentially the sixth man on a team that featured three NBA players, won the Big East and earned a No. 1 seed in the 1999 NCAA Tournament.

In the Big Dance, Mouring continued to prove his value for the Huskies. In a Sweet 16 win over Iowa, Mouring came off the bench and knocked down a trio of three-pointers, scoring 11 points and grabbing three rebounds in 15 minutes of action.

Mouring played sparingly in Elite Eight and Final Four triumphs over Gonzaga and Ohio State, but Calhoun called on him again in the NCAA championship against Duke. On the biggest stage of his basketball-playing career, Mouring showed up. In 17 minutes, he connected on 3-of-4 shots for six points, grabbed three rebounds and also blocked a shot. Mouring's most important basket came with 16 minutes remaining in the game, when he hit Duke defender Chris Carrawell with a crossover and swished a short jumper over him that cut the Blue Devils' lead to three points. That was during a 12-4 run for UConn

UConn went on to win 77-74, capturing the first-ever national championship in men's basketball for the Huskies. With the two teams separated by that tight of a margin, it's easy to argue that UConn may have not won without the contributions of *The Man* from Jonestown.

With All-American Rip Hamilton off to the NBA, Mouring seized a starring role as a junior. In the second game of the season, UConn had a rematch with Duke at a neutral site and won again, led by Mouring's 22 points. He averaged 13.9 points per-game as a junior and made the All-Big East tournament team. Mouring flushed 86 three-pointers that season, a mark that was second best in the deeply talented Big East. In the NCAA Tournament, he had 14 points, five rebounds, two assists and two steals in a win over Utah State, and 17 points and three rebounds in a loss to Tennessee.

UConn went 20-12 and just 8-8 in the Big East during Mouring's senior year, but the Caroline County product continued to pour in the points. Mouring just edged out future NBA All-Star Caron Butler as the Huskies' leading scorer, averaging 15.1 points, 3.2 rebounds and 1.7 assists per-game. In his final game for the Huskies – a disappointing and underwhelming NIT loss to Detroit Mercy – Mouring had eight points, three assists and two steals.

Mouring had a 111-29 record as a player at UConn and scored 1,214 career points. "It was an awful nice run for me. I got a championship ring...

got a lot of wins," Mouring told the Hartford Courant after his final game. Mouring went on to play professionally overseas in Poland, Austria, Israel, Turkey, Finland, Iran and Bahrain. He also played in the United States Basketball League and was its Player of the Year in 2003, averaging 28.4 points per-game with the Oklahoma Storm. The league folded in 2008.

Mouring is still etched in the UConn history books as the owner of the best career free throw percentage in Huskies' history with an 84.2% mark; the product of all those lonely hours spent on that court in Jonestown, shooting through the monkey bars.

Colonel Richardson graduate Albert Mouring shoots over two Syracuse defenders while playing for UConn. UConn Athletics.

GRAYSON HURLEY:
A BIG MAN WITH A BIG HEART

"More than a coach, he was a great father figure. That was one of the best times in my life man, just being around him."
– Hanee Camper

David Insley apologizes before he begins to answer my question. We're sitting in the Plaza Tapatia in Cambridge and – over nachos, white sauce, fish tacos and cervezas – I had just asked him about Grayson Hurley, the ultra-successful basketball coach of the Cambridge-South Dorchester High School Vikings from 1982 through 1997. Insley covered high school sports on the Eastern Shore for the Dorchester Banner in 1989 and 1990, then again for the Banner in 2003 through 2005, and then for 14 years for the Star Democrat in Easton. He's seen countless games and spent an uncountable number of hours with a lot of coaches on Maryland's slice of the Delmarva Peninsula.

Insley takes a sip of his Coors Light and says, "I'm about to make the world's worst analogy here."

I eagerly lean in, moving my tacos out of the way so I don't get sauce on my shirt.

"Fighting against the Nazis, Joseph Stalin used a system, especially around the Battle of Stalingrad," Insley tells me in a history lecture of sorts. "Stalin used this method that's been referred to as min-maxing; minimum amount of troops for the maximum amount of effort… And Stalin gave them just enough to hang on by their fingernails and to tie down the maximum number of troops while they prepared for this massive counter-offensive that absolutely crushed the Germans.

"Grayson was the same way. He min-maxed with his words. He could get something done with his kids that would take five words or two sentences, that would take someone else five sentences or a two-minute chat."

To be perfectly clear, Hurley was nothing like Stalin, the ruthless Russian dictator. Hurley was jolly, cool and cheerful – a genuine and decent human-being who had great taste in food, and would do almost anything for someone in-need. But Hurley did have a unique bond with the young men he coached in basketball. He didn't need to bark or deliver grand speeches to get something done on the court. And Hurley was consistently able to draw out every ounce of talent and every drop of effort from every single player he ever had.

"He just had this magnificent gravitas where the kids listened and people liked him," Insley said. "He just glowed. He was such a pleasant guy to be around. Always laid back, never got worked up, never saw him break a sweat."

Cambridge head coach Grayson Hurley talks to his team during a timeout in 1989. Cambridge-South Dorchester yearbooks.

***

Cambridge had enjoyed success in boys basketball before Grayson Hurley arrived as head coach.

In 1955, the Cambridge High School Raiders won a Class B State Championship under the guidance of head coach Ed Sidaris, a West Virginia University graduate. The Raiders beat Oxon Hill 47-37, thanks to Sidaris' shape-shifting 2-1-2 defense, 15 points from David Bromwell and an 11-point, nine-rebound effort from Hurley, who also played inspired defense against 6-foot-7 Oxon Hill center Joe Horn. Hurley was a senior that season and went on to Maryland State Teachers College – one of the many former names of Salisbury University – where he played soccer, basketball and baseball.

After college, Hurley went to work for a company that manufactured conveyor belts. When he was struck in the eye by a steel rod on the job one day, Hurley went back to school at the age of 26 to pursue a career as a minister, like his grandfather. But at Norman Junior College, a small Baptist school in Georgia, his professors noticed how well he worked with kids and encouraged him to become a teacher instead. So, Hurley went to Valdosta State in south Georgia, where he pursued a teaching degree and assisted the basketball team. He soon returned home to Cambridge, to teach and coach, and worked on earning his degree from the University of Baltimore.

***

The new high school in Cambridge – Cambridge-South Dorchester High School – opened its doors in 1976. The school changed its mascot from the Raiders to the Vikings, but success in athletics continued. In 1979, the football team coached by Doug Fleetwood went undefeated and won the Class B state championship. At the time, it was the first state football championship won by a team from the Eastern Shore. A few months later, many of the same students that powered CSD to that football title also plowed their way through the basketball playoffs.

Coached by Kenny Edgar, the Vikings lost the Bayside Conference Championship in 1980 to Bill Cain's Crisfield squad for the second straight year, but CSD rolled through the Class B playoffs without having to play the Class C Crabbers. In the state semifinals, Cambridge topped South Hagerstown 62-59 behind six points, six assists and 11 rebounds from Darnell Clash, and 17 points from Jeff Churchwell. In the final, it was Skeeter Nichols who played the role of hero, pouring in 26 points, 11 rebounds and two assists in a 55-47 triumph over Southern.

"Skeeter Nichols and Darnell Clash and those guys … they were stacked. They were a very good team," said Brian Butler, who started on the Wicomico High School team Cambridge eliminated in the playoffs. "And they were really good football players too."

A star running back on the CSD football team, Nichols went on to play for Penn State, where he totaled 550 yards of total offense and two touchdowns for the Nittany Lions in 32 games. Nichols rushed five times in Penn State's 1983 Sugar Bowl win over Georgia. Clash was a defensive back and punt returner at Wyoming, where he racked up 2,286 yards on 153 returns, and seven interceptions in 34 games. Clash went on to play in the Canadian Football League, where was an All-Star and Grey Cup Champion in 1985 with the BC Lions.

"I doubt there's any town on the Eastern Shore that has had as many athletes come out of it as Cambridge," said longtime Wi-Hi head coach Butch Waller. "They were always tough."

***

Grayson Hurley came from a coaching family. His father, Grayson Levi Hurley – a World War II Navy veteran who died in 1979 – was one of the first managers for the Cambridge Little League. When the CSD boys basketball job became open, Hurley seemed like the natural fit. Not only because he was an alum of the old Cambridge High School and had helped them win a championship in 1955, but because coaching came so easy to him. And Hurley had been an assistant at North Dorchester under Dale Carrier for several years, and for one year under Kenny Edgar at CSD. Administrators at CSD at the time pushed Hurley to apply for the vacancy left by Edgar.

Hurley's debut as the Vikings head coach came on Dec. 10, 1982, a 56-55 loss to Merrill Morgan's Colonel Richardson Colonels at American Corner. Over the next 15 seasons, Morgan would have much more trouble beating Hurley as the two became friends, and as Hurley's teams got much better.

By 1985, Hurley had the Vikings contending again. They made the state semifinals that season and in 1988, and then appeared in the Bayside Conference title game in 1986 and 1987, losing both times to Crisfield. Hurley was a calm coach who – for the majority of each game – remained seated. He'd unfold his arms and voice his opinions only when irritated by a referee.

The 1989 season would be different. Hurley installed a 1-3-1 zone-trap-press that tormented opponents, and Cambridge finished the regular season with a 14-6 record and then stormed through the playoffs. In the Class 2A Region IV semifinals, Hurley notched his fifth straight win over Waller as the Vikings beat the Wi-Hi Indians 68-43 behind 17 points – and a trio of thunderous dunks – from Radford-bound Tyrone Travis, who averaged 21.4 points and 13.1 rebounds per-game that season. The strong, athletic collegiate prospect followed up that performance with 23 points, 13 rebounds and seven blocks in a 70-45 victory over James M. Bennett for the region crown. In the state semifinals, Hurley's Vikings upset top-seeded Calvert, 55-47 behind 14 points and eight boards from Jerome Harris. In the final moments of the game, CSD outscored Calvert 12-4. Hurley told the Washington Post: "This ballclub has done one heck of a job (and) has taken everybody by surprise."

After a quiet and contained outing in the semifinals, Travis was unleashed in the Class B title game in College Park. Entering the fourth quarter, Hurley had a simple message for his players: "Give the ball to Tyrone." The muscular No. 51 with broad shoulders and a hi-top fade responded by pouring on 31 points and 16 rebounds in a 77-73 win over Hammond. Travis' final points scored as a Viking – two free throws with 44 seconds remaining – put the game on ice for CSD.

Tyrone Travis was the star on the Cambridge team that won a state title in 1989, averaging 21.4 points and 13.1 rebounds per-game. Radford Athletics.

Travis would later say of Hurley: "He'd make you believe that you could be anything in the world."

***

Over the next seven seasons, Grayson Hurley's teams competed for six Bayside Conference Championships, winning four of them. The Vikings also went to the state tournament three more times, winning it all again in 1996 behind the play of Antwan Lake, Tyron Anderson, James White and Hanee Camper.

"The best player I played against was probably Hanee Camper. Hanee was the truth, man," said Doug King, Wi-Hi's point guard in the mid-1990s. "Hanee was a pro. He was like a 6-foot-5 LeBron James. He played the point, but was about 230 lbs. and bigger than everybody. He loved the game. He could do everything and anything he wanted to do. Hanee could do more than Albert Mouring."

Before the Bayside Conference and the state of Maryland were introduced to Camper, Merrill Morgan and Tom Corsey were aware of him. In the mid-1990s, kids from Colonel Richardson and Cambridge often played AAU basketball together in the summertime, and were often driven around by Hurley in his ubiquitous and iconic van at his own expense. Camper recalls playing against the likes of Lamar Odom and Steve Francis on those circuits. On one occasion, Morgan, Hurley and Corsey were all unavailable to coach the team, so Morgan deployed his sons Jeff and Steve to guide the team during a day of games near Washington, D.C. With Lake, Anderson, Camper, Mouring and Kevan Johnson, Jeff and Steve didn't have to do much coaching. The exceptional athletes just went to work. The result was a blowout, in favor of the boys from the Mid-Shore.

"They were outstanding and could've beaten anybody in the state," Morgan said.

"We probably had enough to beat a junior college," said Corsey. When he talked about the team, Corsey still identified Anderson and Lake by their nicknames: Ding-A-Ling and Big Bird.

In the spring of 1993, Cambridge was back in the state final and matched up against a powerful Dunbar team. The Vikings were 23-0, but Dunbar was ranked nationally as the 17th best high school team in the country by USA Today. Dunbar had a remarkable history in basketball – producing eight NBA players to that point – but the Poets hadn't won an MPSSAA state championship. That's because, before 1993, Baltimore City schools competed in their own postseason tournament.

Dunbar was led that season by Keith Booth, an All-American guard who had committed to the University of Maryland. Surrounding him were four other players who were 6-foot-4 or taller. And Dunbar won that day, 65-59, but most folks from the Shore don't remember the final score, or even that Dunbar won.

All they remember is how a Cambridge freshman – Hanee Camper – strapped up, talked trash and frustrated Booth all day long. Booth had just announced he was going to Maryland five days before the game, but Camper could've cared less.

"Times were different then. I didn't know what a McDonald's All-American was or none of that," Camper said. "Keith Booth didn't matter to me. I said some things to him. I'm a dog on the basketball court. I talked trash to him."

Camper stole possessions and shots from Booth. If the Dunbar Poet had lunch money stuffed in his sock that day, Camper would've taken that too.

"Hanee vs. Keith Booth was like two grown men playing," Corsey said. "Hanee wanted him. He wanted that match-up. Dunbar couldn't believe he was only in the ninth grade. The boy was good."

Camper had only been on the varsity team at Cambridge for three games, spending the majority of his freshman campaign dominating on JV, but that day, he was all over Booth – like white on rice in a glass of milk on a paper plate in a snowstorm. Booth struggled mightily while being shadowed by Camper, turning the ball over seven times, and scoring just 14 points on 5-of-19 shooting. Camper had 13 points, five steals and three rebounds. And Cambridge had respect from its peers.

"I was very confident as a basketball player. No one man could stop me," Camper said. "In Cambridge, even before my time, that's how we were. It was embedded in us, in our hometown. That's the way we were."

After the game, reporters from west of the Chesapeake Bay wondered where Camper was going to play college ball. They had no idea he was only a freshman.

"Hanee was the best player on the court at the state final that year," said Morgan, who watched the game with Corsey. "It was ridiculous how much better he was (than the Dunbar players)."

"We took them for granted," Booth told the Baltimore Sun.

And no one would make that same mistake about Camper or Hurley's Vikings ever again.

***

Just a day after his team went to triple overtime with Crisfield in the regional semifinals, Merrill Morgan and his Colonels had another monumental test ahead of them. On Friday, March 1, 1996 at the Wicomico Youth & Civic Center, they had to face Grayson Hurley, Hanee Camper and the Cambridge-South Dorchester Vikings.

"When Colonel met CSD the next night, I would say that is the biggest crowd I have ever seen at the Civic Center for a high school game," said David Dodson, a CSD graduate turned Bayside Conference videographer and walking encyclopedia.

When tip-off for the 1A East Region Final rolled around, there was still a line waiting outside of the Civic Center to get in. Box office representatives, conference and state officials went to Morgan and Hurley and asked them if they could push the start of the game back 15 minutes. That would give folks in the building enough time to open up seating in the upper deck – and give them more time to sell tickets.

Morgan and Hurley agreed. Still, Merrill's daughter was way back in line, and there wasn't a certainty she would be able to get in the building to see the game. Word got to Hurley, and he quietly went to the back door of the Civic Center and snuck her in. The next season, ahead of a sold-out regular season game between Colonel and Cambridge at American Corner, Morgan repaid the favor, sneaking Hurley's wife in through one of the back doors at the old southern Caroline County school. The two coaches had many heated battles over the years, but had immense respect for one another and were friendly. "He and I were on good terms," Morgan said. "His teams were always exceptional."

And perhaps none of Hurley's teams were more phenomenal than the one he had in 1996. By then, Camper had established himself as a walking double-double, a dangerous defender and the Bayside Conference's top player.

"Just coaching against Cambridge, period, was difficult, because they had athletes coming out the gazooba," said Vic Burns, then the head coach at North Dorchester. "Hanee was a man among boys. The kid could get down the court in three dribbles. He had a man's body and was a super player. And a good kid, too. He's one of the best players that the Bayside has produced."

Flanking Camper was Tyron Anderson, James White and Antwan Lake – the latter of whom was about 6-foot-4 and 300 lbs. By then, he was well on his way to securing a football scholarship at West Virginia. With Camper and co. leading the way, the Vikings ended the regular season with just one loss and then spanked Wi-Hi in the Bayside Championship, 86-41, giving Hurley his fourth conference crown.

"Yea. It was bad," said Wi-Hi guard Doug King.

Bill Weber, who ran the scoreboard and clock at Wi-Hi for decades, added: "That was a Grayson Hurley-coached team, and if you're talking about Hall of Fame coaches on the Eastern Shore, you got to throw his name in there. Cambridge always had athletes around then."

Cambridge had squeaked by Colonel two months prior to their playoff meeting, with the Vikings taking a 76-73 victory on Jan. 19, but in the regional final, Colonel had no answer. In front of a crowd of about 3,000 people, Camper went head-to-head with Albert Mouring and came out on top. Camper had 34 points, Mouring had 33, and CSD won handily, 96-77. Anderson added 23 points for the Vikings.

"Hanee hates to lose," Hurley told the Daily Times. "I just roll the ball out there and tell him to go get them."

Camper and Cambridge kept rolling. In the state semifinals, he had 31 points, 14 rebounds, five assists and three steals in the Vikings' 73-63 overtime win over Brunswick. A day later, Hurley won his second state title as a head coach as Camper had 20 points, seven rebounds, four assists and two blocks in a 71-51 win over Williamsport. Lake did the dirty work, with four points, four blocks and six rebounds.

"We were a dominant team at the time. It was a great year," Camper said. "I felt like nobody could stop me. And I felt like my basketball IQ was through the roof."

And on Lake, Camper added: "In basketball, Antwan was the hustle guy. We wouldn't have that state championship without him. He was always the first guy back on defense."

The humble Hurley was overjoyed, but reluctant to take any credit for the triumph. He just wanted to get to Horn and Horn, a smorgasbord buffet in nearby Laurel. "I didn't have anything to do with it," Hurley told the Star Democrat. "I didn't take a shot, dribble or anything. The guys wanted it."

Camper was named an All-American by USA Today in 1996 after averaging around 27 points, nine rebounds and seven assists per-game on the court. He was one of two players in Maryland his senior year to be named All-State in football and basketball. He was twice an all-state selection in basketball and twice named the Bayside Player of the Year.

And during Camper's senior year, he lived with Hurley. The two spent a lot of time together and would break down film after games. Camper would keep track of secondary stats while Hurley analyzed the finer points.

Cambridge's Antwan Lake blocks a shot during a game in 1996. Lake played football at West Virginia University and for three teams in the NFL. Cambridge-South Dorchester yearbooks.

"Oh, man. I loved Mr. Hurley. He was the type that – he was going to do it his way, but he was smart enough to just let us roll the ball out. You couldn't have a better coach," Camper said. "More than a coach, he was a great father figure. That was one of the best times in my life man, just being around him."

Camper went on to play basketball at Polk Community College in Winter Haven, Florida, and then briefly at Delaware State University.

"I lasted a year. I was young and dumb," Camper said. "I played, but I wasn't going to class. My first mistake was grades. I should've done what I was supposed to do."

***

Grayson Hurley – who also taught history, geography, current events, civics and psychology at Cambridge-South Dorchester – stayed there for one more year after winning his second state title as a head coach.

In his final season leading the Vikings, Hurley reached his breaking point. The team was solid, finishing the 1996-97 campaign with an 18-5 record, but CSD principal Mike Asplen asked Hurley to provide written accounts of each assistant coach's role and how each practice was run. Hurley obliged, but did so begrudgingly. And then Asplen presented a proposal to him to resign as head coach.

Hurley accepted. He was done.

"I coach how I feel. If I feel that this isn't working, I will switch to something else," Hurley told Bill Haufe of the Star Democrat in 1998. "I was not happy the last year I coached. I wasn't myself ... I bled for Cambridge. I grew up in Cambridge. I played at Cambridge. I'm a Cambridge person. But I had been wanting to get out. I don't want to be a head coach ever again."

In 15 seasons of coaching the Vikings, Hurley had run up a record of 277-80 – a 77% winning percentage. And in the 1990s, no basketball coach on the Eastern Shore won more than Hurley. In his final six seasons on the job, Hurley's teams went 130-15. In that same stretch, only Pocomoke's David

Byrd had more than 100 wins, coming in with 104. Hurley had one losing season, ever, in 1990-91.

Hurley is also a member of an exclusive club of Bayside Conference basketball coaches that have multiple state championships. Here's the list: Crisfield's Jack Morgan, Somerset's Joe Robinson, Crisfield's Bill Cain, Easton girls' Tom Callahan, Snow Hill's Allen Miller, and Hurley. And only Cain, Butch Waller and Mardela girls' legend Barbara McCool have more Bayside titles than Hurley.

In his final year of coaching at Cambridge, Hurley accepted a new daytime job at North Dorchester. He oversaw the school's "Maryland Tomorrow" program and worked with at-risk students. He described it as coaching off the court.

"You have to remember," Hurley told the Star Democrat. "It's just a game. My main thing was always to see how many kids I could help."

Hurley did return to coaching on the court, but the man with a massive frame, big heart and a great basketball mind tried to remain in the shadows. Ahead of the 1997-98 basketball season, he joined Vic Burns' staff at North Dorchester. In 1999, the Eagles won the state championship behind the play of Reggie Parker and Carlton Dotson. When Burns left ND, Hurley remained as an assistant coach, later working under Dave Monroe.

Burns and Hurley were a bit of an odd couple, or like yin and yang. Burns was loud, animated and aggressive as a coach, while Hurley was cool and collected. When Burns might've been arguing with an official, Hurley might be leaning over to the scorekeeper for a recommendation at the concession stand. The team in 1999 belonged to Burns, no question, but Hurley brought structure to practices and levity to every tense situation.

"Not that I'm some kind of tyrant, but they called us ice and fire. Grayson was a gentleman," Burns said. "He brought that match-up zone defense in and we used that all year long."

***

Grayson Hurley did eventually follow in his grandfather's footsteps. In 2004, he became a minister, preaching and teaching Sunday school at churches in East New Market and Cambridge. In August of that year, he was diagnosed with cancer.

And then, on Feb. 16, 2005, Hurley suffered a heart attack and died in his home in East New Market at the age of 67. At his funeral, Antwan Lake, Hanee Camper, Tyrone Travis and Reggie Parker were among the pallbearers.

"I loved Mr. Hurley," longtime Colonel Richardson assistant Tom Corsey said. "He put the time in and was like a father to them; whatever those boys needed."

Said Camper: "He was a great guy. He could relate to us. He was funny and he loved basketball. We were a lot alike."

Like Camper, Lake lived with Hurley while he was in high school too. After starring on the football field in Morgantown at West Virginia University, Lake enjoyed a six-year career in the NFL with the Lions, Falcons and Saints. Lake admitted, years later, he might have never made it out of Cambridge if it wasn't for Hurley's kindness and generosity.

"He took me in and basically carried me to the person that I am today," Lake told the Star Democrat after Hurley's death. "He was like an angel."

RAMS ON PARADE

"The man is knowledgeable about everything... He's particular about his style, but he's raised generations of young ladies."
– Shawn Tucker

Of the three public high schools still standing in Salisbury today, Parkside High School was the most recent to open its doors in the mid-1970s. The project to build Parkside on a 55-acre site next to Shumaker Pond along Beaglin Park Drive cost around $6.5 million, according to news reports at the time. It was initially slated to open in December 1974, but delays in the delivery of materials – specifically steel – caused Charles Brohawn and Bros. Inc. of Cambridge to fall behind schedule in the construction of the school.

Parkside was needed largely due to overcrowding at Wicomico and James M. Bennett high schools. In 1974, Bennett had nearly 100 more students than it had lockers. Construction on Parkside High School began in June 1973, and it finally opened – albeit incomplete and without air conditioning – in September 1975.

New school district boundaries were drawn to allow Salisbury's growing population to be split evenly among its three high schools, but Parkside also absorbed the enrollment of Pittsville High School – a bit more than 200 students – despite a petition signed by nearly 1,000 people from the modest community located about 14 miles away. Alas, the efforts of the folks from Pittsville were unsuccessful as the Wicomico County School Board voted unanimously to close Pittsville High School and turn its building into an elementary school. Ninth through 12th graders that live there are bused to Parkside now.

There was briefly a debate as to whether or not Salisbury's newest high school should be named for Royd A. Mahaffey. The superintendent of schools for Wicomico County for 18 years, Mahaffey died at age 52 after a battle with leukemia, just two months before Parkside opened. The board rejected the idea of renaming the school for Mahaffey, because it "was known" that Mahaffey "opposed naming schools for individuals" and "he wouldn't have wanted it," according to reports in the Salisbury Daily Times. While Mahaffey wouldn't get the same treatment as his predecessor James M. Bennett, leaders at Parkside found another way to honor him: they used his initials – R A M – to inspire the nickname for the school's sports teams. However, the moniker "Rams" wasn't officially adopted until after it was approved by a committee, forcing Parkside's football team to play its first game, at Kent County, nicknameless. The other top contender was "Patriots," allowing the committee to go for some alliteration. The Daily Times first referred to Parkside's teams as the Rams on Sept. 19, 1975.

When it came time to pick uniform colors for the various varsity sports Parkside sponsored, that decision fell to Anthony Sarbanes, the school's first principal.

The Wicomico County School Board pried Sarbanes away from his post as principal at Wicomico High School to lead the new school. Sarbanes is the younger brother of Paul Sarbanes, who was a congressman from 1971 to 1977, and then a U.S. senator from 1977 to 2007. Both Anthony and Paul were avid basketball fans – Paul was a standout player for Sam Seidel at Wi-Hi in the 1950s and later played at Princeton, while Anthony was also a solid player at Wi-Hi and played collegiately at Western Maryland College. Anthony later coached at Wi-Hi for two seasons, from 1963 to 1965, going 31-7.

And Anthony Sarbanes also loved watching the Boston Celtics. He attempted to rationalize his thinking on Parkside's colors to the Daily Times in 1991, saying, "You want to pick colors that are standard so you don't have to pay extra when ordering uniforms. We couldn't use blue since Wi-Hi has it, couldn't use red since Bennett has it. Mardela is green and gold, but they aren't in the city."

Make no mistake: Parkside wears green and white because that's what Red Auerbach's boys wore while Sarbanes watched them pile up championships.

***

Unfortunately, Parkside has not remotely had the same success in basketball that the Celtics have had. If there is a Boston Celtics of Wicomico County, it's Wi-Hi, considering the Indians' 27 appearances in the boys' state final four – a stage that the Parkside boys have never been on. Parkside's boys basketball team didn't make its first region final until 2017, after it beat Wi-Hi in historic fashion in the 2A East Section II final behind the coaching of Dave Byer and the stellar play of Raequan Williams and Paul Morgan.

But in girls basketball, the story is a bit different. In that sport, the Rams have had stretches of real dominance, especially in the 1980s and 90s. From 1987 through 1991, Parkside captured five straight Bayside Conference championships in girls basketball (in 1989, they were named co-champs with Cambridge after the game was scrapped due to bad weather). In that same span, the Rams went to four state final fours and appeared in the title game once, in 1991.

Those teams were coached by Lance Lewandowski and powered on the hardwood by Kesha Camper, one of the best women to ever hoop in Bayside

Conference gyms. Over Lewandowski and Camper's four years together, Parkside went 87-11.

In winning her fourth Bayside title, Camper racked up 42 points and 17 rebounds in a lopsided 85-48 victory over North Caroline, completing a 22-1 regular season for the Rams. Camper – who averaged 23 points and 12 rebounds per-game her senior season – and teammate Yumika Church finished one and two in Bayside Player of the Year voting in 1991.

"I give a lot of credit to Kesha Camper," said former Mardela star Tia Jackson. "She was a phenomenal talent, and arguably one of the best ever to come out of the Eastern Shore."

Parkside routinely trounced its competition in the Bayside Conference, consistently besting Jackson's great Mardela teams, tough squads from Pocomoke and Snow Hill, and North Caroline, which was dominant in the north. Camper won each of her four high school matchups with Jackson, averaging about 24.2 points and 14.4 rebounds per-game across those battles.

But, similarly to Jackson's Mardela teams, Parkside had trouble winning big in the postseason, particularly at the state final four. Camper's last chance to capture a state title for her Rams came on March 9, 1991. And she put up an excellent effort in Catonsville with a game-high 26 points and 12 rebounds, but Parkside fell in their first state final appearance to Mt. Hebron, 60-52. It was the sixth title in 12 seasons for Mt. Hebron, and just the next in a string of unfortunate and untimely season-ending defeats for the Rams.

Kesha Camper was a co-captain and led the Maryland Terrapins in field goal percentage her senior season. At Parkside, she tallied more than 1,500 points and 1,000 rebounds. University of Maryland Athletics.

Camper went off to Maryland, where she became a solid contributor to Chris Weller's program almost right away. In a win over Florida State her freshman season, Camper scored 12 points and grabbed eight boards in just 18 minutes of action. Camper was an All-ACC Freshman Team selection as a rookie and the Terps made the Elite Eight. As a senior, she was the co-captain of the Terps and led the team in field goal percentage, making 46.1% of her 282 shot attempts. Her best game came her junior year against Howard, where she tallied 33 points and 12 boards in a victory.

Without Camper, Lewandowski led Parkside to two more state final four appearances in 1993 and 1995, but still couldn't win the big one over western shore foes. After winning more than 300 games, Lewandowski resigned as the head coach of the Rams' girls basketball team ahead of the 1996-97 season.

"Parkside had a pretty strong culture of winning," said Kelley Gibson, whose Easton team beat Parkside for the Bayside Championship in 1994. "It was always tough. Those were always pretty tough games."

Lewandowski's successor would be one of his assistant coaches, Warren White. A James M. Bennett graduate, White – who played on the 1968 Bennett boys team that made the state final four – started coaching basketball in the local youth leagues, then began helping out the boys and girls teams at Parkside when his daughters began attending school there. White told the Daily Times in 2007, "My roots are founded in the Salvation Army boys club, which is very crucial in helping our kids. I'm proud to say I got my start there." In high school, White was also a standout triple-jumper in track and field, and he played basketball collegiately at Delaware Tech. A prominent figure in Salisbury's Black community, White has also been the president of the Wicomico County NAACP.

Warren White has coached the Parkside girls team since 1996. Photo by Mitchell Northam.

After a brief dip in his first season on the job in 1996-97 – in which Parkside finished with an uncharacteristic 11-13 record – the Rams returned to their winning ways. But under White's direction, the Parkside girls weren't just as good as they once were; they were better. By March 1998, the Rams were contending again. Parkside hosted the 2A East Region Final that year, but had to play it without three starters due to disciplinary reasons, according to the Daily Times. Without them, the Rams fell 53-45 to the Baltimore Polytechnic Institute. And the Rams missed 20 free throws, which made the loss sting just a bit more. "We knew we had to go without them and it would be a monumental task," White said. "We had our opportunities at the free throw line and could not convert. That hurt."

Indeed, the defeat was deeply felt. But Parkside's confidence and potential could not be ignored. They finished the season with a 20-3 record and the Rams would return all of their key players the next season. The 1998-99 campaign would be different. White knew he had talent, and he knew what they were capable of accomplishing.

***

The 1998-99 high school basketball season was Warren White's third season at Parkside High School and he was entering the year with a pretty talented squad. In the backcourt was senior Beth Houck and junior Rene Wallace, who averaged 22 and 18 points per-game, respectively, the previous year. The duo paced the offense and set the tone defensively, and they were surrounded by solid role players in Ebony Ballard, Aileah Morris and Kema Dashiell.

Additionally, a few sophomores and freshmen were joining the varsity ranks. Rookie Kim Davis proved to be a valuable contributor to the team right away and would be a key part of the Rams' success.

"We have good size without a true center. We have a lot of quickness," White told the Daily Times in December 1998. "We have an excellent chance for a great season."

White also had an experienced staff that was invested in seeing Parkside and its players succeed at the highest level. Kesha Camper had returned to the sidelines and worked under White, and so had Shawn Tucker, Parkside's all-time leading scorer for boys basketball.

After graduating from Parkside in 1994, Tucker went to Salisbury University and played one season. He was a good player, no doubt, but he thought he was better than the Sea Gulls; he convinced himself he was Division I material.

"I'm thinking I'm higher than what I am. I didn't really understand it," Tucker says. So, he went a bit further down Route 13 to the University of Maryland Eastern Shore and tried to walk-on with the Hawks of the MEAC. "I didn't have a shot, and then I ended up breaking my foot," Tucker says. "I struggled." Tucker joined the Coast Guard and served his country for several years between active and inactive time, and played a bit of basketball while he was enlisted too. He came home around 1998 and knew he wanted to be involved with basketball. When he went back to his alma mater, White pulled him aside and said, "Boy, you're going to coach with me."

"Basketball saved my life," Tucker says. "Because basketball is one of those few sports that you can relate to life. You can be up one minute, down the next minute, and you just have to make adjustments after adjustments. It's saved lives around the Shore."

Shawn Tucker is still the all-time leading boys scorer at Parkside with 1,350 points. After stints as the head coach at Mardela and an assistant at his alma mater, Tucker became an assistant coach at Salisbury University. Photo by Mitchell Northam.

***

Red and black balloons floated in the air behind the James M. Bennett bench. It was head coach Amy Fenzel-Mergott's birthday, and her players wanted to celebrate her. Unfortunately, the Bennett Clippers played the Parkside Rams that night on Dec. 11, 1998 and there were a lot of sad faces stationed in front of those balloons when the final whistle sounded. Parkside never trailed en route to its fourth win of the season, as Houck's 21 points powered the Rams to a 54-46 win over their city rival. "Parkside is a very talented team," Fenzel-Mergott said after the game. "It would have been nice to win this game on my birthday, but some things are just not meant to be." While Bennett's coach was disappointed about not getting a victory on her special day, Warren White was a bit miffed that his team scored below its average of 75 points. "The difference was finishing off our running game with baskets. I know we can play better," White told the Daily Times. "But sometimes, being good instead of great is good enough."

As the year turned from 1998 to 1999, Parkside was often great and only twice were they not good enough. The Rams won the Bayside South and entered the conference championship game – a matchup with Colonel Richardson – with a 21-2 record.

"Beth Houck, Kim Davis... I mean, we were loaded," Tucker said. "We had some really good guards."

On Feb. 24, 1999 at the Wicomico Youth & Civic Center, Davis broke out and tallied 19 points, leading Parkside to its first conference title since 1994, a victory that reestablished the Rams as a power in girls basketball on the Eastern Shore. "We did not play well, but we played well enough to win," said Houck, who had 18 points and nine boards in the 69-56 triumph over the Colonels. "I've waited a long time for this win." It was a total team effort with everyone pitching in. Wallace had 14 points, four steals and four assists, Dashiell added 10 points and Morris corralled 14 boards. Parkside turned the ball over 27 times, but it didn't matter. "Every time Colonel Richardson made a run at us, the girls found a way to put it down," White said.

Colonel Richardson head coach Darnell Lake didn't think the Rams played poorly at all, heaping praise on them after the game. He told the Easton Star Democrat: "They're like a Duke team to me. They have it all."

Parkside's only two defeats of the regular season came during a holiday tournament against non-Bayside Conference teams, so the Rams were confident entering the early stages of the 2A East playoffs. Their first postseason opponent in 1999 was Stephen Decatur, a squad the Rams had bested soundly twice before. Their third meeting was no different. Parkside never trailed, jumped out to a 31-9 lead and then coasted to a 24-point triumph. Wallace had 20 points and seven steals (which put her over 100 thefts for the season), and it was clear that the Rams were head and shoulders above the local competition. "The scoreboard speaks for itself," a dejected Dawn Andrews, Decatur's head coach, told the Daily Times.

In the regional semifinal, the Rams appeared to be shaken early on, falling behind 11-4 in Centreville after Queen Anne's opened the game with a trio of three-point baskets, two of which came from Damika Baker. White called a timeout, and then the Rams got on a roll. 70-34 was the final in Parkside's favor, as they forced 27 turnovers and pulled down 50 rebounds, 22 of which were from the offensive glass. After the contest, Queen Anne's head coach Jody Hyde summed up what made the Rams so great to the Star Democrat, saying, "The thing with that defense is, any mistake you make, they can take advantage of it. They show a 2-3 zone, but they're just waiting for you to get in their spider's web.

"They're like black widows: and there you are – you're dead."

For the second straight year, Parkside earned the right to host the 2A East Region Final. And again, the Rams' opponent was a team from Baltimore;

this time, it was the Dunbar Poets. And while Dunbar's girls program didn't have the same reputation as its boys, the Poets were still a talented bunch with a 20-4 record. Dunbar jumped out to a 7-2 lead on Parkside, but the Rams didn't fret. Wallace sank a three-pointer that sparked a 9-1 run from the Rams. In the end, Wallace, Houck and Davis – the freshman sensation – combined for 60 points, leading Parkside to a 75-68 win and its first final four appearance since 1995. "I'm happy beyond tears," Houck told the Daily Times after the emotional victory.

Heading into the state semifinals in Catonsville at the University of Maryland-Baltimore County, Parkside had four players averaging double-digits in scoring with Houck's 18.4 points-per-game, Wallace's 16.2, Davis' 11.8 and Kema Dashiell's 11.1. But the reputation the Rams had earned wasn't for their offense. "I've heard they get a lot of points off their defense. We'll have to do a good job of not making turnovers," Central head coach Eugene Cowser told the Daily Times just days before the state semifinals.

Ahead of the matchup at UMBC, Parkside felt like most Eastern Shore teams that make the trip over the Bay Bridge – they felt disrespected and overlooked by their peers. That was enough motivation to not only beat Central, but to do so in a dominant fashion. Behind Houck's impressive stat-stuffing effort of 28 points, 13 rebounds and eight steals, the Rams won 81-62, punching their ticket to the state final for just the second time in school history. And indeed, Parkside lived up to their defensive expectations, forcing Central into 32 turnovers and giving the Falcons from Prince George's County their worst defeat of the season. Davis added 23 points and seven boards too for the Rams, who seemed fearless and unbeatable heading into the final. And finally, they felt like they earned recognition from the western shore folks.

"People kept talking about how easy the Bayside was, and how our girls might be good on our side of the bridge, but would not stack up to the competition over here. I think we stacked up very well," White told the Daily Times after the game.

In the 2A state final, Parkside faced Urbana of Frederick County, and capturing the ultimate trophy wouldn't be as easy as some of the Rams' other postseason accomplishments.

After the first period ended with a tied score of 15-15, Parkside fell into an awful slump, making just 1-of-11 shots in the second quarter. In total, Urbana out-rebounded the Rams 30-15 in the first half and forced Parkside into 14 turnovers to take a 12-point lead at intermission. Houck and Wallace, the Rams' veteran scoring duo, were held to just 10 points combined. Daily Times columnist John Evans noted that Urbana fans had already started their victory party, and scribes from Frederick County were polishing off their game stories declaring Urbana as the champs. "Only trouble was," Evans wrote, "nobody told the Lady Rams they were dead."

The Rams talked it out and got back on track. "We go in at halftime and we're like, 'There's no 20-point shot.' We got to chip, chip, chip away," Tucker said.

"We just talked about winning the game," Houck told the Daily Times, and she opened the third quarter by swishing a three-ball to cut the deficit to nine points. By the end of the third quarter, Parkside still trailed, but only by seven points and it was apparent that the Rams had figured out Urbana's press. The lead was within reach. And in the final period of the game, White handed the keys of the offense to Davis, the freshman who had scored just two points in the previous three quarters. White told the Daily Times: "She's 5-foot-4, but she's very strong. We knew when we started sending Kim inside that they would not be able to stop her."

White was right. Davis ripped off 15 points in the fourth quarter, a run that included her scoring the game-winning basket. Urbana's Jennie Orelli had swished a three-pointer with 21 seconds left to give her team a 59-58 advantage. Five seconds later, Parkside fired up a quick shot that missed, but Davis grabbed the rebound and lofted up a putback shot while falling away. It sank, and Parkside led 60-59 with 14 seconds to go. Orelli tried to fire a long pass up the court on the next possession, but it sailed over her teammate's head. Davis was fouled on the next possession and missed both free throws, but then grabbed her own rebound off the second miss. She was fouled again and – again – missed both charity stripe shots. Call it freshman jitters, but ultimately, it didn't matter. Urbana's half-court effort at the buzzer was off the mark.

At long last, the Parkside Rams were champs. And nobody could tell them nothing.

"We are the beast of the east, and we'll wear it well after today," White told the Daily Times. "People have to respect us now. That was what this was really all about."

***

Parkside joined Snow Hill and Easton as the girls basketball programs from the Eastern Shore to win state titles in the modern era, a group that Pocomoke would join years later too. They remain the only girls team from the Shore to win a state title in the 2A class, as of 2021.

Beth Houck finished her career at Parkside as second on the all-time scoring charts, just behind one of her coaches, Kesha Camper. The 5-foot-11 shooting guard was an all-state selection her senior season and signed a national letter-of-intent to play at Division II Catawba College in – seriously, of all places – Salisbury, North Carolina. Before heading to the Tar Heel State, Houck joined a group of 15 American youths to play in a summer basketball tour in Holland.

In 2000, White's Rams won their second straight Bayside Conference championship with a 66-60 win over North Dorchester behind 58 combined points from Davis, Wallace and Dashiell. The victory was Parkside's 34th consecutive victory against fellow Bayside teams. The Rams made it to the state final four again, but failed to defend their state championship, losing in the semifinals by three points to Linganore, another squad from Frederick County. Wallace finished her career at Parkside as the holder of the single-season steals record with 135 thefts and went on to play at the University of Maryland Eastern Shore.

Kim Davis continued to climb the scoring charts at Parkside, eventually passing Houck and Camper, finishing her prep career with 2,192 points. She signed her national letter of intent to play at Hagerstown Community College with Camper sitting to her left, smiling. "She's a tremendous athlete, one of those players that loves that game of basketball," White told the Daily Times of Davis in 2001, after she was honored with one of her countless Athlete of the Week awards. "She's a joy to coach."

Camper kept coaching, and eventually succeeded the late, great Barbara McCool as the head coach at Mardela. Between 2010 and 2014, she guided the Warriors to four state semifinal appearances and a pair of Bayside Conference championships.

Kesha Camper succeeded Barbara McCool as the head girls basketball coach at Mardela. She led the Warriors to four state semifinal appearances. Photo by Mitchell Northam.

Dashiell finished her career at Parkside with 1,406 points, good enough for top five on the school scoring charts, and went on to play at Cecil Community College.

White, as of 2022, is still the head coach at Parkside and still coaches the youth every now and then at the Salvation Army in Salisbury. In May of 2021, his former understudy Shawn Tucker – now an assistant coach for the men's team at Salisbury University – held a youth basketball clinic at the old gyms on the corner of Oak and Elmwood streets, and White was there to help out.

For Tucker, being an assistant on Parkside's state championship squad helped crystalize his path for him.

"It was amazing and I was like, 'This is what I'm supposed to be doing,' That was when I knew I could coach, when we got (to states) and I could make adjustments and I could feel it," Tucker said. "So, 1999 with Coach White, I give all props to him. He's not only a coach to me, he's like a father figure to me that I didn't have. He's an amazing coach."

Tucker continued singing White's praises, saying: "The man is knowledgeable about everything. And he's connected. He knows how to get what he wants out of the players and he knows his style. He's particular about his style, but he's raised generations of young ladies. He's that guy."

Since winning his second Bayside title in 2000, White has added two more conference crowns to his collection, beating Kent Island in 2013 and Easton in 2020. His Rams reached the state semifinals again in 2005 and 2009. On Feb. 10, 2020, Parkside walloped Crisfield 63-12 at home to give White his 400th career win. He's over 70 years old now, but doesn't plan on hanging up his whistle anytime soon. His granddaughter became a freshman at Parkside during the 2020-21 school year, and White told the Daily Times she demanded that he be her basketball coach. And so, he says, "If I'm healthy and ready to go, I'll be here."

And so will that green and white state championship basketball banner from 1999 that hangs in Parkside's gym.

CARLTON DOTSON: THE FALLEN STAR

"I love Carlton, even today, no matter what he did. He's paying the price, dearly. That's not going to stop me from feeling the way that I always have about him." – Vic Burns

During the COVID-19 pandemic, when everyone was locked inside and had time to reflect and argue, a thing folks from the Eastern Shore liked to do was talk about high school basketball on social media. There would be long threads on Twitter and Facebook of people going back and forth about who was the greatest player, which team was the most talented and which era was the best. A decade or two ago – hell, even just weeks before March of 2020 – these would've been arguments they might've had with their buddies at the bar at Brew River in Salisbury, or at Joe Rocks Barber Shop in Federalsburg.

When these debates happen, there's typically one extremely talented player that is always omitted from the conversation. This player, by Eastern Shore standards, reached the highest of highs. He brought his high school a championship and went on to play big-time college basketball in the Big 12.

However, many say he also brought some shame and unwanted attention to the Shore.

On May 9, 2020, during a casual Facebook Live chat, Nick Purnell and Andre Collins – two of the top basketball minds on the Shore, who both played and coached – decided to talk about him, briefly.

Purnell: "A name that goes without mentioning in the 90s was a gentleman by the name of Carlton Dotson from North Dorchester, who went and won a state championship."

Collins: "Carlton was on the AAU team that I was on. His name doesn't get mentioned enough."

Purnell: "His name don't get mentioned. And the reason why it don't get mentioned is because of the trouble that he got into, so people done threw him in the back burner. That kid could play."

Collins: "Yes, he was very skilled. Carlton's name can come up, because he did get to that college level... But they won't speak on his ability because of what happened during his time in college. But Carlton definitely had the ability to do whatever he wanted. Carlton was a pro. I don't know what level, but he was a pro."

In 2017, Showtime produced a documentary called "Disgraced" that won a Sports Emmy. It's a compelling, comprehensive and unsparing piece of journalism and filmmaking. In it, director Pat Kondelis explores the lives of Carlton Dotson, Patrick Dennehy and Dave Bliss, and the events that have them linked together forever. The three are intertwined through basketball at Baylor University, a pay-for-play college athletics scandal, an attempted scapegoat scheme and a murder in a field near a gravel pit and a creek bed in 2003 that became a nationwide story.

At one point in the documentary, a woman tells the filmmakers: "It's one of those things people around here do not talk about."

For her, "around here" is Waco, Texas, the site of the crime and the home to Baylor University, the world's largest Baptist institution. But she might as well have been talking about the Eastern Shore. It is difficult to get folks from the Shore to talk about Dotson, his career at North Dorchester High School, his playing days at Baylor, or the summer of 2003 – when law enforcement, TV cameras and reporters swarmed the Delmarva Peninsula looking for him.

The story of Dotson, Baylor and the summer of 2003 has no silver linings, no lessons to be learned, no grand narrative and no happy endings. There is only pain, lies and wonderings of what if?

Long before that summer though, Dotson was just a kid in northern Dorchester County, dribbling a basketball, thinking about his hoop dreams.

***

In 1801, 66 cents was all it cost to buy an acre of land in the slice of northeastern Dorchester County known today as Hurlock. The town really started to grow in 1890, since it was the home of the intersection of two major railroads: the Baltimore, Chesapeake and Atlantic Railroad, and the Delaware Railroad. The town was incorporated two years later, and the town's motto to this day is still, "On track since 1892." Not many trains go through Hurlock nowadays. Just once a year, during the town's annual fall festival on the first Saturday in October, it runs two historic passenger cars to Federalsburg, about seven miles away.

Hurlock isn't exactly a destination on the Eastern Shore. For most folks, Hurlock is a place you drive through trying to get to somewhere else. If you're in Preston and need to go to Cambridge, you go through Hurlock. If you're in East New Market and need to get to Seaford, Delaware, you go through Hurlock. If you're in Denton and need to get to Vienna, you go through Federalsburg and then Hurlock. In this way, Hurlock isn't unlike most communities on the Eastern Shore.

The Hurlock High School boys basketball team in 1931. Courtesy of the Talbot Historical Society, Easton, Maryland.

The town of about 2,000 people is stationed between the Choptank River and the Marshyhope Creek, two poultry plants – Perdue and Amick – and B&G Foods Inc., a pickle plant. The town has one stoplight, its tallest structure is a water tower, and the best eats near there is about six miles west of town at Suicide Bridge Restaurant. The seafood spot on the water near a bridge with an ominous history is a popular venue for celebration dinners – wedding rehearsals, graduations, birthdays, whatever – and a place where young boys with a bit of cash take their high school prom dates.

North Dorchester High School opened its doors in the fall of 1954. It was the last of three public high school projects to be completed that decade, following the construction of South Dorchester High School and a Black school, Mace's Lane. North Dorchester was built about three miles south of Hurlock, near an unincorporated community known as Shiloh, and it absorbed students from previous high schools in Hurlock and Vienna. The school's first Black student was Larry Pinkett, who voluntarily integrated North Dorchester in 1963. That same year, in July after six people were shot amid racial protests and riots, Gov. J. Millard Tawes assigned more than 400 rifle-carrying National Guard troops in nearby Cambridge as limited martial law was imposed. Pinkett starred on the football, basketball and track teams, and was essentially North Dorchester's Jackie Robinson.

It took 20 years for the North Dorchester Eagles to achieve real success in team sports. Coached by Denis Lamparter, the Eagles' boys basketball team breezed through its regular season with a 20-1 record and seemed like real contenders in 1983. One of the leaders on the team was Carlton Dotson Sr., a 6-foot-3 forward. For the second straight season, the Eagles appeared in the Bayside Championship game, but lost by a single possession. Their girls team did win the conference crown though, beating Snow Hill 42-40.

Behind Dotson's 16.6 points and 9.6 rebounds per-game, the North Dorchester boys powered through the playoffs and topped Flintstone 56-54 in the semifinals in College Park behind 15 points each from Dotson and Wayne Batson. The state final didn't turn out as well, as Hammond stifled Dotson with a zone defense and went on to win 73-51, capturing the first state boys basketball title for Howard County. Despite tallying just six points and four boards in the title bout, Dotson was named Bayside Player of the Year by the Easton Star Democrat.

Carlton Eric Dotson Jr. was born in 1982, just months before his father competed for a state championship. The child's mother was Gilreatha Waters and she too was a high school student, just 16 years old. Gilreatha gave custody of her child to her grandparents, Gilbert and Mildred Waters, who raised Dotson in a small brown cinderblock bungalow with a gravel driveway on a rural road north of the railway town, surrounded by woods and wheat fields.

When reporters showed up to the home in July of 2003, Gilbert – then 80 and retired from working on the railroad – and Mildred still lived there, and a broken-down basketball backboard laid on its side behind the house.

***

In the fall of 1988, Denis Lamparter accepted a new job within the Dorchester School District and resigned as the head coach of the boys basketball program at North Dorchester. Leaders at the school tapped Vic Burns, a 1970 Cambridge High School graduate, to replace him. An Eastern Shore native, Burns was also a graduate of Salisbury State College. "And the name changed three times I was there," he said with a chuckle. Burns got his start in teaching in special education in Charles County. In 1980, he returned to Dorchester County to teach and coach at Shiloh.

The boy varsity basketball job was one Burns was heavily interested in, but he didn't think the opportunity would come so soon. Burns had been working at North Dorchester for eight years at that point as a physical education teacher and had previously coached the boys JV basketball team, the girls varsity basketball team, and the track and field teams at North Dorchester. In 1985, Burns guided the boys cross country team to a Class C state championship.

Heading into his first season on the job as the head boys varsity basketball coach, Burns told the Star Democrat: "I would like to finish above .500. And I would definitely like to get back to the playoffs."

A decade later, Burns had much loftier goals for his team. At some point in the mid-1990s, Burns heard there was a middle schooler who was 6-foot-1. His name was Carlton Dotson. And his class, and the class one year ahead of him, was loaded with athletes. Burns knew that, pretty soon – if all those kids stayed in the North Dorchester system – he would have a supremely talented team. "You knew something special was going to happen with that group," Burns said.

The Eagles ended the 1997-98 season with a 55-51 loss to Pocomoke in the region final, a game that had its outcome derailed by a controversial call. Referees gave North Dorchester a technical with under five minutes left because Grayson Hurley – then an assistant coach for Burns – stood at the scorer's table for too long. "Grayson went up to find something out, and the next thing I knew, he had a T," Burns told the Star Democrat. Pocomoke used the technical free throws to grow its lead to 10 points, then coasted to a four-point win and a spot in the state final four.

Despite the loss, Burns had the core of his team returning for the 1998-99 season, including steady and savvy point guard Reggie Parker, stout center Bill Blackwell and the versatile and ultra-talented 6-foot-6 Carlton Dotson, who could deliver bruises in the paint and soft, precise shots from beyond the arc. On the sidelines guiding the team once again was Burns, rocking his trademark mustache, and a jolly and relaxed Hurley.

"Any coach knows that if you have a really good point guard and a big kid, that's the start of any kind of successful season. You can build around that," Burns said. "Blackwell was like our Dennis Rodman, getting a lot of the rebounds and trash and putbacks. And Tarrod Jackson, he didn't score a whole lot, but he was sort of our missing piece to the puzzle. He transferred in from Florida. He was always where he needed to be. He hit some big three-pointers for us."

In its 1998-99 season-opener in Shiloh, North Dorchester exacted revenge from its playoff loss to Pocomoke, beating the Warriors 57-42. In the first five minutes of the game, the Eagles jumped out to a 13-3 lead, a run punctuated by Parker feeding Dotson for a dunk that shook the lone set of bleachers in North Dorchester's tiny gym. "Anytime you beat Pocomoke, I don't care how good or bad they are, it's a good thing," Burns said after the game.

"Dotson was a freakin' stud for the Eastern Shore. A good player," said former Pocomoke head coach David Byrd. "Dotson was just so big. He was hard to handle, and built."

The first job Will Graves landed when he finished up his education at West Virginia University in 1997 was as a sports reporter for the Easton Star

Democrat newspaper. For the 1998-99 high school basketball season, one of Graves' assignments was to cover the North Dorchester Eagles.

"It was very obvious from early on in his career that Carlton was a special player," said Graves, who grew up in Waldorf, Maryland. "You could just tell that he was at a different level than everyone else out there. He was so big and athletic."

Typically, when a coach in the Bayside Conference inherits a player with any kind of real height, they stick them in the paint and just feed them balls in the post. With Dotson, Burns didn't do that. He allowed Dotson to play freely, to take three-pointers, to handle the ball and to play along the perimeter.

"Vic knew that kid was going to be a Division I talent and that he needed a diverse game," Graves said. "I mean, they could've put him on the block and Carlton would've averaged 45 points a game if he wanted to. Vic gave him that freedom to just play."

The Eagles finished the regular season with just two losses and met Wicomico High School in the Bayside Championship game, its first appearance in the conference bout since 1991. But Curtis McNeal scored 20 points for the Indians and Wi-Hi stifled the Eagles to take a 47-38 victory.

"Vic Burns and I are just good friends. Vic knew the game, but sometimes he had an odd way of doing things," Wi-Hi head coach Butch Waller said. "When we played them in that Bayside Championship – to this day, I still don't know what defense he was running. It was some sort of junk defense. It was a close game and that defense gave us trouble. I didn't make a very good adjustment because I didn't know what the hell he was doing."

Burns gives credit for North Dorchester's defensive scheme that season to Hurley, his assistant coach. Burns described it as a "match-up zone" scheme which "looked like a 1-1-2-1." While it didn't beat Wi-Hi that day, it gave opposing Bayside teams fits all season long.

"Nobody knew what it was," Burns said. "We just went out and pressured the ball. Sometimes we doubled in half-court and sometimes not. It confused a lot of people that year." By season's end, North Dorchester had allowed opponents to score just 48 points per-game while it was scoring an average of 72.5 points per-game on the other end. Often, the Eagles left opposing defenses feeling lost and bewildered, like blindfolded cows wearing roller-skates.

Luckily, North Dorchester didn't have to see Wi-Hi in the playoffs with the Indians being in a classification above the Eagles. Burns' side rolled through the early rounds of the playoffs only to see Pocomoke again in the 1A East Region Final. To beat the Warriors once more, all the Eagles needed was Hurley's defense and the offensive prowess of Dotson. When the Eagles' 14-point third quarter lead vanished inside Parkside's gym and Pocomoke tied the game at 39-39, Dotson put the Eagles on his broad shoulders. Amidst an 11-0 Eagles run that put them in front for good, Dotson swished a three-pointer and drained four free throws. "I had to score," Dotson told the Salisbury Daily Times. "My team looks up to me. I didn't have a choice."

By this point – near the end of Dotson's junior season – he was being sought after by Division I college coaches. Cincinnati, USC, Georgetown, Georgia and several Atlantic-10 schools had all expressed varying degrees of interest in the tall kid from Hurlock, and he had a box full of recruiting letters. Like his father before him, Dotson had powered a North Dorchester team to the state final four, and his talents were about to be seen on a much larger stage.

In the week leading up to the semifinals, Burns didn't stress out his players with preparation or try to over-manage them. He assigned Hurley – who had guided Cambridge-South Dorchester to a pair of state titles – to run the players through a series of shooting drills.

"Grayson and I were very good friends," Burns said. "And it was a tough situation for him, because he had been very successful at Cambridge. The main thing that he brought was great relationships with the kids."

In the semifinals, Oakland Mills High School of Howard County was the Eagles' opponent. Mills was armed then with a pair of 6-foot-7 players and many thought they were the favorite to win the 1A state title.

While many teams would have attempted to devise a scheme to stop Dotson, Oakland Mills focused its defensive efforts on trying to rattle Reggie Parker, North Dorchester's 5-foot-8 point guard who was much more than a name filling a space on the depth chart.

"Carlton was the best player, but Reggie really ran that team," Graves said. "There were better players than Reggie, but there wasn't a more important player. He couldn't shoot, but he was a really good distributor, a good defender, smart and did a really good job of controlling the tempo."

Parker was the Eagles' steady hand, conductor, defensive leader, quarterback and passing wizard. During the school day, Parker often wore elevated shoes to strengthen his leg muscles. He and Burns spent a lot of time together, as the coach would often give his point guard rides home from practices and games.

"Reggie had Division I handles," Burns said. "He could handle the ball against anybody. And he was just a tough kid. He was thick, strong and had a pretty good basketball head on his shoulders. And he was unselfish. He never looked to score points. He always wanted to dish. He was just trying to make people around him better. He could do anything with a basketball."

Against Oakland Mills, Parker fought through a full-court press and triple teams for 32 minutes. He played a clean and efficient game, and finished with nine points, six dimes, four rebounds and zero turnovers in a 53-50 win.

Dotson – who claimed after the game he had bronchitis – scored 29 points, and flushed a pull-up jumper from the left elbow with 34 seconds to play to give his squad the go-ahead basket. "Parker was the key to the game," Oakland Mills head coach David Appleby told the Star Democrat. "He was as advertised – a good ball handler and he controlled things. We got down to the nitty gritty and he was the one who had the poise."

Against Pikesville in the state final, North Dorchester played even better. By the third quarter, the Eagles had built an insurmountable 23-point lead by way of a 30-6 run across eight minutes. With less than five minutes to play in the final period, Bill Blackwell was grabbing Parker at midcourt, gazing at the scoreboard with joy and telling his teammate: "This is it."

Parker tallied 10 points and a Maryland state final record 13 assists. Blackwell piled up 15 points, 16 boards and four blocks, and Dotson added 22 points, seven rebounds and four blocks while facing a box-and-one defense. In a dominant dismantling of Pikesville, the Eagles captured a 73-42 emphatic victory.

"The ease in which they won the title game with was kind of remarkable," Graves said. "They expected to win. You would think there would be all this pressure, but once they got to the final, they were so relaxed. They were very chill about it for 16 and 17-year-old kids."

The Eagles held Pikesville to 28% shooting, and Blackwell's defense – and Hurley's scheme – were a big reason why. Blackwell blocked 96 shots in the 1998-99 season, an average of 3.7 swats per-game as the Eagles finished the season with a 23-3 record.

"All year long, we've been the underdog," Blackwell told the Star Democrat. "We weren't supposed to beat Easton, and we beat them twice. We weren't supposed to beat Cambridge, and we beat them twice. We weren't supposed to come here and win, and we came here and did it… I could never put into words what this means. It's special."

Parker was named the Star Democrat's Mid-Shore Player of the Year after averaging a Bayside-leading 7.4 assists per-game along with 11.3 points, 4.9 rebounds and 3.6 steals. Every team the Eagles faced tried to pry the ball out of Parker's hands. Most of them failed as he delivered dimes to Dotson.

While being interviewed for the *Disgraced* documentary, Burns reflected on the ride back from College Park to Hurlock: "It was a big deal for our community. I'll never forget coming through town that night. We were escorted in with the Hurlock police and sheriff's departments, sirens going. People (were) out on their front porch waving to us. It really did something for the kids."

Dotson signed the 1999 championship ball with his number and a moniker: 55 "King of Da Court."

***

When the 1999-2000 school year started, Carlton Dotson wasn't enrolled at North Dorchester High School. He was at Colonel Richardson, and seeking help with SATs from Merrill Morgan, a guidance counselor and the longtime boys basketball coach at the school outside of Federalsburg.

"He lived close to the (Caroline-Dorchester) county line," Morgan said. "But he was only at Colonel for about three or four days, and then he transferred back. He belonged over there. His mom just wouldn't leave him alone and wanted him back (at North Dorchester). I don't know. I like to think, maybe if he stayed at Colonel... Maybe he would've went in a different direction."

Added Graves: "His home life was not great, I knew that. Carlton was a good basketball player and that was his ticket out of there."

North Dorchester head coach Vic Burns was blindsided by Dotson's move to Colonel. Said Burns: "Yea, that was a mess. That even surprised me. I got to say, I was really ticked off over that. I was close to Carlton, and for him to do that without saying anything to me, was not cool. It hurt me. Supposedly, Carlton went there to try football. Whether that's true or not, I don't know."

Dotson never played in a football game for Colonel Richardson and was soon back at North Dorchester. He and Burns reconciled and geared up for one more season, one in which college coaches were closely watching Dotson as he continued to work on his academics and his basketball skills.

Entering the 1999-2000 season, Reggie Parker and Bill Blackwell had graduated, but Dotson was back in the fold, as was sharpshooting junior Tarrod Jackson. And as long as Dotson was on the floor and Burns was on the sidelines, North Dorchester was still viewed as a contender.

But in their season opener, the Eagles' inexperienced guard play was exposed, and Crisfield's Andre Collins scored 23 points in a 63-60 Crabbers win in Shiloh. Dotson had 22 points and 14 rebounds in the loss to his AAU teammate.

"Carlton was a big guy who could play down low, but could also shoot. He was one that didn't do a lot of talking. He was a really good player," Collins said. "Having his height around here is rare, and then he could handle the ball, shoot it, and was a pretty decent defender."

The Eagles finished the regular season of Dotson's senior year with just three losses. But in the playoffs, North Dorchester didn't quite have the same amount of talent required to beat Pocomoke again. In the 1A East Region semifinals, the Warriors held Dotson to 10 points and won 63-52. Pocomoke's Byrd told the Daily Times: "I don't think any one man can guard (Dotson). Every time he touched the ball in the post, we tried to double him. He's a great player."

Dotson was named Mid-Shore Player of the Year by the Star Democrat, and Burns was named Coach of the Year. "Vic was a good coach," Morgan said. "We had some good battles." Dotson, often seen back then as a jokester, was voted "most athletic" and "biggest flirt" by his classmates. To his senior prom, he wore a white jacket and two-toned shoes, and he carried a cane and wore a black hat.

Earlier in the year, Dotson had initially verbally accepted an athletic scholarship from the University of Buffalo, but failed to qualify for the school academically. Many of the teams from the Atlantic-10 Conference were interested in him too, and then-UMass head coach Bruiser Flint came to see Dotson play one night at Colonel Richardson. That night, Burns says, the game was closed off to fans because of fights at the time between kids from Federalsburg and Hurlock, so Bruiser sat in the stands, nearly alone, and watched Dotson play at American Corner.

Without the right combination of grades and test scores he needed, Dotson – instead of jumping to Division I right away – went to Paris Junior College, a school about 110 miles northeast of Dallas.

Around the same time Dotson went to the Lonestar State, Burns went to the Sunshine State, accepting a teaching and coaching job in Umatilla, Florida. He left the school south of Hurlock with more than 150 wins and one memorable championship.

"He was a really good dude," former Star Democrat sports reporter Will Graves said of Burns. "He just had a really special way with those kids and he would always try to downplay his impact."

***

Dotson spent two seasons at Paris Junior College, regularly leading the team in scoring. In his second season, he averaged 12.7 points and 7.1 rebounds per-game and was named to the All-Region XIV team while leading Paris to a 24-9 record and an appearance in the regional championship game. "He knew his role. He was a very skilled player," Paris coach William Foy told the Dallas Morning News. "Unselfish. Very coachable. He was a guy you could count on." While he was at Paris, Dotson met Melissa Kethley, a softball player from nearby Sulphur Springs. In late 2002, they were married.

By the fall of 2002, Dotson was enrolled at Baylor University, brought in by head coach Dave Bliss who was attempting to turn around the Bears' struggling program. A Bobby Knight disciple, Bliss had been a head coach in Division I college basketball since 1975 and had stops at Oklahoma, SMU and New Mexico before coming to Baylor. Along the way, he won more than 500 games and developed a penchant for turning his teams into winners quickly. Bliss' teams had made the NCAA Tournament within four years of his hiring in each of his previous three stops.

At Baylor, the turnaround wasn't moving quickly. In his first three seasons, Bliss hadn't posted a winning record in the Big 12 and hadn't made a postseason appearance yet. In the summer of 2002, he brought in Dotson and Patrick Dennehy, a pair of long, rangy and adaptable forwards who could score inside and out.

While they were from opposite coasts, Maryland and California, Dotson and Dennehy bonded right away over action flicks, hip-hop and basketball dreams. Dotson was able to play right away for Baylor since he was coming from junior college, but Dennehy had to sit out a season due to NCAA transfer rules. He was coming from a fellow Division I, New Mexico, where he was kicked off the team after disrupting a practice, according to the New York Times. In his sophomore year at New Mexico, Dennehy averaged 10.6 points and 7.5 rebounds per-game while shooting 50.8% from the floor, and he was also seventh in the Mountain West in defensive win shares with a 1.3 mark.

Bliss said this of Dennehy and Dotson on Showtime's *Disgraced*: "Terrific player. Agile. (Dennehy) looked like he had all of the attributes that might allow him to be an NBA player... Carlton was very, very skilled offensively. Somebody I thought would be good for part-time minutes."

Dotson played far more than just part-time at the start of the 2002-03 season. By all accounts, things were going well for him, and the Hurlock kid looked like he belonged at the Division I level. Dotson's fourth game at Baylor was an 18-point outing in a win over Southwest Texas. He followed that up with seven points, four boards and two blocks in a 79-74 win over Louisiana-Monroe. Through his first six games at Baylor, Dotson was playing 21.5 minutes a night, averaging 8.5 points and 4.3 rebounds per-game. "Carlton Dotson, I think, continues to be the surprise of our newcomers," Bliss told Baylor's student newspaper after a Dec. 5 game.

And then, for whatever reason, Dotson's playing time declined. He had good performances here and there – scoring 10 points in a Jan. 25, 2003, loss to Oklahoma, and notching six points and three rebounds in a loss to Iowa State on Feb. 2 – but he spent the majority of his time on Baylor's bench. Far too often, his stat line in the box score looked like this one from a Feb. 23 win over Nebraska: eight minutes, three points, one rebound, two fouls.

In all, Dotson played in 28 games in the 2002-03 season at Baylor, starting once. He averaged 4.4 points and 2.6 rebounds per-game while shooting 38.5% from the floor, 35.1% from three-point range and 88.9% from the charity stripe.

What happened next is fuzzy because of conflicting reports from the time, but it was apparent Dotson's days at Baylor were over. The Dallas Morning News reported Dotson "didn't plan to return" to Baylor next season, while the Salisbury Daily Times was told by a Baylor University official that Dotson was released from his scholarship. But Baylor spokesman Scott Strickland told the Washington Post that Bliss and Dotson "agreed that he should transfer to a school where he might get more playing time." Then Andy Katz at ESPN reported Dotson was dismissed from the team in May 2003 for not showing up for a second drug test after failing a previous one. Finally, the New York Times wrote Dotson planned to transfer after Bliss told him he would "play little" in the following season.

Either way, by the late spring, Dotson's time at Baylor was essentially done. However, around that same time, according to multiple reports, his marriage to Kethley had fallen apart in just eight months and the two became estranged. Kethley would later tell the Fort Worth Star-Telegram that Dotson abused her and he had described himself to her as "a prophet."

While Dotson was trying to plot his next move in college basketball and fix his marriage, he moved in with his friend and former teammate, Patrick Dennehy, at the Sterling University Parks Apartments, room No. 11308.

***

In the spring of 2003, Bliss brought in Harvey Thomas, another lanky junior college transfer who could rebound and score inside and out. Thomas, of Fredericksburg, Virginia, spent his freshman season at Georgetown and his sophomore year at a JUCO. When he arrived at Baylor, he brought his cousin Larry Johnson with him.

Evidence presented in interviews on the Showtime documentary *Disgraced* points to Thomas and Johnson having a beef with Dennehy and Dotson. According to stories Dennehy told to his teammates, coaches and girlfriend, Johnson allegedly pulled a gun on him and Dotson in their apartment. Dennehy also claimed $300 was stolen from the apartment, and a third roommate says in the documentary he once saw Thomas through the peephole of the front door, brandishing a gun. Thomas has denied that he or his cousin threatened Dennehy or Dotson. On June 10, Bliss asked Thomas if Johnson had a gun, and then declined to look further into the alleged incident.

But three days prior, Dotson and Dennehy had acquired weapons: a .22-caliber rifle, a .32-caliber pistol and a 9 mm handgun. On June 10, Dotson and Dennehy went out to a farm owned by Tammy and Darren Cox to fire their new guns. On June 11, Dennehy spoke to his girlfriend on the phone and promised to call her back, but never did. On June 12, Tammy Cox saw Dotson and Dennehy outside of a Taco Bell in Waco. On June 15, Valerie and Brian Brabazon were bewildered when Dennehy didn't call his stepfather on his birthday. On June 16, the third roommate at apartment 11308 found Dennehy's prized pit bulls locked up in the bathroom – the dogs hadn't eaten in days and there were feces everywhere. On June 19, Dennehy's parents called the police in Waco to report their son – a 21-year-old communications major with a bright future in basketball – missing.

By then, Dotson was back home in Hurlock, 1,542 miles away from Waco.

On June 23, Dennehy's dark blue 1996 Chevrolet Tahoe was found abandoned in a parking lot in Virginia Beach, not far from the Chesapeake Bay Bridge-Tunnel, one of the structures linking Delmarva to the rest of the world. A week later, one of the peninsula's tiny towns was about to be turned on its head.

***

News doesn't always break. Sometimes it just oozes, and the details just keep stacking up, like layers on a Smith Island Cake.

According to an affidavit released by Waco police on June 30, an informant told investigators in Delaware that Dotson told a cousin he shot and killed Dennehy with the 9 mm handgun after Dennehy had aimed a gun at him.

Before the sun rose on the first day of July 2003, Hurlock was flooded with print reporters, photographers, TV trucks and news anchors. They were all looking for Dotson, but many of them settled on talking to folks who knew – or claimed they knew – the former North Dorchester basketball star. And naturally, they all wanted to think the best of their native son who had made it out of the one-stoplight town to play college hoops on the highest level.

"I don't believe it," one resident told the Dallas Morning News. "For him to pick up a gun? A basketball yes, but not a gun."

"It's unreal," then-North Dorchester principal Greg Meekins told the Salisbury Daily Times. "This is uncharacteristic of the student I remember."

"Carlton's not the type of person to do anything crazy," a former classmate and waitress at the Hurlock Family Restaurant told the Baltimore Sun.

"Other than being an athlete, he was a normal guy," a woman claiming to be Dotson's senior prom date told the Associated Press.

By this time, Vic Burns was back on the Eastern Shore too, having just completed his second season of coaching the boys team at Queen Anne's County High School after a brief stay in Florida. When Burns first heard about what Dotson might have been involved with at Baylor, he and his wife were sitting on the beach in Ocean City. A newspaper reporter from New Mexico called him. The reporter asked Burns if he had heard the news.

"No. I don't even know what you're talking about," Burns told the reporter. But the former North Dorchester coach quickly found out. Because after the reporter from New Mexico hung up, his phone kept ringing. The next call was from the Maryland State Police. Then the next call was from ESPN. Burns' phone kept buzzing. "It was kind of ridiculous," Burns said.

Burns still felt a close bond to Dotson. He told the Star Democrat: "I loved the kid. And when I say love, I use that word strongly. I always felt like he was kind of like one of our own kids." Years later, Burns would later tell the filmmakers of *Disgraced*: "He spent the night at my house, you know, ate at my house, messed around with my kids. I would be proud if he married my daughter."

For the next week, television crews lined the streets of Hurlock. Locals smiled a bit on July 6, when a truck from WMAR-TV in Baltimore broke down in front of the police station and had to be towed away.

Dotson emerged from hiding on July 17 and voluntarily met with the FBI at the Dorchester County Sheriff's Office in Cambridge. The filmmakers behind *Disgraced* obtained a recording of the statement Dotson gave to the FBI that day. It was far from normal. A sampling: "There are things taking place that are unexplainable. People are trying to take me out... My faith is so strong. I have been taken over by a higher power." Dotson then giggles before saying, "My family is a family of prophets... All men (inaudible) sin, but there is time to repent. Time. To. Re. Pent."

No charges were filed that day and Dotson was picked up from the sheriff's office in a burgundy pickup truck driven by Burns, his high school coach. The sheriff's office had called Burns after they failed to get in touch with Dotson's father. Burns drove Dotson to his home, and a flock of reporters were waiting by his mailbox. Burns quickly phoned his wife and asked her to make room in the garage so he could pull his truck in without being hounded by media members. "He was a mess, to be honest with you," Burns said. "You could tell he hadn't slept. Some of things he was saying was just totally off the wall."

Burns says on *Disgraced*: "I was very concerned about his mental health at that time. I tried not to ask a lot of questions. I just wanted to talk to him and just make him know that I was there for him. He was talking about seeing angels. He was crying some. Talked about Jesus. Talking about the devil. He had said that he saw me in heaven... I told Carlton that, if there was something that was going on, that he needed to get off of his chest, that he needed to take care of that."

After seeing the documentary, Burns said, "I think it was fair."

Others interviewed in the documentary described Dotson at this time as someone who "said he was Jesus Christ" and went from room to room in his house reciting Bible verses and repeatedly sweeping the floors, over and over again. At the time, Dotson's lawyer Grady C. Irvin Jr. told the Washington Post his client had not slept for "several days."

On July 21, Dotson was some 55 miles away from Hurlock in Chestertown, a historic and mostly affluent community on the Chesapeake Bay in Kent County. Dotson walked into a grocery store and dialed 911 from a payphone. According to police, Dotson claimed he was hearing voices and asked to speak with the FBI. Inside a hotel room in Chestertown, Dotson confessed to the murder of Patrick Dennehy but suggested it was in self-defense. The FBI contacted police in Waco, an arrest warrant was issued and Dotson was charged with the murder of Dennehy.

Journalists raced – literally – toward Chestertown. Police in the town issued half-a-dozen speeding tickets to reporters on Route 213 and High Street. Todd Dudek, a veteran photographer with the Daily Times, made it to the Kent County District Court Commissioner's Office unscathed. His photo of Dotson – wearing blue jeans, a white Phat Farm shirt and handcuffs while being escorted by three law enforcement officers – appeared in newspapers across the country, from California, to New Mexico, to Texas, to North Carolina. While being transported, Dotson told one reporter: "I didn't confess to anything. Call the FBI."

Four days after Dotson confessed and was arrested, Dennehy's remains were found a quarter-mile down a dirt road off Junction 3400, near a rock quarry southeast of Waco. The scalding hot sun had baked his body into the Texas terrain, but dental records confirmed his identity. The autopsy report raised doubts about Dotson's claim of self-defense, as one of the two bullets that struck Dennehy entered behind his right ear.

A family in California continued to mourn, and a basketball community on the Eastern Shore began to grapple with its fallen star.

"I was shocked. Just because I spent so much time with him, on the road, in the summertime, sometimes two weeks at a time," said Dotson's former AAU teammate Andre Collins. "He was, you know, a funny kid. Quiet. Didn't have any altercations ever. So, I was pretty shocked when that happened."

"It was a shame," said longtime Wi-Hi head coach Butch Waller.

Will Graves was working in Florida in 2003 for the Naples Daily News. The night Dotson was arrested, longtime Star Democrat sports editor Bill Haufe called him and told him to turn on the TV. Graves flipped to MSNBC. "We were stunned at what happened. And then we were stunned at everything that happened after that," said Graves, now a sports writer for the Associated Press in Pittsburgh. "It's sad and unfortunate for all involved."

***

As Dotson sat in a jail cell, things were unraveling at Baylor. Dennehy's murder prompted a closer look at the men's basketball program, and Dave Bliss had plenty to hide.

"Let me explain something to you," former Baylor assistant coach Abar Rouse tells the filmmakers of *Disgraced*. "Nothing – there is nothing that happens without the head coach's knowledge. Ever. It doesn't happen."

Indeed, Rouse is largely correct. In big-time Division I college athletics, especially in football and men's basketball – high revenue sports – the head coach knows everything. Bliss knew who was doing drugs. He knew who had weapons. He knew who was getting paid. And he knew the NCAA was coming after him.

So, he began to devise a plan to cover his own ass. He didn't want the NCAA to find out he was paying Patrick Dennehy under the table, so he plotted to paint Dennehy as a drug addict and drug dealer, just another young man lost to drug culture. Bliss turned to his players and an assistant coach to help him do it. Only problem for Bliss was that assistant coach was Rouse, and he had a conscience. Rouse began secretly recording meetings with Bliss on July 30.

"There's nobody right now that can say that we paid Pat Dennehy because he's dead. OK?" Bliss is heard saying on one of Rouse's recordings, which was played on *Disgraced*. "So, what we have to do is, create the reasonable doubt. I got like 30 years; I've never talked to an NCAA investigator. OK? So, I mean, that stands for something. And the thing about it is, what the lawyers want to do is, all they got to handle is $2,000 for the down payment, and then $7,000 on his tuition. And what we've got to create here is drugs."

Bliss was caught on tape telling two of his players to lie to the NCAA and police. "What we have to do here is to create the perception that Pat was a dealer," Bliss says to the players as he hands them a tape recorder so they can practice telling the fables he's inventing. Bliss wanted his players to fight on his lies. Bliss was a man who would rather live in shit than have the world see him work a shovel.

On Aug. 7, Bliss shook the hand of Dennehy's stepfather at a memorial service for him. The next day, Bliss – getting a whiff of what was coming his way – resigned as Baylor's head coach. An investigation found Bliss was directly involved in paying tuition costs for Dennehy and another player, and drug tests by his players were not properly reported.

And then, on Aug. 15, Rouse handed three days' worth of recorded meetings with Bliss over to the Fort Worth Star-Telegram. The bombshell story, penned by Danny Robbins, was published the next day on the newspaper's front page. The above-the-fold headline read: "BLISS PLANNED COVER-UP."

Bliss never spent a day in jail and was only handed a 10-year show-cause by the NCAA. In disgusting fashion, some college coaches rushed to his defense and besmirched the character of Rouse, who – by all accounts – was the only person on the Bears' coaching staff who had any sort of a conscience. In a roundtable interview with ESPN's Jeremy Schapp, Duke's Mike Krzyzewski said he would never hire a coach like Rouse, who secretly recorded the head coach. Syracuse's Jim Boeheim and then-Oklahoma head coach Kelvin Sampson said Rouse "did the wrong thing."

Rouse would learn, as Butchie tells Omar in The Wire, "Conscience do cost." Rouse never coached in college basketball again, but Bliss did, getting a gig with Southwestern Christian University of the NAIA. He resigned from that post in 2017, shortly after *Disgraced* made its debut on Showtime. In the documentary, Bliss remained delusional, doubling down on his baseless claim that Dennehy was selling drugs "to all the white guys on campus." Bliss added: "He was the worst… They were so busy hanging me. He was a druggie."

It was a sad charade of flat-out lies and fabrication. Dennehy was never charged with a crime.

***

Nearly two years after Patrick Dennehy was murdered, Carlton Dotson pleaded guilty to the crime.

Dotson's guilty plea was unexpected, as it came just five days before his trial was set to begin in June of 2005.

In the fall of 2004, Dotson was sent to a Texas mental hospital after three doctors determined he was not competent to stand trial. However, the head of the psychiatric unit where Dotson was held for four months said otherwise, even though that doctor recommended he continue to take anti-psychotic medication. The psychologist also noted Dotson's claims of hearing voices seemed "suspect." Dotson's court-appointed attorneys Russ Hunt and Abel Reyna – both Baylor graduates – said they would not pursue an insanity defense, and State District Judge Ralph Strother never asked Dotson if he was competent enough to stand trial.

One of those attorneys, speaking anonymously, later told the Washington Post there was evidence to suggest both Dotson and Dennehy were using meth-laced marijuana. The Showtime documentary insinuated both attorneys wanted the trial to be put to bed quickly because it continued to embarrass Baylor.

Dotson plead guilty to the murder of Dennehy on the advice of his attorneys and his mother, and without any promise from prosecutors of a reduced sentence. At the age of 23, the slender kid from Hurlock with a smooth jumper who had dreams of playing in the NBA was sentenced to 35 years in prison for shooting and killing his former roommate and teammate. At the sentencing, Dennehy's stepfather held up a picture of his son and screamed "Remember him!" at Dotson while also calling him an "instrument of the devil." Dennehy's mother wanted a longer sentence and said the family would attend all parole hearings.

Dotson was eligible for parole for the first time on Dec. 15, 2020. It was denied then, and denied again on Feb. 7, 2022.

***

Since being sentenced to prison, Carlton Dotson has not spoken publicly often. He declined to be interviewed for the Showtime documentary and efforts to reach him for this book were unsuccessful. Dotson's old high school coach, Vic Burns, exchanged letters with him for the first few years of his incarceration and sent him books.

Burns lives in Naples, Florida as of this writing, and after coaching the boys basketball teams at North Dorchester, Queen Anne's, Washington and Cambridge, he left the Eastern Shore with more than 260 victories. The one season which is still sharpest in his memory is his 1998-99 campaign with Dotson and the ND Eagles.

"I love Carlton, even today, no matter what he did," Burns said. "He's paying the price, dearly. That's not going to stop me from feeling the way that I always have about him."

In 2008, Dotson spoke to veteran sports columnist Mike Wise, then a reporter with the Washington Post. At that time, Dotson's mother and her husband had just sold their home and antiques and moved to East Texas, living in an RV with a broken water pump. Gilreatha Stoltzfus wanted to be close to her son, and she was obsessed with conspiracy theories and visiting the scene of the crime, according to Wise.

While talking to Wise, Dotson frequently looked over his shoulder and would lower his voice to a whisper. He'd often say, "I've already told you too much." But Dotson never wavered from the same claim he made to the FBI, that he shot and killed Dennehy in self-defense.

According to the story Dotson told Wise, Dotson said he and Dennehy – both high on marijuana, he said – went to the gravel pits for target practice and Dennehy turned his gun on Dotson.

Per the FBI report given to the Associated Press, when Dennehy's gun jammed, Dotson said, "Father, please forgive me," and shot his roommate in the head at close range.

When Dotson told the story to Wise, he said Dennehy fired a few shots behind him and then reloaded. Dotson thought the next shot was for him and panicked, so he shot Dennehy. Dennehy didn't go down right away, so Dotson shot again. "It was like slow motion," Dotson told Wise. Dotson moved the body, then took the keys to Dennehy's Tahoe out of his pocket and made the long drive straight to the Eastern Shore, tossing the guns in a lake along the way.

"It had to happen," Dotson told Wise. "That's the only thing I could think of when you ask if I have a regret about that day. It had to happen. My only regret is getting in the car. I wished I hadn't gotten in that day. I wish I'd said no... But I didn't plan this. It had to happen."

Wise wrote on Twitter in 2017: "When I last sat and spoke with Carlton Dotson in 2008 in prison, I felt he was a disturbed man who probably shouldn't be in a regular prison."

Only two people and God really know what happened on that blistering hot June day in 2003 in a field outside of Waco. One is dead and the other is in prison.

Dotson is now incarcerated at the John B. Connally Unit, a maximum-security prison that takes up 813 acres of land in Karnes County, Texas, and has a capacity of 2,232 inmates. The prison became infamous in 2000 when a group of inmates – known as the Texas Seven – broke out and went on a crime spree.

Less than four months after Dotson's first parole hearing was denied, Baylor won the national championship in men's college basketball, beating Gonzaga 86-70 in Indianapolis. The championship came nearly 18 years after Scott Drew was hired to clean up the mess left by Dave Bliss, which included NCAA penalties of reduced scholarships and a probationary period.

As of 2022, the 1999 North Dorchester squad is still the last basketball team from a north division school in the Bayside Conference to win a state title.

In Shiloh, inside the high school's gym, Dotson's name still hangs on a banner listing the Eagles who have scored at least 1,000 career points.

He is eligible for parole again in February 2023.

ANDRE COLLINS: THE KID FROM CRISFIELD

"For me, I was doing this for myself, my school, my city and my brother." – Andre Collins

The boy could see the basketball courts from the door of his family's humble apartment.

He'd step outside each morning, feel the wind blowing off the marina and breathe in the saltwater air coming from the Tangier Sound. A basketball would be tucked under his left arm, and as he jogged from Somers Cove Apartments, down Charlotte Avenue and to the courts protected by a chain-link fence, he'd hum the whole way. Even when he entered the courts, with the cracked and discolored concrete beneath his feet, the tune was still purring from his lips as he ran two laps, and then worked himself through drills as if he was preparing to play a game for the local storied team with a devout following.

The song was one Crisfield High School's pep band played at each boys basketball game. And the boy who had memorized it would grow up to be – arguably – the greatest basketball player in the Crisfield Crabbers' decorated and illustrious history.

He would lead the Crabbers to a state title and score a shipload of points along the way, entertaining and inspiring a small hard-working community filled with watermen and dreamers, located on the Chesapeake Bay and on the outskirts of the poorest county in Maryland.

"I'd literally be out there by myself, going through the lay-up line," the boy, now all grown up, says. "So, for a kid that cared as much as I did, to have won a state championship my senior year – especially after losing my freshman year when we got there and seeing how it affected my brother… For me, I was doing this for myself, my school, my city and my brother."

Gary Williams of the Maryland Terrapins came to learn about the kid from Crisfield, and convinced him to trade in his purple and gold Crabbers' kit for Terrapin red and white. After winning a national championship, he transferred to a lesser-known school but saw his profile grow as he turned into one of the top scorers in Division I college basketball. He then enjoyed an acclaimed career overseas, and then came back to Crisfield – to coach and to give back.

The boy was Andre Collins.

In many ways, he is the epitome of the basketball success story on the Eastern Shore. He was raised in the southernmost incorporated city in

Maryland and began perfecting his game on those old courts near the Somers Cove Marina when he was just four years old. Those slabs of concrete were his escape. In the sun, in the rain, in the snow or in the dark, Collins could always find his way to those courts. The cheap metal fence surrounding the court protected him from trouble and kept him focused. And over time, he became excellent at making sure a ball fired from his fingertips found the bottom of the basket – on those courts and many others, across the Shore, the state of Maryland, and eventually, around the planet.

At Crisfield, Collins was a high school All-American, a three-time all-state selection and racked up 2,152 points while leading the Crabbers to a pair of conference titles and state crown in 2000. At Maryland, he was part of a national title-winning team – the only one in the program's history. Then, at Loyola, he shared headlines with JJ Redick and Adam Morrison as one of the nation's leading scorers. After college, Collins went overseas and kept doing what he had grown accustomed to: scoring points and winning trophies.

After nearly a decade of playing abroad, Collins came home to the Eastern Shore. Since 2016, he's had stints as the head coach of boys basketball teams at James M. Bennett and Crisfield, he's organized camps for the youth, he's put on celebrity basketball games to raise money for charity and awareness against gun violence. Collins has also been an entrepreneur, opening an athletic training facility called "The Lab" in Parsonsburg, and a boutique sneaker shop – "Downtown Sneaks" – in his native Crisfield.

When I sat down with Collins for this book, I interviewed him just steps away from his childhood home and those outdoor courts he spent so much time on.

What follows is our conversation, which took place inside a tiny office in the Col. Woodrow T. Wilson Community Center on a fall day in 2020.

Was your brother the guy you looked up to the most?

"Absolutely. He's always been talented. He's the reason I started playing basketball, just following behind him to hang with the big brother. That was what he did. So, I took a liking to it. Luckily, I got the chance to be on the same team as him. It probably was the only time I was on the same team as him – my freshman year and his senior year."

Where did you hone your game at? Was it on the outdoor courts around (Crisfield) or in the men's leagues or just playing with your brother?

"It was a bit of both. They actually had a youth league around here. We're trying to start it back up… I think that's part of the reason why the basketball in Crisfield was always at a high level because we started really young. By the time I got to middle school, my old coach, Mr. Phil Rayfield, he did a Crisfield summer league, and it was a men's league. I started planning that when I was about fifth or sixth grade, and that was with grown men. I started playing there because one team needed an extra player. I played good, and from there played every year. I rarely played with kids my own age. I think that's what helped me be competitive, helped me be tough on the basketball court, and definitely honed my skills."

So, eventually, you become this Division I prospect. When did recruiting start for you? When did you start to get letters, or at least think you could play in college?

"I think I started getting letters in about 10th grade. And it wasn't necessarily what I did in the Bayside Conference, it was mainly what I did on the AAU circuit. Well, back then it wasn't really a circuit. It was, you know, it was a lot different than what it is now. It was easier for us to go to the big-time tournaments, because all you had to do pretty much was pay a fee. Now, you have to pretty much have a shoe deal to get on a circuit.

"It's funny because, probably up until middle school, until I started going to my mentors – who lived in Washington, D.C. in the summertime – I would go up there with them and they took me to a couple of college games. Up until then, I always thought it was kind of like scripted, right? I'm watching on TV; I thought the NBA was scripted with actors. I thought college ball was actors. And I think it's weird to think that way, but it's easy to think that way when you come from Crisfield and you don't really get the opportunity to get out. You know, it's easy to think that type of way, because it's on TV. So, once I started meeting these types of people and started seeing it from my own eyes, it opened my mind up and I was able to get more serious and think about it. Like: this is what I want to do.

"Probably once I started getting college letters is when I really, really took it more seriously, because baseball is actually my first love. I was pretty good at baseball when I was younger and I played in high school. I was a shortstop. My dad was a really good baseball player and played back with Harold Baines. And eventually, when I started getting recruited in basketball, I stopped playing baseball because I made the choice to fully commit myself to basketball, because this is what I wanted to do. Baseball is in the spring, and that's when AAU is fully starting up."

So, you eventually decide on Maryland. But before, were there any other serious contenders? Did you talk to any other coaches or go on any visits?

"St. Joe's was on me and recruiting me pretty heavily. Villanova was recruiting me. Temple was recruiting both me and (Sussex Tech's) Brian Polk. Delaware, Texas, Rutgers… It was so long ago. And eventually North Carolina, when I went to Hargrave (Military Academy) and reopened my recruitment."

Oh, you reopened your recruitment at Hargrave?

"Yea, it was a split second and North Carolina jumped in. Eventually, one of Maryland's assistant coaches flew down to Hargrave and we had a conversation and I pretty much recommitted."

Your senior year, you win the state title and beat Pikesville. You also won Bayside's. It was the first state title for Crisfield since 1982. You grew up here, your brother played here, and it was the first state title in 18 years. Did that mean a lot to you? What was that day like?

"It meant so much to me. Coming from Crisfield, that's the only thing that mattered. It was either a state championship or bust when I was growing up. For a long time in Crisfield, people would literally try to book their hotel rooms for states at the beginning of the season. It was a normalcy for us. Back in the 80s, or even the 70s, the runs that we had – those were really strong teams. A lot of times, it would come down to one play and we would match-up against a tough Pocomoke team or Snow Hill. And it's hard to beat a team three times in one season. But for us, it was expected."

At one time, in 1904, Crisfield was the second largest city in the state of Maryland; second only to Baltimore. Its seaport was busy and it was able to export oysters, crabs and more by boat and train, as a branch from the Pennsylvania Railroad system ran through the town. Crisfield quickly became known as the Seafood Capital of the World. Other towns in the country and around the globe have attempted to take on the same moniker, but Crisfield has clung to it. According to Jason Rhodes' 2012 book on Somerset County, Crisfield was shipping out as much as 47 train cars full of oysters and fish per-day in the 1920s. In the early 20th century, Baltimore and New York were the only ports in the country with more boats registered than Crisfield.

Crisfield's population, economy and wealth dwindled over the next 100 years, as the health of the Chesapeake Bay declined and folks began using trucks to transport watermen's catches, rather than steamboats and trains.

Still, Crisfield always had pride in its local sports teams, largely because they were incredibly competitive, talented and successful, especially in boys basketball. The Crabbers have made 19 state final four appearances, and only Dunbar, Gwynn Park, Wi-Hi and Annapolis have made more trips to College Park. Crisfield has won eight state championships in boys hoops, which is the most of any Eastern Shore team – boys or girls – and is fifth-most of any school in the state.

"Crisfield is a basketball town," Butch Waller told the Salisbury Independent. "Here they are, right on the water, like a separate country. And you walk in there and they got eight championship banners. Eight."

The Crabbers first state championship came in 1957, under the direction of Nick Scallion, the all-time leading scorer at Washington College in Chestertown. Scallion also led South Hagerstown to a state title in 1974. After Scallion, Jack Morgan coached Crisfield to a pair of state championships in 1961 and 1964. Morgan was a former University of Maryland basketball player and an Eastern Shore Baseball Hall of Fame inductee. He was later the principal at Crisfield High School too.

And then, in a 10-season span, Bill Cain coached the Crabbers to four state championships, bringing the gold back to Crisfield in 1973, 1978, 1980 and 1982. In that same stretch, Cain's teams won five Bayside Championships, and then won two more – in 1986 and 1987 – under Larry Miles. In 1990, Phil Rayfield took the reins and led the Crabbers to three conference titles in 1991, 1998 and 2000 – the latter of which was the same year Crisfield won its most recent state title.

On the court, that squad was led by Andre Collins. As a senior in the 1999-2000 season, the 5-foot-9 Collins averaged 30.5 points, 9.9 assists, 5.1 steals and 4.9 rebounds per-game. Trying to guard him one-on-one was a fool's errand. Few players on the Eastern Shore could effectively slow him down. For most, it was like wrestling with a ghost. His quickness made it difficult for defenders to keep track of him, his precision made him lethal from behind the arc, and his craftiness and toughness allowed him to get to the basket and finish, often with ease. His jumper was purer than a country sunset, and Collins' court vision allowed him to crack defenses like a crab leg.

Greg Bozman was the girls head coach at Crisfield by the time Collins was leading the Crabbers' boys team to states. He remembers Collins as the fearless and skilled kid who used to come into the high school gym to play with older boys and grown men. Collins wanted to run with the wolves come night, so he couldn't spend his days sparring with puppies.

"He used to ride his bike over from Woodson – which was the middle and elementary school in Crisfield – and he'd play with us. How it worked at Crisfield was, the old guys played against the young guys, and as we played against them, we're kind of teaching them," Bozman said. "By the seventh grade, you knew Andre was special. He learned how to play the game with us. I'm sure he hated us – you would not believe how many times he got yelled at and cussed out, because he would dribble, dribble, dribble."

Crisfield lost just three games in the regular season in 1999-2000. After thrashing Easton 77-54 in the Bayside title game, the Crabbers muscled their way through the tough 1A East Region playoffs, beating Kent County, Cambridge and Pocomoke along the way to earn a spot in the state final four. Collins had 23 points and Mitchell Sterling added 14 points and 12 boards to lead the Crabbers to a narrow victory over Williamsport in the semifinals. In the Class 1A final, Pikesville – which had just been bested by Eastern Shore side North Dorchester a year prior for the trophy – awaited.

Your state final against Pikesville, that was a pretty low-scoring game for that stage – and for y'all that season: 42-37. Did Pikesville try to throw a box-and-one or some other defense at you?

"Man, they threw the kitchen sink at me. Box-and-one, triangle-and-two, they mixed it up and made it really difficult for me. It was a rugged and ugly game – a lot like the national championship game my freshman year at Maryland. But at the end of the day, for me, winning meant more to me than anything, which is why my assists numbers were high my junior and senior year. Because it didn't matter if I scored 30 or 16 or 15. You know, I just wanted to win. I was very competitive. Even in sprints, I didn't want to lose. I don't think I lost a sprint my entire four years of high school. It was just a drive and a work ethic, and it passed down to the entire team; everybody had that same mindset, same idea. And that's why I think we were able to pull it out with me scoring 15 points less than what my average was."

Crisfield held Pikesville to 16-of-51 shooting from the floor in its first state championship victory in 18 years.

What kind of coach was Phil Rayfield? What did he mean to you?

"Mr. Rayfield meant the world to me. He was, for me, more than a coach. He was a mentor, a father figure, and he was the perfect type of man to be in a kid's life. He's impacted so many kids, not just from Crisfield, but as well as people that didn't play for him. I think that's why now, I try my best to provide the youth now with things that I had, as well as things that I didn't have. He's definitely one that gave me so much. When I look back on everything that I'm doing now with the youth, he's one of the ones that is at the center of attention."

Like Collins, Phil Rayfield was born, bred and raised in Crisfield. The son of Charles and Eloise Ruark Rayfield played basketball for the Crabbers and was the valedictorian of his class in 1965, while lettering in every sport he played. He tallied 13 points and six rebounds in Crisfield's second state boys basketball championship victory in 1964, a 74-64 triumph over Hancock.

After earning degrees from Towson and Maryland Eastern Shore, Rayfield returned to Crisfield High School, where he would stay for 31 years, working as a teacher, administrator and coach. In 1990, after coaching the Crabbers' girls for a few seasons, Rayfield moved over to coach the boys. He returned the program to prominence and dominance. Over the next 20 years, with Rayfield at the helm, Crisfield won three Bayside championships and one state crown – with Collins leading the way – in 2000. Rayfield became one of the few coaches in the Bayside Conference to have a state championship ring as a player and a head coach.

The first time sports reporter David Insley covered a game at Crisfield during the Rayfield-era, the two got talking once about how Insley's grandfather, father and several of his uncles were watermen. "My dad fed us by working on the water," Insley said. Rayfield, being the thoughtful and giving man that he was, told Insley if he called ahead by three hours before every time he covered a game at Crisfield, Rayfield would have a freshly made crab cake sandwich waiting for him, wrapped up and ready to go. "For seven years, whenever I covered a Crisfield boys home game, there was a crab cake there."

Years after that first delicious crab cake and years after Rayfield had captured a state championship, Insley asked the Crisfield coach why he kept coming back. Rayfield told Insley, "I've always told myself that if I didn't feel that fire in the fall, that I'd hang up my clipboard."

"And the only thing that put that fire out," Insley said, "was fucking cancer."

Rayfield won more than 300 basketball games as a head coach at Crisfield and Holly Grove, but he was a cultured man of many interests. He was heavily involved with his community in Crisfield, was an artist and a supporter of arts councils up and down the Eastern Shore. He was also a man of faith, who taught Sunday School and was a youth leader at the Pleasant United Methodist Church in Crisfield. And he was heavily into music. Rayfield could play the guitar and the piano, and was also a fan of jazz. He implored the young folks he coached to explore a world outside of basketball. His message to them was: "God first. Then family. Then academics. Then basketball."

On Sunday, Feb. 9, 2014, Rayfield died at the age of 66 at Mercy Hospital in Baltimore.

"Phil really cared and worked really hard with those kids," said Pocomoke athletic director David Byrd. "He was well-respected, and a good friend."

But long after his death, the life Rayfield lived and led has continued to inspire people. People like Andre Collins. If you look closely, you can see Rayfield's fingerprints all over what Collins is trying to do on the Shore in his post-playing career.

"For me, when I look at Mr. Rayfield – I think a lot of people, with me being successful, a lot of people maybe think that I should focus everything on Crisfield. But that's not what Mr. Rayfield did," Collins said. "He focused on whoever he could help. So, with me, my biggest thing is to focus on the entire Eastern Shore, to have my hands on the entire Eastern Shore. That is one thing he definitely did. Mr. Rayfield, for me – I feel like I owe him everything."

Who's the best player you played against in high school?

"I would say, one my freshman year, I really liked Doug King, just as a point guard and as a leader and how he ran the show at Wi-Hi. I enjoyed playing against him. I enjoyed playing against his younger brother, Jamaal. A player that I really, really, really loved playing against was Curtis McNeal. He was at Wi-Hi and a lot of people don't bring his name up. Carlton Dotson, Brian Polk... Most of the guys that I would say were the best players that I played against were the same guys that were on my AAU team.

"I know that when I was in high school, I felt like I had a tough matchup every single night. And I really didn't pay attention to all the other players. You know, I focused more on us and what we had to do. And I was more like – a lot of people called me an asshole when I was on the court. They would try to talk to me and I would literally be mute. Just in a zone."

So, you weren't really a talker then.

"I didn't. I just kind of smirked and said, 'OK.' And then I scored 40."

When you were playing, and still today, Pocomoke is one of Crisfield's big rivals. What were those David Byrd teams like?

"I mean, just the fact that it was Pocomoke. In the 1A, there's usually one of three teams that went (to states): Pocomoke, Crisfield or Snow Hill. There were probably about three teams that I really got up for, and it was those type of games. It was the Snow Hill's, the Pocomoke's, and the Wi-Hi's. Just because I knew I had to be on top of my game in order for us to compete with those teams and to pull out wins. Their fans were always talking, but I definitely thrive for those games. I loved going to those games … David Byrd's teams were feisty. I knew I was going to be trapped. I saw that from my sophomore year on. Throughout high school, I don't think I saw a regular defense – and at Loyola it was about the same."

How about Butch Waller? I mean, you've coached against him now. What's that like?

"His teams now play the same way they did back then; they play fast. But I will say the talent that they had back then was (better). To be able to compete with Crisfield back then and to beat Crisfield, especially if you came down here, you had to have had a really good team. Like that 1997 Wi-Hi team that came down here and beat us."

What was it like being the home team in Crisfield?

"It's the same gym now, but it's a different feel. Our games would be standing room only. Every game. We would play Mardela and it's standing room only. I remember if we played Pocomoke or Wi-Hi or Snow Hill, you should get there when school lets out to start lining up. And our games back then, we didn't play until 7 p.m. If you were traveling from a far place, it'd be tough for you to get in."

After prepping for a year at the Hargrave Military Academy, Collins was off to the University of Maryland. At Hargrave, he averaged 15.6 points and 8.1 assists per-game while leading the team to a 27-1 record. That year, under the direction of Kevin Keatts in 2000-01, Collins was one of 11 Hargrave players to land Division I scholarships. The school in Chatham, Virginia, has produced four McDonald's All-Americans and more than 30 NBA players, including Montrezl Harrell and David West.

As a freshman in College Park, Collins didn't play much at just 3.8 minutes per-game, but that was because there was a trio of super talented guards in front of him on the depth chart in Juan Dixon, Steve Blake and Byron Mouton. Those three, along with Chris Wilcox and Lonny Baxter, powered the Terps to the 2002 National Championship. Along the way, Collins was serviceable when called upon, scoring two points and getting a steal in the Terps' NCAA Tournament win over Wisconsin, and scoring eight points in an ACC tournament win over Florida State. "I guess I'm probably the only person from Crisfield to score in the NCAA Tournament. To be on the shortlist of guys from the Eastern Shore that have done that is pretty amazing," Collins said.

Andre Collins' 2002 National Championship ring was on display at the Wicomico Youth & Civic Center in an exhibit in December 2021. Photo by Mitchell Northam.

And indeed, the list of Eastern Shore folks who have won national championships in college basketball is short. It's Collins and Colonel Richardson's Albert Mouring, who won in 2000 at UConn.

That's it. That's the list.

Collins is seen often in a commonly-used photo of the title team; after the win, Collins was captured crying tears of joy with Dixon's arm around him. The victory took the kid from Crisfield to big celebrations in Atlanta and Baltimore, and to the White House. "It was one of the biggest accomplishments of my life," Collins said.

Earlier that season, Collins got his name written in the history books too. On March 3, 2002, the Terps played their last game ever in Cole Field House, which had been the team's home since 1955. Collins became the last Division I men's player to ever score in a game in the historic venue when he flushed a three-pointer at the buzzer in a 112-92 victory over Virginia. Williams told Collins to hold the ball, but Dixon, Blake and those guys told him to fire up a shot. He obliged his teammates, and Williams wasn't too mad. The next day, Williams teased Collins for his newfound fame, calling him the "Man of the Hour."

During a reunion event with the 2002 Terps, Collins told ESPN's Scott Van Pelt, "I got some bad advice. I was listening to my teammates. Gary was pissed off at me." The crowd laughed, and then Collins continued to reminiscing: "Just to close out Cole – such a historic place – it was just a great moment. It was really important for us to go undefeated in Cole that year... For me as a kid growing up on the Eastern Shore of Maryland, in high school, our No. 1 goal was always to get to Cole Field House. So, to be able to do that in high school and then come here and actually win the last game here – 16-0 in Cole – it was just a great experience."

***

Collins expected to play more as a sophomore for the Terps, but his minutes only went up slightly. He shined in some moments, such as an eight-point, three-assist outing in a road win over North Carolina, but never found consistent playing time under Williams. Even in his junior year, Collins got the nod to make his first collegiate start against George Mason, but logged just 14 minutes of playing time. Six games into his junior season in College Park, Collins left the Terps. With one season of collegiate eligibility left, he plotted his next move, and he continued to work.

In April of 2004, a private Jesuit school in Baltimore – Loyola University Maryland – hired Terps' assistant Jimmy Patsos as its head coach. The Greyhounds had endured 10 straight losing seasons in the Metro Atlantic Athletic Conference. As Patsos was getting settled in his new gig, his old boss Gary Williams gave him some advice: recruit Andre Collins. "He's going to be great for your program," Williams told Patsos. "You need a guy who can score." And after sitting out a season due to NCAA transfer rules, Collins scored an awful lot for Loyola.

Andre Collins won at every level of basketball; leading Crisfield to a state title, being part of a Maryland team that won a national championship and then winning a championship in Italy. Larry French, Loyola University Maryland Athletics.

When you decide you're going to leave Maryland, was it always Loyola, or did you have a few other places in mind?

"I thought about St. Joe's. I thought about Delaware. I also entertained the idea of coming home and playing at UMES, just for the idea of being able to play in front of the Shore. But, at the end of the day, I thought the best decision for me was Loyola – especially when Patsos took over. I didn't even visit the campus. I just committed to play for him."

Your senior year there, you were fourth in the country in points per-game, seventh in points scored. Do you remember who was ahead of you?

"I want to say Adam Morrison (Gonzaga), JJ Redick (Duke) and I want to say me and Keydren Clark (St. Peter's) tied."

Yea, Clark had 0.1 points more than you, according to Basketball Reference anyways... So, what was that year like?

"I remember doing an interview, and I wasn't trying to be disrespectful, but it was kind of reminiscent of high school. Just getting the opportunity and being able to do what I normally do and put my talent on display, as well as leading Loyola to its first winning record since like Skip Prosser (in 1994). The year before that, they won six games. The year before that, they won one. They were pretty much the laughing stock of the MAAC, the laughing stock of college basketball. And they went to being respected, to having a legitimate shot of making the NCAA Tournament."

Collins brought instant credibility to Loyola and helped jumpstart Patsos' rebuilding project. In his Greyhounds debut, he dropped 22 points on Towson in a road win. Less than a month later, he scored 39 against Manhattan. On Dec. 23, 2005, against old ACC foe Virginia, Collins had 16 points, a season-high 10 assists and two steals against the 'Hoos. Against

Providence, Collins tallied 39 points, five steals and three assists. Just like he had done at Crisfield when he played against teams from across the Bay Bridge, or when he got to play in the Capital Classic, Collins proved once more he could play with anyone, anytime, anywhere.

In his final season of college ball, Collins averaged 26.1 points, 4.7 assists, 3.6 rebounds and 2.4 steals per-game while shooting 36.6% from three-point land and 90.2% from the free throw line. His charity stripe shooting percentage was seventh-best in the nation.

After impressing across the Chesapeake Bay, the Crisfield kid traversed the Atlantic Ocean to take his talents to the country shaped like a boot.

Collins was a success right away in Italy. For him, the game was the same, it just got more fierce. With Carife Ferrara, he was named MVP of the league in his second season while averaging 19.2 points and 3.4 assists per-game. His team won its regular season title and was promoted to Serie A, the top league in Italy. Collins was also named Guard of the Year and Import Player of the Year. Just like he had done at Crisfield and Loyola, Collins established himself as one of the best players in his league. This time, instead of the Bayside or the MAAC, it was in Italy.

"It was at a time when my confidence was really, really high. I felt like I still had something to prove to get to where I wanted to be at," Collins said.

In one game in Italy, Collins got the chance to go toe-to-toe with Earl Boykins, who would play 13 seasons in the NBA.

"I remember everything about that. At the time, the team that he was playing for (La Fortezza Bologna) was like, one of the best over there. That team was always a top two or three team. Back then, a lot of NBA players would go to that program. And that's where I wanted to be," Collins said. "And for me, it was like – this is a top name, an NBA guy, a chance to prove myself. They came to us in the spring and I had a great game. I was motivated and I wanted to prove I belonged there, that I could play on that level."

Collins finished that contest with 25 points, five rebounds and five assists in a 93-84 win for his side in April 2009.

Over the next several years, Collins played in a EuroCup, and featured for teams in Italy, Belgium, Germany and Turkey.

In the summer of 2016, Collins held his first youth camp for Eastern Shore kids at Bennett Middle School. For five days, he coached kids in Fruitland, teaching them about basketball and life. Near the end of the camp, Collins was still unsure about the future of his playing career overseas. He had offers – and a contract in-hand from a team in Germany – but he was also 34 years old, had children, and had discovered a newfound love for teaching. On the final day of camp at Bennett Middle, Collins was supposed to talk to his agent about his next potential move overseas. As Collins was backing out of his garage that day, with a duffle bag packed for the gym for his next workout, he looked up. His son was standing on the steps, crying. He didn't want his father to leave again. Wherever he was going, the boy wanted to go with him.

"He was getting to an age where he started recognizing and realizing when it was time for me to go back overseas," Collins said. "And he was getting to the point where he would really show his emotions. You could tell ... seeing him standing on those steps – he's hurt, because he thinks his dad is leaving to go back for 10 months."

Collins called his agent: "I can't do it anymore."

By December, Collins was the head coach of the boys team at James M. Bennett High School, after he had turned down an opening at Sussex Tech. He won in his coaching debut, 63-53 over Colonel Richardson at home. He spent three years leading the Clippers, then one year at his alma mater, sharing head coaching duties at Crisfield with former Pocomoke standout David Arnold.

Crisfield great Andre Collins returned to Bayside Conference basketball in 2016, becoming the head coach at James M. Bennett. Photo by Mitchell Northam.

"As far as coaching, it's funny, I always said I never wanted to coach high school just because I saw what Mr. Rayfield went through with parents and politics," Collins said. "But I did develop a passion for teaching kids."

Chesapeake Bay water is practically in Collins' blood. After his playing career ended, he could've lived anywhere and done anything he set his mind to. But Collins chose to come back to the Delmarva Peninsula and decided to give back to the communities that raised him through the game of basketball. It is abundantly apparent Collins believes basketball is of the utmost importance to the Eastern Shore. But putting the reason why it's so crucial into words can be difficult.

"It's just something that's in the water. You know what I mean? It's just something that we do," Collins said. "For Crisfield, it's definitely the most important sport. A few other places have football, but I think – by a longshot – basketball is the most important sport, the most dominant sport. There's this swag about the game of basketball. And the Shore, at least when I was coming through, was known for shooters. I think it's just in our genes. It's in the DNA on the Shore.

"I try to do everything kind of around basketball, because I know that's something the majority of people know me for. My goal is trying to get the basketball of the Eastern Shore back up to the standards that it used to be."

As long as the Eastern Shore's basketball community, history and culture is shepherded, promoted and cared for by folks like Andre Collins, it's in good hands.

School	G	MP	FG%	3P%	FT%	TRB	AST	STL	BLK	PTS
01-02 Maryland	22	3.8	.667	.500	.778	0.5	0.9	0.2	0.0	2.2
02-03 Maryland	19	5.7	.516	.400	.500	0.4	0.9	0.6	0.0	2.2
03-04 Maryland	6	8.8	.467	.143	.000	1.2	1.7	0.2	0.2	2.5
05-06 Loyola (MD)	28	38.1	.414	.366	.902	3.6	4.7	2.4	0.1	26.1
Overall	75	17.5	.429	.367	.860	1.7	2.4	1.1	0.1	11.1

WINNING, THE BUTCH WALLER WAY

"If I was going to do it, it was getting everything I had."
– Butch Waller

It would be easy to consider Butch Waller as the Yoda of high school basketball on the Eastern Shore. All he's missing are pointy ears and a green lightsaber.

He's old, wise, and bald, with an excellent sense of humor. He can still relate to young people, and he can still outcoach anyone. Hell, he's done it more than 800 times at this point across more than five decades.

Waller has been patrolling the sideline at Wicomico High School since the Nixon administration. Joe Biden's presidency is the 10th Waller has coached through.

He's armed with a great laugh, an inviting smile and an encyclopedic mind. Waller also has an eye for talent, with the ability to spot a superb basketball player through the window of an airplane 32,000 feet in the air.

Waller is the all-time winningest coach in the history of public high school boys basketball in Maryland. And he has an obsessive nature when it comes to preparing for competition.

When I first met him, it was after a victory in which he hit a historic milestone – win No. 700. Back then, I was a community college student and an out-of-work sportswriter, trying to figure out how to do this damn thing I've tried to make a career out of. That night, I sat on the old bleachers in Wi-Hi's gym – a place everyone calls the Waller Dome – right behind the visitor's bench. I was keeping notes and stats, and it felt like every nine seconds I was writing down: "REB - T. BROWN." That was for Thomas Brown, a 6-foot-4 power forward who was an athletic bulldozing rebounding machine, and the centerpiece of a Wi-Hi team that was a buzzer-beater away from winning a state title in 2013, which would've – and perhaps should've – been Waller's second state championship.

Two years later, Waller invited me to ride with him, Doug King and Scot Dailey, two of his former point guards turned coaches, to scout a first-round 2A East playoff game between North Caroline and Easton. In that packed gymnasium in Ridgely, I got to see up-close just how meticulous Waller was in his preparation. His Indians would face the winner of that game. He sat down in the bleachers and pulled two index cards out of his pocket, one for each team, and as the game wore on, he covered them front and back in notes, detailing strengths, weaknesses, and tendencies for both sides.

Waller has done this his entire career. During regular seasons, if his team is off, but there is a decent game being played at Bennett, Parkside, or even as far as Crisfield, he'll climb into his pickup and drive to check the competition out and fill up a page of notes, even if they're just mental ones. Waller says the only other Bayside coach he regularly ran into on these impromptu scouting trips was Colonel Richardson's Merrill Morgan, usually by himself with a clipboard in one hand and a pen in the other. Waller always respected that.

"I'm a big believer in driving out on these cold nights and driving to Pocomoke or Snow Hill or Decatur or Denton or wherever, and sitting my ass in those stands and watching an opponent that I'm not real sure of," Waller said. "I was looking at what defense they were running. I wasn't trying to figure out the offense, because they're all going to the same place; the basket. If they have an outstanding player, see if they want to go left or right, that kind of stuff."

Butch Waller, with Doug King and Wayne Warren behind him, closely watches his Wi-Hi team during a 2017 regular season game at Pocomoke. Photo by Mitchell Northam.

Instead of spending his off nights in gyms across the Eastern Shore, Waller could have been home, spending time with his wife, his son, or his dog. But perfection drove him and his competitive nature ate away at him. To satisfy both, he has spent countless hours studying every opponent he's ever faced on a basketball court.

This overly-obsessive ultra-measure of super preparedness is how Waller attained staying-power in a sport that recycles coaches like Coke bottles. It's how he's led his teams to 13 state final fours and won more Bayside Conference titles than any other basketball coach on the Delmarva Peninsula. Being regimented, detailed and conscientious isn't just a habit for Waller; it's his way of life. He decided, long ago, while a team might be more talented than his, and while their coach might be a bit savvier with X's and O's, they weren't going to out-plan him. Waller has a mental book on every team he goes up against on the hardwood.

"His preparation, man, he's always on it. You're not going to tell him to do something and him not be prepared for it," said Doug King, who has been Waller's assistant coach for nearly two decades. "When it comes to basketball, he can coach, but he's just more prepared than any other coach. He knows what the other team is going to do before they do it. He's organized. He knows what he's doing."

***

Florence Ellis Waller gave birth to her only son, William Howard Waller Jr., on April 21, 1940, at Peninsula General Hospital in Salisbury. He was named after his father, but a few days after he was born, his sister Pat leaned over the bed he was lying in and said, "He looks like a Butch."

And the nickname stuck. Forever.

Years later, college professors would call out his first name, William, for roll call, and Waller would say, "Where the hell is William?"

And then, "Excuse me sir, my name is Butch."

Waller grew up on Monticello Ave. in Salisbury. His mother worked at the Wicomico County Health Department. His father was a road building contractor and a member of the Old Green Hill Episcopal Church. In 1957, between Butch's junior and senior years of high school, his father died of a heart attack at the age of 73. His father's brother, Robert Fulton Waller, was a Maryland state senator from 1941 through 1946.

Like all boys, Butch Waller dabbled with Tonka toys, chased girls and messed around in the mud, but sports always caught his interests and soaked up most of his time. If it had a ball and a scoreboard, Waller played it. And he wanted to win.

In 1956, he was the only underclassman on the Wicomico High School football team, featuring at tailback. However, a week before that season started, Waller was tackled during practice and an offensive lineman stumbled and fell on him. "Paul Lord. I'll never forget his name," Waller says. "He stepped on my damn leg ... I heard it snap." Waller's coaches, Charlie Berry and Denver Knapp, didn't exactly believe him. So, he walked home – more than two miles – and then his mother took him to the hospital. An X-ray revealed what he already knew and felt: two broken bones. "I was out and that damn team went undefeated. I wore a cast the rest of the year," Waller said. He got back on the football field as a senior, scoring the first touchdown in a 26-0 win over Edgewood on Nov. 1, 1957. Waller's score came on a two-yard off-tackle scamper into the end-zone. Waller wore a helmet which looked a little bit too small for his head. It didn't have a facemask and was held on his noggin with a thin white leather chin strap. Under the helmet wasn't much padding. It was on a football field when someone first told Waller his hair was receding.

"I am convinced that Waller never had hair," said former Easton Star Democrat sports reporter David Insley, half-joking.

On the baseball diamond, Waller was a left-handed pitcher. As a youngster, he played in the first little league and pony league programs in Salisbury.

And on the basketball court, he was a guard, coached by Chesty Squires, a former Virginia Tech football player who also taught industrial arts at Wi-Hi. "He was a guy who everybody respected," Waller said.

Waller graduated from Wi-Hi in 1958 and enrolled at East Tennessee State University. Waller's sister went there and liked it, so Waller thought he might too. But then, the Salisbury boy got homesick.

"I transferred to Maryland with most of my friends. Big mistake," Waller said. "There was too much going on and I almost flunked out after one semester."

After surviving in College Park by the skin of his teeth, Waller pressed pause on his academics and joined the workforce. He landed a job with a cable television company, and his co-workers taught him how to climb a pole while wearing cleats. "That was a lot of fun," Waller says. He then got a gig driving a bulldozer and helped build a housing development, Canal Woods, right off Route 13 in Salisbury. And then Waller thought to himself, "You know, I don't want to be doing this for the rest of my life." So, like the trucker Darius Rucker sings about in his rendition of "Wagon Wheel," Waller was headed back to Johnson City, Tennessee.

Once he got back to East Tennessee State, Waller refocused and got involved with a fraternity and sports to fill his free time. "I matured and I stayed there and got my bachelor's degree," he says. And then Waller stayed around a little longer and earned his master's degree. While he was pursuing that, he taught and coached bowling, gymnastics and archery at ETSU. Waller, admittedly, didn't know one thing about archery, but he had the Tennessee state champ of the sport in his lectures, "and he pretty much ran the class. He got an A."

When he finished his master's degree, Waller considered pursuing a Ph.D. or going to Florida. But then he got a letter from his old high school football coach, Charlie Berry.

"He was renowned in this area," Waller said. "And he wanted me to come back."

Waller was married by then, had a son, and needed a job. And his wife was from Salisbury too.

Butch met Sandy in middle school. During a baseball game, a buddy tugged on his shirt and said, "Hey Butch. That girl likes you." And that was all Waller needed to hear. "That's how it started. And it carried on right through high school," Waller said. "We were together at least 10 years, and then right around when we were 25, 26, everyone was getting married." So, Butch and Sandy got married. She moved to Johnson City, they got an apartment, and soon, Sandy gave birth to her only child, a son named Spencer.

In 1966, the Wallers moved back to Salisbury. Butch intended to stay at Wi-Hi for a year and then find something better. He accepted a job teaching physical education and – somewhat begrudgingly and somewhat humbly – took on coaching duties of the JV boys basketball team and the varsity baseball team.

Initially, Waller coveted the head football coaching job at Wi-Hi. It was the gig he really wanted. But back then, before Parkside existed, the football teams at James M. Bennett and Wi-Hi agreed to have an equal number of coaches. The Indians already had their five, so Waller was frozen out of football. "I often look back at times and think about what kind of career I would've had in football," Waller says. "I would've still been doing it."

Still, after a stint at East Tennessee State, Waller was happy to be back home.

Like scrapple and blue crabs, he belonged to the Eastern Shore.

***

Coaching baseball was effortless for Butch Waller. In his first four seasons as skipper of the Wi-Hi Indians, the team went 50-13-1.

"I thought I was hot shit. Baseball was easy. It was so easy to win around here then," Waller said. "Baseball came so natural to me. It was almost dishonest, the way we beat teams."

In 13 years of coaching baseball at Wi-Hi, Waller went 183-39-1 and captured two Bayside Conference Championships in 1974 and 1979. He briefly returned to coaching the Indians' baseball team in 1983, leading them to a 16-3 record and a Bayside title. Waller then became a high school and collegiate umpire, something he did in the spring for more than 35 years. In 2014, he was inducted into the Eastern Shore Baseball Hall of Fame. Waller also started the Wi-Hi golf program in 1977.

Coaching basketball seemed to come naturally to Waller too. In his first season coaching the Indians JV boys in 1966-67, the squad went 16-1. Waller's only loss came to Milford, in Delaware.

"I thought, shit, there ain't nothing to this. I guess we were that good, or everybody else was that bad," Waller says of his inaugural season on the court. "I was young and dumb and full of piss and vinegar."

By the fall of 1970, Wi-Hi needed a new varsity basketball coach. James Cassaday, who had been the coach for three seasons and was a math teacher at Wi-Hi, left the country and moved to Switzerland. "His wife's father was big in the banking business," Waller said. "He left in a little bit of a huff ... but he was a good coach."

Waller applied for the head basketball coaching job, and others did too, including Colonel Richardson's Merrill Morgan. But Waller had an advantage. He was already in the building, he was born and bred in Salisbury, and his old football coach Charlie Berry – the athletic director for Wicomico County – was making the hire.

"He was the closest thing to Vince Lombardi," Waller said of Berry, who, in 2007, had the football field at Wicomico County Stadium named after him.

In August 1970, Berry told the Salisbury Daily Times and the Baltimore Sun that Waller got the job.

But Waller didn't have the same immediate success in varsity basketball like he had in the JV ranks and on the baseball diamond. Waller won in his head coaching debut on the hardwood, 77-73 over Easton, but guided the Indians to a mediocre 11-11 record. Those early struggles pushed him to adapt and improve. Coaching basketball was difficult for Waller in the beginning, and he viewed it as a challenge.

"I was pissed. In my mind, I thought, if we lose, it's on me. I'm doing something wrong," Waller said. "That's when I really started getting into it and analyzing the game and what I was doing, and, was it fitting the kids that I had?"

In the summer of 1971, Waller attended Morgan Wooten's annual coaching clinic at DeMatha Catholic High School for the first time.

Once Waller found the place – nestled just outside of northeast D.C. near Hyattsville, Maryland – he wasn't very impressed. "It was just a bunch of brick buildings," Waller said. "I walk in the gym and said, 'This is DeMatha? My gym is better than this.'"

But then, Waller walked down the hallway. And he saw DeMatha's trophy case, which is as long as the Wicomico River. Wooten was the coach at DeMatha for 46 years, and by the time he retired in 2002, he had a record of 1,274-192, a winning percentage of 86.9%. A countless number of Wooten products went on to play Division I college basketball. In 1965, Wooten's Stags beat Power Memorial Academy of New York City, which then featured

7-foot-2 wonder Lew Alcindor – later, and better known as Kareem Abdul-Jabbar. In 2000, Wooten was inducted into the Naismith Basketball Hall of Fame. Boston Celtics' cigar-smoking legend Red Auerbach once said of Wooten, "He was the best at what he did … he was always in control without being a boisterous type."

"I got the picture then," Waller said. "And Morgan and I just hit it off, and I went to every one of his clinics."

***

After attending Morgan Wooten's clinics and getting his feet wet in coaching varsity basketball, Butch Waller had the Indians competing for championships by his third season. At Wooten's sessions, Waller would fill up legal pads full of notes, jotting down things about each speaker – what surprised him, what impressed him – and then he would apply some of those takeaways to his practices.

Waller was especially an admirer of North Carolina's Dean Smith. The two exchanged letters once, discussing planning and defense.

"I was a big fan of Dean Smith because he was always prepared – unlike Lefty – at end-of-the-game situations," Waller said. "I've seen Lefty Driesell piss away so many games, God almighty."

For decades – night, after night, after night – Waller would sit in his office at Wi-Hi and pour over his painstaking notes, trying to figure out his plays, his system, his team and his opponents. Because the Wi-Hi varsity boys often practiced from 6:30 to 8:30 p.m., Waller usually didn't get home at nights between November and March until well after 9 p.m. He rarely had time to catch "The Rockford Files" or "Hawaii Five-O" on television.

And charting, diagramming, graphing and record-keeping became a habit of his too. Near the Wi-Hi locker room is one chart showing how many charges each player has taken in the current season. On another bulletin board is the Bayside standings, updated each game-night by Waller. Near the entrance of Wi-Hi's gym is a large sign showing all of the program's record holders, etched in Waller's handwriting. And the walls in Waller's office soon became covered with papers and mementos: newspaper stories, photos, diagrams, inspirational quotes, business cards, records, posters, letters and more. It's cliché to say it at this point, but Waller's office really is like a living Bayside basketball museum. And beneath it all, there's still this sort of golden Wi-Hi glow to it.

"The Waller Dome has to be my favorite gym," said former Star Democrat sportswriter David Insley. "I sat at the scorekeeper's desk with my feet on the floor. I felt the most-welcomed there out of any sports venue. I can't count how many times Butch handed me a Gatorade that had my name written on the lid."

See? Waller writes on everything, from drink tops to notecards.

And everything Waller's teams do – every play, every defense, every break – has a name, number, or a color assigned to it.

Wi-Hi's gym, commonly referred to as "the Waller Dome" has hosted a number of high-profile Bayside Conference over the past several decades. Photo by Mitchell Northam.

"That was so important to me, that I was putting it all together in my mind," Waller said. "If I didn't understand it, I couldn't portray it."

In the spring of 1973 – around the same time he became chairman of the Bayside Conference – Waller had the Indians headed toward College Park, set for a Class A state semifinal bout with Fort Hill. Leading the way for Waller's side was Ed Lashley, Marion Ennis and Harris Strozier, the latter of which ended his Wi-Hi career with more than 1,000 points and 1,000 rebounds.

"Ed Lashley was a prolific scorer at Wi-Hi," said Paul Butler, then a local middle-schooler who watched Wi-Hi games with his parents. "And Harris Strozier was just a monster. He could not only score, but he averaged about 20 rebounds a game."

Paul's brother Brian added: "Lashley was the best basketball player at Wi-Hi in the '70s and I wanted to be like him. I always thought he was an amazing player."

Strozier still holds the Wi-Hi record for most rebounds in a season with 417. Ennis that season averaged 17.1 points and 10.4 rebounds per-game. But despite 21 points from Ennis and Strozier's 18 points and 16 boards at Cole Field House, the Indians fell 72-65, marking the first of – unfortunately – many long bus rides home for Waller, heading back across the Chesapeake Bay empty-handed.

Lashley was selected in Major League Baseball's 1975 amateur draft by the Baltimore Orioles in the 32nd round and played one season of minor league ball. His son played basketball at Snow Hill and Wi-Hi, and also at Saint Joseph's.

***

Butch Waller's relationship with Morgan Wooten led to what would become known decades later as the Governor's Challenge, the largest high school holiday basketball tournament in the country. In 2019, the tournament – held annually at the Wicomico Youth & Civic Center and surrounding venues – spanned six days and featured 129 boys and girls teams from 13 different states, as well as Puerto Rico and Canada. It now features a dunk contest, a three-point shootout and a skills challenge.

It all started in 1980. Waller believed the winter break for public schools in Maryland was too long to go without playing any basketball. Teams around the Shore had held their own little Christmastime tournaments here and there, but they were always against other Bayside Conference teams. Waller wanted his players to be tested against someone unfamiliar. So, he called up Wooten, who had declined an offer just months prior to become the head coach at N.C. State, according to John McNamara's book "The Capital of Basketball." The DeMatha Stags had a talented team that winter led by Adrian Branch, an All-American who was an All-ACC forward at Maryland and an NBA champion with the Los Angeles Lakers, and Bob Ferry, who averaged 13.5 points and 3.6 rebounds per-game in four seasons at Harvard. Wooten liked the idea of coming to the Shore for a game and agreed to split the gate 50-50 with Waller, after expenses. Under Wooten, DeMatha was an incredibly disciplined team. As the Indians and Stags ran through lay-up lines, Waller blew the horn to get the game started with about two minutes remaining in warm-ups. A DeMatha assistant, dressed in a full suit, approached him and said, "Coach, we need the full 20 minutes to warm-up." Waller politely obliged, and added time back to the clock.

Wi-Hi jumped out to a 2-0 lead initially on Dec. 13, 1980, but then the Stags ripped off a 13-0 run. Branch didn't play, but Ferry had 23 points and 10 assists in the 78-53 victory for DeMatha.

"We played on the tile floor that time. There wasn't no wood," Waller said. "And the kids didn't come on a bus. Morgan, he came in some sort of limo."

The next year, Waller and Wooten agreed to run it back. But, to make it a real event, Waller had an idea for a double-header. So, Waller called Bill Cain, the coach at Crisfield, and Wooten called Joe Gallagher, the longtime head coach at St. John's College High School who had given Wooten his start in coaching. Both Cain and Gallagher agreed to a game in Salisbury. On Dec. 12, 1981, in front of a crowd of about 4,000 people, St. John's edged out Crisfield 64-56 and DeMatha had thrashed Wi-Hi 97-56.

"Crisfield gave St. John's all they could handle," Waller recalled. "Joe Gallagher went fucking bananas up and down that court. He was into it."

But the scores didn't really matter. Brian Butler, a star on those Wi-Hi teams of the early 1980s, says those games against DeMatha were the only time he heard Waller say that he didn't expect to win. He just didn't want the Indians to get embarrassed. "Coach wanted those games because he wanted the publicity for Shore basketball," Butler said. "DeMatha was just too deep. They would rotate a new five in and they were all Division I players. I don't think the Eastern Shore fans had seen a team like that."

What was important was the start of a tradition. And Waller, a man of routine and habit, wanted to keep his little winter non-conference tournament rolling. In 1982, the field grew to six teams for a triple-header: Wi-Hi, James M. Bennett and Cambridge-South Dorchester of the Eastern Shore, and Gaithersburg, West Nottingham Academy, and Ballou from across the bay. Wi-Hi played Ballou, making it the first time Waller coached against a woman, as Ballou was guided by the groundbreaking Wanda Oates. "They were impressive," Waller said of Oates' Ballou team.

In 1983, Waller enlisted the help of the local Lions Club to market, organize, operate and grow the tournament. "It was a lot of work. I was coaching, teaching and soon-to-be athletic director," Waller said. "I couldn't have done it all by myself. It turned out to be almost a year-round job ... we just kept plugging along."

Then, in 2010, Wicomico County's Recreation, Parks and Tourism division took the reins and rebranded the tournament as the Governor's Challenge, pitting teams from Maryland against teams from Delaware at the crossroads of Delmarva. Then-governors Martin O'Malley of the Old Line State and Jack Markell of the First State wagered a tasty baked treat on whose teams would win. Up for grabs was a Smith Island cake and a peach pie. Delaware won the first three years, with Maryland finally taking the cake – or, rather, pie – in 2013.

James Simmons soon became the director of the tournament, and in 2014 it partnered with DMVelite – a company based out of Bowie, Maryland, specializing in event management, media and scouting, with a focus on covering and promoting youth basketball in D.C., Maryland and Virginia. The partnership gave the Governor's Challenge new credibility. As Simmons said of DMVelite, "every coach in the Baltimore and D.C. area knows their name." The tournament grew to 53 teams and added a girls' division that year for the first time ever.

In 2015, the Governor's Challenge really took off with a full investment from Chris Lawson, Edgar Walker and Marcus Helton of DMVelite, the steady direction of Simmons, and Waller's institutional knowledge and connections. More than 100 boys and girls high school teams played in the five-day event and a JV tournament was introduced. The tournament partnered with WMDT47 for a selection show where it unveiled the schedule, and the tournament landed big-name sponsors in Dr. Pepper and Under Armour. The 2016 tournament brought a $1.2 million economic impact to Wicomico County.

Stephen Decatur's Kevon Voyles goes up for a dunk at the 2016 Governor's Challenge at the Wicomico Youth and Civic Center. Photo by Mitchell Northam.

As more teams have entered the tournament, more talented players have too. Some of the Governor's Challenge alumni include NBA players Nic Claxton, Saddiq Bey, Immanuel Quickley, Obi Toppin and Patrick Williams, and 2021 Denver Nuggets draft pick Nah'Shon "Bones" Hyland of Middletown, Delaware.

Before it was called off due to COVID-19, the 2021 tournament was expected to attract more than 130 teams to Salisbury. And it all started with this little idea Waller had some 40 years ago. As the tournament doubled, tripled, quadrupled and boomed in size over the decades and changed hands in orchestrators, Waller always had one simple request: "Do not leave the local kids out."

And no one has dared to defy him yet.

***

Around the time Butch Waller was introducing those annual Christmastime games that would later evolve into the Governor's Challenge, he had an incredibly talented team. Despite getting trounced by DeMatha in

1981 and 1982, Waller's squad was building toward another run at the Maryland state title.

"Butch's '80s teams were really good," said Derrick Fooks, then a player at Stephen Decatur. "Stacked, some of them."

Those Wi-Hi teams of the early 1980s were built around someone who could do just about anything he wanted to – and anything Waller told him to do – on the basketball court. His name was Brian Butler, and in his debut game as a freshman, he scored 32 points against Easton. Butler wasn't supposed to start that game – and was probably one of the first freshmen to ever do so back then under Waller – but the man in front of him on the depth chart, Jerome Mitchell, had gotten into a fight in school the day before the season-opening contest. So, Butler was inserted into the starting five and his spot was cemented for four years with the Indians.

"After that first game, I just felt like I belonged. And I felt like I could play with older players," Butler said. "Coach was kind of courageous to put me on varsity. I was pretty good, and I felt like I could play, but not many (freshmen) played varsity back then. But he was an excellent coach. He knew what my strengths were. He knew what I needed to work on."

Brian's older brother Paul played for Waller too, and their parents were Indians superfans. From 1974 until Paul Butler Sr.'s death in 2020, he and his wife Doris attended every Wi-Hi home contest and a countless number of away games too.

"They bleed blue and gold just like we do," Paul Butler said of his parents.

Paul graduated from Wi-Hi in 1980. Long before he was one of the most recognizable broadcasters on the Delmarva Peninsula, Paul was a shy, skinny kid at Wi-Hi who didn't say a whole lot. But Waller, in his down-to-earth and relatable nature, brought the older Butler brother out of his shell on the basketball court by injecting him with some assurance. Waller told him, "You can shoot the basketball with anybody in this conference. And we're going to need you, night in and night out, to help us win games."

Hearing that from Waller – having someone verbalize that his skills on the hardwood were needed – boosted Paul's morale and gave him some newfound poise and tenacity when he slipped on the blue and gold Wi-Hi jersey. "He would hold you accountable too," Butler said. "If you were not getting the playing time you felt like you deserved, he would say, 'Look. You got to earn it.'"

Paul earned his minutes as a pure jump-shooter. Considering he was shaped like a beanpole, he often avoided driving toward the basket. Paul planted himself along the perimeter and turned himself into a real weapon out there, someone Waller could count on when the inside game wasn't working.

"You know, Paul was one of the best shooters I ever played with," Brian said of his older brother. "We used to call him 'Iceman' like George Gervin, because he was really smooth. He could really shoot the ball."

"We didn't have the three-point line back then, but from the wing, the corner or the top of the key, those were my favorite spots," Paul said.

Paul Butler continued: "Everybody that I know that plays for Coach Waller will say nothing but good things about him. Not only was he good at the fundamentals of the game or the X's and O's, but he taught you how to play the game the right way. The other thing was, he let every player know that there was something in your game that could help the team, whether you were the superstar or the 12th man on the bench ... I've never had a coach that was like that. He instilled in them, 'Listen. You've got some talent that I can use, that can help us win games. So, just be ready when your time comes.' He just made you believe in yourself."

In the 1979-80 season, Paul's senior year and Brian's freshman campaign, the Indians had an efficient basketball team and often won in entertaining fashion. Paul shared the backcourt with point guard Scott Smith, big man Jackie Walls patrolled the paint, and Brian Butler and Marcus Carr manned the forward positions. Paul led the team in scoring with 14.3 points per-game and they finished second in the south Bayside with a 16-8 record. In the playoffs, unfortunately, Wi-Hi ran up against a Cambridge team led by Skeeter Nichols and Darnell Clash which went on to win the state title.

After graduating from Wi-Hi, Paul made it to the final round of cuts at the University of Maryland as a walk-on, but Lefty Driesell wasn't particularly impressed by his defense. After being snubbed by the Terps, Paul transferred to Division III University of Mary Washington, where he played a season. He then finished out his academics at Salisbury University before embarking on a career in radio and television.

Brian Butler played as forward in his first two seasons at Wi-Hi, but Waller knew he was Division I material. So, before his junior year, he moved Butler to point guard. At 6-foot-4, Butler was a big forward in the Bayside Conference, but in college, he'd be a perimeter player. Waller knew that, and wanted Butler to improve his court vision and have the ball in his hands a little more. Butler's parents didn't initially agree with Waller, but the plan worked. Butler says now that Waller "probably changed the trajectory of my career." And that change was for the better.

"Brian just had an all-around game. He was built. Not only was he big, but he could handle the ball," Paul Butler said of his younger brother. "Not only did he turn into a good three-point shooter, but he loved dishing out the assists, and he loved taking charges. He could rebound, played great defense, just hustled. If there was a loose ball on the floor, he was going to get it. He was just relentless. He had a monster game."

Brian Butler began attracting interest from college coaches during the summer between his junior and senior years, when he held his own at the 1982 Five-Star Basketball Camp against the likes of Muggsy Bogues and Reggie Williams from Baltimore's Dunbar High School, and future college and NBA stars like Kenny Smith and Pearl Washington. The camp was operated by Howard Garfinkel, a longtime basketball scout, and was typically held in either Virginia, the Poconos or Pittsburgh. From 1966 to 2008, this is where the country's best high school basketball players congregated every year. To attend the showcase, players needed an invitation or a recommendation from a trusted coach. Butler got into the camp due to Waller's efforts and connections.

After Wi-Hi's season ended in the spring of 1982 with a state semifinal loss, Waller was looking for a way to drum up some collegiate interest for his standout pupil. He called up Lefty Driesell at Maryland, and made the case that Driesell should recommend Butler for an invitation to the camp. Driesell obliged and called Garfinkel. Soon, the Terrapins' coach was one of the dozen or so coaches vying for the services of Butler, just a few years after he had cut his brother as a walk-on.

"That's where my name kind of got national in terms of being recruited by a lot of different schools around the country. That was the first time I had big exposure," Butler said. "I started getting a lot of letters and calls from a lot of different people, including Maryland ... I started to get headaches because I had so many people calling. I told my parents I wanted to sign early. We were getting calls all the time."

Waller arranged meetings for Butler with Driesell at Maryland and in Annapolis with Navy coach Paul Evans. But Butler didn't think he could maximize his playing time at a big school like Maryland, and he didn't want to spend a year at the Naval Academy Prep School either. Before Butler attended that Five-Star Camp, Waller got a call from Gerry Gimelstob, who had been coaching at George Washington for a season after working as an assistant under Bob Knight at Indiana. He asked Waller to set-up an intrasquad scrimmage so he could see one of Butler's teammates, Tony Bateman, play. Instead, Butler was the one that stood out. Bateman landed on the roster at the University of Maryland Eastern Shore.

"I didn't know it at the time, but that was illegal," Waller says. "But he sees Brian and bites him up ... and Brian loved GW. He was a first-class kid. You don't get many like him."

Butler also took visits to Holy Cross, Hofstra, Maryland, Navy and had a trip planned for Clemson, but ultimately decided on George Washington before his senior season got underway. In hindsight, had Butler gone to Maryland, he would've played with the late Len Bias. And had he gone to Navy, he would've played with NBA Hall of Famer David Robinson. At the time though, Butler wanted to go someplace he was comfortable and somewhere that he could play right away and often.

In addition to being a talented scorer and passer, Butler was a relentless and savvy defender too. He still holds the Wi-Hi record for most charges drawn in a season with 39. Whatever it took to win, Butler was going to do it. Which made him the perfect player for Waller.

"With Coach Waller, charges are huge. In practices, that's one of things he talks about – how can we have more possessions than the other team? One is offensive rebounding. Another is drawing charges. When you draw a charge, that's a turnover, and so you're taking a possession away," Butler said. "I just had no qualms about putting my body in front of somebody. It was just something I liked doing. Drawing a charge gave me the same kind of feeling, that high, as dunking."

As Butler got better at playing point guard, dishing passes, dunking balls and frustrating opposing players, Wi-Hi improved too. The Indians started the year 5-0 with Butler averaging around 26 points per-game, but then he sprained his ankle at Crisfield and missed about 12 games. Still, the Indians kept rolling. Butler came back and they pushed their way to the state final four for the second straight year. After beating Einstein High School of Kensington 72-66 in the semifinals behind Butler's 28 points and 14 rebounds, Wi-Hi found itself playing for a state championship for the first time since 1951, back when Sam Seidel was the head coach.

In the final, the Indians fell in heartbreaking fashion, losing 75-67 to Southern in double overtime at Cole Field House.

"That game is one that still haunts us to this day," Paul Butler said.

"Tom Albright was the coach of Southern and he was very good," Waller said. "Played country and western music during warm-ups, and played a 1-3-1 zone during the game."

Brian Butler has a more blunt, honest and sobering self-assessment of his remembrance of that championship defeat. In his final game in an Indians uniform, he logged 19 points, nine assists and two steals, but he still feels like he could've done more.

"I didn't play well. We didn't win the state tournament because I didn't play well. I was the best player on the court – the only Division I player on the court – and I didn't play well," Butler said. "I underachieved that game. If I had played the way I had played in the first game, we would've won. I think I should have taken the ball more. I should've just said, 'Give me the ball.'"

Butler was named Bayside Player of the Year as a senior and made the All-State team after averaging 21.3 points, 3.7 assists, 1.5 steals and 6.1 rebounds per-game while shooting 55% from the floor and 75% from the charity stripe. Butler played in 103 games at George Washington over four seasons.

In one of his first games his freshman year, Butler got a little cocky when playing against Virginia Tech and decided to bark a bit at a guard by the name of Dell Curry. Gimelstob often deployed Butler as his "defensive stopper" against opposing two-guards. On that night though, there was nothing Butler could do.

"It was my first experience of truly being 'lit-up' by somebody," said Butler, who shot 1-for-8 in that game while Curry dropped 23 points. "When I got in, I trash-talked... I don't know why. I knew he was good. I wanted to get him off his game. He, probably within a three-minute period, hit three or four straight jumpers in my face with my hand in his face. I got taken out and cursed out by my coach. His shot was just like Steph's shot. So smooth, so effortless."

Butler was a real asset to the team by his senior year, starting in 14 of the 28 games he played in while averaging 8.9 points, 2.5 rebounds, and 1.4 assists per-game. Butler was also a legitimate weapon from behind the arc as a senior, knocking down 43.6% of his attempts from there. He was 10th in three-pointers made in the Atlantic-10 in 1987.

Brian Butler still holds the Wi-Hi record for most charges drawn in a career with 80. He played in 103 games at George Washington and shot 44% from three-point range as a senior in the 1986-87 season. George Washington Athletics.

"It took me some time to adjust. Although I had the talent and skill – the athletic talent – I didn't have the true guard skills yet," Butler said. "And I'm seeing the guys who are playing, they can score. They might not play any defense, but if they score, they're going to get in the game. So, I just spent crazy hours working on my outside shot. So, I just became a three-point specialist."

On Jan. 5, 1984, Butler's GW squad played a game against West Virginia University, which at the time carried Crisfield's Greg Bozman on its roster. Both Eastern Shore boys played as WVU won, 69-66.

"He was fabulous, a tremendous player," Bozman said of Butler. "He was one that you knew could adapt to the next level. Had handles, an all-around game, athletic, could shoot the ball. And his brother Paul could play too; could shoot the lights out."

Bozman added: "And Waller is just a legend. I love him. He's just a good guy. His record speaks for itself. He's a winner."

After his career at George Washington ended, Butler played one season in England for the Oldham Celtics. Near the end of the season, he suffered a knee injury and went through two surgeries to repair the damage. "That was it for me," Butler said. With his playing days behind him, Butler took a job as a substitute teacher and eventually carved out a career in education, following in the footsteps of his father who was a reading teacher at Berlin Middle School and before that a principal at Cedar Chapel in Snow Hill. At 56 years-old in 2021, Butler can feel all those charges he took in a Wi-Hi jersey when he wakes up every morning in the form of knee and hip aches, and his name is still etched on the record holder's chart outside of the Waller Dome.

"Brian Butler was my star," Waller said. "A great kid. Was he the best point guard I ever had? No. But he was impressive. He was an easy sell."

***

Because of how good Washington was in the 1970s, and how consistently great Crisfield and Pocomoke were in the 1970s and 1980s, it took Butch Waller a while to win his first Bayside South division title outright. It happened for the first time in 1988. And once Waller's Indians got a taste of the Bayside Conference Championship game, they kept going back. And they often won.

Between 1988 and 2007, Wi-Hi went to nine Bayside title games and took victories in all but one of them. Waller added to his collection of conference championships in 2015, 2018, 2019, 2020 and 2022, for a total of 13 Bayside crowns. In the 2018 and 2019 regular seasons, Wi-Hi didn't lose to a Bayside opponent.

For his first Bayside title, Waller's Indians faced a tough Easton team, led by 6-foot-8 center Wes Cornish, at the University of Maryland Eastern Shore in 1988. Before the game, Cliff Mister – then the sports editor at the Dorchester Banner – had conducted a poll of Bayside coaches, asking them who would win. Every single one, except for Cambridge's Grayson Hurley, picked Easton. Mister went to the Wi-Hi locker room and dropped off a stack of papers, giving Waller ammunition for motivation.

"Boy, I really used that. I gave this big Knute Rockne speech. I stomped on the papers," Waller said. "I'm telling you what, they were about to peel the paint off the wall. And then we went out and kicked their ass."

Wi-Hi won 77-71 thanks to a match-up 2-1-2 zone defense, 32 points from Mike Cole and a dazzling effort from point guard Tommy "Mooney" Williams, who had 11 points, 11 assists and nine steals.

Still, for all the success Waller had in the Bayside Conference, a state title

Doug King was a standout point guard at Salisbury University for Ward Lambert. King scored 1,087 points for the Sea Gulls in just two seasons. Salisbury University Athletics.

continued to elude him as he entered his third decade of coaching basketball at Wi-Hi.

***

On the last day of February in 1996, Butch Waller was sitting at the front of a school bus, stewing, as it drove over the Chesapeake Bay Bridge, back to the Eastern Shore. His Wi-Hi Indians had just been handed another playoff loss by Southern and coach Tom Albright's suffocating 1-3-1 defense. 63-47 was the final score in the 2A East Regional semifinal. Waller decided it was time for a change.

He said to himself: "Butchy Boy, that's it. We're not walking the ball up the floor no more. We're running. We're going up-tempo. We're going Loyola-Marymount."

Waller started watching tape and researching the run-and-gun offense Paul Westhead ran in the late 1980s with Bo Kimble and Hank Gathers at LMU.And then he asked his friend, Ward Lambert, who ran his own version of the system at Salisbury University, to come speak at practice.

"His philosophy was: no plays. He burned the boats," Waller said of Lambert. "Don't worry about defense, let them have the lay-up, you're going to go down and get three ... Ward's practices were nothing but running, but he had a way to sell it."

The group of players Waller had around then were a bunch he affectionately referred to as the Kiddie Corp. The players had all started together on varsity since their sophomore year, and point guard Doug King was one of the team's leaders. Like Waller, King was born and raised in Salisbury. And like Waller, he loved basketball. It was all he played since he was 8 years old, when he took his first dribbles in the Salvation Army league.

"I grew up in a basketball area. I stayed on the eastside, and eastside kids went to Wi-Hi," King said. "My first encounter with Waller was – I had him for gym in second period, and we played ping-pong."

King was the perfect player to orchestrate Wi-Hi's new offensive attack. He was a smart point guard who knew the game well, was quick with or without the ball in his hands, and knew just when to dish it off to teammates, like Damien Johnson.

"Lambert came and showed us how to run it. We were running all the time," King said. "It was a little project, but it worked."

Indeed. Wi-Hi started the season bumpy, falling to Colonel and Crisfield, while adjusting to a new style of play, but it didn't take long for King, Johnson, Al Hankerson and co. to settle in. By the end of the regular season, Wi-Hi was 20-2 and set to face Easton in the Bayside Conference Championship. Behind 31 points, 11 rebounds and a pair of electrifying two-handed dunks from Johnson, the Indians won 78-76. King had 11 points and seven assists.

Wi-Hi seemed destined to at least make the state tournament that season, but in the 2A East Regional Final, they ran up against Baltimore City College and suffered a 72-68 defeat. City often held possession and slowed the tempo of the contest to a crawl in an attempt to knock the run-and-gun Indians off their groove.

"It's difficult in the 2A," Waller said. "There's always some Baltimore team, and they're all so doggone good."

King still owns Wi-Hi's career records in steals (255) and assists (775). King dished out 347 assists as a senior, an average of 13.3 dimes per-game – which might be a Bayside record, if only someone in the conference kept those sorts of statistics.

The Kiddie Corp. laid the groundwork for the new era of Wi-Hi basketball. King and his crew won big and won often. They showed Waller a fun, fast-paced offense could work, and they captured the city of Salisbury's attention.

"When we played at home on Fridays, it was a show. It was like going to the club," King said. "People would go to the mall, get their clothes, then come to the game. Standing room only."

Waller kept working on perfecting his new offensive strategy. And in 2002, he finally had the horses to run the best version of it. The team was loaded, top to bottom. Bubby Brown ran the offense, Jermichael Mitchell was the lock-down defender, Craig Winder played the role of walking highlight-reel, Carl Miles protected the paint, and John Wolff, Kyle and Darnell Camper and Maron Brown were more-than-solid players who provided depth and timely play-making. Wi-Hi boat-raced through the Bayside that season, plowed through the playoffs and remained stout at states. They were truly unstoppable and brought Waller his first state championship.

His players lifted him up and paraded him around Cole Field House after the triumph, after completing the pristine season, something Waller had long strived for.

But he wasn't at peace. Waller wanted more.

"After we won that 2002 state championship, my thinking was, let's go win another one," Waller said. "You win one, everybody says you're lucky. You win two, you're not lucky. That's why I keep driving, to get another one. And a little bit of it is ego; no doubt about it."

***

Ahead of the 2002-03 season, in December, the Salisbury Daily Times sat down with both Butch Waller and Pocomoke's David Byrd for a lengthy in-depth interview. Both men had coached at their schools since the 1970s and both had just won their first state championships in March of 2002. The reporter for the Daily Times asked Byrd and Waller: "How long do you guys see yourself coaching?"

Waller: "That's easy. That's not hard."
Byrd: "That's easy for me... At Pocomoke High School, this is my last year."
Waller: "At Wicomico High School, this is my last – well, you never say never, don't burn any bridges – but unless something unforeseen happens, this is my last year."

Byrd kept his word, handing the reins of his team over to longtime assistant Derrick Fooks after losing in the 1A state final to Dunbar. Waller's Indians fell in the 2A East region final to an underdog James M. Bennett team. And so, Waller came back.

And he kept coming back, season after season after season after season. The 2022-23 basketball campaign will be Waller's 52nd year as the head varsity boys basketball coach at Wi-Hi. In April 2022, he turned 82 years-old.

"I've been around longer than anyone else," Waller said. "That wasn't necessarily the plan, but that's how it's worked out."

Waller is a bit like Bodie from HBO's The Wire. When Marlo's goons come for him near the end of Season Four, a defiant Bodie yells, "This is my corner!" And Wi-Hi is Butch Waller's corner. And he ain't going nowhere.

"Waller is insane," former Star Democrat sportswriter David Insley said. "We know he's always going to coach."

In his 56 years at Wi-Hi, other schools and other teams have called Waller, trying to pry him away from his sanctuary on Long Avenue. Bennett and Parkside have both offered him coaching jobs, and so has Salisbury University and his alma mater, East Tennessee State University. Waller at least listened to the college offers. In the interview for the Salisbury job, he felt a bit insulted. Ward Lambert had just left, and there wasn't anyone who really knew basketball in the interview. One Salisbury coach asked Waller,

"Well, what's your system?" And he proceeded to cover a chalkboard, breaking down every detail. The room was speechless.

"They didn't know shit from Shinola," Waller said. "I didn't want that job. I was making more money (at Wi-Hi) and I didn't want to go out on the road and recruit."

And on the ETSU job: "I just couldn't relive the past. I had been there and done that. And you know what? I'm happy. I don't need to be a big fish. I think I'm helping kids around here and I'm having fun. Plus, I was getting older. And I didn't want to do basketball year-round. I like to umpire baseball, play golf, go to the beach. That's a job for young, single guys."

When Waller's friend Morgan Wooten declined the N.C. State job in 1980 to stay at DeMatha, he said: "As for climbing mountains, they are where you find them."

Wooten's mountain simply wasn't in college basketball. And neither was Waller's.

"I got a lot of pride in this school," Waller said of Wi-Hi. "This is where I went. This is my school."

***

In 2012, Butch Waller finally stopped going to Morgan Wooten's clinics.

That summer, Wi-Hi guard Jamaal King Jr. transferred to Bishop O'Connell, where Wooten's son Joey was the head coach.

"Joey Wooten came down here to the (Governor's Challenge), saw Mar-Mar, and stole him. Something about that pissed me off," Waller said. "It hurt my feelings. It did. But for Mar-Mar, it worked out. That's the trend now… Wi-Hi plays a maximum of 28 games, if we go all the way. At O'Connell, they played 38, and some of them are on television – it's a no-brainer. That sort of started a lot of local kids going other places."

King, whose father still holds the Wi-Hi record for most steals in a single season with 138 in 1998-99, comes from basketball royalty of sorts in Salisbury. His dad played for Waller, and so did his uncles Doug King, and Bubby Brown. Like them, it was noticeable right away King was a talented player, destined to play college ball.

"I don't think a lot of people understand that I really was born into a basketball family," King said. "They didn't force it on me. I was just born with it. I never felt the pressure. That's who I am – I'm Jamaal King. I'm Bubby's little nephew, I'm Dougie's little nephew. I'm my dad's son. AJ Spencer is my uncle… And then it was my turn. I was like the basketball prodigy. Coming from a basketball family, I loved it. That's what we're known for. And I hope it doesn't end with me."

Jamaal King Jr. – the nephew of Doug King and Bubby Brown - played at Wi-Hi and then finished his high school career at Bishop O'Connell. Photo by Mitchell Northam.

In his varsity debut for the Indians his freshman season, he scored 13 points in a Dec. 8, 2011 win over Cambridge. King also helped lead Wi-Hi to a pair of wins over Queen Anne's that season, a year in which the Lions were anchored by 6-foot-9 future Terrapins center Damonte Dodd. King had 26 points in a regular season win over QA and 20 points in a playoff win over the Lions. King was just the fifth freshman ever to start on varsity for Waller.

"I remember my freshman year like it was yesterday," King said. "Bubby, Doug and Waller were the coaches. It wasn't overwhelming, but it was really cool. But I didn't get that Wi-Hi vibe. We were mediocre that year, at best. It didn't feel right."

Wi-Hi fell to Easton in the 2A East region semifinal on March 1, 2012. Not long after, King landed on the DC Assault AAU team – the same squad that produced NBA players like Michael Beasley, Nolan Smith and Quinn Cook. And soon after, he transferred to Joey Wooten's Bishop O'Connell.

"I felt like I was the best player around here. I know that. I believe that whole heartedly. I had to go over there and show the world my talent," King said. "Salisbury is small. It doesn't get that exposure. I had to keep my name out there ... O'Connell didn't have to take me. I'm really big on opportunities – taking them and running with them."

King shared the backcourt at O'Connell with future Maryland Terrapin Melo Trimble. He played on national TV a few times, often faced off against other Division I prospects, was twice a Washington Catholic Athletic

Conference First Team selection, was written about in the Washington Post, and saw his star rise as a recruit. By the fall ahead of his senior year, King had garnered scholarship offers from Hawaii, Maine, Robert Morris, Rider, Radford, Southern Miss and, where he ultimately committed to, St. Francis (Pa.).

More than once, King flirted with the idea of returning to Wi-Hi, but it never happened.

"My senior year, I wish I could've come back and gotten all that love. I feel like I would've turned the city up, just like Jorden Duffy and Kory Holden did. I would've given Salisbury a show," King says. "I was already locked in with St. Francis and I was thinking about going back to Wi-Hi. It would've been headlines here. But at the moment, I felt like, I came to O'Connell and I'm going to finish it. I didn't owe them, but my loyalty stuck. And with D.C. Assault, I was in the politics game a little bit. I could've come home my senior year, but would O'Connell have stamped me, if I needed them to? I might need Coach Joe later in the long run. I chose loyalty."

Transferring away from Wi-Hi and staying at O'Connell worked out for King. When he had issues with his transcripts, the coaches at St. Francis stuck with him. "They rolled with me," King said. "My road could've gone different, so I'm grateful and blessed."

At St. Francis, Wi-Hi's Jamaal King Jr. led the Red Flash to an NIT appearance in 2019. He was a two-time All-NEC First Team selection. In a 2018 game at No. 7 UNC, he had 21 points and three rebounds. Photo by Mitchell Northam.

A wicked quick 5-foot-10 guard with a knack for scoring, King started in 93 of the 115 games he played in at St. Francis, averaging 13.2 points and 3.4 assists per-game. As a senior, after scoring 21 points in the Dean Dome in a loss to UNC, he was named First Team All-NEC while leading the Red Flash to a regular season NEC championship – just their second ever – and a trip to the NIT.

After playing two years overseas in Bulgaria and Serbia, King decided to follow in the footsteps of his uncles to become a coach. He returned to St. Francis as a graduate assistant coach in 2021 – another example of the connections King made, and the loyalty he cultivated, shining through.

"When I got back from overseas, I was homesick. I was playing good. It wasn't about basketball; it was the little stuff. Just the food, like, they don't have cheese over there," King said. "There were things that I missed. And I felt like, if I was going to commit, I needed to be over there for 10 years. I don't like half-assing shit. I committed to O'Connell, I committed to St. Francis. I'm always going to put all my eggs in one basket. It was a big decision. Putting the shoes down, it hurt me and it hurt a lot of people."

Nobody told King he wasn't good enough to play basketball anymore. No one forced him to unlace his sneakers for the final time. But basketball is a young man's game; he wasn't going to play forever. So, King left the court on his own terms. He just felt like, at the age of 24, getting a head-start in coaching was the right move.

Jamaal King Jr. returned home in the summer of 2021 to share his story with kids in Salisbury. King plans to go back to St. Francis (PA) to pursue a master's degree and start a career in coaching. Photo by Mitchell Northam.

"It's a grown-man decision. When you look at the bigger picture... My resume just has basketball on it. I've never really had a job or an internship... And now I can go back to school, get my master's for free and coach basketball. This is giving me a chance to jump ahead of the curve. And I didn't even ask for this. It's bigger than me. I'm a little kid from a small town who did a lot of sacrificing, who did a lot of things that made him uncomfortable to get to where I am today. I don't regret none of it."

Instead of being the next Albert Mouring, someone who starred in foreign leagues, King could be the next Oliver Purnell or Butch Waller – someone who puts the Eastern Shore on the map through coaching.

"Maybe I'm that person who can catch us up. Maybe we can get a nice Eastern Shore AAU team," King said. "Those kids ain't better than us down here. They might have more money, funding, exposure – but skill wise? No. It's nobody's fault. It's just where we're born and where we live."

***

After Jamaal King Jr., a few more players would flee Wi-Hi for what they thought were greener pastures. Halfway through the 2018-19 basketball season, Wi-Hi football player Dominic Bailey – who was also Butch Waller's starting center on the basketball team – opted to transfer to St. Frances Academy in Baltimore for his senior season. But Bailey already had exposure. Penn State, UNC, Pitt and several other schools had already offered him scholarships and he was evaluated as a prospect by the national recruiting site 247sports. Still, he went to St. Frances. Bailey wound up taking an offer from Tennessee. "He came in my office and said, 'Coach, I'm leaving.' We were playing Crisfield that day," Waller said. "He was nice enough to come tell me... But he had the scholarship to Tennessee when he was at Wi-Hi."

For every success story like Dominic Bailey and Jamaal King Jr., there are other examples where a player thinks he's better than he really is, gets bad advice, or ends up in a less-than-ideal situation. To Waller, that's Jaden Baker. Indeed, Baker was a talented guard with excellent grades – whom Waller was talking to coaches at the Naval Academy about – but Baker decided to re-class and transferred to a private college-preparatory co-ed boarding school in Virginia. "He made a horrible mistake... He had to pay. He had to leave his friends. But that seems to be the trend," Waller said, sighing. "His mother was pissed off at me because I didn't get Mike Krzyzewski to come look at him." Baker wound up playing at Division II Bentley University in Massachusetts, where he averaged 1.1 points per-game as a freshman in the 2021-22 season as his team won the Northeast 10 conference title.

Said Doug King, who has been Waller's assistant since 2002: "Waller is a good dude. He gets a lot of flak because some people say he doesn't help the Black kids get into college. I've been there for 18 years. He helps them. And you know, we don't really have college kids. We don't have Division I kids."

When King said that, he meant in terms of basketball talent. It's true that, recently, Wi-Hi hasn't produced a basketball player who has gone straight to Division I from high school.

But Waller's players have gone to college. The 2015 team is just one example. After the Indians won the Bayside title and made the 2A state semifinals, each of Waller's five seniors on that squad – Nelson Brown, Trevell Jones, Lionel Batson, Xzavier Branyon-Sims and Ryshaun Taylor – graduated on-time with grade-point averages above 3.0, and each went to college. Brown landed at Lenoir-Rhyne University where he played football, Jones and Branyon-Sims went to Cheyney University, Batson went to Harford Community College where he played a season of basketball, and Taylor landed at Maryland Eastern Shore.

Said Jones, back in 2015: "Waller would surprise you in your classroom every now and then. He still does it even though the season is over and we're graduating. He's just checking on you and checking on your grades, him and King. They won't tell you always, but they're checking."

And Waller has had Division I talent, but they often ended up transferring away for whatever reason, like King's nephew Jamaal, like Bailey, like Baker.

Despite talented players coming and going over the last decade, Waller has still extracted every last ounce of talent and effort out of every team he's had. The unit Waller had in 2012-13 – which would've been Jamaal King Jr.'s sophomore season – the Indians were a last-second floater away from winning a state title. Instead, they fell to Edmondson, 56-54.

"Edmondson. Oh my God, man. That team had all the pieces. And we had a beast at power forward. We had so many opportunities," Doug King said. "And the last play, it was a charge… And if my nephew was on that team, we would've punished Edmondson. It wouldn't have been close."

While transferring has become more popular, and as basketball culture on the Eastern Shore has changed, Waller has adapted. The players come and go, and Waller keeps winning.

In the summer of 2021, two of Waller's All-Bayside guards Antwan Wilson and Taiwan Hardy transferred to Cross Christian Academy in Seaford, Delaware. After he broke the news on Twitter, Travon Miles – a Wi-Hi grad turned WMDT47 sports director – said this: "It's going to take more than a few transfers to get Butch out of the gym."

***

Both Butch Waller and Doug King are a bit tired, by the way, of talking about Waller and the 'R' word – retirement.

"What the hell am I going to move on to? I'm not a big fan of retirement,"

Waller says. "From November to March, I'm at Wi-Hi seven days a week. That's what I do."

King has been with Waller for 20 years. After playing for Waller on those Kiddie Corp. teams, he went on to Cecil College and then Salisbury University where he was a starter and a captain. When Dave Byer left to become the Parkside head coach in the fall of 2002, Wi-Hi had an opening and King filled it.

He's made it known he wants to be a head varsity basketball coach, but King is in no rush. Wi-Hi is Waller and Waller is Wi-Hi. When the time comes, there is an unspoken mutual agreement the job will be King's.

Waller has asked King, more than once, "Doug, am I in your way?"

King says, "You stay as long as you want."

After playing for Cecil College and Salisbury University, Doug King returned to Wi-Hi to become Butch Waller's lead assistant. He's also the head coach of the JV boys team. Photo by Mitchell Northam.

"I want to be a varsity coach. Hopefully, one day, Waller will get out of there," King said. "I'm comfortable at Wi-Hi. If I was going to leave, wouldn't I have already been gone? I can't see myself coaching at Bennett. I've been at Wi-Hi this long, I might as well wait. I'm like 98% sure I would get the job when it's time… And me and Waller are close. He's like my friend. He's old, but he's cool. I'm not trying to run him out. We have a good relationship."

Waller said of King: "He's smart and knows the game. He's a big help and big sounding board. We work really good together."

As long as Waller is coherent, has his health and can walk and talk, it's likely he'll be coaching basketball at Wi-Hi, and King will be by his side. As evidenced in his decades of coaching, Waller is a man of routines and habits and preparation. In the spring, he umpires baseball. In the summer and the fall, he golfs and spends time with his chocolate lab. And from November to March, he's around basketball. These routines have become particularly important to Waller since 2018, when his wife of 54 years, Sandy, died.

"Coaching basketball has been a huge part of my life," Waller said. "It's cost me a little relationship with my son. I probably wasn't that good of a father. Ever since I started coaching varsity, it's 'What should I have done?' It eats at me. That's why I'm overly organized.

"If I was going to do it, it was getting everything I had."

***

On March 16, 2018, a Friday afternoon, Wi-Hi principal Don Brady had scheduled a meeting with Waller and Wi-Hi athletic director Stosh Schtierman about the new floor in the gym. Waller had an opinion about how one of the feathers on the floor was painted. After that brief exchange, Waller grabbed his truck keys and headed for the door. "Hold on," Brady said. "We got one more thing." Waller responded, "Christ, don't you guys know it's Friday?"

The three men went out the back door of the school, across the field and toward the intersection of Long Avenue and Glen Avenue. Waller saw police lights and assumed there must've been a bad accident. Then the men got closer, and Waller heard Wi-Hi's band playing. And as they inched closer to the crowd, Waller started recognizing a lot of familiar faces. He turned to Schtierman, his former assistant coach, and said, "What the hell is going on here?"

What was going was, the people of Salisbury and Wicomico County – particularly Paul Butler, Donna Richardson and Mayor Jake Day – decided it was time to put Butch Waller's name on something, for all the kids he has coached and for all the lives he's impacted in a positive way. Day proclaimed March 16 as "Butch Waller Day" and Long Avenue – the street Wicomico High School sits along – was renamed as Butch Waller Way.

"He's an amazing guy," said Butler, then working for the Wicomico County Board of Education. "I love him to death. We're still great friends … I've never had a coach that was like Butch Waller."

Waller was pleasantly shocked, surprised and humbled by the honor.

"I'm pretty swift in picking stuff up. I don't know how they pulled that off without me knowing," Waller said. "I must be getting dumber than a clam's ass."

Waller, jokingly, told Day he'd like to put a toll booth on the street and charge every driver a dollar, with the money going toward Wi-Hi athletics.

He then told David Insley of the Star Democrat, "The only thing that would've made it better would've been if a 6-foot-8 kid had walked up and said, 'Coach Waller, I'm a junior and I've transferred in.'"

***

Butch Waller didn't have any Division I basketball players on his 2015 squad, but they won a regional on the road and made the state final four again. Photo by Mitchell Northam.

Butch Waller never did get a 6-foot-8 transfer, but his teams have kept on winning. In March of 2020, his Indians had a 25-1 record and were Bayside champs and were boarding a bus to head to College Park for the state final four when a school administrator rushed outside. Because of COVID-19, the state tournament was called off, and all Waller and Doug King were left with were what-ifs and a busload of disappointed teenagers.

"What a blow," Waller said. "I thought we had a shot. The other three teams were good, but we had them all scouted."

The Bayside Conference didn't play basketball in the 2020-21 school year due to the pandemic. But when 2021-22 rolled around, after vaccines had been rolled out and injected into the arms of millions of Americans, Waller was ready to get back to coaching. Once again, Wi-Hi had a successful team, finishing the regular season with just one loss – to James M. Bennett, coached by Bubby Brown, a former Waller understudy. Brown was named Coach of the Year after leading the Clippers to the 3A East Regional Final.

Wi-Hi won the Bayside's and the 2A East regional title – a thrilling 62-61 triumph at Liberty in Eldersburg in Carroll County. The Indians trailed by as many as 18 points in the second quarter, then broke off a 20-0 run to take the lead. After the game, players and staff took turns cutting down the nets to celebrate the regional crown and Wi-Hi's 27th trip to the state final four – only Annapolis has more, making 28 appearances. Waller climbed the ladder last, trimmed the final bit of nylon off the iron rim, and hoisted it in the air as his players and surrounding fans gave him a thunderous applause. As he gingerly stepped off the ladder, one of his players said, "Waller. You got to dance."

Waller, bemused, said, "Dance?" As if it was something he didn't do.

When he reached the floor, the players began clapping and chanting a tune. A grin grew across Walker's face. The old coach stepped in his time machine, chugged his arms and moonwalked through the group of teenagers. Laughter ensued. It was a joyous moment – one that only comes on the heels of crucial victories. It's one of the reasons why Waller still does this.

Waller has 877 wins, more than anyone else who has ever coached public high school boys basketball in the state of Maryland. He passed former Annapolis coach John Brady for the record – win No. 773 – on Jan. 5, 2017 with a 78-64 home win over Easton. Along the way, Waller has made some adversaries, but by and large, he's loved, appreciated and respected among the majority on the Eastern Shore.

"He's one of the great basketball minds we have," said Pocomoke head coach Derrick Fooks.

"Butch is a fine coach and a good man," said former Colonel Richardson coach Merrill Morgan.

When Waller finally does call it quits – or, as he says with a laugh, drops dead in the Wi-Hi gym and is "swept up by the janitors" – basketball on the Eastern Shore won't quite feel the same. It'll be like if the Whopper suddenly fell off the Burger King menu, or if Bugs Bunny disappeared from the Looney Tunes, or if Iron Man left the Avengers. It'll be really weird. But at some point, it'll happen, and the sport and community will have to adapt to his absence. However, because of the impact Waller has made on basketball on the Shore over the last five decades, his legacy will live on long after he leaves the bench at Wi-Hi.

"I make a point to tell all the kids, whatever I'm coaching, what we're playing for. It's not just to show off for your girlfriend or family," Waller says.

"Let's have some fun today, and I want to win something."

AN ORAL HISTORY OF PERFECTION: THE 2002 WI-HI INDIANS

> "We started to sense it in the fourth quarter. The clock is ticking down and we're just looking at each other like, 'Yo, we won.'"
> – Craig Winder

Each year since he started running the scoreboard at Wi-Hi, Bill Weber can expect a call from Butch Waller on Oct. 15. Waller always asks the same question – "Are you in for this year?" – and Weber says yes, and then they talk about the team. Most years Waller will tell Weber his team is no good and he'll be lucky to get 10 wins.

"You could set your watch by it," Weber said.

But on Oct. 15, 2001, Waller didn't pull any punches.

"I got horses," he told Weber. "This is my year. I'm going for this one."

Waller wound up being absolutely right. From Dec. 5, 2001 to March 9, 2002, Wi-Hi was dominant every single time its players stepped on the basketball court. Waller brought back a roster from the previous season that lost the state title narrowly to the mighty Dunbar Poets of Baltimore, and he was adding to it. Waller would have a team littered with Division I talent, players who could shoot, dunk, pass and defend as well as anyone in the state. He had dogs – ultra-super competitive and talented players – throughout his squad, from stars Craig Winder and Bubby Brown to the 12th man on the bench.

The Indians' two warm-up songs that season were "Danger" by Mystikal and "We Right Here" by DMX. On the DMX track, the hook flowed:

Bring it!
What?
We right here
We're not going anywhere
We right here
This is ours and we don't share
We right here
Bring your crew, 'cause we don't care
We right here, uh, uh, uh

It was fitting, because every other team in the Bayside knew Wi-Hi was coming, and the other teams knew they couldn't assemble a crew to compete with the Indians.

What unfolded over the 2001-02 season for Wi-Hi was Waller's lone perfect season, culminating in his first – and only, as of 2021 – state championship. It gave him the lone boys basketball state championship banner hanging in Wi-Hi's historic gym.

The journey to that joyous moment began almost exactly a year before. Before the Indians could experience accomplishment and happiness, they had to feel pain. They had to get their hearts broken by basketball.

This is the story of the pursuit of perfection; of Wi-Hi's 2002 boys basketball team – perhaps the greatest team ever assembled on the Eastern Shore.

"I don't think Butch has ever had a team like that," Weber said. "And I'm not sure if he'll ever have one like that again."

Wi-Hi's Butch Waller finally won his state championship in 2002, as the Indians went a perfect 28-0. His players carried him around Cole Field House after the big win. From the collection of Todd Dudek.

SHORE HOOPS

***

PART ONE: BROKEN ZONE RESULTS IN FRUSTRATING LOSS

March 10, 2001 – Dunbar 45, Wi-Hi 43: 2A State Championship Game, Cole Field House

BUTCH WALLER, WICOMICO HEAD COACH: I really felt we should've won, but there were some issues with us breaking that 1-3-1 zone. Dunbar was holding the ball and we were in a 1-3-1 zone. Without saying any names, a couple of our players decided to come out of it, because they got frustrated.

BUBBY BROWN, WICOMICO JUNIOR GUARD: We kind of caught Dunbar off-guard. We were in the game at halftime, playing a 1-3-1 defense. With four or five minutes left in the third quarter, (Dunbar) went to stall ball. We stayed in the zone and they stalled until the end of that quarter and into the fourth. They were trying to shorten the game.

JERMICHAEL MITCHELL, WICOMICO JUNIOR GUARD: It was a coaching decision made to stay back and not put as much pressure on the guard – and his name was Kenny, we actually played against him in AAU, so we knew him and some of the Dunbar guys – and we were down, but not by much. I felt like we could have pressured the ball a little bit more, but we went with his coaching decision and stayed back in the zone.

ERIC LEE, DUNBAR HEAD COACH (to The Baltimore Sun): They had a great scheme. We knew if we got up, our game plan was to bring them out of the zone.

BUTCH WALLER: We were telling the players to stay put, because Dunbar was doing us a favor. We had been scoring on almost every trip. They held it, and every time we came out of the zone, they got a lay-up, because we were out of sync. We were two points down, then four, and we're yelling at them to stay in. Then we went down six points and we had to go man-for-man.

JOHN WULFF, WICOMICO JUNIOR FORWARD: The zone was definitely weird, because we sat there for five to six minutes. Just sitting in the zone, waiting for Dunbar to do something.

KENNY MINOR, DUNBAR SENIOR POINT GUARD (to The Baltimore Sun): Like we've done the whole season, we outhustled them. We outran them on a lot of loose balls. They could have had us, but they weren't hustling as much as we were.

BUBBY BROWN: Their best player, Kenny Minor, got hurt the night before and was playing on a bum ankle, so that might've been why they went stall ball too. Typical Baltimore basketball.

BUTCH WALLER (to The Baltimore Sun): For the most part, we tried to shorten the game in order to get into the fourth quarter. I thought they were a little bit stronger on the boards, and that seemed to be the case on offense.

JERMICHAEL MITCHELL: It was devastating. I cried. We were that close.

JOHN WULFF: It was awful. It was heartbreaking, but it definitely lit a fire under us for the next year. We all made a promise to each other that we would be back the next year.

Bill Weber has been running the scoreboard at Wi-Hi for Waller's games since the 1980s. Over those three-plus decades, Weber grew to become a friend of Waller's and a fan of Wi-Hi basketball. His son Josh did too. When Josh was about 10-years-old he started helping his dad do the games and by the time he was 14, Josh did his first game by himself.

Both were in College Park that day, hoping to see Waller win his first title.

BILL WEBER, WI-HI SCOREBOARD OPERATOR: Butch out-coached the guy, but Wi-Hi just didn't have that extra gear to get it done. Once a couple of calls went against him and Dunbar got the lead, they took the air out of the ball. Butch had used that tactic many times to his advantage and this was one of the times where it went against him.

JOSH WEBER, WI-HI SCOREBOARD OPERATOR: Darnell Camper broke the zone. It was the 1-3-1, he was at the top. Dunbar pulled the ball back out to the corners and they're just sitting there watching the clock tick away. James Poorman, the senior center, he was getting a little antsy. They wanted to play, but Waller was like, "No, you sit there."

BILL WEBER: Late in that game, Wi-Hi had a chance to tie it up. Bubby shot a corner three in front of Wi-Hi's bench, and a Dunbar kid basically planted him into the water cooler. No call, shot misses and that's pretty much how it ends. I was pissed off because the Eastern Shore was getting hosed again.

BUTCH WALLER: As soon as that game was over, I was caught between frustration, anger and trying to look ahead, because I was going to have almost all of those kids back. I pulled them in a huddle right there on the floor at Cole Field House and I said, "Look you guys, we screwed up. We gave this game away. Let's make a deal right now, that 365 days from now, we'll be on this same floor again and we'll win."

BUBBY BROWN: (Waller is) big on dates and days, so he said, "365 days from now we're going to be back on the same floor."

JERMICHAEL MITCHELL: Bubby didn't shed a tear. He was the leader for us, since we were kids. And he turned to us and was like, "Next year man. We're going to come back and we're going to win it."

BILL WEBER: I had been with Butch for about 17 years or so at that point in time. Knowing how bad he wanted one – and considering who else had won one on the Shore – you felt he was robbed. He lost in 1983 by a point, he had another chance in 2001 and just didn't get a break.

In the stands at Cole Field House was a young man who would soon be a member of the Indians. Craig Winder grew up with several of the Wi-Hi players, but played at Mardela Middle and High School until after his junior year. Mardela was abysmal as a boys basketball program back then, but Winder was an outlier as someone who had massive talents as a hooper.

After a stop at Cecil College, Craig Winder landed at Texas where he played with NBA All-Stars Kevin Durant and LaMarcus Aldridge. The Longhorns went to the NCAA Tournament both years Winder was there. University of Texas Athletics

BUTCH WALLER: Winder went to Mardela, and nothing was going on there, basketball-wise.

BUBBY BROWN: Carl Miles didn't play that year either. He was ineligible and was in the stands with (Winder).

JERMICHAEL MITCHELL: If we had (Miles), we would've won the state championship by 10 or 15 points.

CARL MILES: I wasn't eligible that year because I had gotten into some trouble. I was there though, and it was tough. I was upset because I wasn't out there. I was needed.

CRAIG WINDER, MARDELA JUNIOR GUARD: All the guys on the team were my friends, through AAU basketball and just hanging out, so I felt that loss just as bad as they felt it. Bubby, Jermichael, John (Wulff) – all of those guys.

BUTCH WALLER: When we were going in the back door at Cole Field House to face Dunbar, Craig tried to come in with us and I said, "Craig, this is just for the players. If you want to be a player," – and this is my recruiting pitch – "then you come to Wi-Hi with us next year." He went around front and bought a ticket and next year he transferred in.

CRAIG WINDER: The thing was, my brother and sister had already graduated from Wi-Hi, my grandmother just didn't let me go there yet. So, I felt like I was supposed to be there. I never understood why I wasn't able to go. When we moved to Wi-Hi's district, my grandmother kept me at Mardela.

BUBBY BROWN: I was trying to get Craig to Wi-Hi since we were sophomores. His grandma wouldn't budge.

JERMICHAEL MITCHELL: We got Craig because, if you went to Mardela, they didn't have football. So, for real, if you said you were trying out for the football team at Wi-Hi and you didn't make it or didn't like it, then you were good to stay at Wi-Hi because you tried out.

JOSH WEBER: When Wi-Hi played Mardela, you knew Wi-Hi was going to win by 80, but Winder was going to score 30 or 40 – basically all of Mardela's points.

BILL WEBER: Winder came and played at Wi-Hi in his junior year, and I think he dropped 30 points in the first half. He was taking almost every shot, but he was the only player Mardela had. Whatever way Winder wanted to score – dunks, three's – he scored. He was a freak athlete.

BUBBY BROWN: My first time meeting Craig was when I drafted him at a pick-up game at the Salvation Army. I didn't even know him. He walked in the gym, we had the first pick, and he just looked like he could ball.

***

PART TWO: THE TONE IS SET

In winning his 773rd game in 2017, Butch Waller passed John Brady of Annapolis to become the all-time winningest coach in the history of boys public high school basketball in the state of Maryland. Photo by Mitchell Northam.

BUTCH WALLER: I kept 12 players and I knew who the top six were.

We didn't go into tryouts very long that year. I knew what my team was going to look like.

BILL WEBER: Every year on Oct. 15, I was getting a call from Butch asking, "Are you in?" and every year he would tell me that the team wasn't very good and then they would go play for the Bayside title or something. But that year, the 01-02 season, he didn't pull any punches.

BUBBY BROWN, WICOMICO SENIOR GUARD: We actually cut about three good players in tryouts. There was another kid who came with Craig from Mardela, and he ended up going to Bennett and playing there the day after he got cut. We had a kid from Cambridge who got cut too. We had like eight seniors, so it was tough.

JERMICHAEL MITCHELL, WICOMICO SENIOR GUARD: There were two other kids too. Jason Cotton and Chris Johnson, who actually played football for Wi-Hi, but both of those guys ended up transferring out because they didn't make the basketball team.

CRAIG WINDER, WICOMICO SENIOR GUARD: I was just trying to figure out where I fit in. These guys already had a routine and I didn't want to mess anything up. Waller just told me to play my game and have fun. He was all about trying to do everything stress-free.

BUTCH WALLER: All the practices were good because they really wanted to win. They would get after each other in practice.

CRAIG WINDER: I knew we could be special, just from what we were doing outside of high school from AAU and growing up. Bubby and I won a championship at the boys' club, so I'm thinking it's just like old times again.

JERMICHAEL MITCHELL: We knew Craig was coming and I had to take a backseat. I had to give up my starting spot when Craig came.

BUTCH WALLER: The most vocal leader was Bubby Brown. Bubby was a very smart basketball player, like a coach on the floor.

BUBBY BROWN: Funny part is, and Waller was mad at me for this, WMDT47 interviewed me before the season and I told them straight-up, "We are going undefeated and we are going to win the state championship." Waller was really mad about that, but that's just how I felt.

JERMICHAEL MITCHELL: He made that statement and Butch was not happy. Butch was so mad. We weren't cocky, but we were very confident. And now we had a couple pieces that we didn't have from the year before.

Doug King is a former player of Waller's who still holds Wi-Hi records for most career assists and steals. He went on to play at Cecil Community College and Salisbury University. During the 2001-02 season, he hung around some practices and helped out his old coach.

King, a standout point guard in his playing days, noticed something right away out of Bubby Brown during scrimmages.

DOUG KING, FORMER WI-HI PLAYER: In the fourth quarter, nobody touched the ball but Bubby. He either passed it to you and you scored, or he scored. He didn't let anyone else carry the ball. It was amazing. He just took over.

CRAIG WINDER: Bubby was one of the most skilled growing up. He was a floor general. He kept everyone in place from running wild. If you watch tape of us, Bubby was always the calmest.

JOSH WEBER: Bubby was cerebral. Bubby was that guy where, if you were on his team, you were going to win. In practice, in pick-up games, whatever. He had the skills, the grades. Maybe his numbers weren't that great, but he was a winner. He could do a little bit of everything. If you needed Bubby to play the four or five and get some rebounds, he could do that. If you needed him to lock-up the other team's best guy, he could do that. If you needed him to go hit four (three-pointers) because you were down by 15, he could do that. He was so versatile. He wasn't tall, but he was tall enough. He wasn't quick, but he was quick enough. He wasn't fast, but he was fast enough.

During his playing days at Wi-Hi, Bubby Brown was a fierce and versatile guard. He never shied away from the spotlight; in fact, he relished and thrived in it. If there was a crucial shot to be taken, the ball would likely be in the hands of the swaggy kid with cornrows, black Adidas sneakers and a No. 32 Indians jersey.

Dec. 5, 2001 – Wi-Hi 91, James M. Bennett 48: Game One, Regular Season, at James M. Bennett (Craig Winder – 19 points)

BUBBY BROWN: It was 30 to zip to start that game.

BUTCH WALLER: I don't remember why Jermichael didn't play. Maybe he was ill. There weren't any discipline problems with that team, that's for sure.

BUBBY BROWN: Jermichael got hurt during football season and missed that game. He had hip problems.

JERMICHAEL MITCHELL: Well, I tore my MCL in football, so I missed the first few games actually. I only played football my senior year.

CRAIG WINDER: We'd play around sometimes at practice. If the coach wasn't looking, you'd throw a cheap elbow or something. It was a loose group. But if it got out of hand, we would solve the problem ourselves.

BUBBY BROWN: We played around a lot. I mean a lot. We wrestled all the time. It was a fun team. Our pre-game ritual was turn off all the lights in the locker room, put some DMX on and play fight. It was dangerous, but that's what we did. We were crazy. We would slap box. We were really close.

Dec. 7, 2001 – Wi-Hi 89, Parkside 31: Game Two, Regular Season, at Wi-Hi (Craig Winder – 25 points)

The score was 30-2 after the first quarter.

BUTCH WALLER: We pressed a lot. They were hungry and I had to feed them.

BILL WEBER: How many high school teams had five guys who can dunk? Not many. You don't see it. But these guys, they could all throw it down. It was Dunk City when they got the chance.

Dec. 11, 2001 – Wi-Hi 89, Snow Hill 64: Game Three, Regular Season, at Wi-Hi (Craig Winder – 27 points)

JERMICHAEL MITCHELL: Those were our rivals. Nowadays, Wi-Hi's rivals are Parkside and Bennett, the city teams. But we never worried about them. We knew we were going to be City and County Champions. Our rivals, when I was in school, was Pocomoke and Snow Hill. The guys we played with in the summertime on our AAU teams. We knew we had to bring our 'A' game against them.

BUTCH WALLER: We knew we had a dream team and I knew I had to stay on my toes. I had to keep challenging them every week. We were killing people and I couldn't let them get stale.

Dec. 14, 2001 – Wi-Hi 119, Washington 47: Game Four, Regular Season, at Washington (Bubby Brown – 23 points)

Brown connected on seven three-pointers.

BUTCH WALLER: Bubby has the record for most three's in a game. He hit eight in one game in his junior year. He was a very good shooter.

John Wulff added 18 points on six-of-six shooting and six-of-six from the free throw line.

BUTCH WALLER: I talked to John Wulff right at the beginning of the season and I told him, "I know you're a great perimeter player, but I really need you inside." He said, "Coach, wherever you need me. I'm there." Wulff was a great team player.

JOHN WULFF: Me and Carl were the two biggest gentlemen on the team, so with the addition of Craig and some other guys, (Waller) needed me to be a rebounder and have more of a presence down low.

JERMICHAEL MITCHELL: Wulff came over from Parkside. He had played AAU with us and then came over to Wi-Hi. There was a lot of us who were at Wi-Hi that could've went to Parkside and been the best player there.

BUBBY BROWN: Wulff was someone you would love to play with. He was a high-energy, loved to get the crowd in it, but he was skilled to. Had a nice pump fake and he would try to dunk on you. Plus, he was the only white boy on the team. He had all the fans from the student section. They used to always chant Wulff's name.

JOHN WULFF: I wouldn't say all the fans, but I got a "Great White Hope" cheer every once in a while.

Dec. 18, 2001 – Wi-Hi 86, Crisfield 51: Game Five, Regular Season, at Crisfield (Bubby Brown – 17 points)

BUBBY BROWN: Crisfield wasn't too tough that year. They played hard; Phil Rayfield had that 3-2 zone. My sophomore year was the hardest against Crisfield, when they had Andre Collins. But they still had the band in that small-ass gym.

BUTCH WALLER: If someone was going to beat us down here in the Bayside it would've had to have been a really good team. I pretty much knew about most of the teams. The biggest threat was Pocomoke.

***

PART THREE: THE FIRST TEST

Dec. 21, 2001 – Wi-Hi 73, Pocomoke 67: Game Six, Regular Season, at Pocomoke (Carl Miles – 15 points)

BUBBY BROWN: Pocomoke always played hard, and we all played AAU together, but when we faced off, we didn't like each other. We almost threw blows.

JERMICHAEL MITCHELL: Back then they had these small gyms. So, you only had half a side of bleachers, and then a wall you didn't want to run into, and it was loud. If your fans didn't get there early enough, you were in Pocomoke with no fans. You got booed, but it was fun.

BILL WEBER: If you weren't in line for Pocomoke's band box by 3'o'clock then you weren't getting in.

DAVID BYRD, POCOMOKE HEAD COACH: Yea, we lost to (Wi-Hi) twice last year, but I didn't have my starting point guard either time. I keep telling (Waller) that.

BUTCH WALLER: David Byrd always says, "Well I didn't have my point guard that game." That's BS. Pocomoke had a very good team.

DAVID BYRD: We go back a long way, Butch and I. I was playing basketball at Pocomoke when Butch was coaching JV at Wi-Hi.

Pocomoke's Eddie Miller and Tyrone Northam combined for 40 points.

BUBBY BROWN: Eddie was tough. Always smiling. Eddie hit some big shots.

JOSH WEBER: Eddie was always going to get 20 points, at least. He was too good of a shooter to not to.

BUTCH WALLER: Eddie Miller was a great player and went on to play at Fresno State. Ty Northam was a good inside player too.

CRAIG WINDER: Ty and Eddie played with us in AAU, so we knew what they were about and what they could do.

BUBBY BROWN: Ty Northam was just a dog. Always played hard.

CARL MILES: Guarding Ty was cool, because we played AAU together, so I knew him well. He was really active down there in the paint.

Bubby Brown had a poor shooting night, finishing with six points and just two-of-10 from the free throw line.

JOSH WEBER: That's how good they were. Bubby could be trash and they could still pull out the road victory. That's how deep they were. You had guys coming off the bench who ended up playing college ball.

BUBBY BROWN: I just couldn't hit nothing that game. I got some good looks, but I just couldn't hit nothing. And then when you're playing with Craig and he's always asking you for the ball, that makes it like five-times harder. He's running up to me like, "I got a mismatch! I got a mismatch!"

BUTCH WALLER: We knew that was probably the biggest game on our schedule for the regular season. Byrd did his homework.

The Warriors and Indians were tied 36-36 at the half, then Wi-Hi went on a 19-13 run in the third quarter. This was the smallest margin of victory for Wi-Hi all season.

Dec. 28, 2001 – Wi-Hi 81, Delmar 70: Game Seven, Christmas Tournament, Wicomico Youth and Civic Center (Craig Winder – 24 points)

BUTCH WALLER: A lot of times the Christmas Tournament is where I can find out what team I really have. Not that year. I already knew. My biggest concern in the Christmas Tournament was trying to get some of the non-starters some playing time.

Dec. 29, 2001 – Wi-Hi 88, Sussex Central 55: Game Eight, Christmas Tournament, Wicomico Youth and Civic Center (Maron Brown – 14 points)

BUTCH WALLER: Maron came off the bench for us and was a solid role player for us that season. He was a 6-foot-4 left-handed player and started for me in seasons after 2002. He started some.

BUBBY BROWN: Getting Maron Brown eligible was another key addition to the team. That was his junior year, and he hadn't played the past two years.

BILL WEBER: One night its Wulff, one night its Maron, one night its Kyle. They didn't care who scored. They just wanted to win.

JERMICHAEL MITCHELL: We ran through the Christmas tournament. After that, we were together every night, even when there wasn't basketball. Me, Bubby, Craig and a couple others, we were like brothers. Bubby kept saying, "Yo man, we are not going to lose."

PART FOUR: NEW YEAR, SAME WI-HI

Jan. 2, 2002 – Wi-Hi 104, Stephen Decatur 54: Game Nine, Regular Season, at Wi-Hi (Bubby Brown – 25 points)

BUBBY BROWN: That's when I scored my 1,000 points. That's the school my mom went to, so I remember that day. The funny part is, I left my shoes at home, so I had to wear Waller's shoes in that game. They were a pair of black Nikes that were about a half size smaller than what I usually wear, so I put them on with no socks on.

BILL WEBER: Bubby was the best pure shooter on the team, and with Kyle, Craig and those other guys, he didn't shoot a lot of contested three's.

JOSH WEBER: I remember looking up at halftime and seeing Bubby's shoes like, "What is he wearing?"

Decatur's Jamar Purnell scored 20 points on the Indians. While his side won handily, Waller made a note in the scorer's book to ensure that Purnell wouldn't score so easily again. He wrote above Purnell's name, "Next time: Kyle" to remind him that Kyle Camper would guard Purnell the next time the two sides met.

Something else happened around this game too. Jermichael Mitchell, who's minutes had dwindled due to the arrival and rise of Craig Winder, was growing frustrated.

JERMICHAEL MITCHELL: My points went down, my assists went up, but it was rough. By mid-season, we were getting ready to play Decatur, and I'll never forget it because my mom came to that game, but I was ready to quit. It was tough for me. We were undefeated, but I wasn't getting the same numbers that I was the year before. I had to check myself. I had a meeting with Butch, we had a great conversation, and I ended up being a big help towards the end of the season. Sometimes your ego can get in the way, but I had to realize it was about the championship.

BILL WEBER: Jermichael, to me, was the unspoken leader of that team. He led by defensive example.

Jan. 7, 2002 – Wi-Hi 137, Kent County 56: Game 10, Regular Season, at Kent County (Carl Miles – 18 points)

BUTCH WALLER: The players used to always get on our center, Carl Miles. They would say, "Carl you should've had that rebound man, let's go."

JERMICHAEL MITCHELL: Carl Miles made a big difference. He had to get eligible. But even though he wasn't on the team the year before – and back then it was a little different – Waller made sure he was still around in the gym with us. We made sure he had that feeling of, "If you were here, this is what it could be like."

BILL WEBER: Carl was a space-eater inside. He was just a beast. He wanted to mix it up inside. He wanted the rebound.

CARL MILES: I was the enforcer. I brought the defensive presence.

Jan. 8, 2002 – Wi-Hi 125, Mardela 32: Game 11, Regular Season, at Wi-Hi (Carl Miles – 19 points)

This was the largest margin of victory for Wi-Hi in 2002.

BUTCH WALLER: Well, everybody played and everybody scored.

CARL MILES: Most of my points were really from put-backs and dunks.

BUBBY BROWN: There was about 10 dunks from us in that game.

JOSH WEBER: Almost everyone on that team could dunk. You don't see a lot of high school squads like that. And they could dunk easy, in the half-court, not just on a fast break. Wulff could pump-fake a (three-pointer) in the corner, dribble-drive past you and tomahawk it on your head.

While running the clock and scoreboard at Wi-Hi and the Civic Center with his father, Josh Weber has seen dozens of incredible games in the Bayside Conference over the last two decades. Photo by Mitchell Northam.

Jan. 11, 2002 – Wi-Hi 69, Cambridge-South Dorchester 61: Game 12, Regular Season, at Wi-Hi (John Wulff – 17 points)

BUTCH WALLER: Carl Miles was very rough and a defensive guy. He wasn't the type of guy you could post up and throw him the ball. John Wulff was. John could catch and hit the opponent with a post move.

JERMICHAEL MITCHELL: We didn't play North teams that much. Butch had a great scouting report, but it's different from playing guys that we knew and played against all the time.

JOSH WEBER: Recently it's been Easton, but back then, Cambridge was Wi-Hi's biggest rival from the North.

BUBBY BROWN: It was just one of those high-profile games, north versus south, and Cambridge was always good.

Chavar Tripper tallied 17 points for the Vikings. In his notes after the game, Waller wrote, "We shot poorly. Especially inside!"

CRAIG WINDER: Cambridge had a tough team that year, but for me, whenever we had a close game, it wasn't what the other team did right, but what we did wrong. Maybe it was bad shots or frustration. We thought, if we lost, it would be because we beat ourselves.

Jan. 17, 2002 – Wi-Hi 67, Pocomoke 60: Game 13, Regular Season, at Wi-Hi (Bubby Brown – 22 points)

Craig Winder had an off-night offensively, finishing with just three points. Still Waller had to keep him on the floor. The coach knew he could get offense from somewhere else, whether it be Brown, Wulff or Miles, but he needed Winder for his defense

BUTCH WALLER: Craig could play both ends of the floor. Really, all of those guys could. I needed Craig for defense in that game though.

CRAIG WINDER: When you're not scoring, you try to find different ways to affect the game. I was having a rough game, the ball wasn't going in for me, so I just focused on defense.

DAVID BYRD: All the best players in Salisbury go to Wi-Hi. We know that. (Waller) had good guards when they transferred from Mardela.

BUBBY BROWN: The spark in that game came from Jermichael. He came in the second quarter and hit three straight jumpers from the left side. And on defense, he was just great.

JERMICHAEL MITCHELL: I knew Bubby could shoot, Craig could score, Kyle Camper could score, so it was like, what can I do to get in the game? What can I do to make sure that I'm on the floor at the end of the game? Defense ended up being my specialty. Put me on the other team's best playmaker, and I'm going to give you at least my five fouls to make it tough on them.

JOSH WEBER: Jermichael was kind of the sixth man on that team, but in the close games, he played a lot of minutes. He was the lock-down guy and the key to the 1-3-1 zone that they ran back then. He was the guy on the baseline, in the back of the zone, running corner to corner. Usually, the back of that zone is a big man, a shot blocker, but that's not how Butch did it because Jermichael was the best guy at drawing charges, that I have ever seen anyways. He didn't have to sell it like a Duke flop, he just beat you to that spot and let you hit him.

BILL WEBER: As much talent that Wi-Hi had, Eddie Miller was probably the best player on the court. But for Pocomoke, it was just one or two Division I players going up against the four Wi-Hi had.

Going into the fourth quarter, the Indians and Warriors were tied 54-54 and Eddie Miller and Tyrone Northam had combined for 36 points.

But in the fourth quarter, Wi-Hi put its foot down. Neither Northam or Miller scored in the final eight minutes.

BUTCH WALLER: We paid attention to Eddie. We knew where he was. He was a classic shooter, but could put it on the floor too.

CRAIG WINDER: Eddie Miller was a great shooter with a lot of bounce. He could get his shot off very quick, so you had to do your work early and try to deny him the ball. His shot was so sweet. Still is.

BILL WEBER: Miller got shut down at the end by Jermichael. The nights where the ball wasn't going through the basket for the other team, Jermichael was playing defense, drawing charge after charge after charge.

Brown took over, scoring nine of Wi-Hi's 13 fourth quarter points.

BUTCH WALLER: When we got down into crunch time, the rest of players knew it was time to give it to Bubby.

CRAIG WINDER: Bubby had the handle, the shot and it was his team. When he needed to, he took over.

BUBBY BROWN: In that game, I hit a three and got an And-1 off of it. There was like a minute and 30 seconds left. Then a few plays later, I hit a lay-up and got another And-1. I made my free throws down the stretch in that one.

JERMICHAEL MITCHELL: It was a lockdown situation. Those Pocomoke-Wi-Hi games were the best games.

DAVID BYRD: They had a great team. We had a good team too. We won the 1A and beat Dunbar and they won the 2A so we celebrated together. It was good for the Shore. Wi-Hi and Pocomoke have gone across the Bay a lot, but it's hard to win over there.

Jan. 23, 2003 – Wi-Hi 79, Parkside 32: Game 14, Regular Season, at Parkside (Maron Brown – 22 points)

In this game, no Parkside player scored in double-digits.

JOSH WEBER: Maron was instant offense off the bench.

Jan. 25, 2002 – Wi-Hi 70, Snow Hill 62 (OT): Game 15, Regular Season, at Snow Hill (Bubby Brown – 20 points)

BUTCH WALLER: That was a battle in that little band box gym.

JERMICHAEL MITCHELL: There was this big box on the wall there, and a lady would beat and bang on it the whole game. From start to finish. She had her cowbell and everything. It was like a college atmosphere.

CRAIG WINDER: It was tough to play there. It was a real small court. They played just as hard as us.

BUBBY BROWN: Waller flirted with the lineup that game too. Someone was sick, I think it was Wulff, and we started all guards.

CRAIG WINDER: We were down 20 at halftime, and Waller told us not to worry about the score, just play basketball. That was one of our first big tests. We were always up at halftime and beating people up.

BUBBY BROWN: Jerrell Harmon came out on fire and Tony Harmon was a mismatch for us because he was like a big 6-foot-5 guard. They were first cousins and they gave us fits.

JERMICHAEL MITCHELL: Tony Harmon and them were unreal.

Snow Hill led by 10 points after the first quarter and by three points going into the fourth. Jerrell and Tony Harmon combined for 44 points for the Eagles.

Late in the game, momentum had stalled for Snow Hill. The Eagles scored just four points in the fourth quarter and only seven points in overtime. Wi-Hi would score 15 points in overtime, led by Brown's nine points in the extra period.

BUTCH WALLER: During a timeout in overtime, I said to Craig, "Now look, this is tight. We have to pull this out. Don't get nervous." He looked me in the eye and said, "Coach, I don't get nervous."

CRAIG WINDER: That was always my mindset. I just played hard. Nervous or being scared was never in my basketball vocabulary.

This was the first time Wi-Hi had shot better than 70% as a team from the free throw line, making 13-of-17 of their shots from the charity stripe.

BUTCH WALLER: Allen Miller was a good coach. He would come up with a box-and-one or a triangle-and-two, three out and two in, something like that.

JERMICHAEL MITCHELL: David Byrd, Allen Miller, Butch Waller – those guys were just different. They always had their teams prepared. It was a different atmosphere in those gyms and a different breed of kids playing for them.

BILL WEBER: You look back on then, and you had, what I would consider to be four Hall of Fame Eastern Shore coaches at that time: Butch, Phil Rayfield, Byrd and Allen Miller.

CRAIG WINDER: It seemed like we always got a test at the right time, between Snow Hill, Pocomoke and Crisfield. The biggest for us was in Snow Hill. Once we won that, we really felt invincible. It was like, "Okay. What can we do now?"

JOHN WULFF: I thought we might have a hiccup once and maybe not go undefeated, but I didn't think we would lose more than once. I knew we would get back to Cole Field House.

Jan. 29, 2002 – Wi-Hi 74, Crisfield 47: Game 16, Regular Season, at Crisfield (Craig Winder – 17 points)

BUBBY BROWN: Craig scored the first five points of that game. He scored off the jump ball, then stole the ball, laid it up, got fouled and made the And-1.

BUTCH WALLER: Phil Rayfield was big on the 1-2-2 zone and you could almost count on it. You could never get him man-for-man.

CRAIG WINDER: It was still a tough place to play and they had a pretty decent team. Their zone was very good. It was mean.

Jan. 31, 2002 – Wi-Hi 78, Stephen Decatur 62: Game 17, Regular Season, at Stephen Decatur (Craig Winder – 16 points)

As Waller planned, Jamar Purnell didn't go off again as he was being guard by Kyle Camper and Jermichael Mitchell.

CRAIG WINDER: Jermichael was lockdown dude. He'd get up on you, 94 feet, and not let you go. His job was whatever (Waller) asked him to do.

JERMICHAEL MITCHELL: That was definitely one of my roles, to be a defensive specialist. I took a lot of charges. That's one of the things Butch bred into us, to take charges.

But another Seahawk exploded. Torrez Spence dropped 30 points with 15 of them coming in the fourth quarter to help keep Decatur in the game. Still, the Indians pulled away with ease.

Feb. 6, 2002 – Wi-Hi 87, North Dorchester 62: Game 18, Regular Season, at North Dorchester (Craig Winder – 13 points)

Feb. 7, 2002 – Wi-Hi 87, Easton 40: Game 19, Regular Season, at Wi-Hi (Anthony Robinson – 12 points)

BUTCH WALLER: Anthony was a solid man off the bench for us.

BUBBY BROWN: Anthony Robinson was like our 11th man, but he started some playoffs game. Just a tough guy who was in the program all four years.

Six Wi-Hi players scored in double-digits. Winder had 10 points in the first quarter.

Feb. 8, 2002 – Wi-Hi 108, Washington 35: Game 20, Regular Season, at Wi-Hi (Carl Miles – 16 points)

BUTCH WALLER: Carl Miles was a get the rebound and put it back guy. He led the team in rebounds by far. Very few teams got a second shot on us.

The Jaguars were having trouble this season and entered this game with just six players. Colin Thomas had 18 points for them. Six Wi-Hi players scored in double-digits and most of the Indians' points came in the paint as Wi-Hi connected on just two three-pointers in this game.

BUBBY BROWN: They had like three or four players go to some prom or winter formal down in Cambridge. I guess they knew they were going to lose, so they didn't even come to the game.

Feb. 12, 2002 – Wi-Hi 123, Mardela 37: Game 21, Regular Season, at Mardela (Craig Winder – 22 points)

Seven Wi-Hi players scored in double-digits and the Indians connected on 12 three-pointers.

CRAIG WINDER: We knew what was going to happen at Mardela. We knew it was going to be a victory and the score would be pretty bad.

Feb. 14, 2002 – Wi-Hi 89, James M. Bennett 63: Game 22, Regular Season, at Wi-Hi (Bubby Brown – 22 points)

John Holmes led the Clippers with 17 points. A year later, he would lead them to a 2A State Championship and then go on to enjoy a career at Bethune Cookman University.

BUTCH WALLER: We made a point to put guys like Holmes on our radar. They were leading scorers for their team for a reason. Jermichael was really our stopper. I could put him on pretty much anyone. They were all pretty good defenders. They took it personal if someone got by them or scored on them. It also helped that they had Carl Miles behind them to swat shots away.

***

PART FIVE: PLAYOFF MODE

Feb. 20, 2002 – Wi-Hi 104, Cambridge-South Dorchester 60: Game 23, Bayside Conference Championship at Salisbury University's Maggs Gymnasium (Craig Winder – 27 points)

BUBBY BROWN: It was a lot different from the first game against Cambridge. The crowd was gone at halftime. It was packed too.

JERMICHAEL MITCHELL: By the time the Bayside game rolled around, we knew everything about Cambridge. Who could and couldn't dribble, who could and couldn't shoot.

CRAIG WINDER: Coming up, that was a place we always snuck into. Salisbury's gym just felt like another home court for us, especially for me, Bubby and Jermichael. We'd sneak in and try to get the college kids to play us for money.

BUBBY BROWN: We were in that gym all the time. We always wanted to play against Salisbury.

JERMICHAEL MITCHELL: We snuck into there and UMES all the time. I had a car at 15, so we could get places and we would travel and play ball against men. We would go into SU and hoop with their team or whoever was in the gym.

The Indians connected on nine three-pointers in their 23rd consecutive win of the season. Still, there were more games ahead. They had won one championship, but a bigger title still eluded them.

Feb. 26, 2002 – Wi-Hi 92, North Caroline 56: Game 24, 2A East Region Quarterfinals, at North Caroline (Craig Winder – 28 points)

The playoff system for the MPSSAA was a little different in those days. So, despite having a perfect record, Wi-Hi never hosted a playoff game.

BUBBY BROWN: I tell people that all the time. We didn't play one home game in the playoffs.

JERMICHAEL MITCHELL: It was one of the weirdest things. We were like, "How do we have a season like this and not get a home playoff game?"

BILL WEBER: At that time, if I remember correctly, the first couple of teams got a bye, and there was a rule in place that if a team traveled in the first round, they got to host the second round. So, the lower seed got to host. And then at that point, they played all of the 2A East region semis and finals at Chesapeake College.

BUBBY BROWN: North Caroline wasn't bad. They had three big boys. We just clicked that game.

CRAIG WINDER: We really buckled down when playoffs started. There was no playing around or cheap shots in practice behind coach's back.

BUBBY BROWN: It was the playoffs. We just had a different mentality.

All season long, Wulff had started for the Indians despite a nagging pain in his lower back. Upon further discovery, he found out it was very serious. That, combined with an ankle injury, caused him to miss four of Wi-Hi's playoff games.

JOHN WULFF: I had a cracked vertebra in my lower back, just from years of playing. So, I was getting treatment for that the whole time we were in the playoffs. And then I tweaked my ankle in one of the last regular season games.

Feb. 28, 2002 – Wi-Hi 90, Kent Island 52: Game 25, 2A East Region Semifinals, at Chesapeake College (Craig Winder – 21 points)

There were 47 total fouls in this game and Wulff did not play. Kent Island missed 12 free throws. Even if they had made them, the Buccaneers had very little chance of derailing the Indians' mission.

BUTCH WALLER (to the Daily Times): We were just too quick for them. They've got size, I can see why they've won 15 ballgames, but they just couldn't handle our quickness and the game was pretty much over in the first half. The second half, it got a little sloppy. This game won't help us much for Saturday, except for the fact that we will be playing Saturday.

March 2, 2002 – Wi-Hi 75, Edgewood 57: Game 26, 2A East Region Finals, at Chesapeake College (Carl Miles - 17 points)

BUTCH WALLER: We knew some people up around Edgewood who did some scouting for us. We checked The Baltimore Sun for some box scores and tried to notice a pattern. I spent a lot of time researching the coach.

BUBBY BROWN: That game was a dogfight.

BILL WEBER: There was fan support for Wi-Hi at Chesapeake out the ying-yang. Everyone knew that they were going for the title.

At the end of the first quarter, Edgewater had a one-point lead. At the half, they were tied with the Indians. Wi-Hi then erupted in the third quarter, going on a 13-0 run.

BUBBY BROWN: That was a game of quarters. I had a good first quarter, Kyle Camper had a good second quarter, Winder had a good third quarter, and then we went to the 1-3-1 defense. We played man in the first half.

BILL WEBER: Those Harford County teams sort-of played a Princeton style. Set a lot of picks, shoot threes. It was just a different style than the Bayside and they kept Wi-Hi from penetrating.

What changed for the Indians? They switched defenses at halftime. Edgewater had hit six three-pointers in the first half and were held to none from behind the arc in the second.

Oh, and Carl Miles dominated. Dwayne Howell was 6-foot-6 and Harford County's leading rebounder. Miles pulled in a double-double of 17 points and 10 rebounds while holding Howell to two boards.

BILL WEBER: Butch is the master at halftime adjustments. There have been many nights where he'll walk by and tell me he's switching something up and then say, "I'm either going to lose by 30 or win by 10," and most nights he'd win by 10.

BUTCH WALLER: The 1-3-1 allowed us to cover the perimeter effectively. You have to have certain type of athletes to run a 1-3-1 zone. It helps if they're big and long and your bottom man is usually a guard because he has to run corner to corner – that was Jermichael a lot of times. The concept is to have three guys between the ball and the basket and it does clog up the middle. It's not really popular. The team has to be smart.

JERMICHAEL MITCHELL: Back then, we either played a 2-3 zone into a press, man-to-man, or that full-court 1-3-1.

BUBBY BROWN: In the 1-3-1, we were so long that it was hard to pass over or around us.

BUTCH WALLER (to the Associated Press): The only number that means anything is 28. We're at 26 right now. We've got a lot of momentum. I say we've got heaps and heaps and heaps of momentum.

***

PART SIX: BACK AT COLE FIELD HOUSE

March 8, 2002 - Wi-Hi 68, North Hagerstown 61: Game 27, 2A State Semifinals, at Cole Field House (Kyle Camper – 19 points)

JERMICHAEL MITCHELL: Kyle played very well for us up there on that big floor.

BUTCH WALLER: Kyle was a 6-foot-3 wing player who could put it on the floor and had a nice jumper. His brother Darnell was a smaller point guard who was tough and skilled too.

Wi-Hi had a comfortable lead at halftime, leading 46-21, but then the Indians relaxed. North Hagerstown outscored the Indians 40-22 in the second half, but ultimately the Indians' first half lead proved to be too large.

Still, Waller was furious with how the Indians played in the second half. They were so close to winning a title and relaxing now was not an option.

BILL WEBER: They took their foot off the throttle. Wi-Hi could've won that game by 50. They decided to play around a little bit and that wasn't like them.

BUTCH WALLER: That game really pissed me off. I was steaming. I let them have it after the game. They had that team on the ropes and they let them off.

BUBBY BROWN: I don't put a lot on Waller, but I'm going to put that one on Waller. We played man the whole first half and we had a lead. Then in the second half, we go to a zone and tried to change it up and they got comfortable. The game slowed down on us, we couldn't hit any shots, we started playing one-on-one, and their best players started hitting shots. We were tough-minded.

JOSH WEBER: Those guys were always trying to play man-to-man.

CRAIG WINDER: We figured, we were up big, so let's play around a little bit. We took some quick shots, took some plays off, tried for some highlight stuff, and then they ate our zone up. They started hitting shots late.

BUTCH WALLER: They had a kid who was 6-foot-6 and he always went around to the top of the zone to shoot threes. We knew that, and he got hot and we couldn't stop him.

CARL MILES: I wouldn't say it was difficult, but yea, that dude could ball. I held my own though.

JERMICHAEL MITCHELL: North Hagerstown had a big man who could really shoot the ball and that was different for us. All season long, we never faced a big who could stretch the floor. We were thinking he was going to beat and bang in the paint, but they had another kid who did that.

BUBBY BROWN: There was only one game left, so there was no need for us to harp on it.

JERMICHAEL MITCHELL: We had a flashback of the state title game the year before. We were happy we won though and we came all the way back to the Shore, because Butch wasn't a fan of staying overnight there, got refocused and got ready for Saturday.

March 9, 2002 – Wi-Hi 72, Central 50: Game 28, 2A State Finals, at Cole Field House (Kyle Camper – 20 points and 10 rebounds)

JERMICHAEL MITCHELL: Central's coach was about to retire, they had two players who were supposed to play Division I, and they had two 6-foot-9 guys, and we were supposed to get beat by 20 points. That's what we kept hearing.

CRAIG WINDER: That was the only game we were really worried about going into it. We were just so focused because we didn't want to lose. They had been there, and we didn't want to lose this time. We were kind of surprised, because we thought it was going to be a tougher game.

BUTCH WALLER: Some reporter from The Washington Post got me in the tunnel on the way out to warmups and asked me, "How do you pronounce this name? Week-oh-meek-oh?" I said, "No, it's WHY-COM-ICK-OH. It's a county in the state, you know, down on the Eastern Shore?" And then I was getting a little irritated, because I wanted to get out on the floor. Then he asked me how good we were and what kind of team we had and I said, "Well, we're good enough to get here." Then I guess he got pissed off and he says, "Well you know you're probably a 20-point underdog." I told him, "Well damn, if I had known that we would have never showed up."

BUBBY BROWN: We didn't really know too much about Central. Back in that day, we always thought PG County teams were soft. So, when we're playing some team from PG County, we thought we could out-tough them. We thought they were pretty boys.

Central was on a mission: It wanted to send its longtime head coach Walter Fulton out on top with his fourth state championship. Instead, Fulton's parting gift was a double-double from Kyle Camper in a 22-point defeat.

Years after playing at Wi-Hi, Bubby Brown became the head coach at Bennett. Photo by Mitchell Northam.

JERMICHAEL MITCHELL: A lot of people slept on Kyle, because it was always about Craig and Bubby. So, a lot of people, to me, slept on him throughout the season. He wasn't on the scouting report, but he killed it.

BUBBY BROWN: We went to Kyle in the post a couple of times. A lot of his points came from hustle plays.

JOSH WEBER: His best position was point guard, but he never got to play it until his senior year. He was so tall, they would just put him on the blocks.

Camper began his college career at the Division I level, playing two seasons at Iona. But at Slippery Rock, he became a Division II star. In the 2008-2009 season, he averaged 10.5 assists per-game. Slippery Rock would later retire his No. 10 jersey.

BUTCH WALLER: Central had some scorer that was pretty good and we put Jermichael Mitchell on his side, because we knew he was a driver. In the first half, Jermichael drew three charges on him.

BUBBY BROWN: Jermichael did get three charges on him in the first half, but I got the first.

After the third quarter, Wi-Hi had a 12-point lead. Waller feared the Indians would lay back once again, but the players didn't. They kept playing hard in the final eight minutes and used a 21-11 run to close out the fourth quarter and a championship win.

After missing the previous playoff contests with injuries, John Wulff returned to the rotation and grabbed nine rebounds for the Indians.

JOHN WULFF: I got in for most of that last game. We were all lucky to be there.

BUTCH WALLER: Central just couldn't do anything against the zone. The players wanted me to cut them loose and play man-for-man, but I said, "Why? You're killing them."

DAVON WEST, SENIOR CENTRAL FORWARD (to the Washington Post): We just didn't come out like we wanted to win. It's real disappointing. We couldn't make shots because we had pressure. We were just trying to go out and continue the cycle instead of going out to win first.

BUTCH WALLER: In the fourth quarter I kept going over to the water jug, thinking that when I turn around there would be another minute off. The fourth quarter seemed like forever.

BILL WEBER: I remember looking at my wife, with about four minutes left, and going, "He's got it. There's no way he blows this lead this late."

CRAIG WINDER: We started to sense it in the fourth quarter. The clock is ticking down and we're just looking at each other like, "Yo, we won."

BUBBY BROWN: I knew that game was over when, with about four minutes left, Tyson went up for a lay-up and Carl Miles blocked his shit into the stands. That took the air out of their whole team.

Brown, as he had done for most of the season, orchestrated the closeout for Wi-Hi. He scored 18 points and connected on 11-of-12 free throws. Winder added 11 points and spectacular defense.

BUBBY BROWN: Jermichael was sitting on the bench crying, because he's very emotional, so that's what he does.

JERMICHAEL MITCHELL: I cried tears of joy. It was great feeling. It was really a blessing.

BUBBY BROWN: There's like 1:16 left and Waller took us all out. So, we're on the bench and I'm talking to my teammates and Waller told us his childhood dream was to be picked up and carried around Cole Field House. So as soon as the game was over, we found him, picked him up and carried him to half-court.

BUTCH WALLER: I got the trophy and went over to the bleachers and our fans were going crazy. It was cool. Somebody picked me up and carried me around. It was really cool.

BILL WEBER: It was just pure joy for Butch. You could see the weight come off his shoulders and the kids were happy to be the ones that did it. He talked a lot about putting a banner in the corner, and they were the ones that did it.

CARL MILES: It was exciting, and I was so happy to be out there because I couldn't the year before.

CRAIG WINDER: It was big for me, just coming from Mardela where it was loss, loss, loss, loss, and then winning a championship. That's one of the best feelings.

BUTCH WALLER: After the game I looked for that guy, the Washington Post reporter, and I couldn't find his ass. I looked for him and went to the press section. He wasn't in the post-game press conference either. I was going to let him have it.

Josh Mitchell penned the game story for the Post that day. He did not mention Waller in his story, nor did he quote anyone from Wi-Hi.

BUBBY BROWN: WMDT interviewed me after the game and I was just like, "I told y'all we were going to go undefeated and win states."

Pocomoke was also in Cole Field House on March 9, 2002, which happened to be head coach David Byrd's 50th birthday. His team extracted some revenge for Wi-Hi. Dunbar had moved down to the 1A class and the Warriors beat them 88-70. For Byrd, it was his 400th win, his first and only state championship, and a big win for the Shore.

John Hall, then sports editor for the Daily Times, penned the 1A centerpiece on Sunday, writing: "Forty years from now, Eastern Shore basketball fans will still be talking about what happened Saturday at Cole Field House."

BILL WEBER: The Shore felt like they were slighted. For Wi-Hi and Pocomoke to win on the same day, it was an Eastern Shore thing. There was a major standing ovation. For both teams.

DAVID BYRD: The differences in those two teams were not a lot. So, I'm glad they won and I'm sure Butch is glad we won. That's a good thing for the Eastern Shore. That doesn't happen.

JOHN WULFF: It was great to show off the talent we had, because I feel like across the bridge, we get neglected a lot. They don't think we're much competition. But that year we showed them the Shore was a force.

JOSH WEBER: I remember wishing I should've gone. If I could go back and change like five things in my life, that's one of them, probably.

BUBBY BROWN: We got back to Salisbury and we all stayed at my house. We walked up to the gas station and the store was closed, but we saw the newspaper man dropping off some papers. Needless to say, one of those stores didn't get no newspapers that day, because we took the whole stack.

JERMICHAEL MITCHELL: It was really late and we went to the store and grabbed the papers. We had the paper clips before anyone else did.

CRAIG WINDER: That season taught me how to play with a good team, and how to gel with a team quickly and find your spot and role, no matter what. That really helped me in college and the pros, going from team to team where, in one spot I might be a leading scorer and, in another spot, I might be a defensive guy, or someone who specializes in offensive rebounds.

JERMICHAEL MITCHELL: We met so many people and got awards and stuff after. Meeting the mayor, the governor, senators. It was the first boys basketball title for Wicomico County. That was the first time around here anybody had seen a state championship ring.

BUBBY BROWN: I still wear my ring when playoffs roll around.

JOHN WULFF: I have my ring, but it's in a box in my closet. Once or twice a year, I'll go in there, look at it, put it on and wear it around the house. I don't take it out of the house too often.

CRAIG WINDER: I gave my rings to my dad. There's that one from Wi-Hi, the Elite Eight ring from when I was at Texas, a D-League title ring, and then two trophies from overseas winning championships.

JERMICHAEL MITCHELL: I don't wear mine. It's a keepsake. I actually lost mine and had to order another one, so I don't wear the new one at all.

JOHN WULFF: When we walked in to graduate that year, (Waller) was the first person there and he had a box full of rings for us. He is a great coach and a great man.

BUTCH WALLER: This school, realistically, with a little bit of luck, we should have about four state championships.

Wi-Hi's Craig Winder landed in the NBA G-League and won a championship with the Rio Grande Valley Vipers. Winder averaged 10 points and 2.9 rebounds per-game across 128 appearances. University of Texas Athletics.

DOUG KING: Everybody is always like, 'Who would win, 1997 or 2002?' And I'm like, it doesn't matter. They're the better team because they won the state championship. How do you argue with that? They brought it home. I kill that argument real quick all the time… We had an alumni game where we played against them. It was trash. I was old. They started pressing us. They were too serious about it.

CRAIG WINDER: Butch Waller was all about making basketball fun. At Mardela, we lost a lot, so I just tried to score as much as I could to have something to talk about. At Wi-Hi, it was just play and have fun. I've kept that with me in my career, playing in some cutthroat leagues overseas. That kept me going: have fun, have fun, have fun.

BUTCH WALLER: I'm not much of a jewelry guy, but when we have tryouts every year at the beginning of the season, I always wear that 2002 ring. The players all want to look at it and I tell them, "This is what you're playing for." We had a talented group, but more than anything they were hungry and intelligent basketball players.

A heavily condensed and altered version of some of the contents of this chapter appeared in the March 19, 2017 edition of the Delmarva Daily Times. All writing and reporting was done by the author.

2003 BENNETT, THE UNLIKELY CHAMPIONS

"When Bruce won, we were happy." – David Byrd

Entering the 2002-03 season, off the heels of the Wi-Hi and Pocomoke boys capturing state titles, many around the Shore expected both squads to contend again for championships. And indeed, both teams still had an abundance of talent.

Returning for his senior season to lead David Byrd's Pocomoke Warriors was the sharp-shooting Eddie Miller. Big man Tyrone Northam had graduated, but reinforcing Miller on the squad was a tough, defensive-minded guard in Jovan Schoolfield and a play-making point guard in Tony Tull who always took care of the ball, turning it over just once in 2002 1A state championship game against the mighty Dunbar. Byrd had a team of mostly guards, but they were a well-balanced and veteran group who put defense first. In the paper's preseason rankings, the Salisbury Daily Times pegged Pocomoke as the No. 1 team in the region.

And while Bubby Brown, Craig Winder, Jermichael Mitchell and five other class of 2002 seniors had moved on from Wi-Hi, the team was still bringing back Maron Brown and Kyle Camper; two guys who had long been itching for a chance to show the rest of the Bayside what they were made of. Camper was a versatile player who could play nearly anywhere on the floor, possessing the ability to handle the ball like a guard while also being able to post up like a big. He led the Indians in scoring in both games at Cole Field House the previous season, combining for 39 points across both contests in the state final four.

"Kyle Camper was a hardnosed player," Winder said of Camper. "That defensive core was tough and Kyle was a big part of that. He was very skilled and really a point guard playing the three."

Brown was a 6-foot-4 lefty who came off the bench for instant offense for the Indians in 2001-02. Near the end of that regular season, Brown dropped 22 points in a whooping the Indians delivered to Parkside.

"Maron was a little bit of everything. He was a walking double-double," Bubby Brown said of Maron. "He could get the rebound and go coast to coast. You might as well stop at half-court, because once he started dribbling, he wasn't going to pass it."

The Daily Times had Wi-Hi as the third best team in the Bayside entering the 02-03 season, behind Pocomoke and Cambridge South-Dorchester. And then down at No. 7 in their rankings was James M. Bennett, a squad coming off a mediocre 14-12 season.

Entering his third season as the head coach of the Bennett Clippers was Bruce Wharton, a 47-year-old native of Accomac on Virginia's Eastern Shore. Known to some of his friends as "Bingo," Wharton was a devoted and proud member of the Kappa Alpha Psi fraternity, which he joined while attending Barber-Scotia College in Concord, North Carolina. Before he was a high school coach, Wharton founded what would come to be known as "the Kappa League," a youth outdoor summer league which soon became part of the fabric of the Shore's basketball culture.

Wharton began his career as a high school coach in 1995, when he joined Jim Rayne's staff at Bennett. Rayne had coached Bennett to a pair of Bayside titles in 1983 and 1984, and to one state semifinals appearance in 1984 as well.

And that's sort of where Bennett's history as a basketball school ended. The Clippers' girls team won Bayside championships in 1976 and 1998, but the school never had a state crown of its own in hoops. Bennett was a football school and won three state championships on the gridiron in the 1980s under the tutelage of John Usilton. The Clippers had also been to eight state tournaments for field hockey by then, winning it all in 1993. Basketball was an afterthought at the school. No one paid any mind to the fact that Wharton – who became head coach of the boys varsity basketball team prior to the 2000-01 season – was 0-4 vs. Butch Waller and his Wi-Hi Indians.

But something was different about *this* Bennett team. As the 2002-03 season went on, the Clippers established themselves as contenders, they attracted fans, they captured the attention of the city of Salisbury and the Shore, and they pulled off something few people thought was possible.

Bennett's fortunes changed in the offseason when the school welcomed in two transfers from out of state. One was Alfred Little, a senior guard from New York who was athletic, gritty and didn't back down from anyone or any challenge. In his lone season playing football at Bennett, he tied the school record for receiving touchdowns with nine.

The other newcomer was Steve Parham, a 6-foot-6 senior big man from Chicago, who gave the Clippers confidence and toughness. Parham had come to the Shore for his senior year of high school to live with his cousin Tim, who was an assistant coach down Route 13 at the University of Maryland Eastern Shore. In Chicago, Parham says he went to a school that "wasn't really known for basketball" and when he got to the Shore, he was supposed to go to Wi-Hi, but his cousin lived in Bennett's district and had high praise for Wharton.

"Bruce sort of reminded me of my uncles," Parham said. "Really good guy. Always willing to help and really cared for his players. He knew some strategy for basketball. I wouldn't say he was the best, but he had a pretty good idea of his X's and O's."

With the size advantage Bennett was going to have, there was little need for some intricate and fancy offense. With Parham, John Holmes and Cornell Johnson, the Clippers had three players taller than 6-foot-4. Throw in Greg Wellinghoff, Eric Farrare and Little, and the Clippers had as much talent as anyone. It just didn't mesh right away.

Even if the offense wasn't there, Bennett's dominance on defense showed immediately. In their first game of the season, they rolled over Queen Anne's, winning 68-27. In his Bayside Conference debut, Parham tallied an easy double-double with 10 points and 10 boards.

"We didn't have an offense, per se, but all of our scores were in the low numbers," Parham said. "So, I think we knew we had to beat teams by making them play our style, which was kind of slow. We had the biggest size advantage out of all the schools on the Eastern Shore. The only issue is, all those other schools – the Pocomokes, etc. – all had really good guard play. So, we had to slow them down and make them play at our pace."

Indeed. Bennett was at its best when it could keep the opposing team below 50 points. Their first loss of the season came in Game 3, when Edwin Lashley and Snow Hill rolled into Salisbury to deliver a 57-54 defeat to Bennett. Lashley finished with 27 points, and a photo of him gliding by Parham for a lay-up landed on page 32 of the Daily Times the next day. It was after that game that roles became more defined for the Clippers. Parham opted to give all of his energy to the defensive end, and he'd allow Johnson and Holmes to carry the scoring load. This was something Wharton embraced. He knew he only had Parham for one season and he wanted the kid from Chicago to do what he did best. Holmes was an athletic freak who hadn't hit his peak yet and he needed to touch the ball.

"Steve is a hard worker. He's very focused in the locker room. Some guys listen to music or something else. Steve usually just sits in the corner and gets himself focused," Wharton told the Daily Times. "John is still making the transition to guard, and I'm extra hard on him because I know he can play at the next level."

Parham added: "I could score, but I have always made my thing to play defense. John was more athletic than me, for sure, and he could get to the rim and get to the foul line. I was more concentrated on getting rebounds and blocking shots and doing some of the dirty stuff that other guys weren't really trying to do … with John, we were cool. I don't try to get in pissing contests. In practice, me and him would always go at it, but we made each other better, in my eyes, and I brought a type of grittiness that they didn't have. Coming from Chicago, I wasn't afraid of anybody. I was ready to go to war every time I got on the court."

The Clippers won their next five games, and entered a match-up with city rival Wi-Hi with a 7-1 record. Despite leading at halftime at home, Bennett couldn't hold off Wi-Hi, losing 56-44. Kyle Camper — who would become a McDonald's All-American nominee this season — dropped 20 points and had 13 boards, while Maron Brown had 22 points and 13 boards. The seasoned Waller knew what Bennett's strategy was, saying after the game, "They want to keep the score in the 40s, evidently." Bennett executed that plan in the first half, heading into intermission with a 20-17 advantage, but the Indians got on a roll in the second half and never looked back. More problematic than Wi-Hi's scoring was Bennett's lack of it. Holmes was held scoreless and Johnson had just two points. Parham poured in 16 points, seven rebounds and six blocks — and that was a day after he was in a car accident. Neither coach was particularly happy with the performance.

"Both coaches ought to apologize to the fans, because that was one sloppy, poorly played game," Waller said.

Doug King, who was in his first season as Waller's assistant that year, took it a step further and bluntly assessed the talent on Wi-Hi's roster: "We had two players that year, Camper and Maron Brown. We had two stars, two decent players, and the rest were horrible."

The second meeting between the two teams on Valentine's Day at Wi-Hi would prove to be much more entertaining — if you were a Wi-Hi fan.

This time, Holmes showed up and led the Clippers in scoring with 21 points. However, with the game tight near the end of the fourth quarter, both he and Greg Wellinghoff fouled out with 1:35 to play. And on any other night, Bennett might've had the lead in-hand, as Wi-Hi shot 56% from the charity stripe this season, but on this night, they made 13-of-14 shots from there. And so, it would come down to the final possession. As the clock winded down, the ball ended up in Parham's mitts. He lofted up a three-point attempt and the ball fell through the hoop.

Tie game. Overtime.

Or, so he thought.

There was a whistle and the referees met for about five minutes while confusion ensued in the Waller Dome. Eventually, the ruling was Parham's foot was on the line and there were a few ticks remaining on the clock. So, the shot counted for two points and Wi-Hi had the ball and a one-point lead. The Indians inbounded safely and ran the clock out. And the Clippers were enraged, but also full of some newfound confidence.

"After that game, I felt like we had a chance," Parham said.

"This is the first time we've played with that kind of intensity for four quarters," Wharton said. "Hopefully, if we can play with this kind of intensity, we can play with anybody."

A few days after that narrow heart-wrenching defeat at Wi-Hi, something else happened that Parham said changed the course of Bennett's season. One day, the Clippers couldn't get into Bennett's gym to practice. But instead of everyone going home, the players gathered up and went over to the gym at Salisbury's YMCA. And instead of actually practicing, the Clippers just played pick-up against whoever showed up – other kids, college students and grown men. And the Clippers just clicked and dominated for hours.

"We just ran the gym. Everyone was talking and communicating. That's when we started feeling like we were really gelling together," Parham said. "We were just like, 'Man, we are too good and we have too much size.' We just weren't playing our style."

It was almost as if – until they came within a questionable call of beating Wi-Hi – the Clippers had not really considered what they were truly capable of. After running the floor at the YMCA and reflecting on the Wi-Hi game, Parham, Holmes and the boys had all the confidence they needed; as if they felt they could take on hell with a Super Soaker.

At the next official practice, Wharton decided to implement a 3-2 zone defense, which allowed Bennett to maximize its length and use its advantage in size as a weapon in the guard-dominated Bayside. The defense allowed the Clippers to shrink the court and make scoring a tough chore for opponents.

And from then on, Bennett didn't lose another game. They rounded out the regular season by thumping North Dorchester by 19 points outside of Hurlock. Wharton and his team set their sights on the playoffs and eyed another meeting with Waller and the Indians. After beating Joppatowne 50-48 on the road in the 2A East Region Semifinals – a win sealed by a steal by Holmes with four seconds left – the Clippers had set-up that rematch. For Wi-Hi and Bennett, a trip to College Park was on the line on March 7 at University of Maryland Eastern Shore's Hytche Center.

"The prevailing opinion was that the regional championship between those two was the default state championship. They were both just so good," said sportswriter David Insley, then working for the Dorchester Banner.

Wi-Hi was coming off a 73-69 playoff win over Aberdeen, a game which saw Maron Brown rack up 27 points and 21 rebounds, and featured a Kyle Camper triple-double. Both of Waller's stars were playing well and the Indians eyed another trip to College Park.

Josh Weber was a junior at Parkside High School, but his father Bill had long been the scoreboard operator for Waller at Wi-Hi home games. Josh often tagged along or assisted, and over time became a fan of Wi-Hi basketball, getting an up-close look at the program for many seasons. He attended the regional final at UMES, which was played in front of a sell-out crowd.

"I'm not saying Wi-Hi would have won states," Weber said. "But they were definitely better than that Bennett team in my 17-year-old opinion."

Indeed, Wi-Hi seemed like the better team on-paper, and on the court for its past two meetings with Bennett. But, as Parham says, "You're not beating the same team three times in one season. It's just not happening."

The game was tight from the beginning, like AC/DC in 1978. And the referees would play a role in its outcome. By the end of the third quarter, Wi-Hi led by two points, but Camper – the Indians' star – already had four fouls. And the chippy calls weren't one-sided. Parham and Greg Wellinghoff also had four fouls apiece by the end of the third. Midway through the fourth quarter, Camper stole the ball and launched an assist up the court to Brown to give Wi-Hi a 44-43 lead. It would be Camper and Brown's last combination together in a Wi-Hi uniform. Because on Wi-Hi's next possession, Camper was whistled for an offensive foul, "using his left arm to ward off the defender with 2:52 left in the game," according to the Daily Times' game story.

"Kyle always had this one move where he would dip his shoulder and try to get around guys," Parham said. "And it would sort of knock them over."

Weber describes Camper's final two fouls a bit differently.

"It was a weak-ass hand-check foul after a sideline inbound and then an even worse charge-push off (call) on a Wellinghoff flop," Weber said. "Kyle was the best all-around player in the Bayside that year. For him to get fouled out like that was just crazy. He was not a hot head or a talker. So quiet and composed… they could never just let the kids play and it played right into Bennett's strategy because they were Duke-flopping and playacting all over the place."

Added Waller: "We had a little problem with officials that game. That was one that always felt like it slipped away… we had a couple officials that didn't particularly care for me that season."

Wi-Hi assistant Doug King had a more sobering recall of the game: "Bennett played this long-behind zone. We struggled."

Nonetheless, Camper was gone with just eight points and four assists to his name on the night. And then, with 52.8 seconds left, Maron Brown was whistled for his fifth and final foul while fighting for a rebound with Wellinghoff. On the next Wi-Hi possession, Nate Luther dribbled off his foot. Still, with 1.8 seconds left, Wi-Hi had a chance, but Valdase Morris slipped while receiving the inbounds pass and time expired.

For Bennett, the boogeyman was dead.

"I tried to have this passionate hoo-rah speech in the locker room afterwards and I couldn't even get my words out. I was just happy for them," Parham said. "I wasn't really into that rivalry. I was only there a year. I just knew that Wi-Hi won states the year before and I knew the talent we had."

"We got tired of everyone talking about us, that we couldn't beat Wi-Hi,"

Cornell Johnson, who had 19 points and nine rebounds, said after the win. "Our main key was to get their star player in foul trouble and that's what we did."

2003 was the first year the state semifinals and finals were held at the newly constructed home for the Maryland Terrapins, the Comcast Center. For the next several years – even after the arena became the Xfinity Center – the phrase "going to Comcast" meant a team was heading across the Bay Bridge to represent the Eastern Shore in the MPSSAA final four.

First up for the Clippers in the 2A state semifinals was Fort Hill, a historic program from Allegany County that won three state championships between 1948 and 1958. And 2003 marked the Sentinels third trip to the state semifinals in four seasons. But it quickly became apparent they were no match for the Clippers as Bennett built a 32-15 halftime lead.

However, for some strange reason, Bennett stopped clicking in the third quarter. The Clippers took their foot off the gas and couldn't find the bottom of the net. JMB was held to just two points in the third quarter, but the hole Fort Hill had dug themselves into proved to be too deep. Bennett went on to win 51-41 behind 12 points, eight rebounds and four steals from Cornell Johnson, but Wharton had mixed emotions. He expected more.

"I'm upset, but I'm happy," Wharton said. "I'm happy to be in the finals and hopefully we'll get a chance to play a little better tomorrow night... I thought we came out flat in the second half."

What changed the momentum of the game and put Bennett's chances at a victory in jeopardy was the technical foul Wellinghoff picked up, his third in three straight playoff games. Wellinghoff was a talented guard and an exceptional all-around athlete who stood at about 6-foot-3, but was known to have a temper. Weber, who played soccer against Wellinghoff, said he could be an "asshole," but "he had a lot of natural athletic ability." Weber recalled a soccer practice where Wellinghoff was playing goalkeeper and while defending a corner kick, Wellinghoff leapt into the air and bicycle-kicked the ball into his own goal "just because he freaking could."

Sometimes, teams from the Shore will head back home after winning the state semifinals, just to turn around the next morning for another two-hour-plus bus ride back to Comcast. Bennett decided to stay overnight in a hotel, and Parham and Alfred Little wound up rooming together. The two out-of-town boys got their hands on some game film on Central and stayed up all night dissecting it. At one point, Little turned to Parham and said, "I don't care what happens, but we cannot lose this game. Whatever we got to do."

During warmups on the floor of the Comcast Center, Parham knew. He turned to a teammate and said, "I'm going to have a good night tonight."

But Central High School of Prince George's County did its homework too. The team that lost to Wi-Hi in this same game the season before decided it was going to go at Wellinghoff and attempt to provoke him into picking up a technical foul or two. Wellinghoff was a key part of Bennett's defense, and having him on the bench would make things easier for Central's scorers. But Wellinghoff kept his cool despite Central's obvious tactics. Instead, three of their players would wind up fouling out and Wellinghoff played exceptional defense in the final quarter, anchoring a unit that held Central to 3-of-17 shooting from the floor.

"The fouls were killing me and my legs got cut four times, but it wasn't worth it this time," Wellinghoff told the Daily Times.

In the regular season and for the majority of the playoffs, Parham put defense first. On offense, he made the extra pass, he passed up decent scoring looks and conserved his energy for the other end, where he could block shots with authority and grab rebounds in bunches. However, in the state final, Parham went all out, and showed off on offense, scoring the first seven points of the game. He led the Clippers in scoring and rebounding, totaling 18 points and 14 boards, and put the game on ice for Bennett with 25.4 seconds left, when he swished a turnaround jumper in traffic to push Bennett's lead to two possessions. Little connected on the back-end of a one-and-one with 7.6 seconds left to seal the win. Soon after, Parham was dancing up and down the sidelines.

The Clippers won, 56-52, capturing their first ever state basketball championship in school history. As of 2022, it remains their only state title for hoops, boys or girls.

"When Bruce won, we were happy," said Pocomoke coach David Byrd. "I rooted for the Eastern Shore, and Bruce was a great guy."

For Holmes, who finished the game with 16 points and 10 rebounds, the victory gave him something to talk about with his folks at family gatherings when everyone was bragging about their hardwood accomplishments. His mother played on the 1979 Snow Hill team that won states, and his brother Sherman was a member of the 2000 Crisfield team. After JMB's win, three people in the family had rings.

"I can go to the dinner table now and sit around and talk about it," Holmes told the Daily Times. "When I get older, I can show my grandkids my ring, show them my trophies. Me and my buddies can sit around and talk about the times we had."

When Wharton was hired as the head coach in 2000, he told Bennett's administrators he hoped to make the team competitive in three seasons. Indeed, he had done far more.

Wharton's Clippers finished the season 19-5, brought another title back to Salisbury and hung the first state basketball banner in Bennett's gym.

"This is the most wonderful feeling I've ever had," Wharton said after the win. "People said all year long that we weren't playing to our potential... it goes back to that second Wi-Hi game. I think that was the turning point for us. We lost the game by one point, but we haven't lost since."

Parham would join Kyle Camper, Maron Brown, Tony Tull and Javon Schoolfield on the All-Bayside team. Wharton was named Coach of the Year while Pocomoke's Eddie Miller took home Player of the Year honors. In his final game representing Bennett, Parham tallied 13 points, 10 rebounds and five blocks in a win for the South in the Bayside Senior All-Star Game.

The next year, Parham went on to Cecil College, but took a redshirt season after fracturing his left foot in a pro-am game in Chicago. One day, he received a call from Wharton, who was in need of an assistant coach for a game. Parham went down to Bennett and sat on the bench. As of this writing, he's a youth basketball coach and scout around Chicago.

"We ended up winning the game and that was my first experience of being on the sideline in a game as a coach. And I loved it," Parham said. "It kind of changed my perspective of my basketball career. I knew I was talented and I knew I could play Division I if I wanted to, but I liked coaching more. He kind of opened that door to me."

John Holmes' star continued to rise, as he was named Bayside Player of the Year in 2004 and often graced the front of the Daily Times' sports section with his thunderous dunks. He went on to play at Bethune-Cookman, where he averaged 11.9 points, 5.8 rebounds and 1.3 assists per-game across 63 contests, and he created a few more highlights at the Hytche Center in MEAC clashes.

Wharton coached Bennett to a Bayside title and another appearance in the state semifinals in 2004. Prior to the start of the 2006-07 season, he resigned as Bennett's head coach. Wharton remained active in the local basketball community on the Eastern Shore and continued to shepherd the Kappa League until his death on July 27, 2020.

"He was a good dude. He was a local legend around here. A good man who knew the game of basketball and treated kids right. Him passing, that hurt me," said Wi-Hi assistant coach Doug King. "He was a community man. Everybody loved Bruce."

The state championship Wharton led the Clippers to was mentioned in the third paragraph of his obituary.

DAVID BYRD'S TITLE TOWN

"He's going to go hard for you, as long as you go hard for yourself. He may not be the most lovable guy on the court, but you're going to love him no matter what." – Eddie Miller

The team James M. Bennett forward Steve Parham knew the Clippers had no chance of beating in the 2002-03 season was Pocomoke. When asked about how Bennett – the 2003 2A state champs – matched up with the Warriors that season, Parham just laughed.

"We got destroyed by Pocomoke," Parham said. "That was one of our losses that season where I was like, 'Okay. We're really not good.' Pocomoke was small but they picked up 94 feet, they trapped all over the court, and they had small guys but they all played well together."

Bennett and Pocomoke were supposed to play each other twice that year, but their second meeting was snowed out. In the first game, the Warriors won easily in what Parham called "Pocomoke's little crackerjack gym." In later years, when they were teammates together at Cecil College, Eddie Miller teased Parham and told him that Bennett was scared of a rematch.

We'll never know, but Bennett would've likely lost a second bout by a landslide at their gym too. Led by Miller, Pocomoke went on to have one of its best seasons in school history in its 2002-03 campaign, going undefeated in the regular season. Miller dropped 30 points in a win over Wi-Hi at the University of Maryland Eastern Shore, hung 33 points on Stephen Decatur, and then tallied 17 points, nine rebounds and two assists in a win over Snow Hill that wound up being the final home game for him and longtime head coach David Byrd.

With Byrd's guidance and Miller's play-making abilities, Pocomoke seemed poised to repeat as 1A state champions in 2003. But replicating their run from 2002 would be easier said than done. Still, Pocomoke's campaigns in 2002 and 2003 – Byrd's final two seasons at the helm – would go down in school history as being some of the best basketball the mighty Warriors had ever played. Even in the previous year, in 2001, Pocomoke was pretty good too, making the 1A East Region Final.

For Pocomoke, the journey to those incredible and record-setting years began all the way back in 1977. It was just several weeks before the high school basketball season was about to begin. And, because of one man's dream to become a dentist, Pocomoke High School suddenly had an opening for its boys varsity basketball coach.

***

The Pocomoke River runs from the Chesapeake Bay, all the way inland past Snow Hill and nearly up to Willards, a small community about halfway between Salisbury and Ocean City. English settlers first navigated the river as early as 1608, according to a book penned about Pocomoke City by Norma Miles and Robin Chandler-Miles. By 1670, Lord Baltimore sent his representatives to that area of the Delmarva Peninsula to claim and develop land. Col. William Stevens created a ferry crossing along the banks of the Pocomoke River. That settlement pushed out most of the Native Americans there – the Algonquin tribe – and it would soon become what is known now as Pocomoke City. For those natives, the word "Pocomoke" meant "black water."

Shipbuilding became a successful business in the settlement, and boats filled with furs, tobacco and lumber sailed along the river. Pocomoke City was officially incorporated in 1878. Ten years later, tragedy struck again. A fire broke out and destroyed 79 buildings in the town. Two more large fires came in 1892 and 1922, the latter of which torched about 75% of businesses there.

In 1996 and 1997, the town received more bad publicity when Pfiesteria – a toxic organism deriving its name from a Latin word meaning "fish killer" – infected the water in the river. According to the Baltimore Sun, the outbreak killed "uncountable numbers" of fish and cost the state seafood industry millions. Some watermen who were exposed to it experienced memory loss. "When you put your hands in the water, it was about like you were getting a shock," Marion East of Crisfield told the Sun. Scientists concluded runoff of chicken manure from Eastern Shore farms contributed to conditions that led to Pfiesteria growing and turning toxic. Ultimately, it sparked a massive initiative to clean Chesapeake Bay.

The thing that became synonymous with Pocomoke are its sports teams at its only high school – which is the ninth smallest in the state out of 198 public high schools. While some call Pocomoke "the Friendliest Town on the Eastern Shore," others simply call it "Title Town," for the parades that storm down Market Street after state championships are captured. And if it wasn't for the Byrd family, hardly anyone would call it that.

Alan Byrd coached the Pocomoke Warriors' boys soccer team to 12 state championship appearances, capturing eight victories. He won four straight between 2005 and 2008. His sister, Susan Pusey, won a share of 16 field hockey state championships, winning 13 of them outright. Her 1994 team is regarded as one of – if not the best – high school field hockey teams ever assembled in the state of Maryland, as it went undefeated, scored 82 goals on the season and allowed zero. The Warriors also won state titles in girls basketball in 2008, softball in 2009, and two more field hockey crowns in

2015 and 2021 under the direction of Brandi Castaneda.

And for all of those titles, Alan and Susan's older brother David was the athletic director at the high school. And from 1977 through 2003, he coached the boys basketball team, winning three Bayside Conference titles and one illustrious state championship in 2002. We'll get to that in just a few moments.

The Byrds were born, bred and raised in Pocomoke. The black water the Algonquin tribe spoke of runs in their veins. And sports do too. David Byrd's mother, father, three uncles and mother-in-law all played basketball at Pocomoke High School. And he was a fine player too, starring for Marvin Detwiler and Ronnie Ross.

A photo of Byrd, with thick black rimmed glasses and his dark hair pushed over, first appeared in the pages of the Daily Times newspaper in Salisbury on Jan. 15, 1969. He had 13 points and six rebounds in an 81-65 home win over Washington. As a senior, Byrd was more of a focal point on offense for Ross. In the first-year head coach's debut, Byrd led the team with 21 points in a 59-50 win over Northampton on Dec. 9, 1969. In Byrd's final high school game – a 91-84 overtime triumph on the road in Crisfield – Byrd notched 22 points.

Byrd went off to the University of Maryland, but College Park proved to be too far from his beloved hometown. As a sophomore, he enrolled at Salisbury State College. A strong athlete in any sport involving a ball, Byrd found his way onto the soccer, basketball and lacrosse teams for the Sea Gulls. Soccer wound up being his strongest sport. In 1971, he was named to the All-Delaware Valley Conference team as a sweeper while also helping the team to a 7-4-2 record and a conference title. During a win over Eastern College on Nov. 2, 1972, Byrd had four assists in a single match. But while Byrd shined on the pitch, there was something different for him about basketball. He was hooked on the sport played on the hardwood.

After finishing his education, Byrd returned to Worcester County and became a physical education teacher at Berlin Middle School. He began guiding the JV soccer team at Pocomoke, but still yearned for a chance to coach basketball. Two months into his fourth year teaching at Berlin Middle, opportunity knocked.

"I forgot what happened," said Byrd, digging through his memory. "But they moved me from there to here (Pocomoke High School) and it was almost basketball season."

What happened was former head coach Chip MacDonald was resigning after just one season on the job. Off the heels of winning a state championship in 1976, then-Pocomoke head coach Carey Reece went out on top and handed the reins of the squad over to MacDonald, a biology teacher at the school and the JV boys basketball coach. But after a year as the varsity skipper, in which the team went 6-16, MacDonald pursued a career change. He told the Daily Times: "I think it's time to go after what I've always wanted – dentistry."

And of course, the world needs dentists. But it also needs basketball coaches.

Pocomoke principal William McComb and vice principal Marvin Detwiler huddled to decide who would inherit the boys basketball program. Detwiler recommended one of his former players, who was teaching just up the road. On Oct. 1, 1977, the Daily Times announced Byrd's hiring and quoted McComb saying, "We're confident he can do a fine job with the basketball program." The author of the story noted he had no previous coaching experience in basketball. But what they didn't know, and what they couldn't quantify, was his love for the game and his knowledge of it.

Former Pocomoke head coach David Byrd remained close to the game of basketball by serving in various leadership positions with the MPSSAA and the Bayside, and by calling UMES men's games on the radio for more than a decade. Photo by Mitchell Northam.

"I wanted to be a physical education teacher. I like all sports, I've played them all, but I like basketball the most. I was really into basketball," Byrd said. "I was just lucky to be in the right spot at the right time. And then for the next 20 years, I went to Morgan Wooten's basketball camps and the Mason-Dixon basketball camps. And basically, that's where I learned how to coach basketball."

Byrd lost in his head coaching debut, 69-64 to Easton, but bounced back quickly with a pair of wins over Washington and Snow Hill, the latter of which came in an 75-72 overtime thriller. Snow Hill had a first-year head coach that season too in Bob Mitchell, as did North Dorchester and St. Michaels. Neither one of them would have the same success or longevity as Byrd. When folks think of longtime boys basketball head coaches on the Eastern Shore, they typically think of Byrd and Wi-Hi's Butch Waller. The two first met when Waller was the head JV coach at Wi-Hi and when Byrd was a player. But on Jan. 3, 1978, they met as adversaries for the first time down near the Maryland-Virginia line. With a 75-64 score, Byrd took the W in the first chapter of what would become a long rivalry, but also a lengthy relationship of mutual respect and admiration.

"David Byrd was a good coach," Waller said. "He dotted all the I's, crossed all the T's and was well prepared. He had really good way with his players, and had good players. He ran a nice program."

While Byrd and Waller had lastingness and success on the court in common, they were very different creatures in the way they prepared. On off nights, Waller would drive to games across the Eastern Shore to examine the competition and he's known for keeping meticulous hand-written records and notes.

Byrd did most of his scouting via the telephone.

"I sent people. I was preparing here, so I'd send people to games all across the state and they'd call me," Byrd said. "I'd call into (former Daily Times sports editor) Cliff Mister every night and give him our box scores. Not only because I liked the guy, but because I was getting the scouting report at the same time. He had everything. Who the best free throw shooter was, who the top rebounder was. Had it all."

And Byrd didn't hunker down in his office to draw up plays and plans for games and practices. No, most of that was done in the early winter mornings from a deer stand. While Byrd waited for targets to appear, he'd have a yellow legal pad with him that he'd scribble on, charting out practices or scheming up nifty inbounds plays.

"I did most of my planning when I was deer hunting. I'd sit in the deer stand and I'd plan out practices. What I wrote down was what I learned from going to basketball camps and watching 9 million hours of college basketball. I was a practice-planning guy," Byrd said. "I wanted practice to start at 7 o'clock on the nose. For the first month, we'd go two hours. Then it'd go down. And if you didn't make your foul shots, we were running."

Byrd developed a few more habits while he was coaching the Warriors. The first is he never used a whistle in practice. When he needed the players' attention, his voice did the job. "I can't whistle during the game, so I wanted them to know my voice when I stood up," Byrd said.

And after he destroyed one-too-many of sports coats, Byrd had to change up his game-day wardrobe.

"I always sweated through my damn shirt. I ruined many of jackets, because I sweat right through the whole thing," Byrd said. "And you got to throw that away. And I didn't have a lot of money in those days. So, I changed to sweaters and pullovers."

The third habit Byrd adopted was not standing much during games he coached in. In part because standing and pacing led to more sweating.

"I'm not a stander," Byrd said. "I like to sit down when I coach. When I stood up, I wanted somebody to pay attention to me – players or referees.

"I was kind of a dictator too. It was my way or the highway. I think the kids appreciated that though. I would do anything for them, they would do anything for me. We won a lot of games."

Byrd had his fair shares of ups and downs through his first few seasons on the job in Pocomoke, but in the 1980-81 season things came together quite nicely. At the Wicomico Civic Center on March 2, 1981, Byrd guided the Warriors to a Bayside Conference Championship win over Easton, 77-68. Pocomoke's defense was outstanding. Easton attempted 26 more shots than Pocomoke, but made five fewer. Byrd employed a 3-2 zone and pressed often on the defensive end, and offensively the Warriors got 22 points from DeAngelo DeShields, 21 points from Darryl Dennis, and 18 points from 6-foot-6 center David Betterton, sporting his trademark thick white wristbands.

"Darryl Dennis probably had the best hands, as a defender," said Derrick Fooks, who played at Stephen Decatur in the early 80s. "I mean, he would strap you up. And when you got home, you'd wonder where you got all these cuts. Because he would touch you."

The Warriors stormed their way through the playoffs and beat Crisfield 52-50 for a spot in the state semifinals. But in Byrd's first trip to College Park's Cole Field House as a coach, the Warriors couldn't survive another nail-biter. Dennis – who would be Byrd's first Division I player, going on to play at the University of Maryland Eastern Shore – picked up three quick fouls in the first half of a semifinal matchup with Valley High School of Allegany County and fouled out with plenty of time left on the clock. Dennis played just eight minutes and Valley topped the Warriors 59-58. Betterton and Jimmy Schoolfield combined for 50 of Pocomoke's points, but Betterton missed a five-foot bank shot with less than 10 seconds to play. And by then, Schoolfield had fouled out too. Pocomoke finished the year 21-4.

Despite the semifinal loss, Betterton was named Bayside South Player of the Year after averaging 20.7 points and 14.5 rebounds per-game as a senior. Byrd called his star center "hard-working" and "coachable." He played at Allegany College before starring in men's leagues on the Eastern Shore. Betterton died at the age of 35 in 1999 due to complications from Marfan syndrome.

Dennis, DeShields and Schoolfield also made the All-Bayside South Team picked by the Daily Times.

"On a personal level, I think Darryl Dennis was one of the best defenders and all-around players that I faced," said Greg Bozman, who played at Crisfield at the time. "He was a late bloomer, but he was incredible."

***

In 1986, David Byrd had another talented squad, and again he ran into Valley High School in the state semifinals at Cole Field House. This time, the game went into double-overtime, but Valley's 6-foot-3, 250-pound Chris Winner hit six free throws in the second extra period to give his squad a 70-65 win, ousting Pocomoke again. Gerald Croswell scored 26 points for the Warriors, but the more glaring statistic was the fact Pocomoke squandered a 12-point lead. Dejected, Byrd told the Daily Times after the game: "We should have won it a couple of times. We made a lot of mental mistakes we normally don't make."

That was true. Nearly a decade into his tenure as the head coach of the Warriors, Byrd's Pocomoke teams became known for a few things. First, most of the time, they were incredibly disciplined. Second, their defense was going to be top-notch; they'd press the hell out of you. And third, it was going to be very difficult to beat them on their home floor.

Pocomoke's home court, like Snow Hill's, was not the same size as the other Bayside schools. It was smaller by width and length. There wasn't a lot of room for error.

"If you sat on the bleachers, on the bottom row, your feet were touching the sideline," Byrd said. "And we had people standing against the wall. The fire marshal was non-existent."

Opposing players who had to travel to Pocomoke over the years agreed. Winning there was no easy feat.

"The toughest gym I had to play in would be Pocomoke's," said Doug King, who played at Wi-Hi in the mid-90s. "That place is just tough. Especially when they're good, in that small gym."

"They'd press you in that little gym and there was nowhere you could go," said Greg Bozman, who played at Washington and Crisfield in the late 70s and early 80s.

"The toughest road gym was definitely Pocomoke," said Nick Purnell, who played at Snow Hill in the late 80s. "And it was a rival. We felt like we were battle-tested because we played at Pocomoke."

"Pocomoke was in your face all the time," said Fooks, a Decatur player who later became an assistant under Byrd, then succeeded him as Pocomoke's head coach. Byrd likes to remind Fooks, while he was playing at

Decatur, he lost to Byrd's teams four times. "Some of these teams – David's had midgets. Small kids. And they just competed and pressed."

The way the crowd chants at Pocomoke games – that thundering "P-OH, P-OH, UH-OH, UH-OH" – is like a sound that takes on its own physical life form, living on as an echo as the Warriors storm up and down the court, almost as if they really are playing with six men.

For Byrd, the overall respect opposing teams had for Pocomoke's gym, defense and professionalism was especially meaningful.

"The most important thing is – and what I'm most proud of – if anyone told you they were playing a Pocomoke high school team, especially one that I coached, they'd say you had to strap 'em up every night," Byrd said. "When you play Pocomoke, you're going to get pressed when you step off the bus. And it's going to be high intensity. And we're going to play very, very hard. We got a good reputation for that. That got us a lot of W's. But we also had a lot of very good players; kids that would run through a wall for you. I coached a lot of great kids."

***

One of the most talented players to ever walk through the locker room doors at Pocomoke High School was Mike Roberts.

Growing up, Roberts honed his basketball skills in his yard in Pocomoke, on a hoop hanging from three two-by-four planks driven into the dirt. He was one of the few four-year starters on varsity for David Byrd and passed the 1,000-point scoring mark as a sophomore. At 6-foot-2, he often played like he was six inches taller.

"Mike put it on me," said Shawn Tucker, who played at Parkside. "He was the first person to put 20 and 10 on me in the first half. Mike was really good. Right away I was like, 'He's a D1 guy.'"

The boy wearing the gold jersey with No. 44 emblazoned on it in navy gave headaches to teams across the Bayside Conference. When Roberts laced up his white Converses, the opposition was in trouble. With a strong jaw, a sharply cropped fade and broad, muscular shoulders, Roberts often bulldozed his way through opposing defenses. Not only was Roberts a tenacious rebounder and a crafty inside scorer with his left hand, but he was superb three-point shooter too. He did everything and anything for Byrd's squads in the late 80s and early 90s.

Andre Collins, who'd go on to score his own share of boatloads of points on the Eastern Shore, called Roberts, "a walking bucket." That's not exactly an exaggeration either. Points per-game, Roberts averaged 13.5 as a freshman, 24.6 as a sophomore, 29.1 as a junior and 32.8 as a senior. In all, he finished his high school career with 2,611 points. The Maryland Public Secondary Schools Athletic Association does not keep individual career statistics or records, but unofficially – as far as Byrd and this writer knows – Roberts is still the state's all-time leading scorer among boys public school players. In a 1992 Daily Times story, sports editor Dave Broughton noted Roberts' career three-point shooting mark at Pocomoke was 47%.

"If he played in the Bayside right now, he'd score 50 a night," Byrd said. "They'd foul the hell out of him and hang on him, and then he'd step out and knock the three down. And he still holds the school record for most threes made in a game, nine. We gave him the basketball and he carried us."

Mike Roberts scored 2,611 points across his four years at Pocomoke, which is still unofficially the all-time career scoring record by a boys basketball player at public schools in Maryland. Colgate Athletics.

Added Derrick Fooks: "Mike Roberts did everything. He was unguardable. He was phenomenal."

Jeff Levan was an assistant coach at Snow Hill during each of Roberts' four seasons at Pocomoke. Levan said, "I would be willing to bet that no one ever scored more points against one opponent than he did against us. Between the 1A playoffs and the John Coleman Christmas tournament, we would sometimes meet three to four times a year. He put up huge numbers in most of those games."

Once, against James M. Bennett, Roberts scored a school record 52 points, grabbed 21 rebounds, blocked four shots and had three assists. He might as well have taken tickets at the door too.

After a Jan. 23, 1991 game, in which Roberts scored 33 points in a road win, Parkside head coach Andy Hall told the Daily Times: "He's just a fantastic player. He's so strong that there's really no one player on our team who can guard him."

A month later, Easton head coach McKinley "Mac" Hayward had to agree, telling the Star Democrat after he gashed Easton for 34 points and 18 rebounds: "He's probably one of the strongest ballplayers I've seen down low like that for a long time. We were so worried about him. We would double-team him and then he'd slide through."

Roberts' junior season, his lowest scoring output was 21 points. His highest was 49 and he shot 69% from the floor and 86.5% from the charity stripe, an impressive mark for any player at any level. He also averaged 15 rebounds per-game in the 1990-91 season. Roberts' awesome skill and productivity powered Pocomoke back to the state final four at Cole Field House. And this time, they didn't falter in the semifinals. Against Brunswick, Roberts scored all seven of Pocomoke's overtime points – while nursing a sprained ankle – to push the Warriors into the 1A state final with a 75-72 victory. In all, Roberts finished the game with 29 points and nine boards.

Unfortunately, Roberts' talent alone wasn't enough to net Byrd his first state title. The Warriors fell to Joppatowne, 67-47. Roberts finished the game with 19 points. A week later, he was named Bayside Player of the Year, an award he'd hang onto as a senior too. In 1992, Roberts would guide Pocomoke back to College Park, but they lost in the semifinals to Milford Mill, 66-39. In his final game as a Warrior, Roberts scored 20 points. He led all scorers in the Bayside All-Star Game with 26 points.

For his college ball, Roberts went north to Hamilton, New York and starred at Colgate of the Patriot League. By his sophomore season, he was playing regular minutes at the Division I level, 16 per-game. As a senior, he was a starter, playing 28.2 minutes a night. As a junior, Roberts averaged 10.1 points, 3.3 rebounds,

At Colgate, Pocomoke's Mike Roberts helped the Raiders appear in a pair of NCAA Tournaments in 1995 and 1996. Colgate Athletics

1.1 assists and almost a steal per-game as Colgate won the Patriot League and made the NCAA Tournament for the first time ever. Colgate lost its opening tournament game, but Roberts had 12 points and three rebounds against Kansas. As a senior, Roberts helped the Raiders win the Patriot League again, averaging 11.1 points and 3.2 rebounds per-game while shooting 36.6% from the floor. Colgate was again defeated in the first round, and Roberts went out with seven points, two rebounds and two assists in his final college game.

***

Under David Byrd's tenure, Pocomoke didn't just produce incredible athletes. Iconic voices came through the school and his program too.

Every offseason, Byrd would meet with the JV players and tell them what they needed to work on to compete on the varsity level. But when sophomore Pat Doughty walked into his office in 1985, he had a different kind of advice. He didn't tell Doughty to improve his ball handling, or he needed to be a better jump shooter, or he needed to attack the glass with more tenacity.

"I thought I was an athlete," Doughty said.

No. Byrd told Doughty that he needed to put the basketball down and pick up the microphone.

"Pat Doughty. I need you to find something else to do. I don't need a 5-foot-8 power forward," Byrd told him.

But Doughty loved the game of basketball. Living in a place like Pocomoke City, how could you not? The kid that grew up on Laurel Street needed to stay close to the game. So, he grabbed a seat at the scorer's table and snatched up the mic. He took over announcing duties from the school's vice principal that winter.

"Once I heard my voice the first time go out over the loudspeaker, and I heard people's reactions, it was a shot of adrenaline," Doughty told WBOC. "I was hooked."

Doughty would call games through the rest of his high school days at Pocomoke and he continued to hone his craft just up the road at the University of Maryland Eastern Shore. Doughty then joined the Navy, and even aboard a nuclear-powered guided-missile cruiser, he found his way to the microphone, manning the ship's PA system, reading wire news reports during the first Gulf War. After being discharged in 1992, he worked for a gravedigging company on the Eastern Shore until the folks at UMES reached out in 2000, needing a new voice at the Hytche Center. He soon became a well-known voice in the MEAC, his voice booming through Princess Anne every time a Hawk dunked or drained a three-pointer.

And then, when the NBA was brought back to Charlotte, North Carolina in 2004 – then as the Bobcats – they needed a public address announcer. Someone to deliver messages, introduce the players and get the crowd involved. Doughty saw the opportunity and grabbed it with both hands. He started leaving voicemails for folks who worked for the expansion franchise. They noticed his persistence and invited him to make the drive down – Route 13 to 58 to 85, in his 1986 Lincoln Town Car – to audition.

Out of more than 500 people vying for the job, Doughty was one of two finalists. But before the Bobcats hired him, he started calling games for the WNBA's Charlotte Sting, which played in the same arena. Eventually, Doughty got the NBA gig too, and he's been the voice of the NBA in Charlotte – from Bobcats to Hornets, from Gerald Wallace to LaMelo Ball – ever since.

A Pocomoke High graduate, Pat Doughty is now the public address announcer for the Charlotte Hornets. Photo by Mitchell Northam.

"I do it all. Everything that needs to be informative during the game – for those three hours, I've got your attention. I'm talking the entire time," Doughty said. "It's surreal."

In 2010, Michael Jordan bought controlling interest of the Bobcats and changed the name back to the Hornets in 2014. So now, Doughty's boss is the greatest basketball player of all time. One of the most famous people in the entire world knows him well. Jordan's nickname for Doughty is typically either "P" or "Big Guy."

"It's absolutely wonderful," Doughty said. "You're in awe the first few times you meet him, then you see him and it's in passing and, it's still Mike, but you know, he's a good guy. He doesn't want you to call him Mr. Jordan, he wants you to call him MJ or Michael, and he's very personable. Good guy."

One of Doughty's signatures when calling Hornets' games is to use his VoiceTone processor to produce an echo effect on his calls. They sound a bit like: "BUUUZZZZ CITYYY! GET ON YOUR FEET AND GREET YOUR CHAAAARRRLOTTE HORNETS-HORNETS-HORNETS-HORNETS," with the last word trailing off, bouncing off the walls throughout the Spectrum Center.

Doughty came back to Pocomoke's gym in 2016 and announced a sold-out girls game between the Warriors and Stephen Decatur. His niece, Shayla Jones, was on that Pocomoke team and helped lead the Warriors to the state semifinal in Gail Gladding's final season at the helm. He's returned to the Shore dozens of times to MC celebrity all-star games too.

***

While players like Mike Roberts, Darryl Dennis and David Arnold didn't walk through the doors of Pocomoke High School every year, Byrd's program – by the mid-90s – had established itself as one of the Shore's best and most-respected. Regardless of who was on the roster, the Warriors were going to be competitive. They wouldn't just roll over for anyone due to lack of talent or size.

"Pocomoke was always going to be in the hunt. It's very seldom that we're not," Byrd said. "You have to adjust. Some years you have good scorers, some years you have good ball handlers, some years you get a big man. Pocomoke has been noted for having very good guards over the years. I've played teams with five guards. Size has not been one of our attributes."

Still, as good as Byrd's teams were and as often as they won, the ultimate trophy still eluded him. Byrd won his second Bayside Conference Championship in 1995, but his brother and sister were beginning to stack up state titles in boys soccer and girls field hockey. On the basketball court, Pocomoke was admired and feared on the Eastern Shore, but they still didn't have statewide recognition.

In 1998, Byrd and the Warriors had another shot. That season, he passed the 300-win mark and the Warriors beat a tough Crisfield team in overtime in the regional semifinals, then topped North Dorchester for a ticket to College Park. It would be Byrd's seventh time there as a player or coach. The Monday before the Warriors boarded the bus to cross the Bay Bridge, Byrd was awake past 3:30 a.m. watching a Big Sky Conference game between Boise State and Eastern Washington. He was – and still is – a total basketball junkie.

"I live it. I breathe it," he told the Daily Times. "The only thing more important is my family, and I think they question that sometimes."

His wife Peggy told the paper: "He obviously doesn't coach for the money. He does it because he loves it and he wants to see the kids succeed."

The Warriors barely beat South Hagerstown in the semifinals, 70-69, largely due to two factors: the Warriors were excellent from the charity stripe, making 18-of-23 attempts, and Mirko Humbert and Brandon Holden combined for 40 points and 11 rebounds.

In the final, against Forest Park, the Warriors were beyond unlucky. The result proved agonizing, leading many to believe the Warriors were simply snake-bitten. With the game tied at 43-43, Forest Park had the ball with 8.1 seconds left after a timeout. The Foresters scrambled, looking for a decent shot against the Warriors' stingy defense. Eventually, the ball wound up in the hands of Jamie Higginbotham, who had shot just 1-of-8 from the floor up until that point. With about eight-tenths of a second remaining, he launched an off-balance shot.

Swish. Buzzer.

Pocomoke loses – again.

"It was a heartbreaker," said Derrick Fooks, then an assistant coach on the team. "It was a Hail Mary. Kid is falling on the ground, heaves something up and it goes in. That was for the marbles."

To add to the Warriors' sorrow, the game-winning shot was set-up by a controversial call near the Pocomoke bench. The ball went out of bounds during a scuffle for possession, and officials said it last touched a Warrior. Byrd was adamant the call should've went the other way, telling the Daily Times, "It was out of bounds on them and they got the ball. I got the best look at it because it almost hit me in the face." Byrd didn't blame the call for the defeat. He conceded Forest Park's 2-2-1 press gave Pocomoke problems, and giving up 24 offensive rebounds to the Foresters didn't help either.

***

If you ask Derrick Fooks now, when he thought the 2001-02 Pocomoke team had what it took to win a state title, he'll tell you it was the year before.

"We lost to Snow Hill. A call here or there," Fooks recalled. "We actually should've won three in a row. That's the heartbreaking part of it. That was a three-year run where we were really, really good."

Indeed, from December of 2000 to March of 2003, Pocomoke went 72-6. Simply put, they were a fantastic basketball team. But a few teams were able to best them. On March 2, 2001, in the 1A East Region Semifinals at the University of Maryland Eastern Shore, that team was Snow Hill.

Pocomoke led in the fourth quarter, but Allen Miller's Eagles broke off a 9-1 run to end the game and squeaked out a 60-57 victory. Snow Hill, powered by Tony Harmon, Jessie Bratten and Buddy Johnson, would go on to win the state title that year, giving Miller his second championship while Byrd still searched for his first.

But the following season, 2001-02, would be very different. Speaking to the Daily Times for its season preview, Byrd said, "We're going to press people and run the floor. We'll be fun to watch." But Byrd, nor the writer of the preview piece, said much about Eddie Miller, who would prove to be the difference maker for the Warriors.

Derrick Fooks won his 300th game as Pocomoke's head coach in 2020. Before taking the reins of the program, he was David Byrd's assistant. Photo by Mitchell Northam

Miller was born just a hop, skip and a jump down Route 13 in Nassawadox, Virginia. He moved across the Maryland line as a kid and was raised in Pocomoke, but didn't truly discover his love and talent for basketball until he was about 13 years old. Playing in the Salvation Army leagues, he looked up to Crisfield's Andre Collins, Wi-Hi's Bubby Brown, and Pocomoke's Josh Hickman and Harvey Davis.

"It was an inspiration watching those guys," Miller says. "I was always shy to play, but I developed a love for the game."

Miller also quickly grew a knack for scoring at all three levels. He could jump and dunk with anyone, but he was also an expert marksman from behind the three-point arc. He didn't talk much when he played, leading some to call him a silent assassin. For that 2001 regional semifinal against Snow Hill, Miller spent most of the game on the bench. It was evident early on in the 01-02 season Miller wouldn't spend much time on the bench at all. In Game Two, an 89-61 win over Crisfield, Miller knocked four three's in the first half and helped power Pocomoke to a victory.

"They were like lay-ups for him," Fooks said of Miller's three-point shooting. "You thought they were all going in."

But the 2002 team wasn't just Miller. Patrolling the paint was 6-foot-3 Tyrone Northam, despite lacking a few inches, there weren't many post players – on the Shore or in the state – who could guard Northam one-on-one. Built like a football player, his grit was unmatched, and his quickness and craftiness routinely surprised opponents.

"He was very skilled," Miller said of Northam. "And not many players were left-handed. He was a mobile five. He could put it on the floor and take it to the rack."

Playing in the other frontcourt position was often either Gerry Laws or David Wilson. Byrd called Laws a rebounding forward at 6-foot-1 and "probably one of our best athletes." Wilson was a 6-foot-4 exchange student from Nottingham, England. Said Byrd: "He was a skinny white kid, but he did what he was supposed to do; rebound and set picks."

Joining Miller at the guards were Jovan Schoolfield and Tony Tull. Schoolfield was a versatile do-it-all guard who could handle, create for himself and others, and play defense the Pocomoke way. Tull – whose father Anky played on the 1976 state title team – was the floor general.

"Tony was the guy who could say anything and everyone would listen to him," Fooks said.

By the time the annual holiday tournament rolled around, Pocomoke was 5-1, with its lone loss coming against Wi-Hi. At the Wicomico Civic Center, the Warriors were tested by Sussex Tech, but triumphed in overtime with a 72-71 victory. Byrd wasn't happy afterwards, because Pocomoke shot just 23-of-40 from the free throw line. He told the Daily Times: "I think a blind nun could shoot free throws as good as we did tonight."

A few weeks later, Pocomoke improved at the charity stripe, but turned the ball over 28 times in a game at Parkside. Still, their talent was too great. The Warriors rolled, 70-58, behind a combined 50 points and 23 rebounds from Miller, Northam and Wilson. For their 11th win of the season, Pocomoke extracted revenge from rival Snow Hill, taking a 72-68 victory. Schoolfield was the star in that game, pouring in 23 points and swiping several possessions away from Snow Hill. Eagles head coach Allen Miller said after the game, "That's the best I've ever seen Jovan Schoolfield shoot. He played really well... The bottom line is, Dave and I want to see one or the other go across the bridge. He's going to root for me and I'm going to root for him."

If 2001 was Miller's year, 2002 belonged to Byrd. At least in 1A anyways. In the 2A on the Shore, it was apparent Wi-Hi was the top dog. Still, after the Indians narrowly beat the Warriors again, both Butch Waller and Byrd were glad they wouldn't have to see each other in the postseason. Waller told the Daily Times: "I had at least five people come up to me and say, 'Butch, this was a great game for your team. You needed a game like this,' and I'm going to tell you, I did not need a game like this."

Said Eddie Miller of Wi-Hi: "We wanted them to win as bad as they wanted us to win. Just not against each other."

Pocomoke was 12-2 at this point in the season and Miller was emerging as one of the Bayside's top talents. He was leading the conference in scoring with 18.7 points per-game. And Northam was averaging 16.1 points and 9.3 boards per-game.

"Eddie always set the tone. He was really freaking good player," Byrd said.

While some of the players may have had their own motivations that season, many of them also wanted to win it for Byrd. Miller described his high school coach as "inspirational" and being like "a father figure."

"He was somebody you can model your life after, to be like him. He was not only your coach, but he was a guidance," Miller said. "He's going to push you and make you want to be a better person and a better player. He's going to go hard for you, as long as you go hard for yourself. He may not be the most lovable guy on the court, but you're going to love him no matter what."

Pocomoke rolled through the rest of the regular season unscathed. And in the regional semifinals, Snow Hill was waiting for them again at the University of Maryland Eastern Shore. At the end of regulation, it looked like a familiar scene: Pocomoke was about to lose at the buzzer. In the last second, it seemed like Tony Harmon had a successful tip-in, but the ball rolled in, around and out of the basket. In the huddle after the buzzer, Byrd asked his team: "Do you want to go to College Park?" In overtime, Schoolfield had 10 of Pocomoke's 17 points as they bulldozed their way to a 70-59 win. In the regional final – also played at UMES – Colonel Richardson was no match for the Warriors who were indeed determined to reach College Park. The Colonels were outhustled, outclassed and outmatched in every way. The Warriors won 91-52 behind 23 points from Miller and 19 points from Gerry Laws. And so, for the eighth time in his basketball career at Pocomoke, Byrd was bound for Cole Field House – and for the last time too. Maryland was opening a new basketball arena and the state tournament would be moving there.

"I had several really good teams that lost at College Park. The one that won it all was a team," Byrd said. "We had depth. We had all these ingredients. We had good kids, good players, good athletes. We weren't big. We had Eddie Miller who could shoot the lights out of it. I had really good guards that were coaches on the floor, too. They excelled by going beyond what we asked them to do."

In the state semifinals, Pocomoke ran into South Hagerstown. The Warriors made quick work of them, capturing a dominant 82-58 win behind 23 points from Miller and 19 points and 11 boards from Northam. The Warriors forced 21 turnovers, and Tull was credited with seven steals.

Awaiting Pocomoke in the final was the formidable Dunbar, who had just reclassed down to 1A in the offseason. In 2001, they beat Wi-Hi for the 2A state final. Dunbar was respected and feared across the state. They gained fame in the early 1980s for their teams coached by Bob Wade. From 1981 to 1983, the Poets went 59-0 and had 11 players from those teams go on to play Division I college basketball, and four of them – Muggsy Bogues, Reggie Williams, David Wingate and Reggie Lewis – would play in the NBA. Between 1993 and 2001, Dunbar won seven state championships. And now, another team from a region of the state that former Governor William Donald Schaefer referred to as a "shithouse" stood in the Poets' way.

"They did not take us seriously," Byrd said of Dunbar. "We were from the Eastern Shore. They thought they were going to run over us."

In the semifinals, Dunbar beat Chesapeake by 75 points. Pocomoke did not lay down in the same way. Pocomoke started the game off on an 11-2 run, and highlighting that offensive spark was a play from Northam that set the tone for the entire game. Northam received a pass from Tull and lured Dunbar's 6-foot-10 center Michael Thompson out to the top of the key. Northam turned and faced him, then blew by him and dunked with a ferocity that shook Cole Field House. Northam then swished an 18-footer over Thompson a few moments later.

Dunbar fought back, but Pocomoke retained a two-point lead at halftime. The Pocomoke locker room was calm, quiet and confident. And in the second half, they unleashed every ounce of energy they had left. At the end of the third quarter, Miller drained a three-pointer to push the lead to eight points. In the fourth quarter, Dunbar couldn't catch up. 88-70 was the final. Schoolfield had 29 points while Miller scored 26. Laws and Northam scored in double-digits too, and point guard Tony Tull had just a single turnover.

"Beating Dunbar was amazing," Miller said. "We wanted that game so bad. They weren't ready for us. They didn't realize the heart we had."

Dunbar had long been the Mike Tyson of boys high school basketball in Maryland. They won a lot, and often with relative ease. But on March 9, 2002, the Poets met their Buster Douglas. It was Pocomoke, and in the Warriors' corner was David Byrd.

"This is going to sell a lot of newspapers in Ocean City tomorrow," Byrd told the Baltimore Sun. "There are going to be a lot of people at home who want to read about how we beat the mighty Dunbar."

A Pocomoke team coached by David Byrd had finally done it. His wife cried and cheered from the stands. Derrick Fooks hugged him. And his son Spencer – a reserve player on the team who never missed a practice – hit the final shot of the final boys high school game ever played at Cole Field House.

It was a storybook day for Byrd. On his 50th birthday, in his 25th season of coaching, his first state championship victory was also his 400th career win.

And finally, he'd board a school bus back to Pocomoke, and he'd go over the black water river and down Market Street, and he'd see Pocomoke City the way his Alan and Susan had: as a champion.

"Coaching in a small town, the town gets behind you. It's a community thing. When I go into Ace Hardware today, they still call me 'Coach.' I haven't coached in 18 years. You know what I mean? There's still that connection," Byrd said. "Every holiday – Christmas, Thanksgiving, Easter, stuff like that – I get emails or texts. And then every Father's Day I get bombarded with 'Happy Father's Day' from all previous basketball players."

***

Back on the Shore, David Byrd was named Bayside Coach of the Year and Northam landed Player of the Year honors after averaging 15.9 points and 10.2 boards per-game. He'd go on to play at Division III Virginia Wesleyan, and Northam and Miller also made the All-Mason Dixon Team. While Northam moved on to college, the rest of the team's core returned. Miller, Schoolfield, Tull and Wilson geared up for the chance to win back-to-back state crowns.

Pocomoke sprinted through the regular season with an undefeated mark. This time, not even Wi-Hi could stop their full-court, full-speed attack. With a guard heavy lineup, the Warriors flew up and down the court and scored in bunches. And they pressed hard and often defensively too. And Miller's skill and confidence was growing. By late February, he was averaging a Bayside-best 25.7 points per-game, along with 7.5 rebounds and 2.8 steals. Wilson and Schoolfield were also averaging double-digit points.

"I put in the work. I felt like I was the best player in the conference," Miller said. "Anybody that stepped in front of me that night just had to deal with it. And as a team, we clicked so well together."

At the end of the 2003 regular season, the Warriors were named co-Bayside champs with Cambridge after the conference championship games were scrapped due to inclement weather. Pocomoke stormed through the playoffs again, powered by Miller. He scored 31 points in a first round win over Colonel Richardson, effortlessly put up 39 against North Dorchester and had 24 points in a region final win over rival Crisfield.

"We could run and get up and down the floor with just about anyone," Byrd said. "It was controlled wildness. And we took good shots."

Pocomoke topped South Hagerstown again in the state semifinals, only to meet Dunbar for the second straight year in the 1A Final in College Park. This time, things worked out better for the Baltimore boys, as they won 72-55. The loss ended a 39-game winning streak for Pocomoke that dated back to the previous season.

"It's not bittersweet at all," Byrd said after the game. "They're a great group of young men... if we beat Dunbar two years in a row, they'd be liable to have to close the school."

In his final game for the Warriors, Miller led all scorers with 27 points while facing a box-and-one defense from the Poets. For Miller, he remembers the 2003 loss to Dunbar more than the 2002 win. Joy doesn't leave scars like pain does.

"They wanted us to play their game and we kind of fell into a little bit," Miller said of the loss to Dunbar. "I don't think we played a bad game. We just got out-played."

***

From there, Eddie Miller was off to Cecil County, where he quickly became one of the best junior college talents in the country. Schoolfield landed at Dundalk Community College and Wilson went to Division III Hood College. Miller took one official Division I visit his senior year at Pocomoke, to Rutgers, but felt the junior college route would be better.

Coached by Bill Lewit, Cecil College was loaded with talent from the Shore. Lewit was a former Salisbury University football and basketball player who created a bit of a pipeline from the lower Delmarva Peninsula to North East, Maryland. Beginning in the mid-to-late 1990s with the likes of Doug King and Rashad Brooks, Lewit would bring in players from the Shore who were under-recruited, under-developed or those who just needed some structure in their life. Along the way, he'd win a mess of games and turn a chunk of those players into Division I prospects. Between 1995 and 2008, Lewit's teams had a 320-87 record and captured five Maryland JUCO titles. The teams Miller and Steve Parham played on at Cecil also featured Wi-Hi's Craig Winder, Maron Brown and Kyle Camper. "He's a great guy," David Byrd said of Lewit. "He should've been the coach at UMES."

Often, Lewit would bring his Cecil team to Chesapeake College in Queenstown or down to Salisbury for a showcase game and allow his Shore kids to play in front of their friends and families. For Miller, a game on Feb. 5, 2004 at Salisbury University against Chesapeake felt like he was back in high school. On the first play of the game, Camper served him up a lob and Miller threw down the alley-oop. He finished with 30 points.

"I just wanted to come out and put on a show," Miller said. "That was our opening play. We tried to start off every game with a dunk that season."

Miller averaged 19 points per-game as a freshman, then took a redshirt in his second season at Cecil, a year in which he and Camper worked out and played one-on-one nearly every day. In his third season, Miller averaged 23.3 points per-game, shot 40.2% from three-point range and began attracting attention from big-time Division I schools. He was named NJCAA Division II Player of the Year and helped Cecil win a national title in 2006.

"Eddie was a good shooter," said Steve Parham, the former James M. Bennett forward who was also at Cecil then. "Not the best ball handler, but he could light it up and was very sneaky athletic. If I was doing a scouting report now, Eddie Miller would be a 'three-and-D' guy. He can play good defense and he can spot up and shoot, and he can dunk on your head. And he was a great teammate."

Lewit once told the Daily Times: "I can't say enough about what it's like to have a shot-maker instead of a shot-taker. Eddie's just that. He knows how to seize the moment."

Before his third season at Cecil began, Miller was already committed to Fresno State. It was the only visit he went on before the season began and, despite it being on the other side of the country, the school in the middle of California felt like home to him.

"Like, as soon as I got off the plane and I stepped foot outside to breathe in air, its surroundings made me feel good. It was a great vibe," Miller said. "You meet the people and everybody is so homey. It's like being here, on the Shore. It felt real. Everything was amazing. Everybody was laid back."

Miller's other offers included St. Bonaventure, Texas, Florida and Indiana. For him, in addition to comfort, the deciding factor was playing time.

"Coming from a JUCO, I got two years to play. And those are amazing, big-time schools, but I wanted to play. I was playing it safer than sorry. I don't regret it," Miller said. "I had an amazing time at Fresno. One thing we can't change is time."

Indeed, Miller wasn't necessarily a star at Fresno, but he did play a lot of minutes and score a lot of points – 817 of them in 2,023 minutes, to be exact. In his senior season for the Bulldogs, he averaged 15 points and 2.9 rebounds per-game while shooting 40.5 percent from behind the arc. In both seasons at Fresno, he ranked in the top two in the Western Athletic Conference in three-pointers made. He knocked down at least seven threes in a single game six times at Fresno, and his 38.7% career three-point shooting percentage is still the fifth-best all-time in WAC history.

"Man, I had fun out there. On the court and off the court," Miller said of his time at Fresno. "The people are great; the coaches did everything they were supposed to do. It was an amazing experience."

After two seasons at Fresno – where he played against the likes of Brook and Robin Lopez, Anthony Tolliver and Jerryd Bayless – Miller took his talents overseas for a few years, playing for teams in France, Poland and Saudi Arabia. In his first season in Poland, Miller played for a team in a city called Inowroclaw. The gym was small, but the rabid fans packed the arena. It felt a little like Pocomoke. "It was extremely small. Every single game was an event," Miller said. "They packed it out. They loved it. And we won; we were one game out of the playoffs."

The star of Pocomoke's 2002 boys state title team, Eddie Miller returned to his alma mater in 2016 as an assistant coach for the girls team. Photo by Mitchell Northam.

***

Eddie Miller would eventually return to the Lower Shore, and got his first high school coaching job as an assistant on the girls team at Pocomoke, helping Corey Zimmer, who succeeded Gail Gladding ahead of the 2016-17 season.

On the same day in 2003 that Bennett's boys won and Pocomoke's boys lost, Gladding and the Pocomoke girls were in Catonsville, competing for their first state title victory, also against Dunbar. But Gladding's Warriors coughed up possessions more than 30 times and missed 14 free throws, and Dunbar's size proved to be too much. Pocomoke fell, 53-48.

"They were big. They are much taller and stronger than we are; a lot more physical," Gladding said after the loss. "… we went after them. We came up to the big city and made a name for ourselves."

And if you're an Eastern Shore team going across the bridge, if you don't win, you at least have to make them respect you and remember your name. In 2003 – and every other time a Byrd, Pusey or Gladding-coached team went across the Chesapeake Bay – the girls and boys from Pocomoke did that. And that was just fine for the tiny basketball-crazed community cheering for the small school with the big legacy nestled near the Maryland-Virginia line.

COACHING ANGRY

"It really means something that your peers can see it. But then to look at my alma mater who couldn't see it – that stuck with me." – Nick Purnell

When Allen Miller took over the boys basketball program again at Snow Hill in 2004, this time from Sean Alvarado, he kept Nick Purnell on as an assistant coach. Miller's former state-championship-winning point guard assisted with both the JV and the varsity boys over the next four years, helping the Eagles go undefeated and win states again in 2008. Then, when the Snow Hill girls needed a head coach, Purnell stepped up and helped shepherd them along.

"Coaching girls was a big-time adjustment for me," Purnell said.

Nick Purnell and Butch Waller watched a Governor's Challenge game together in 2016. The star of that game was Immanuel Quickley. Photo by Mitchell Northam.

Purnell learned a great deal from coaching girls basketball, especially trading tactics against greats like Barbara McCool, Warren White and Gail Gladding. But, deep down, he always wanted to coach the boys team at Snow Hill.

When Miller died suddenly in the fall of 2010, Purnell applied for the job.

Instead, it went to Greg Bozman, who stayed just one season. When the job was open again in 2011, Purnell applied. Again, he was overlooked and the gig went to Byron Arenella, a math teacher at the school.

Purnell was upset. He was an alum; the point guard on the greatest Snow Hill team ever. He had coaching experience, with the boys under Miller and he had been in charge of the girls team for multiple seasons. He felt like he was in line for the job and that it would be a perfect fit. That he wasn't hired – not once, but twice – didn't make sense to him.

"It was always my dream to coach (boys basketball) at Snow Hill," Purnell said. "I had been there for so long. So, I felt as though, somewhat, like it was a slap in my face."

Purnell wasn't just upset; he was irate. And he had a chip on his shoulder that was bigger than the Death Star.

He continued to coach the girls at Snow Hill. And then, in the fall of 2012, an opportunity presented itself. Just 22 miles away from Snow Hill in Princess Anne, Washington High School had an opening. Vic Burns had just resigned and the Jaguars needed a coach. Purnell was dropping his daughter off at college when he got a phone call from his friend, and former Snow Hill assistant coach, B.J. Johnson. The principal at Washington High School had called Johnson to see if he was interested, but Johnson wasn't; he had his eyes on returning to Stephen Decatur. When the principal asked if Johnson knew if anyone else was interested, he thought of Purnell.

"I'm going to be totally honest here: I felt like I had to prove to Snow Hill that I could coach," Purnell said. "So, when the Washington position came up... I was angry."

Purnell called another friend in the local coaching fraternity, Pocomoke's Derrick Fooks.

"(Fooks) gave me some really encouraging words," Purnell said. "He said, 'You should take the job. Because you have so much more to offer in the Bayside in other places than just Snow Hill.' That stuck with me, because everything I had done to that point was in Snow Hill."

Purnell took the weekend to think about the job, and then he pounced on it. He called the Washington principal, accepted the position and then wrote on Facebook about his new gig. If he could do it all over again, Purnell says he would still take the job, but he'd do it differently.

"I caught so much backlash from Snow Hill, mainly because of the way I did it," Purnell said. "They were out of school that weekend, and before I talked to Snow Hill, I posted on social media that I had taken the job. They were upset."

At that time, Washington was a basketball wasteland. The Jaguars hadn't appeared in a Bayside Championship or a state final four since the 1970s.

Their state championship victory in 1975 seemed like eons ago. As the decades went on, the Jaguars just got kicked around by Crisfield, Pocomoke and Snow Hill, and their best players often transferred away.

Shortly after Purnell was hired, he would go to Washington during after-school hours. Basketball practice hadn't formally started yet, but the kids who would be on his team would go into the gym and play ball. Purnell would just sit back and watch. After watching one pick-up session, Purnell called his brother and told him, "You won't believe the hidden treasure I just walked into." In his mind, Purnell began mapping out the system he would play, where the players would be positioned and how they would attack.

"I knew if I could get the kids to play the way I wanted, we could do something special," Purnell said.

When Purnell was hired at Washington, he wanted to do three things: One, he wanted to change the basketball culture there. Two, he wanted to get the most out of his players and he wanted them to be disciplined. And three, he wanted to win.

Oh, and there was a fourth objective too: He wanted to beat Snow Hill, and he wanted to beat them badly.

"I was just an angry man. If you look at some of the scores between us and Snow Hill, it was me lashing out at the administration, at the athletic director and a couple of teachers – because I had heard what they said. And their actions kind of backed up what I heard they said," Purnell says. "So, I had said, when I play Snow Hill – if I'm up 20, I'm going for 40. And if I'm up 40, I'm going for 60. It wasn't against the kids; it was against the adults. And that's what built that Snow Hill vs. Washington rivalry."

Washington played Snow Hill early on that season and the Jaguars won, 73-62. Purnell didn't get the chance to run the score up because he was still learning his players and they were still learning him. But in their second meeting, on Jan. 17, 2013 in Snow Hill, Washington won 72-49 as the Jaguars smothered the Eagles.

In his four seasons as the head coach of Washington, Purnell's teams faced Snow Hill 10 times and went 9-1 – eight regular season meetings and twice in the playoffs. Across those nine victories, Washington won by an average margin of 32.7 points. Three times, Purnell's squads blew the Eagles out by more than 40 points.

For Purnell, it was extremely personal.

"When I was beating Snow Hill, I saw three faces," Purnell says. "When I went up 20, I saw Brenda Jones' face. When I went up 40, I saw (athletic director) Todd Lampman's face. When I went up 60, I saw (principal) Tom Davis' face. And I was like, 'How you like me now?'

"I sent the message. I really did."

That second win over Snow Hill was Washington's fourth straight after the Christmas break in the 2012-13 season. At first, as the players adjusted to Purnell and he adjusted to them, Washington started the season out 3-3, dropping contests to Kent Island, Parkside and Bennett. But the turning point for the Jaguars was at the Governor's Challenge, the annual holiday tournament in Salisbury. There, Purnell was able to experiment with different press defenses and a quicker offense. The trials were successful; Washington clicked and played efficient basketball in a pair of wins over Woodbridge and Seaford at the Wicomico Youth & Civic Center.

After December, Washington lost just two games for the rest of the regular season, both defeats coming at the hands of Butch Waller's Wi-Hi Indians. Wi-Hi had a talented team that year too, led by Thomas Brown, Rashaan Handy, Nelson Brown, Derrick Hayward and Larry Ennis. Wi-Hi was a buzzer-beater away from winning the 2A state title in 2013. "I always measured myself against Butch," Purnell said.

If Wi-Hi was the best team in the Bayside South that season, Washington was certainly the second best. They proved as much on Jan. 24, when they went into James M. Bennett and came out with a victory. The Clippers were very talented that season, strapped with two Division I guards in Kory Holden and Jorden Duffy, but the Jaguars – with zero starters on their squad who would go on to play college basketball – went in and beat Bennett 80-73 to improve to 11-4.

"When we flipped that gym, just like Biden flipped Pennsylvania, it became our home gym," Purnell said. "I'll never forget it. Those guys rallied around one another."

The leaders for Washington that season were Gavaughn Trower, pint-sized brothers Jemir and Marc Jones, Mike Ballard and Shakur Cottman. Trower was a football player, and an undersized forward, but he was versatile, skilled and hardnosed. Cottman had a fearlessness to him and supreme athleticism. Jemir Jones was intelligent and more of a finesse player, while Marc was ultra-aggressive. And Ballard, like the rest of the Jaguars, didn't back down from anyone.

Washington continued to take teams by surprise through February and ended the regular season with an 18-5 record and the No. 2 seed in the 1A East Region playoffs. After discarding St. Michaels and Colonel Richardson, the Jaguars found themselves on a bus heading toward Worton to face Kent County, the northernmost Bayside Conference team.

"That was a long ride," Purnell said, and indeed, Princess Anne to Worton is 108 miles. "It was brutal because your nerves are going, and you just want to get there and play."

When Washington was warming up in Kent County's gym, Purnell heard a few Trojan fans chirping, "They're too small! They can't hang with us! Too small!" Purnell just smirked and shook his head. Despite Kent's size and homecourt advantage, he was confident.

"I've always had this thing in the Bayside, when it comes to the South vs. the North. When it comes to football, the North crushes us. But when it comes to basketball, we crush them. When it comes to basketball – look at who the North plays," Purnell said. "You got St. Michaels twice, you play North Dorchester twice... They're not playing the Wi-Hi's, the Bennett's, the Pocomoke's on a nightly basis. So, I felt we were battle-tested.

"And not to take anything away from (Kent County's Sobaye Scott), but I said to myself, he can't out-coach me."

Sobaye Scott coached Kent County's boys team to its first state final four appearance in 2017. Photo by Mitchell Northam.

At the Jaguars' practice before the regional final, Purnell told his players: "We're going into their house. They're bigger than us. They're going to punch you square in your mouth. Are you going to lay down, or are you going to get up?"

And indeed, Kent County threw a big first punch at Washington, going up 19-6 after the opening tip. During a timeout, Purnell reiterated the message. And then the Jaguars broke off an 8-0 run and kept chipping away at the Trojans. In the second half, the major change in the Jaguars was their defense. Purnell deployed a mix of man-to-man and a 2-3 zone and held Kent's leading scorer MJ Montgomery to just six second-half points. Additionally, Washington guarded the perimeter extremely well, holding Kent to 1-of-14 from three-point land.

On the other end, Kent played man-to-man, but Washington was faster. With Kent trailing on defense, Purnell found one particular play that worked over and over again, often ending with an easy lay-up for Cottman or Trower. The set-up involved a simple screen, and the man setting would delay – allowing his defender to drift away – before cutting to the basket.

Trower carried the load with 30 points and 13 rebounds for Washington. Cottman, who was in foul trouble early and made just two shots in the first half, wound up finishing with 22 points for his third straight playoff game with at least 20 markers. Washington pulled away late and punched its ticket to College Park with an 83-71 win.

The Washington fans that made the trip – the ones who had waited 38 years to go back to the state final four – stormed the court in Worton and danced all over it. Cottman jumped on Purnell's back as they paraded around after the win. Snow Hill didn't believe in Purnell, and nobody believed in these Jaguars. Together, they made history.

"Trower put us on his back and played the game of his life," Purnell said. "I think that the town was so appreciative of the banner going up. But at the same time, I caught a lot of backlash because of the way I was demanding respect, discipline and certain things... Winning solves everything."

David Insley of the Star Democrat asked Purnell after the game, "What were you doing in 1975?" Purnell chuckled. "Watching cartoons." He was just three years old the last time the Jaguars went to states.

Unfortunately, Washington's party did not continue inside the Comcast Center at the University of Maryland. The Jaguars, riding high on their performance on the Eastern Shore, ran into the buzzsaw of all buzzsaws: Dunbar. And in 2013, the Poets were simply bigger, faster, stronger and more talented. The Poets suffocated the Jaguars defensively, forcing Washington into 20 turnovers and holding Cottman, Trower and co. to just two assists. Two players on Dunbar's roster went on to play big-time Division I college basketball: Kamau Stokes at Kansas State and Daxter Miles at West Virginia. 10 different Dunbar players scored as the Poets won 70-41, ending the Jaguars' storybook season.

Days later, Purnell was sitting at a Bayside South coaches meeting. Each year, between the final playoff loss for a South team and the Bayside Senior All-Star Game, the coaches gather to hammer out and vote on the First Team, Player of the Year and Coach of the Year awards.

Derrick Fooks tallied up the votes as Purnell sat beside him. Fooks leaned over and said, "Nick, it looks like you're going to be Coach of the Year." Purnell quickly collected himself and found a way out of Wicomico High School, where the all-star game was held that year. When he got outside, he broke down and cried. Then he called his brother.

Out of nine, Purnell received six votes for Coach of the Year. He voted for Bennett's Dean Sullivan. Two other teams – one of which was Snow Hill – didn't vote for Purnell.

"It really means something that your peers can see it," Purnell said. "But then to look at my alma mater who couldn't see it – that stuck with me."

Under Purnell, Washington was consistently a competitive team in the Bayside Conference. The Jaguars got tough draws in the Governor's Challenge, but always represented the Eastern Shore well. Purnell's teams went 5-3 in the annual holiday tournament, pulling off upsets over much larger schools, like Mervo and Randallstown.

After the 2015-16 season, Purnell was once again bitten by the politics of high school sports. In the fall of 2016, Washington High School implemented a new rule and didn't tell Purnell about it: It wanted all of its coaches to also work within the Somerset County school system. Purnell wasn't a guidance counselor or a teacher though. He worked full-time at the Worcester County Developmental Center as a job coach.

The other thing was, Washington had a new athletic director in Danny Lamb. Lamb, who played his high school ball at Mardela and Delmar, had coached the girls team at Washington, but also coached the Jones brothers, Cottman and others in AAU ball.

"I did not resign. Danny Lamb wanted the job, he pulled his power, he had gotten the AD job, and they came up with a thing where they wanted coaches to be in the building. That was it," Purnell says "I didn't even hear it from the school. They didn't have the audacity to tell me. I had to call the principal and ask, 'Am I being replaced?' He said they sent me a letter in the mail. And then he said, 'Well, there's someone in the building who wants the position.'

"They forced me out. They cut me. Danny Lamb wanted what I had."

Less than 10 days after news broke of Purnell being ousted, Lamb was named the boys head coach at Washington. He had been athletic director at the school for less than two months. Of the rule change – having coaches work full-time within the school system – Lamb said at the time: "It is something that most counties are doing. I think it's great to have your coaches in the building to monitor their athletes every day."

In a lot of ways, Purnell coached like Allen Miller. He was enthusiastic and demonstrative on the sidelines, jumping around, calling out to his players and getting advice from his father who often sat behind the Washington bench. Purnell knew his x's and o's, but he was a motivator too, and he could get his players to run through a brick wall for him. He was never afraid to call out an official or switch up his team's playing style on the fly. And Purnell won, a lot. In four seasons at Washington, Purnell was 70-35 – a 66.7% winning percentage. One of his players landed a Division I scholarship as Montraz Oliver – one of the few opposing players to ever score more than

40 points at Wi-Hi – landed down the road in Princess Anne at the University of Maryland Eastern Shore.

After graduating from Washington, Montraz Oliver went to play for the University of Maryland Eastern Shore. He appeared in 43 games for the Hawks, and was coached by Ace Custis from the Eastern Shore of Virginia. Photo by Mitchell Northam.

And as the years went on, Purnell wasn't so bitter over the Snow Hill situation. In the 2017 playoffs, he was the Eagles' biggest cheerleader, clapping and leading chants during the Eagles' regional semifinal matchup with Pocomoke.

"Over time, the anger started to ease. The Lord started to work on me," said Purnell, who has since channeled the energy he used in coaching toward his grandson. "I think the coaching ship has somewhat sailed, simply because of the politics of it all. It's not what you know, it's who you know. And you have to change the way you do things. If I have to change my style, I can't do it. I am who I am. I can't change it. I'm loud, I got the towel draped over me… If I can't do that, I'm not me."

The first season that Purnell coached at Washington, his brother-in-law got him a gift that Christmas: two towels with "COACH PURNELL" monogrammed on them. Purnell would wear them over his shoulder and they became a trademark of his, akin to Big John Thompson's style at Georgetown, who Purnell's father was a huge admirer of. As of this writing, those towels hang in Purnell's man cave inside his home, just waiting to be dusted off and draped on his shoulders again.

If Nick Purnell ever returns to the sidelines of the Bayside Conference, those towels will too.

POCOMOKE FLOW

"We relied on Tyler to set the tone. We trusted him. It was his team. He was the smallest guy, but he had the biggest heart."
– Anky Tull

Before the 2002-03 season started, David Byrd had decided that it would be his last as a head coach at Pocomoke. It wasn't that he was tired of coaching or sick of basketball. He just simply had too much on his plate. In addition to guiding the boys hoops team at his alma mater, Byrd had also been the school's athletic director since 1981 – a position he still holds as of spring 2021. And along the way, he served in leadership roles in the Bayside Conference and in the Maryland Public Secondary Schools Athletic Association. He had tenures as president in both organizations.

"I was doing a lot of administrative stuff. And I enjoyed it. I met a lot of people and went on a lot of trips out of that, going everywhere around the state," Byrd said. "But I figured I couldn't do justice to that and coach basketball. There were times where my teams hurt a little bit because I was running the region tournaments and the Bayside Championships. There's a lot involved in that.

"It was a good time to stop. I pretty much went out on top, I thought."

Retiring after a three-season run that included a state championship, a co-Bayside title and a 72-6 record is pretty close to going out on top. Plus, Byrd's son Spencer was also graduating in 2003. He didn't have any more of his own kids to coach. The other luxury Byrd had was that he knew the program would be in good hands with his successor, a man he'd known since the mid-70's, when Byrd was a teacher at Berlin Middle School and Derrick Fooks was a student there.

A 1983 graduate of Stephen Decatur High School, Fooks and Byrd rekindled their relationship in 1989 when Fooks walked into his office looking for a student-teaching position. After that stint, he went to Bohemia Manor High School in Chesapeake City for a few years where he taught and coached basketball. And then – just like Byrd did in the 70s after a brief stay at the University of Maryland – Fooks came back to the Shore and back to Worcester County. He's been at Pocomoke ever since.

Fooks already knew a great deal about basketball when he walked back into Pocomoke High School. Before his gig at Bo Manor, he was an assistant coach at his collegiate alma mater, the University of Maryland Eastern Shore, where he also played. Fooks had a growth spurt in college and wound up being a 6-foot-6 forward for the Hawks. In the 1987-88 season, he averaged 5.4 points, 3.5 rebounds, a steal and a block per-game while shooting 42.4% from the floor. But Fooks learned even more about the game by sitting on the bench with Byrd for nearly a decade.

"I'll be honest. He's taught me so much," Fooks said of Byrd. "It started in 1975, in middle school. Who would've thought, this many years later, that we'd still have that connection? I still use his inbounds plays. And they still work."

A true student of the game, when Fooks wasn't coaching the boys or discussing strategy with Byrd, you could find him in Pocomoke's gym with a notepad during the Warriors' girls basketball practices, watching longtime coach Gail Gladding give a masterclass in the game of basketball.

In Year One of the Fooks' era, the cupboard was pretty bare. Eddie Miller, Tony Tull and all of those boys were gone. But the thing that carried over from Byrd's reign was an emphasis on defense. Fooks told the Daily Times for the 2003-04 season preview that the Warriors were going to have a "defensive theme" and "if we stop people, I've got people that can put the ball in the basket." Fooks' first season on the job had its fair share of ups and downs, but the Warriors landed a four-seed in the 1A East playoffs that year and won their first-round game, an 81-52 victory over Washington. Robert Johnson led the way with 16 points and 13 rebounds. In the next round, Pocomoke fell to Cambridge 76-61, and ended the season with a 13-11 record. But this much was clear: Although Pocomoke had a new head coach, the Warriors were still going to be difficult to beat, no matter the year, no matter the roster.

The next season, in 2005, Fooks led the squad to an appearance in the Bayside title game and the state final in just his second year on the job. In the Bayside Championship, the Warriors were beaten by the North Caroline Bulldogs. And at states – yea, you guessed it – Dunbar was there again. Eric Lee's team won 69-56 for the third of what would be four straight titles for the Poets. Fooks guided his teams to the state final four in College Park in 2009, 2011 and 2012 too. And in '09, they lost another Bayside title game to North Caroline. Fooks' teams were good, but a championship was elusive for him.

"Derrick has done a good job down there," Butch Waller said. "He's going to play that 1-2-2 zone and they're going to run you."

***

In the midst of winning boatloads of games and gaining the respect of his peers, Derrick Fooks became known for two things. First, he always had a towel with him on the sideline. Usually blue, he used it to wipe the sweat from his brow and also as a stress ball of sorts. That stress often came from the second thing he was known for: his animated interactions with the referees. As Butch Waller said, "Derrick just spends too much energy arguing with the officials." Former Daily Times photographer Justin Odendhal had a knack for capturing Fooks' sideline reactions and frustrations. One photo shows Fooks pulling the towel down over his head with both hands. In another, he covers his mouth with the towel and it looks like his eyes were about to pop out of his head as he glared at an official.

As the years went on, Fooks wasn't the only coach on the Eastern Shore that had trouble winning the big game. In the late 90s and into the new millennium, teams from the Bayside Conference had great success across the Bay Bridge. From 1996 to 2003, seven boys teams and one girls squad from the Shore won state championships. Entering the 2015-16 season, no team from the Shore had won at states since 2008. Eastern Shore teams were still routinely reaching the state final four, but they were coming home empty-handed.

But there was something different about Pocomoke's squad in the fall of 2015. They were armed with a certain amount of swagger, confidence, determination and motivation. It was apparent during a preseason tune-up scrimmage at North Dorchester. The scoreboard was shut off, but it might've read something like 102-18 in the Warriors' favor had it been lit up. Fooks was chatting with a reporter from the Daily Times as Tyler Nixon stole away an errant North Dorchester pass and fed it up the court to LeAnder Roberts for an effortless dunk. Fooks leaned over and said, "See? I told you. These guys are hungry. This team is going to compete for a state title."

The previous season, Pocomoke lost in the regional final at Joppatowne in overtime. Missed free throws wound up being the recipe for the Warriors' demise – they missed 17 of them and fell short by three points. In the locker room afterwards, Nixon rounded the team up. He vowed that next year, his senior season, would be different. He promised they'd win a state championship. LiCurtis Whitney chimed in too. Pocomoke made it known then, and throughout their 2015-16 campaign, that they wouldn't let an opponent's speed, size or skill get the best of them. And they damn sure wouldn't lose again because of missed free throws. Said Nixon: "I made it personal. We talked about that (Joppatowne) game every day. There's only one expectation: state championship." The bus ride home from Joppatowne that evening was silent, the air full of bitterness. The players didn't even want to stop to eat. They just wanted to get back on the court. "We stopped to eat and guys stayed on the bus," Fooks said. "Tyler Nixon was so mad. It's the quietest bus I've ever been on."

SHORE HOOPS

***

Derrick Fooks had a veteran-laden team entering the 2015-16 season.

The starting lineup was composed of Tyler Nixon, a pint-sized point guard who was maybe 5-foot-6, on a good day with big shoes. But for what he lacked in size he made up for with grit, heart and determination. Nixon was armed with the brains of Will Hunting and the strength of Artis Gilmore, and he was arguably the best defender in the conference that year. For opposing guards, Nixon was like a gnat at a cookout. He was persistent and wouldn't leave them alone. On offense, he was a bit of a wizard with the ball, able to create for himself and others. "And when you stole the ball from him, you might as well look to get hit. He knew how to foul. As little as he was, he was stronger than he looked," Fooks said. "And he was one that wouldn't bite his tongue."

At the other guard position was Tyrone Matthews, who was the youngest starter as a junior. Matthews could score inside and out, and had no backdown in him despite being about 5-foot-7. He was never afraid of the moment, and never met a three-point shot attempt he didn't like. "The kid could play, man. And could play against anybody," Fooks said of Matthews. "He was the next version of an Andre Collins. He could shoot from anywhere. Mid-range, step-out, take you to the hole, knew how to use his body. He had every tool in the box."

Pocomoke's Tyrone Matthews was one of the Bayside's top players in the 2016-17 season. A fearless player, he laid on the floor at Snow Hill briefly after being fouled at the rim. Photo by Mitchell Northam.

LeAnder Roberts often played the four. He was an athletic forward who could run, defend, rebound and finish at the rim in traffic. At times, he was just what the Warriors needed.

And often patrolling the paint was LiCurtis Whitney, who Nixon referred to as Z-Bo after Memphis Grizzlies forward Zach Randolph. Like Randolph, Whitney didn't have much hops or height. He might've been 5-foot-10. But he often played like he was nine inches taller and he had a unique nose for rebounds. Coupled with his unmatched toughness and willingness to do the dirty work, he was difficult to score against. The Pocomoke coaches affectionately and playfully called Whitney, "Fat Man."

"Fat Man could guard anybody," Fooks said.

The other starter on the team was Jerrick Johnson. While the schools in Wicomico County had transfers coming and going off their teams every season, it wasn't often that Pocomoke was gifted with a transfer who was a talented basketball player. But Johnson, coming from Arcadia just over the line in Virginia, was the exception. He was active on both ends of the floor and his length, leaping ability and speed made him an asset on defense. He could score from the arc and inside the paint too.

"We've had a few people come in, but Pocomoke is off the ends of the earth down here. Understand? Nobody is just going to pop up," Byrd said. "Sometimes we get kids from Virginia. Sometimes two or three exchange students, but they're never All-Americans."

Johnson might've not been an All-American or even All-Bayside, but he was good enough and he helped Pocomoke win a lot of games. Additionally, Tyree Thornton and Kwamaine Atkins proved to be valuable players off the bench. The Warriors coasted to a win in their opening game, beating North Caroline in a tip-off event at Chesapeake College. By halftime, they led by 32 points and had forced the Bulldogs into 16 turnovers. Said Matthews: "We get steals, force turnovers and get layups. That's who we are."

"We kind of knew what we had. That group had some of the best athletes around, and they were really close. It reminded me some of my 1976 team," said Anky Tull, an assistant coach under Fooks that season. "Tyler was our everything. He was our quarterback. He was our coach on the floor. We relied on Tyler to set the tone. We trusted him. It was his team. He was the smallest guy, but he had the biggest heart."

By Dec. 21, both Pocomoke and Stephen Decatur were undefeated at 5-0 and the Seahawks came into the Byrd House that night. The Warriors sent them packing with a 72-59 victory. A 9-0 third quarter run proved to be key, and a fourth quarter dunk by Roberts put an exclamation point on the win. "Fat Man made (Keve Aluma) small," Fooks said of Decatur's 6-foot-7 college-bound center.

Pocomoke got its ego checked at the Governor's Challenge, losing both of its games in the holiday tournament to teams that were bigger, faster and stronger. Battlefield, from Virginia, beat them 67-60, and IDEA Charter hung 93 points on the Warriors. "They were grown men," Fooks said of IDEA. "They had to have been 25." Still, Pocomoke continued to roll through the Bayside Conference, until they met Stephen Decatur again. In Berlin on Jan. 26, the Seahawks avenged their defeat earlier in the year and handed the Warriors a 68-47 defeat. To be clear, Decatur was really good this season too. Coached by B.J. Johnson, the Seahawks were powered by 2015 Bayside Player of the Year Torrey Brittingham, who had 12 assists in the win over Pocomoke, and a pair of future Division I college players in Kevon Voyles and Aluma. With Pocomoke being 1A and Decatur being a 3A school, they wouldn't face each other again. But Pocomoke knew it had work to do. Against Decatur, the Warriors shot 12-of-47 from the field. Nixon told Fooks after the loss: "No worries. We needed that. That's motivation. That's getting us ready."

A month later, Pocomoke and Decatur had identical records and the regular season was over. Still, there was a Bayside Championship game to be played. Cambridge won the North's bid outright, but the South's representative would be decided by ... yes, a coin flip. On Feb. 23, Fooks and Johnson – former classmates under Byrd at Berlin Middle – met at the Worcester County Board of Education. Fooks let Johnson call it. "Tails." It was heads. By sheer luck, Pocomoke was back in the Bayside title game.

Pocomoke was supposed to meet Vic Burns' Cambridge team at the Wicomico Youth & Civic Center for the Bayside Championship, but a rare tornado warning for the Eastern Shore pushed the game back a day and forced Bayside Conference leaders to find another venue. They landed on Bennett, the biggest high school gym in Salisbury. The venue or day didn't matter all that much. It was obvious to just about everyone that Pocomoke was going to boat race Cambridge. Despite missing 20 free throws, the Warriors still bested the Vikings, 61-47, for Fooks' first Bayside title and the first for the Pocomoke boys basketball team since 2003. But their charity tripe issues loomed. "We have to get better at free throws," Matthews said after the game.

In the postseason, Pocomoke shifted its focus. It also locked into its defensive strategy. Every game, with a zone press, the Warriors goal was to inflict chaos on the opposing team. Pocomoke thrived in disorder. When the other team was in disarray and trying to think too much, that's when the Warriors raced by them. In the third quarter of a regional semifinal playoff game against Washington, the Warriors created that type of environment with a 14-3 run. And then they cruised to an 80-58 win. "Our defense is a little Helter Skelter," Nixon said. "That's how we like to play. We feed off the crowd and we get after it." Nixon had 14 points, 10 rebounds, seven assists and seven steals.

Pocomoke hosted the region final too, and their opponent was the Kent County Trojans, who had built up a competitive basketball program under Sobaye Scott. In 2016, they were armed with a superb athlete in Marcquan Greene and a future Division I talent in Manny Camper. But Worton to Pocomoke is the farthest trip between two Bayside schools: about 120 miles and about two-and-a-half hours. And the Trojans had to endure that long bus ride – there and back – on March 5, just to get their butts whipped. Pocomoke claimed its 18th regional title, beating Kent County 80-62. The whole time, the crowd chanted: "P-OH, P-OH! UH-OH, UH-OH!" Pocomoke was powered by a 17-4 second quarter run, and Camper was largely neutralized by Jerrick Johnson, a player who matched his size and speed. In the second quarter alone, Johnson blocked Camper's shot twice, stole the ball from him once, boxed him out for three rebounds and held him scoreless. Camper had nine points.

Most times when a basketball team captures a region crown, there is usually a short ceremony where the coaches and players climb up a ladder and take turns at cutting down a net. But on that day at Pocomoke, that didn't happen. Perhaps this was because a girls basketball game immediately followed the boys – Gail Gladding's team won a regional that day too – or, maybe it was because the Warriors hadn't seen the net that they wanted to cut down just yet.

At the Xfinity Center in College Park, the Warriors arrived with a bang. In the state semifinals against Clear Spring, they kicked in the door and broke off a 20-2 first quarter run, then started the second quarter with a 17-4 spark. The 86-65 victory was Fooks' 245th of his career and put him in his third state final game. The Warriors stole the ball from Clear Spring 19 times and forced them into a total of 31 turnovers. Nixon had nine of those steals, and 31 points. Clear Spring was armed with a pair of future Division I athletes who stood over 6-foot-5, but it just didn't matter. "It's very hard to simulate what Pocomoke is," Clear Spring head coach John Hutzell said after the game.

"When we're on the gas, we stay on the gas," Fooks said. "In the first half, the game was over."

Pocomoke would meet a Baltimore city team in the state final. This time, it wasn't Dunbar, but Lake Clifton – a team with four state titles to its name that had lost in the 1A final a year ago. The game started off feeling like those losses to Dunbar, as Pocomoke trailed by 11 points in the first quarter. But the Warriors didn't quit. Specifically, Nixon didn't quit.

When nothing else in Pocomoke's office was working, the tiny point guard just drove inside and drew foul after foul. His senior season, Nixon shot 57% from the charity stripe, a less-than-ideal mark. But on that day in College Park, he was fantastic, making 18-of-22 free throws. The week leading up to the game, Nixon lived at the free throw line, practicing them every day. "Before we would even get to practice, Tyler was in there shooting," Fooks said. Nixon wound up with 23 points, six rebounds, three assists and two steals and Pocomoke won, 64-56. In all, the Warriors shot 81% from the free throw line.

"We had a great point guard. That's why we won it" Fooks said. "Tyler Nixon told us at the region final the year before. So, I knew we were going to come back if we kept everyone healthy. Just from what he said in the locker room that night in Joppatowne. Tyler was that guy."

Matthews, who was sick the night before and was nursed by the coaches, was exceptional too in the final, scoring 14 points and going 10-for-10 from the free throw line.

One of the key moments of the game happened in the fourth quarter, when Lake Clifton was trying to stop Pocomoke's run. With the Lakers leading by a single point, their sophomore center Ronald Lucas attempted a two-handed dunk, but missed and hung on the rim. The refs gave him a technical foul, which was also his fifth personal, fouling him out. With a bit more than four minutes left, the Lakers were without their tallest player. Fooks called for more pressure on defense, and Pocomoke created chaos, leaving Lake Clifton's offense messier than a teenager's bedroom. In all, Lake Clifton committed 20 turnovers and 28 fouls. And despite facing a massive size disadvantage, Pocomoke won the rebounding battle 41-38. Roberts had 14 of those.

Derrick Fooks succeeded David Byrd as Pocomoke's head boys basketball coach in 2003 and led the Warriors to a state title in 2016. From the collection of Justin Odendhal.

"We saw them rattled then," Fooks said. "We saw them shake just a little bit, so we thought we'd shake them just a little bit more, so that's when we put our foot down."

Said LiCurtis Whitney: "Basically, we just got into the Pocomoke flow. Everybody got on defense, we started rotating right, making smart passes and easy buckets. The game was won."

The fans behind the Pocomoke bench started erupting when the game seemed out of reach for Lake Clifton. Fooks, clutching that blue towel in his left hand, pumped his fist, then looked up at the ceiling on the brink of tears and pointed toward the sky. When the buzzer sounded, the players mobbed Nixon, piled onto him and danced around him. Fooks, crying at this point, hugged his floor general. He then sat down on the bench and basked in the moment. David Byrd, his mentor, rushed to his side. And just like in 2002, they shared the victory together.

Fooks and Nixon would be named Coach and Player of the Year in the Bayside Conference. One notable thing about their 2016 squad is that no player from the team went on to play college basketball. Truly, they were just a group of determined kids and coaches that did whatever it took to win.

In the fall before the basketball season, Pocomoke also won a state championship in field hockey – their 19th – under the direction of first-year head coach Brandi Castaneda, following the tragic and unexpected death of Susan Pusey, who died in 2015 from complications after a surgery. In April, Maryland Gov. Larry Hogan came to Pocomoke to give the field hockey squad and the boys basketball team governor's citations. Said Nixon: "Wherever we go, people know who we are. And once you win, that's forever. I've never met the governor before, so that was a new experience."

In 2020, Fooks won his 300th game. Since he's won his championship, and as he's grown in age, he's a bit calmer on the sideline too. During a game that season, a referee came up to him mid-game and asked, "Are you okay? You're not standing, you're not walking, you're not yelling."

As of the spring of 2021, Fooks' 2016 team is the only Bayside Conference squad – girls or boys – that has won a state championship in basketball since 2008. "Remember," Fooks says. "The last team to win the state championship for the Eastern Shore resides down here, in little ole Pocomoke."

"On the Eastern Shore, when you talk about basketball, the same teams sort of keep popping up," Warriors Athletic Director David Byrd added.

Indeed. Year in and year out, Pocomoke keeps popping up. And as long as there is a Byrd, Fooks or Tull on the sideline, the Warriors will be in the hunt. Because of them, the town of less than 5,000 people wedged up against the Virginia border is a crucial part of basketball culture and history, not just on the Eastern Shore, but in the state of Maryland.

KEVE ALUMA:
FROM THE SOCCER PITCH TO BLACKSBURG

"I'm definitely proud to be one of the guys representing the Shore." – Keve Aluma

By the late 1980s, Stephen Decatur High School began to encapsulate a student body that lived everywhere from oceanfront condos to cornfields. The school kept growing over the decades that followed. As of this writing, it's the largest high school on the Eastern Shore, with an enrollment size over 1,000 students.

Between the beach and the farms was one tall boy with bushy hair who grew up loving soccer in the quaint town of Berlin. His name is Oghenekeve Aluma. Everyone shortens his first name though, calling him Keve.

He didn't know it then, when he entered Stephen Decatur as a wide-eyed freshman in the fall of 2013, but Aluma would turn into a stellar high school basketball player, a star on the Eastern Shore, and then someone who would go on to play in multiple NCAA Tournaments, and eventually become a legitimate NBA prospect.

After a hiatus from coaching in the Bayside Conference, Byron "B.J." Johnson returned to his alma mater to be the head coach once again of the boys team at Stephen Decatur at the beginning of the 2013-14 school year. That fall, Johnson stood in the cafeteria as eager freshmen signed up for winter sports tryouts. Boys flocked to the paper hanging on the wall for the basketball team. When Aluma walked in, Johnson couldn't help but stare. As a freshman, he was already 6-foot-4 and had plenty of room to grow. Johnson was certain that this kid was going to jot his name down on the sheet for JV basketball. But Aluma kept walking, leaving Johnson bewildered and perplexed. Johnson approached a group of kids and asked them, "Who was that?"

"Oh," they said. "That's Keve. He doesn't play basketball. He's a soccer player."

Aluma was outstanding on the pitch too. He had played throughout his youth beginning at the age of four, so, despite his large frame, he had the agility, quickness, stamina and IQ to keep up with players that were smaller and faster than he was. He often played centerback, but because of his height, he was also a target on set pieces. Few opposing players could out-jump him. As a sophomore at Decatur, he was the Defensive MVP for the boys soccer team.

"But nobody took me seriously as a soccer player," Aluma once told the Virginian Pilot. "They said I was too tall."

The hardwood was one place where Aluma's size would be respected, but he had zero interest in playing basketball. Aluma had never played the sport competitively before in an organized team environment. Soccer was his thing, even if his biological father was an NBA player.

A native of Lagos, Nigeria, Peter Aluma was a 6-foot-10 star on the court for Liberty University, the private super-evangelical Christian school in Lynchburg, Virginia. In the 1990s, Aluma was twice an All-Big South First Team selection, a two-time Big South Tournament MVP, and led the Flames to their first NCAA Tournament appearance in 1994. When Aluma left Liberty, he had scored more than 1,700 points and owned the program records for blocked shots and free throw attempts. He is still the Big South's all-time leader in blocks with 366. Aluma played briefly with the Sacramento Kings and the Phoenix Suns and also spent a year with the Harlem Globetrotters. A member of Liberty's Athletics Hall of Fame, Peter Aluma died on Feb. 2, 2020 at the age of 46.

Peter Aluma was not a big part of his son's life. Keve was raised in Berlin by his mother and his stepfather, Bruce Copeland. So, while Keve had his father's genes, he didn't always have his influence and his passion for basketball. The fall he entered Stephen Decatur, Keve had dreams of being a defender for D.C. United in Major League Soccer – not being the next Aluma to dunk ball through a hoop.

"I didn't want to play basketball," Aluma said. "They told me, with my height, I should at least try… Soccer was all I played, and all that me and my friends played. I played indoor, outdoor, year-round."

Johnson was persistent in his pursuit of the younger Aluma. After some begging and pleading, Aluma finally agreed to come to the gym. Once there, Johnson had one simple request: "I want to see you run and I want to see you jump."

Aluma obliged, running up and down the court with relative ease and without getting winded. This was nothing compared to the sprints he had ran on the soccer field in the Eastern Shore's unbearable humidity. And then Aluma leapt into the air and – with little effort – grabbed the rim with both hands. He was a natural talent, and Johnson had seen enough. He had coached basketball long enough to know what potential looked like. One of Johnson's first coaching gigs was at Snow Hill, on a team that was powered by the great Sherron Mills.

After working Aluma out, Johnson sought out his parents. His message to Aluma's mother and step-father was simple, but carried a big promise. "If this kid is with me for four years," Johnson told them, "he'll go to college for free."

"I don't know if they believed me at first," Johnson told Ricky Pollitt of the Daily Times in 2020. "It was in his DNA... We made sure to surround him with great people and try to guide him. He put in the work."

After making the NCAA Tournament with Wofford, Keve Aluma followed his coach, Mike Young, and transferred to Virginia Tech. Photo by Mitchell Northam.

***

During the winter of the 2013-14 school year, Keve Aluma found himself on the JV basketball team at Decatur, learning the basics of the game from former Wi-Hi point guard Bubby Brown, then the head JV coach at Decatur. Aluma knew how to run and jump – which is sometimes all you need to be a decent player – but that JV season he learned basketball terminology, he began to understand defensive assignments, how to set screens and how to box out on rebounds. The next season, he was thrown into the fire as a sophomore on varsity. In his varsity debut on Dec. 5, 2014, Aluma tallied nine points and a team-high 14 rebounds in a 55-27 victory over North Caroline. He finished the season with an All-Bayside honorable mention nod.

"That's the first time I practiced basketball and was on a team," Aluma said.

In Aluma's junior season, there was a ton of hype around Decatur. By then, Aluma had grown to about 6-foot-7 and he was expected to put up better numbers on the court. In addition to Aluma, the Seahawks also had athletic wings in Keyon Eley and Kevon Voyles, a tough guard in Darion McKenzie and a hardnosed forward in Ja'Quan Johnson. And at the point, they had Torrey Brittingham, the reigning Bayside Player of the Year who transferred back to Stephen Decatur after spending his junior season at Wi-Hi, in which he led the Indians to a Bayside Championship and a state final four appearance. Brittingham was short and slender, but had a real feel for the game and superb court vision. He wasn't afraid of contact inside, he could hit an open three-pointer and he knew just where to loft the ball up for Aluma to slam it home on alley-oops.

"Torrey was an outstanding point guard who had a clock in his head," said Jeff Levan, an assistant coach under Johnson for those Decatur teams. "I don't think I ever coached a kid who had a better sense of time and score."

Decatur started the 2015-16 season with a 5-0 record, and then ran into a Pocomoke team that was much smaller than the Seahawks. But on Dec. 21, that didn't matter. The Warriors – led by Tyler Nixon – had no backdown in them. They were fast, tenacious, gritty and resilient, and they weren't scared of Aluma or Brittingham. Decatur left the Byrd House that evening with a 72-59 defeat in front of a sellout crowd and an audience that watched the game via livestream on the Daily Times' website. Aluma was held to 10 points and nine boards, even though he was five inches taller than the tallest Pocomoke player. "Size was overrated tonight," Johnson said after the game. Indeed, that night, Pocomoke just wanted it more.

The Seahawks got back on track in the Governor's Challenge, beating a team from Virginia's Battlefield High School 64-59 behind Aluma's 14 points and 19 boards. And then in late January, Decatur got its revenge on Pocomoke, topping the Warriors 68-47 in Berlin. Aluma used his size this time around, scoring 12 points and grabbing 21 boards, while Brittingham tallied nine points and 12 assists.

When the regular season ended, Pocomoke and Decatur had identical records in conference play and split their season series. So, the South representative in the Bayside Championship was decided by a coin flip. Pocomoke won and easily discarded Cambridge-South Dorchester for the conference crown. Decatur, motivated to prove itself, set its sights on the 3A East playoffs. In the first round, the Seahawks spanked Northeast 93-54 behind 20 points from Brittingham. Next up was Hammond, and Decatur prevailed 70-68 in overtime. In the 3A East Regional Final, Decatur hosted Centennial and would not be deterred at home, winning 65-47 behind 15 points from Brittingham and 12 from Aluma to punch the Seahawks' ticket to College Park.

At the Xfinity Center, Brittingham stepped up – big-time – in the semifinals. The point guard stuffed the box score with 33 points, five assists and four rebounds in a 66-61 win over the Seneca Valley Screaming Eagles. Brittingham was the only Seahawk to score in double-digits and he also notched his 1,000th career point that evening on the campus of the University of Maryland. Aluma had nine points, nine boards and five blocks – and a game-defining two-handed dunk in the third quarter that shook the 2002 National Championship banner in the rafters. He and Brittingham's consistent play all season long had powered the Seahawks to their first state final appearance since 1971.

Decatur faced C.M. Wright, a team from Bel Air, in the 3A state final in 2016. And things did not go the way the Seahawks scripted it. Aluma rolled his ankle in the fourth quarter and was sidelined when the game turned to overtime. With the game tied and about 30 ticks remaining on the clock near the end of the first extra period of play, Brittingham had possession of the ball and dribbled it in front of himself as Wright's Chris Lorenzo guarded him closely.

After coaching his Pocomoke team to the 1A state title just hours before, Derrick Fooks stuck around to watch Decatur. He knew what was about to happen as the clock ticked away.

"That defender had watched Torrey do that move the whole game," Fooks said. "I could see him saying, 'Oh, he's going to do it again, right in front of me.' And boom."

Lorenzo closed in on Brittingham at the exact moment he went to crossover. Lorenzo stripped him of the ball, clean, and raced to the other end of the court for a lay-up while avoiding being chased down by Darion McKenzie. Five seconds remained, and Decatur's final shot attempt was off the mark. Wright had won, 51-49. Brittingham hung his head in defeat. B.J. Johnson said after the game that Lorenzo "just made a lucky and great play. We put the ball in the hands of our best player and if I did it all over again, we would've put the ball right back in his hands."

Said Levan: "We'll never get that one back. It was a shame."

***

Torrey Brittingham and Keve Aluma both made the All-Bayside First Team and the DMVelite All-Maryland team. And that summer, Aluma's potential started to become tangible. He joined the Uncommon Bulls, an AAU team that played in the D.C. circuit and in showcases nationwide. By May, he received his first two college scholarship offers: Stony Brook and nearby University of Maryland Eastern Shore.

Interest in Aluma built from there. Robert Morris, NJIT, James Madison, Army and his father's alma mater, Liberty, all made contact with Aluma. Then Howard, Coppin State and Canisus offered, then UTEP and Loyola-Maryland. Most of the college interest came during and after a tournament Aluma played at in Las Vegas.

"That's when I kind of realized that this was the route for me," Aluma said of that summer.

In September of 2016, Wofford's Mike Young – wearing a dark suit – was one of just four Division I coaches who accepted B.J. Johnson's invitation to come watch Aluma work out in Stephen Decatur's gym. Just a few months earlier, that same gymnasium was transformed into a circus as then-presidential candidate Donald Trump held a rally there, sending Worcester County into a MAGA-hat-wearing frenzy. Unfortunately, Aluma's day holding court in the gym was not as well attended. Aside from Young, the only other coaches in the building were Keith Booth – the former Terp who was then an assistant at Loyola-Maryland – and representatives from UMass Lowell and nearby Maryland Eastern Shore.

"I begged Towson to recruit him," Levan said. "And where was Delaware? They didn't give him the time of day."

While Aluma had piled up 10 Division I offers, none were from Power 5 programs and he was still a relatively obscure prospect. He was so unknown that his profile page on the scouting site 247sports didn't feature a photo of him. He was a zero-star recruit. As Winston-Salem Journal reporter Ethan Joyce noted, it would've been easy to call Aluma, "No Name Keve."

But Young – who had been at Wofford since 1989 as an assistant and then as the head coach – did not care about ratings and opinions on websites. He had seen Aluma up-close. And that was enough.

"I think we get too hung up on numbers," Young said. "We get too hung up on four-star and all of this stuff – I don't care about that stuff. I could care less. Can he catch? Can he pass? Can he shoot the basketball? Is he tough? … It'll always be an inexact science."

For Young, Aluma checked all of the boxes, and he offered the kid from Berlin a scholarship and then booked him for an official visit. Less than two weeks later, Aluma was in Spartanburg, South Carolina, touring Wofford College, the private liberal arts school founded in 1854 that carried an enrollment size of less than 2,000 undergraduates. Aluma committed on the spot, sending out a tweet and Instagram post on Sept. 24 announcing that he'd be taking his talents to upstate South Carolina.

"Originally, I had committed there because I thought I would be able to redshirt, get in better shape and learn the game better before I started playing college ball," Aluma said of Wofford. "That was a big part of it. And then there was that family atmosphere, and my family loved Coach Young."

With a scholarship secured – just like Johnson had promised his family – Aluma skipped his senior season of high school soccer to avoid the risk of an injury.

In his final year of high school basketball, Aluma and the Seahawks steamrolled through the regular season. There wasn't a single team in the Bayside Conference that could keep up with the trio of Aluma, Voyles and Parkside transfer Gary Briddell, who had averaged 16.7 points and 9.5 rebounds per-game as a junior for the Rams. Even mighty Pocomoke was no match for Decatur in the 2016-17 season, as the Seahawks blasted them 89-57 on Dec. 21 behind 48 combined points from Aluma and Briddell. The Seahawks even went into Crisfield's "Graveyard" and beat the Crabbers by 25 points.

Kent County's Manny Camper and Stephen Decatur's Keve Aluma clashed in the 2017 Bayside Championship in Cambridge. Both players went on to excel at the Division I level. Photo by Mitchell Northam.

From Cape Charles to Dover, it was apparent early on in the season that the Seahawks were the best basketball team around, and one-on-one, there wasn't a player on the Delmarva Peninsula who could guard Aluma, whose confidence, skill and swagger began to noticeably grow and show. In one of the final regular season games that year, Decatur went north to Worton to play Kent County, and Aluma went head-to-head with another Division I prospect in Manny Camper, who had committed to Siena. Aluma finished with 30 points while Camper had 28 as the Seahawks won by three. Decatur went undefeated in Bayside play, their only regular season loss coming against an out-of-town side in the Governor's Challenge.

A few weeks after beating Kent County in Worton, Decatur faced them again in Cambridge for the Bayside Conference Championship. The Trojans weren't up to the challenge. In the waning moments of the game, Aluma was laughing and launching three-pointers with the game well in-hand. The big man had 17 points, 12 rebounds and six blocks in front of a sold-out crowd in a 71-43 victory for Decatur, capturing the school's first Bayside title in boys basketball. Camper got hurt in the game, and when the Seahawks flipped to a 2-3 zone, they smothered the Trojans in Cambridge's gym. Three years prior, Aluma had been sitting on Decatur's bench as a freshman when they played for the Bayside crown in 2014 at the Wicomico Youth and Civic Center. The Seahawks were ahead by three with 0.7 seconds to play when Easton's Tay'Von Emory hit a half-court miracle buzzer beater to push the game into overtime, and Easton eventually triumphed. So, beating Kent for a trophy was the culmination of so many things for the Seahawks: Johnson had brought his alma mater a banner, Aluma had begun to realize his potential, and the demons of the 2014 title game had been exorcised. Decatur's win over Kent was the most-lopsided conference championship result in the Bayside since 2002, when Bubby Brown's Wi-Hi team beat Cambridge 104-60 in Salisbury.

Then an assistant for Stephen Decatur, Bubby Brown talks with Keve Aluma during a timeout in the 2017 3A state semifinals in College Park. Photo by Mitchell Northam.

Brown remained an assistant coach at Decatur that season and for a few years that followed. In 2020, he was hired as the head coach at James M. Bennett. Aluma still credits Bubby for his development from a soft-spoken soccer player into a Division I basketball talent.

"I think Bubby was a big part of me continuing basketball. Because I didn't necessarily like it and I didn't really understand it. Bubby was able to coach me up, keep me going and keep my spirits up," Aluma said. "Certain people just know how to make men and build confidence, and Bubby knows how to do those things. Having him being able to support me, that was big.

I owe him a lot for being in the position where I'm at now."

Unfortunately, Aluma's high school career would end in tears of disappointment, not joy. He powered Decatur back to the state final four, but the Seahawks ran into the Baltimore Polytechnic Institute. And Poly was simply bigger, faster, deeper and more skilled on March 9 in College Park, beating the Seahawks 74-44 behind Temple-commit De'Vondre Perry's 33 points, nine rebounds, four assists and three blocks.

"We had no business playing Poly," Levan said. "They were just too good. They were the equivalent of what Dunbar used to be."

Aluma, who was named Bayside Player of the Year, closed the book on his time at Decatur with a 19-point, 11-rebound effort against Poly. He buried his head in his jersey as the seconds ran out at the Xfinity Center and took blame for the loss after the game saying, "They just kind of suffocated me."

Over his time in college, Aluma would take the necessary steps to make sure that never happened to him again on a basketball court.

***

When Keve Aluma got to Wofford, he figured he would redshirt as a freshman, sit out a year and then begin his college career in earnest the following season. After all, he had only been playing organized team basketball for four years. In fact, the way Mike Young remembers it, Aluma's mother Bethany "insisted on" him redshirting.

But Young and the coaching staff at Wofford thought that he could help the team out right away. Young phoned Bethany back in Berlin to inform her that, "Sorry, your son has to play right away." So, as a freshman, Aluma became part of the Terriers' rotation, seeing the floor an average of 13.3 minutes per-game.

"I had to kind of roll with it and learn on the fly. But I did similar things to what I was doing in high school," Aluma said. "So, I was crashing the offensive glass, setting screens and playing defense. I was already doing those things at Decatur."

Aluma – who had grown to 6-foot-9 by the fall of 2017 – made his collegiate debut on Nov. 10, 2017 at home against South Carolina, the first basketball game the Terriers played at the sparkling new Jerry Richardson Indoor Stadium – a 3,400-seat facility paid for and named after Richardson, a Wofford graduate who owned the NFL's Carolina Panthers from 1995 through 2017. Aluma played 10 minutes and grabbed a rebound. On the opposite sideline, making his debut for the South Carolina Gamecocks was James M. Bennett product Kory Holden, who landed on Frank Martin's team after leaving Delaware. Holden had two points and two assists in eight minutes. He'd leave South Carolina before the season's end and finish his college career at South Alabama.

After the game, Young doubled-down on his commitment to Aluma's development, saying: "We are big fans of that young man and are thrilled that he's with us… He hasn't played a lot of basketball. He's got big eyes and he wants to learn. He works very hard. He's got great hands and the guy can catch anything. He is going to be a really, really good post player around here and it's going to come sooner rather than later."

Indeed, Young soon found out if Aluma could sink or swim in Division I college basketball. Aluma played 26 minutes against Texas Tech, tallying six points and three boards. Shortly after the new year, he racked up six points, two steals, an assist and seven rebounds in a win over The Citadel. Aluma proved to be a valuable asset off the bench in the frontcourt as someone who excelled at setting screens for shooters like Fletcher Magee, grabbing misses off the offensive glass and defending in the post. Wofford finished the season with a 21-12 record and an 11-7 mark in SoCon play. They went to the CIT tournament, and Aluma had three points and six rebounds in a loss to Central Michigan. The Decatur product finished the year averaging 2.5 points and 3.4 rebounds per-game.

That offseason, Aluma worked out often with Wofford veterans Cam Jackson and Matthew Pegram. "Those guys really helped me," Aluma said. And when his sophomore campaign tipped-off, Aluma was the starting center. The Terriers started the 2018-19 season with a 4-2 record, and then they went into Columbia and beat South Carolina with Aluma piling up 10 points, eight rebounds and an assist. The growth that he made was clear. The former soccer player had slimmed down a bit, added a bit of muscle and wasn't intimidated by anyone. A few weeks later, in a victory over Samford, he had his first collegiate double-double with 12 points, 12 boards, three steals, a block and an assist.

Wofford wasn't just SoCon-good in the 2018-19 season; they quickly turned into one of the best teams in college basketball. After a loss to Mississippi State on Dec. 19, the Terriers didn't lose another regular season game. By Feb. 25 – after a win over Furman in which Aluma had 11 points, seven rebounds and three blocks – they were ranked in the AP Top 25 poll. Wofford won the SoCon's regular season and tournament titles, and landed a No. 7 seed in the NCAA Tournament.

In the opening round, Wofford pulled off an 84-68 win over Seton Hall of the Big East, a victory in which Aluma contributed eight points, four rebounds, two assists and two blocks. Aluma was the first from a Bayside South school to play in an NCAA Tournament since Wi-Hi's Craig Winder featured for Texas in the Big Dance in 2007.

Next up for Wofford was No. 2 Kentucky. Coached by the slick John Calipari, the Wildcats that season were armed with eight players who would wind up getting minutes in the NBA, and they had four players who were 6-foot-9 or taller. In its preview of the game, the Lexington Herald-Leader gave Kentucky the advantage at the center position.

But dammit, Aluma gave the boys in blue all they could handle. He had 11 rebounds – tying Kentucky's Reid Travis for the game-high – to go along with seven points and a block. Aluma kept Wofford's chances of an upset alive with 37.9 seconds left, following up Storm Murphy's missed lay-up with a tip-in that cut the Kentucky deficit to two points. The Wildcats padded their lead at the foul line and Magee missed a three-pointer late that sealed the game. Wofford lost 62-56, but Aluma felt like he had arrived.

"Everyone wants to play well on the biggest stage in the tournament, so being able to do that was definitely a confidence booster," Aluma said. "I remember (the Kentucky game) as – I could've had a double-double. I wasn't really taking a ton of shots. I definitely look back at that as a game that was big for my confidence."

***

Mike Young talks to reporters at the 2021 ACC Tip-Off in Charlotte. He was named ACC Coach of the Year in 2021, and was one of the few to recruit Keve Aluma. Photo by Mitchell Northam.

Mike Young had been an assistant coach at Wofford from 1989 to 2002, and then the head coach for 17 seasons. At the conclusion of the 2019 NCAA Tournament – his fifth time leading the Terriers to the Big Dance – he had spent three decades in Spartanburg, South Carolina coaching college basketball. His stock was high, but few expected him – then 56 years-old –

to leave the school he had spent so much time at.

But Young is a native of Radford, Virginia, which is just southwest of Blacksburg. So, when Virginia Tech came calling after Buzz Williams bolted for Texas A&M, Young jumped at the chance to return home to his native state. Two weeks after Wofford lost in the NCAA Tournament to Kentucky, Young was named the new men's basketball coach of the Hokies.

Aluma was stunned.

"I didn't even know that he was going to leave," Aluma said. "I saw stuff on ESPN, but I just assumed it was rumors."

Aluma has trouble recalling what exactly happened next. He heard, through a grapevine of sorts, that Young wanted him to come to Virginia Tech. Aluma had no plans of leaving Wofford, but he and Young had established a tight bond. The two had an unspoken mutual understanding that Aluma wanted to play for Young, and that Young wanted to coach Aluma. So, on April 24, Aluma entered the transfer portal. On May 5, he announced he was heading to Blacksburg to be a Hokie.

"I definitely wasn't considering leaving," Aluma recalls. "Somehow, I found out that it was an option for me to go with him. I'm not sure exactly how it all came back to me. But once I heard that, I mean, that's not something you pass up on. So, it wasn't an easy decision, but it was the right decision."

At the 2019 ACC men's basketball media days in Charlotte that fall, Young explained Aluma following him like this: "There was no pitch. There wasn't. He let it be known that he wanted to play for me and I love that kid. And I love his family. This was a guy who hadn't played a lot of basketball when we got him, as you know, and he had a pretty good freshman year – a typical freshman year for a big kid. But I'm telling you, I mean, that guy keeps getting better and better. Somebody asked me if we were going to take him (at Virginia Tech) and I said, 'Well, let me do some figuring here – he had 11 rebounds in an NCAA Tournament game against Kentucky, against the biggest frontline I think I've seen in my 34 years in basketball. Yea, we're going to take him.' You 'betcha. Having him on the floor, he helps. He understands. He's a really good player."

And that was that.

Except Aluma couldn't play right away for Young at Virginia Tech. NCAA transfer rules were a bit tighter at that time and Aluma didn't receive a waiver to play right away. So, he had to sit out a season and redshirt.

The year away from games was difficult for Aluma. Here was a young man who, six years ago, had no interest in playing basketball whatsoever. But in the 2019-20 college basketball season, it was hard for him to blend into the background, to stay out of the limelight and to train alone – especially being on a new team at a different school in an unfamiliar place.

"That year was definitely not easy," Aluma says. "I was on the team and a part of it, but I didn't travel to games. It was the little things, like not traveling with them, and being a big part of practice, but not being able to step out on the court."

Aluma soon found a solution: he was going to go to the gym as much as he could. He was going to shoot as much as he could and he was going to work hard to improve his game. These were things that Aluma had not really put a ton of effort into doing before. Dunking, rebounding and playing defense came natural to him. He improved over time in each aspect of his game with practice, but he was often able to get by as a serviceable role player by being fundamentally sound and using his athleticism. His redshirt year, he completely transformed his game. And when the COVID-19 pandemic began in March of 2020, there was little else he could do besides go into the gym and get shots up.

"I was in the gym pretty crazy," Aluma said. "I had never really worked on (shooting) threes and I had never really gotten in the gym in my free time. I was just kind of the role guy and I didn't really need to get in the gym for that. But that year, I just put in tons of hours, and (Young) saw that and he gave me the green light, so that gave me the confidence to take threes."

Young later said, "He took two threes for me at Wofford, neither of which came close to going in the basket. They didn't land in the New River. They were not pretty. But he can shoot over 40% from three now. He's shooting it well."

***

When Keve Aluma first slipped on the No. 22 jersey for Virginia Tech, he looked slimmer, stronger and more focused. He made his Hokies' debut at home against Radford on Nov. 5, 2020, and the change in his game was so obvious that even Stevie Wonder could see it. In 68 games for Wofford, Aluma attempted just one three-pointer and missed it. In his first game as a Hokie Aluma took five shots from behind the arc and sank three of them. He scored a collegiate career-high 19 points in the win.

Three days later, Virginia Tech played a game in Uncasville, Connecticut against No. 3 Villanova, and it was obvious that Jay Wright and his Wildcats obviously underestimated the strides that Aluma had made in his game. The kid from Berlin had 23 points, eight rebounds and two blocks as the Hokies upset the Wildcats, taking an 81-73 win. For his performances against Radford and Villanova, Aluma was named ACC Player of the Week.

"That Villanova game… It all happened so quick," Aluma said. "We were super excited. For us to go in and win, and for me to play well, that was a confidence booster for me and the team."

Jeff Levan, an assistant coach on the Decatur teams that Aluma played for, is Maryland basketball fan, but watched as much of Virginia Tech as he could during the 2020-21 season.

"When they played Villanova, the announcers kept talking about how Jeremiah Robinson-Earl was an All-American," Levan said. "Keve pissed all over that kid. He was much better. Jay Wright was sending double teams at him five minutes into the game… When this COVID started, a lot of kids played Fortnite for six months. Keve went into the gym and became a three-point shooter. And he deserves credit for that."

Aluma kept impressing and the Hokies started the season off 8-1. In their final game before 2020 turned into 2021, the No. 24-ranked Hokies topped the Miami Hurricanes 80-78 behind Aluma's 26 points, six rebounds, four assists and three blocks. Aluma hadn't just become a good player for Virginia Tech; he was turning into one of the best players in the ACC. And he wasn't only Virginia Tech's anchor on defense; he was their top offensive weapon too. He was no longer the big body that set screens for quick little shooters at Wofford – he was the shooter now.

"I think everyone likes to have the ball, but I try to play as unselfish as possible and get everyone involved because I've been part of teams that are the opposite of that," Aluma said. "I like having the ball and being able to make decisions."

Aluma won his second ACC Player of the Week award in February after he poured in 29 points, 10 rebounds and four assists in No. 25 Virginia Tech's 65-51 triumph over rival Virginia, then ranked 15th. That night, there was nothing the 'Hoos could do to contain Aluma. He drew nine fouls in the game and did not commit a single one. Frankly, he outplayed both Jay Huff and Sam Hauser, a pair of All-ACC selections. In the first half, he flushed a three in Huff's grill and dunked on him. In the second half, Aluma worked on Huff in the post with relative ease. Under Tony Bennett, Virginia has consistently had one of the top defenses in the country, but on Jan. 30, 2021, Aluma made them look like St. Michaels' JV team.

Virginia Tech started off 7-2 in ACC play in the 2020-21 season, their best ever start since joining the conference. And Aluma was a big reason why.

"He is really, really good. And to think he was at Wofford," Pitt coach Jeff Capel said of Aluma ahead of a match-up with the Hokies. "He's really good with his footwork and his shot fakes. He's been really good for them all year so we're going to have to try to find a way to slow him down a bit."

Capel's Panthers weren't successful whatsoever in containing Aluma, as he poured in a career-high 30 points along with 10 rebounds, five assists and two blocks in one of the best performances he's ever had on a basketball court. A one-time useless player from behind the arc, Aluma sank 4-of-7 from deep against Pitt and went 6-of-6 from the charity stripe. No, Capel did not find a way to slow Aluma down – rather, his Panthers allowed the Berlin native to get his and clamped down on the rest of the Hokies, as Pitt came away with an unlikely 83-72 victory in Blacksburg.

In 2021, Keve Aluma became the first player from the Eastern Shore to play in an ACC Tournament since 2003, when Andre Collins was playing for the Maryland Terrapins. Photo by Mitchell Northam.

After losing to Pitt, the Hokies beat Miami and then didn't play for a while. The team had a COVID-19 outbreak and didn't play for 17 days. The timing couldn't have been worse for a team that, in February, was really hitting its stride and had its best player playing as well as he could've.

Virginia Tech resumed play on Feb. 23, losing to Georgia Tech. They ended the regular season with a victory over Wake Forest – led by Aluma's 23 points – and entered the ACC tournament with a little momentum. But the Hokies just didn't click against UNC. Aluma – the first Bayside Player to play in the ACC tournament since Crisfield's Andre Collins in 2003 with Maryland – tallied nine points, eight rebounds, four assists, two steals and a block in a loss to North Carolina at the historic Greensboro Coliseum.

At the end of the regular season, Aluma was voted to the All-ACC Second Team. He received three votes for the conference's Player of the Year award and one vote for its Defensive Player of the Year award. Aluma was the first from the Eastern Shore of Maryland to be named to an All-ACC team since Easton's Kelley Gibson did so for Maryland in 1996 and 1999. He was the first men's player – ever – from the Shore to be named to a Power 5 all-conference team.

Before the 2020-21 season started, Young told the Virginia Tech athletics website, "I can tell you right now, if you think (Aluma is) going to average 16 points in the ACC next year, you're wrong."

As it turned out, it was Young who was almost wrong. Aluma more than doubled his points per-game average at Wofford, averaging 15.2 points in 22 games for the Hokies while shooting 49% from the floor and 35.1% from three-point land. Aluma also averaged 7.9 rebounds, 2.2 assists and 1.3 blocks per-game, stats which had also increased from his time at Wofford.

"I'm a little surprised. But I'm not surprised by his toughness. I'm not surprised by his basketball intelligence. The number of mistakes that he covers up with sheer grit and basketball savvy on the defensive end... He's a great person that worked his fanny off," Young said on the Packer & Durham show on the ACC Network. "I'm proud of No. 22... He is a tough hombre."

Virginia Tech received a No. 10 seed in the NCAA Tournament via an at-large bid. The Hokies took the floor at Hinkle Field House in Indianapolis on March 19, facing off against the seventh-seeded Florida Gators. In the days prior, because of COVID-19 protocols, players had to quarantine for multiple days and Virginia Tech didn't get to practice with a basketball. "It was kind of weird," Aluma said. No kidding.

Aluma grabbed the first rebound of the contest, corralling a missed three-pointer from Tre Mann, marking a productive start to the Berlin native's third game in the Big Dance. Two minutes after that board, Hokies' guard Justyn Mutts fed Aluma a nifty pass and he connected on an easy lay-up.

Young's side led 33-27 at the half over the Gators. Aluma had to leave the game briefly in the second half, after he knocked his elbow on Tyree Appleby's forehead while throwing a pass, drawing blood from the Florida guard at the 12:58 mark. Aluma had Appleby in the high-post, took a dribble turned and fired a pass across the court, inadvertently driving his arm through Appleby's face. Aluma was back in the game about 90 seconds later, announcing his return by knocking down a mid-range jumper.

The Hokies would go on to squander a lead that had grown to 10 points. With seven seconds left, Florida led by three points and was at the charity stripe to ice the game. But Anthony Duruji missed both free throws. Aluma grabbed the defensive board and charged up the floor as the clock ticked. Just before he arrived at the top of the key, he dished the ball to teammate Nahiem Alleyne, who swished the game-tying shot from behind the arc with a defender in his grill.

"It was just a crazy feeling," Alleyne said. "I mean, that wasn't really the play – we were supposed to give the ball to (Tyrece Radford), but (Florida) was shading to his side so, Keve passes to me and I just knocked it down."

In overtime, Aluma would foul out and the Hokies would fall, 75-70.

Aluma finished the day with seven points, seven rebounds, two assists, one steal and one block in the second NCAA Tournament loss of his career.

"You always have nerves in the NCAA Tournament. I'm glad we got to play, but I'm frustrated with how it ended," Aluma said. "Most of us are coming back, so we'll be able to go into next year with that to fuel us."

In the 2020-21 season, Stephen Decatur's Keve Aluma was twice named ACC Player of the Week and made the All-ACC Second Team. Aluma also received three ACC Player of the Year votes. Photo by Mitchell Northam.

***

Keve Aluma wasn't always sure that he was going to come back to Virginia Tech for another season. Not long after the Hokies' NCAA Tournament loss to Florida, he declared for the NBA Draft and signed with an NCAA-certified agent. Aluma didn't have any individual workouts with teams, but he did attend the G-League combine and met with coaches and scouts who gave him some feedback. They wanted Aluma's play to be a bit more consistent and they wanted him to get into better shape. "It was good for me to see that. Now I know how to navigate that," Aluma said.

Aluma ultimately decided that it would be best for him to return to Virginia Tech for his senior season.

"I definitely want to improve my handle," Aluma said. "As a team, I just want to win. Winning will help everyone."

And he wants to win for Mike Young too, who has meant so much to him. It was Young who traveled more than 600 miles to come see Aluma work out in-person as a raw high schooler. It was Young who gave him an opportunity to get minutes and start at Wofford. It was Young who brought him to Virginia Tech. And it was Young who believed that the best version of the Hokies' offense was one that ran through Aluma.

"He's meant everything," Aluma said of his college coach. "He's been super important to me on the court. He's helped me be confident. There were ups and downs, and during the downs I was pretty hard on myself. He just believes in me."

Aluma earned his bachelor's degree over the summer of 2021 in human development. He also got Lasik surgery, so he can ditch his contacts when he's playing basketball. Aluma's shooting percentage from his junior to senior seasons went up from 49% to 53.8%. Maybe that was because of his corrected vision, or perhaps it's because Aluma put in another offseason where he absolutely worked his ass off to become a better player.

When Jeff Levan thinks about Aluma, he also thinks about Sherron Mills. Both were tall, powerful forwards from Worcester County, and Levan coached both players, at Stephen Decatur and Snow Hill, respectively.

"Keve and Sherron Mills are very similar in the fact that they were both late bloomers," Levan said. "Keve was the most talented player on those teams and he was the hardest worker – like Sherron was for Snow Hill. (Aluma) didn't question anything you told him. He had a great upside and he's maximized it. That scenario doesn't come along all the time."

Mills and Aluma could soon share something else in common. Aluma could become the first from the Eastern Shore to be selected in the NBA Draft since 1993, when Mills was plucked out of VCU by the Minnesota Timberwolves.

The possibility of being drafted isn't something that Aluma thinks about too much though.

"I don't feel too much pressure. I just want to leave it all out there and be the best player I can be," Aluma said. "I'm definitely proud to be one of the guys representing the Shore."

***

At the ACC's 2021 preseason media day in Charlotte, North Carolina, Mike Young was reminded of the day he stepped foot in Stephen Decatur's gym – way back in 2016, with only a few other colleges coaches around – to see Keve Aluma work out. One reporter asked Young: "Did you ever think he'd become what he is now?"

Young shook his head and laughed. "Nope."

"It always makes me chuckle to think about it," Young said. "I remember him five years ago as slightly overweight, timid, unsure. And to see him now – he's in the best shape he's ever been in. He looks like a million dollars. He's delightful to coach. He's awesome. I'm so proud of him. And thankful to have the opportunity to coach him one more year."

Ahead of Aluma's senior campaign at Virginia Tech, he was named to the All-ACC Preseason Team and the Hokies were picked to finish fifth in the conference. Early in the 2021-22 season, Aluma returned to his home state for a pair of games and shined in front of familiar faces. He and the Hokies played in the Veterans Classic at the Naval Academy, and Aluma notched 20 points and six boards in a 77-57 win over the Midshipmen.

Weeks later, Aluma returned to the Xfinity Center in College Park, where he lost in his final game as a Stephen Decatur Seahawk. This time, his side won as Aluma had 17 points, 12 boards, two assists and two blocks in a 62-58 win over the Maryland Terrapins, in what wound up being the last game Mark Turgeon coached the Terps in.

Again, Aluma was named to the All-ACC Second Team after averaging 15.4 points, 6.5 rebounds and 1.8 assists per-game while shooting 53.1% from the floor and 30.2% from three-point land in the regular season for the Hokies. But for Virginia Tech as a whole, the regular season was an uneven one. Young's side finished it with a 19-12 record and an 11-9 mark in ACC play. They endured a stretch of six losses in eight games, and then won six straight. The streaky Hokies entered the ACC tournament as a No. 7 seed and considered by many as a bubble team for the NCAA Tournament.

And then, Virginia Tech did what just one other ACC team had ever done before – it won four games in four days to win the conference championship, securing an unlikely automatic bid to the NCAA Tournament. Along the way, in Brooklyn, New York, Aluma and the Hokies beat Clemson and Notre Dame, and then got some revenge against UNC, ousting them in the semifinals. Aluma had 18 points, four rebounds and three assists as Virginia Tech made the ACC title game for the first time since joining the conference.

In that title game against top-seeded Duke, Aluma and the Hokies – much to the delight of Maryland fans on the Shore – spoiled what could've been Mike Krzyzewski's final ACC title. Aluma sank a three-pointer late in the first half as the Hokies took a seven-point lead. In the second half, he flushed a pair of free throws to give the Hokies an 11-point lead, then dished an assist under the basket to Justyn Mutts to extend that advantage. In the end, Virginia Tech won its first-ever ACC title 82-67. Aluma nearly had a triple-double, finishing with 19 points, 10 boards and a career-best seven assists. Aluma danced in the middle of the Barlcays Center to the Hokies' anthem – "Enter Sandman" – as burnt orange confetti rained down on him and his teammates while Krzyzewski and the Blue Devils walked off empty handed.

"It means everything," Aluma, somewhat speechless, said in the postgame press conference. "First thing that went through my mind… champs."

Aluma made the All-ACC Tournament First Team after scoring 76 points in four days, and Virginia Tech became the first No. 7 seed to win the tournament. And Aluma became the first player ever from the Eastern Shore to win an ACC title.

Ace Custis, working on Virginia Tech's staff as a special assistant to the head coach, powered up Facebook Live on his phone from the championship podium. He pointed the camera at Aluma, who he calls "Berlin" and the Worcester County native pointed at his ring finger. Long before Aluma came along, Custis – a native of Eastville on Virginia's Eastern Shore – starred for the Hokies in the 1990s.

After beating Duke, the Hokies earned a No. 11 seed in the NCAA Tournament. They were again beaten in the first round, falling 81-73 to Texas despite Aluma's 15 points and six rebounds in Milwaukee, Wisconsin.

***

Not long after the tournament ended, Aluma again entered his name into the NBA Draft pool.

With his Virginia Tech career in the books, Aluma will easily go down as one of the most accomplished collegiate players the Eastern Shore has produced. His resume, as of this writing, features two All-ACC selections, an ACC Championship, a SoCon Championship and three NCAA Tournament appearances. He has started in 95 of the 126 games he's played in, scored 1,227 points and grabbed 761 rebounds while shooting 54.7% from the floor and 33.8% from three-point land.

Aluma could play one more season of college ball because of the NCAA's COVID-era ruling, but it doesn't seem like he'll delay what could be a lengthy and lucrative pro career any longer. Whatever Aluma decides to do – either turn pro or return to Blacksburg for one more ride with Mike Young – he'll have a legion of Eastern Shore folks cheering for him.

One of them will be David Byrd. The Pocomoke High School athletic director is an avid college basketball fan and saw Aluma beat his teams a few times in high school. None of that matters now. Byrd is firmly planted in Aluma's fan section.

"I'm not surprised, because he's worked hard," Byrd said of Aluma's transformation. "He's blossomed since he left Stephen Decatur. He's filled out and he's very smooth. And he's smart. He's inside and outside now, in the ACC.

"He's making the Eastern Shore look good. I'm rooting for him."

School	G	MP	FG%	3P%	FT%	TRB	AST	STL	BLK	PTS
17-18 Wofford	33	13.3	.566	.000	.571	3.4	0.5	0.2	0.4	2.5
18-19 Wofford	35	26.6	.667	.000	.574	6.8	1.0	0.7	0.9	6.9
20-21 Virginia Tech	22	30.6	.490	.351	.722	7.9	2.2	0.7	1.3	15.2
21-22 Virginia Tech	36	30.8	.538	.333	.785	6.5	1.9	0.8	0.9	15.8
Overall	126	25.0	.547	.338	.690	6.0	1.3	0.6	0.8	9.7

Keve Aluma averaged 15.2 points and 7.9 rebounds per-game for Virginia Tech in the 2020-21 season. Photo by Mitchell Northam.

BEST OF THE REST

As I wrote in the intro of this book, this is not a complete and total history of high school basketball on the Eastern Shore. To detail every player, every coach and every team, well, this book would've been longer than Ulysses S. Grant's memoirs and the Old Testament – combined.

With that, I've attempted to construct a list of people and teams who deserve recognition, but weren't covered in the pages preceding this one. Consider this a "Best of the Rest" of Shore Hoops.

Rasheedah Akram, Mardela

Mardela's Rasheedah Akram is still the all-time leading scorer for girls basketball in Maryland public schools. The 5-foot-10 three-time Mason-Dixon Player of the Year earned a scholarship to Pitt. Mardela yearbooks.

Rasheedah Akram's senior yearbook quote was this: "Some are born great, some achieve greatness and some have greatness thrust upon 'em."

She had all three. Akram was a naturally gifted basketball player who had her skills sharpened by Barbara McCool, which in turn made her a walking bucket – one of the most lethal scorers the Shore has ever seen.

When Akram graduated from Mardela in 1997, she was the top scorer in the history of girls basketball at public schools in the state of Maryland with 3,561 points. It is a record that Akram still holds as of this writing. "She could really score. She could do it all," said former Crisfield guard Andre Collins.

Akram stood around 5-foot-10, but her game was much bigger. As a senior, she averaged 36.8 points, 18.3 rebounds and 3.5 assists per-game for McCool's Warriors, leading them to a state semifinal appearance. In each of her four seasons for the Warriors, she averaged at least 36 points and 12 rebounds per-game. Akram was a three-time Mason-Dixon Player of the Year and a two-time Street & Smith's All-

American. She was the fifth Division I player McCool coached, playing collegiately at the University of Pittsburgh and Missouri Valley College.

"She could do whatever she wanted," said former Wi-Hi guard Doug King. "She was skilled. She'd get the rebound, bring it up, score the lay-up. She could play with the boys, for real. She was tough. She could shoot three's handle, break you down. She was a monster."

Akram went on to be an assistant coach at Salisbury University for eight seasons, and then the head coach at Sussex Tech.

Marty Bailey Jr., Easton

Marty Bailey Jr. played and coached at Easton High School and found a lot of success doing both. When he graduated in 1998, he had totaled 1,793 career points and was the all-time leading scorer for the boys program. As a senior, Bailey was named Mid-Shore Player of the Year after averaging 18.9 points, 6.1 assists and 3.6 steals per-game.

"Marty was a really good player with a great handle," former Star Democrat sports reporter Will Graves said. "They were up-tempo and pressing all the time."

Bailey went on to play at Delaware State where he averaged 8.3 points, 2.1 rebounds and 1.3 assists over 108 games. In 2001, he was fourth in the MEAC in three-pointers made with 59. Bailey shot 39.7% from three-point range in his college career.

As the head boys basketball coach at Easton from 2007 through 2015, Bailey guided the Warriors to a trio of Bayside Conference Championships and three state final four appearances. He left Easton with a record of 142-44. In 2018, he became the head coach at Cambridge-South Dorchester, succeeding Vic Burns.

"He's low-key, quiet, but the kids respect him and they do what he says," said Wi-Hi head coach Butch Waller. "He's a blue-collar coach and has done a good job."

Rashad Brooks, Mardela

A star for Mardela in the mid-to-late 90s, Rashad Brooks excelled at Cecil College for Bill Lewit and then landed a scholarship at Louisville. At Cecil, Brooks scored more than 1,000 points. As a sophomore in 1998-99, he averaged 19.7 points, 5.5 rebounds and 5.6 assists per-game and helped Cecil capture its first regional championship.

"When he got to Cecil, he didn't come home," said Doug King, who played with Brooks there. "He was all about his game. He stayed there in the summer and worked. He knew what he had to do, and that's how he ended up at Louisville. He was all about basketball. And it paid off."

In two seasons at Louisville, Brooks played in 61 games and averaged 4.4

points, 1.6 rebounds and 1.3 assists per-game. Then-Cardinals head coach Denny Crum called him "a strong, explosive athlete that plays under control." After his playing career, Brooks was later the head coach at Washington High School and then Cecil College, succeeding Lewit. He was inducted into Cecil College's Athletics Hall of Fame in 2020.

Manny Camper, Kent County

Manny Camper played in 37 G-League games in the 2021-22 season. Photo by Allison Farrand/NBAE via Getty Images, courtesy of the Grand Rapids Gold.

Manny Camper was a member of the first Kent County squad to make the state final four in 2017. A two-time north Bayside Player of the Year, he scored 1,951 career points for the Trojans, and averaged 28 points and 13 rebounds per-game his senior year. Camper was the first person from Kent County High School to receive a Division I athletic scholarship.

He went off to Siena, where he started in 71 of the 92 games he played in. Across his junior and senior seasons, Camper averaged 13.8 points, 10.1 rebounds, 2.9 assists and a steal per-game while shooting 44.4% from the floor. Arguably his best game came on Nov. 20, 2019 against Yale, when he had 22 points, 19 rebounds, two assists and two steals. For the 2020-21 season, Camper was named MAAC Player of the Year as he led the Saints to a 12-4 conference record. The 6-foot-7 forward also had a dunk make it onto SportsCenter's Top 10. Camper declared for the NBA Draft in 2021 and had workouts with the Memphis Grizzlies and Sacramento Kings, but went unselected.

Not long after the draft though, Camper tried out for the Grand Rapids Gold, the NBA G-League affiliate of the Denver Nuggets. The team signed him and he made his professional basketball debut on Nov. 11, 2021, tallying nine points and 19 rebounds in a 103-99 win over the Sioux Falls SkyForce. Camper became the first Eastern Shore native to play in the G-League since Wi-Hi's Craig Winder. Camper played the entire 2021-22 season with the Gold, starting in 19 of the 37 games he played in, averaging 8.7 points, 7.7 rebounds, 1.5 assists and 1.2 steals per-game. After his first G-League season ended, Camper continued to play professionally in Puerto Rico.

Jerry Carter, Crisfield

A 6-foot-2 guard, Carter scored a total of 47 points in two games at the 1978 state final four to lead Bill Cain's Crisfield team to a state title, the fifth in school history.

"He was like Skywalker, man. He was great," said Paul Butler, who played at Wi-Hi while Carter was at Crisfield.

After serving in the Army, Carter joined the men's basketball at the University of Idaho at the age of 27. "He gives us some character out there, more so than the points," Idaho coach Tim Floyd told the Spokesman-Review of Carter in 1987. "He was playing 80 games a year on the All-Army team, and you can't buy that kind of experience."

Carter played in 45 games at Idaho, averaging 2.9 points and 1.1 rebounds per-game while shooting 39.1% from three-point range. He had two points and two steals in the Vandals' 1989 NCAA Tournament loss to the UNLV Runnin' Rebels.

"He was very athletic, but he could just spot up on the wing and shoot the lights out," former Crisfield player Greg Bozman said of Carter. "He would work on his handles every day in practice."

Ace Custis

No, Ace Custis is not from the Eastern Shore of Maryland – but he is, without question, the greatest basketball player ever from the Eastern Shore of Virginia, and someone who has influenced a lot of players on Maryland's slice of the peninsula. And so, he gets mentioned here.

Custis is a native of Eastville, Virginia and matriculated at Northampton High School where he grew to 6-foot-8 and excelled at basketball. Custis once played on the Boo Williams Elite AAU team with Allen Iverson and Joe Smith, two future NBA Draft picks. Custis went on to Virginia Tech, where he became one of the most decorated Hokies ever, becoming just the third player in program history to tally 1,000 points and 1,000 rebounds. Custis started in 94 of the 123 games he played in for Va. Tech, averaging 13.9 points, 9.6 rebounds and 2.3 assists per-game for his career. He led the Metro Conference in rebounding in 1995, and led the A-10 in rebounding in 1997. In 1995, Custis helped lead the Hokies to a win in the NIT Championship over Marquette. In 1996, the Hokies played in the NCAA Tournament. The No. 20 jersey Custis wore is retired and now hangs in Cassell Coliseum.

After a brief stint with the Dallas Mavericks as an undrafted free agent, Custis enjoyed a lengthy professional playing career overseas, featuring with teams in Indonesia, Venezuela, Qatar, the Philippines, Syria, Lebanon and Japan. Since retiring from playing, he has been an assistant coach at Virginia State, Maryland Eastern Shore and his alma mater, Virginia Tech.

Damonte Dodd, Queen Anne's

There were few on the Eastern Shore who could defend Damonte Dodd while he was playing for Queen Anne's. Playing in the guard-dominant Bayside Conference, Dodd scored with ease at the rim. As a senior, he averaged 24.1 points, 16.7 rebounds and 7.4 blocks per-game for the Lions. After a stint at Massanutten Military Academy, Dodd landed with the Maryland Terrapins and became a defensive specialist of sorts. Dodd played in 119 games over four season and left College Park ranking eighth all-time in blocked shots with 141. Dodd helped the Terps make a trio of NCAA Tournaments, including a Sweet 16 run in 2016. Former Indiana coach Tom Crean once called Dodd, "the best screen-and-roll player in the (Big Ten)." Dodd has played professionally in the G-League, Mexico, Poland and the Czech Republic.

Jorden Duffy, James M. Bennett

At one time, Jorden Duffy held the single-game scoring record at the Governor's Challenge with 38 points vs. J.H. Blake in 2014. A 6-foot guard, Duffy averaged more than 28 points per-game as a senior at Bennett and went on to play at San Jacinto College and then at the University of North Texas.

Despite battling six different injuries during his time with the Mean Green, Duffy started in 31 of the 51 games he played in, averaging 9.5 points, 3.8 rebounds and 1.6 assists per-game. In 2018, Duffy helped North Texas win the postseason CBI tournament, averaging 17.8 points, 5.8 rebounds and 1.8 assists across six contests while shooting 51.4% from three-point range. Duffy went on to play professionally in Slovakia, where he averaged 19.1 points and 4.4 assists per-game in the 2021-22 season for MBK Rieker Komarno.

Andre Foreman, Stephen Decatur

"He was a good player in high school and a great player in college," Pocomoke's David Byrd said of Foreman. "He was freaking fun to watch. Andre Foreman is one of the best Division III players ever. He worked at it and blossomed."

Indeed, while Foreman was a solid high school player at Stephen Decatur, he became a legitimate scoring machine at Salisbury University. Foreman was the 1992 Division III National Player of the Year and still holds the record for the most points scored in a career by a Division III player with 2,940.

Foreman also pulled down 1,140 rebounds in his career at Salisbury. During his senior year, the Sea Gulls enjoyed a 27-game winning streak as Foreman averaged 31.5 points per-game. Foreman set 17 records at Salisbury and went on to play professionally in Australia, Hong Kong, Finland and

Sweden. He was inducted into the Small College Basketball National Hall of Fame in 2020.

Since retiring from playing, Foreman has become a coach, guiding the girls' varsity team at St. Andrew's Episcopal School and the 16U squad for Team Takeover in the Nike EYBL.

"Foreman was tough," former Snow Hill player Nick Purnell said. "He was more of a combo-guard type, more of a scorer. He could handle, he could play the point, he had range. He's one of the greats."

Dayona Godwin, Stephen Decatur

Godwin stayed on the Shore for college ball. Maryland Eastern Shore Athletics

A 5-foot-5 guard from Ocean Pines who was often unstoppable in the Bayside Conference, Godwin finished her high school career as Stephen Decatur's all-time leading scorer with 2,081 points. Godwin scored her 2,000th career point at Decatur on a corner three in the 2016 Bayside Conference Championship game against Kent Island. Behind Godwin's 28 points, her Seahawks won their second straight conference crown that day. She was the first to score that many points in a Seahawks' uniform.

Godwin went on to play the University of Maryland Eastern Shore on an academic scholarship, where she featured in 57 contests across four seasons, averaging 2.1 points and 1.3 rebounds per-game. One of her best games came in the 2019-20 season, where she had 13 points, seven rebounds and three assists at Morgan State.

Rockeem "Rocky" Harris, Kent County

Rocky Harris is 5-foot-9, but for what he lacked in size, he made up with in grit, heart and a smooth handle. A 2009 graduate of Kent County High School, Harris was the first 1,000-point scorer in the school's history and the first Trojan to be named Bayside Player of the Year – an award he garnered as a senior after leading the state of Maryland in scoring with 31.2 points per-game. Harris went on to play at Chesapeake College and Salisbury University. For the Sea Gulls, Harris started in 51 of the 56 games he appeared in and averaged 7.9 points, 2.6 rebounds, 1.6 assists and 1.1 steals per-game while shooting 40% from three-point range. He helped Salisbury notch back-to-back NCAA Tournament berths in 2015 and 2016. Harris went on to coach at Chesapeake College and at youth camps. In July 2021, Harris beat professional Kendal Williams in a highly publicized game of one-on-one.

Shelton Hawkins, Easton

While Hawkins was a talented and accomplished player for Easton, his impact as an artist – and using basketball as a vehicle – has been greater.

A military brat, Hawkins spent some time in Germany before he moved to Easton, where he was the ball boy for Shaquille O'Neal's high school team. When Hawkins arrived in Easton, he spent much of his time at Idlewild Park, where he looked up to players like Monte Banks. By the time Hawkins was a high schooler, he was 6-foot-4 and dunking on that court.

Hawkins made the All-Bayside Team as a junior at Easton, averaging 16.7 points and 6.1 rebounds per-game, helping the Warriors start the 1997-98 season with 17 straight wins. Hawkins played his final season of prep ball at Notre Dame Academy in Middleburg, Virginia, and then went on to Weatherford College in Texas. Hawkins then played two seasons at Division II Midwestern State University, where he averaged 4.5 points, 1.5 assists and 1.7 rebounds per-game in 48 contests.

When his playing days were over, Hawkins coached at the University of Maryland Eastern Shore, and then became an art teacher in Charles County. Then, through projects like "Destination Art," "Play in Color," and "Project Backboard" he started designing, creating and refurbishing basketball courts with an artistic and creative touch to strengthen communities. His hometown of Easton has two "Destination Art" courts, one at Moton Park and another at Hawkins' childhood stomping grounds of Idlewild Park. He modeled the design at Idlewild off of a court he saw in Puerto Rico, and finished it with his cousin James Thomas – who died on the court in 2003 – in mind.

"I wanted to do something that would keep his name alive, and that had deep meaning for our family and the community," Hawkins said. "So, the goal was to fix up the local basketball courts and the project began."

As of this writing, Hawkins has designed colorful and unique courts and other art pieces across the globe, working with the likes of Nike, Adidas, Converse, Under Armour, USA Basketball, NBA 2K, Candace Parker and LeBron James. Hawkins was supposed to design a court for use at the 2020 Summer Olympics in Tokyo before COVID-19 intervened. Locally, he has also partnered with James Simmons and the Governor's Challenge, creating the "Hall of Fame Boulevard" exhibit in 2021. Hawkins also has plans for courts in Salisbury, Crisfield and Berlin.

Salisbury Mayor Jake Day once wrote of Hawkins' work: "Shelton's use of vibrant colors creates a feeling of energy and excitement, turning any playing surface into a work of art, and lifting its surroundings with positivity."

In 2022, the Town Council of Easton gave Hawkins the "Image Award" for being committed to preserving communities through art and sport.

Kory Holden, James M. Bennett

A two-time Bayside South Player of the Year and Bennett's all-time leading scorer, Kory Holden played his college ball at three Division I institutions: Delaware, South Carolina and South Alabama. At Delaware, Holden was an All-CAA Rookie as a freshman and an All-CAA second team selection as a sophomore. When he announced his intent to transfer in 2016, ESPN tabbed him as the No. 1 transfer target. In his redshirt year at South Carolina, the Gamecocks advanced to the Final Four. Then, for Holden's final season of college ball, he suited up for the South Alabama Jaguars. In all, across 98 college games, Holden averaged 12.2 points, 3.6 assists and 2.4 rebounds per-game while shooting 40.6% from behind the arc. His 31.4 assist-percentage is third-best all-time in the CAA. Holden went on to play professionally in Georgia and in the 2021 edition of The Basketball Tournament.

While he sat the season out due to NCAA transfer rules, James M. Bennett's Kory Holden was a member of the South Carolina team that made the Final Four in 2017. Photo by Mitchell Northam.

Kim Horsey, Mardela

One of the first great women's players from Mardela, Kim Horsey averaged a double-double as a junior and senior for Barbara McCool's side and led the Warriors to a berth in the 1978 state championship game and back-to-back Bayside titles in 1978 and 1979. Horsey went on to play at UT-Chattanooga where she was a two-time All-SoCon selection and helped the Mocs advance to the final of the National Women's Invitation Tournament in 1984. Before losing to Vanderbilt in the final, Horsey dropped 31 points on Clemson and 18 on Oklahoma. She still holds the Mocs' single-season record for rebounds with 356. In 2002, she was inducted into the UTC Hall of Fame alongside Terrell Owens. Fellow Mardela great Tia Jackson said of Horsey: "Kim Horsey was the player that Coach McCool always talked about. She kind of laid the land at Mardela early. She was phenomenal."

Gordon Jeter, Easton

A versatile 6-foot-5 wing, Gordon Jeter helped guide Easton to three straight state championship appearances in 2010, 2011 and 2012. He went on to play at Salisbury University, where he was the Capitol Athletic Conference Rookie of the Year in 2014 and was a two-time All-CAC selection. Three of the teams Jeter played on at Salisbury went to the NCAA Tournament. Jeter was a 1,000-point scorer at both Easton and Salisbury. For the Sea Gulls, he had career averages of 9.8 points, 6.4 rebounds, 1.5 assists and 1.1 steals per-game while shooting 50.3% from the floor.

Gordon Jeter helped Easton reach the state final four in each of his last three high school seasons. Salisbury University, Jeter was a key member of three teams that went to the NCAA Tournament. Photo by Mitchell Northam.

Bill Jews, Cambridge

A star at Cambridge High School, Bill Jews set the school record for scoring in a single game with 40 points against Colonel Richardson in 1969. For as talented as he was on the basketball court, Jews was better off of it. After studying – and playing basketball – at Johns Hopkins University, Jews became the President and CEO of CareFirst BlueCross BlueShield. While playing for Johns Hopkins Blue Jays, the 6-foot-7 Jews was a three-time all-conference selection and still holds the school record for the best single season scoring average with 21.9 points per-game in the 1972-73 season. He had 1,234 career points and 825 rebounds at Johns Hopkins and was inducted into the school's athletic hall of fame in 1994.

Casey Morton, Mardela

Casey Morton is still fourth in Hawks' history in scoring with 1,230 points. Maryland Eastern Shore Athletics.

After four years at Mardela, Morton finished third in school history in scoring behind Rasheedah Akram and Tia Jackson with more than 2,500 career points. Morton was recruited by Power 5 programs and initially committed to Mississippi State of the SEC, but wound up staying close to home and enrolled at the University of Maryland Eastern Shore. As of this writing, Morton is still fourth in Hawks' history in scoring (1,230 points), fifth in assists (296), fourth in steals (188), third in three's made (131) and first in games started (110) and minutes played (3,481). She is now an assistant for the Hawks under head coach Fred Batchelor.

Cliff Mister

After serving in the Air Force, Cliff Mister was a sports editor of the Salisbury Daily Times and the Dorchester Banner. A Colonel Richardson graduate and member of the school's first basketball team, he chronicled high school sports, specifically hoops, on the Eastern Shore for decades. Mister died in 1996 at his home in Crisfield at the age of 52 after suffering a heart attack.

"Cliff was instrumental in starting the Bayside All-Star Game," said Pocomoke's David Byrd. Following his death, the senior all-star game was named after Mister.

"He covered Eastern Shore sports as a priority," said longtime Wi-Hi head coach Butch Waller. "The NBA and the NFL were way down at the bottom. He knew all the players around here."

Wilbert Mills, Pocomoke

After leading the Pocomoke boys to their first state title in 1971, Wilbert Mills was tabbed as an All-American the following season by the U.S. Basketball Writers Association. In the 1971-72 season as a senior, he scored 590 points, averaging 24.6 points per-game. After scoring a total of 1,319 points during his career at Pocomoke, the record-setter played college ball at James Madison and helped the Dukes reach the Division II national championship twice. He became a teacher and basketball coach at George Washington Carver High in Virginia, totaling an 80-60 record in six seasons before his untimely death in 1983 from an apparent heart attack.

Ty Newman, Easton

Newman led the Bayside Conference in scoring his senior season at Easton, averaging 32.1 points, 4.4 assists and 6.2 rebounds per-game in the 2006-07 season. After a stint at Chesapeake College, Newman became a prolific scorer for Division II Livingstone College, a historically Black institution in North Carolina. He helped the Blue Bears win the CIAA championship in 2015 and secured tournament MVP honors. In 2016, as a senior, he averaged 17.8 points, 2.7 assists and 1.4 steals per-game. Newman had a workout with the NBA's Charlotte Hornets and later played professionally in Bolivia.

Jackie Pinckens

Pinckens coached the girls varsity teams at North Caroline and later – from 2011 to 2016 – at Colonel Richardson. While leading the North Caroline Bulldogs, Pinckens' teams went to the state final four on four occasions; in 1984, 1986, 1991 and 1996. Her Bulldogs also went to seven Bayside Conference Championship games in a span of 13 seasons, winning the conference crown in 1996 with a 61-55 victory over Washington. Pinckens won more than 430 games as a head girls basketball coach in Caroline County.

Andrea Reed, Pocomoke

One of the best players to come out of Gail Gladding's program, Reed led Pocomoke to a Bayside Conference Championship and the 1A East region crown in 2006 while averaging 17.8 points, 8.2 rebounds and 7.4 assists per-game. Reed was a McDonald's All-American nominee and was also part of Pocomoke teams that won the Bayside in 2004 and went to states in 2004 and 2005. After tallying more than 1,700 points, 800 rebounds and 500 assists at Pocomoke, Reed went on to play her college ball at Wagner where she led the NEC in assists as a sophomore and junior. She left Wagner ranking fourth all-time in program history in assists with 499.

AJ Spencer, Wi-Hi

Spencer still holds the Wicomico County scoring record for boys basketball players with 1,775 points tallied in his career. Spencer helped Wi-Hi capture back-to-back Bayside titles and 2A East region titles in 2006 and 2007. He went on to play at Cecil College and then at Alabama State, where he featured in 41 games.

Mooney Williams, Wi-Hi

Tommy "Mooney" Williams was a talented point guard who played for from 1985 through 1988. Williams was an All-Bayside First Team selection as a sophomore, junior and senior. In three varsity seasons, he racked up 941 career points and 514 assists. As a junior, Williams averaged 15.6 points, 7.9 assists and 4.6 steals per-game in the 1986-87 season.

"He went to a Five-Star camp and took it over. They had never heard of Salisbury or Wi-Hi," said former Crisfield player Greg Bozman. "He was one of the best point guards I've ever seen. Had a real floor sense."

"He was one of the greatest, flashiest point guards I've ever seen," said former Snow Hill guard Nick Purnell.

"I thought he was one of the greatest guards ever around here," said former Snow Hill assistant coach Jeff Levan. "He could dominant a game without scoring. He controlled the whole flow of the game. The ball was like string in his hand."

Added Paul Butler, who was Wi-Hi's JV coach from 1986 through 1989: "You talk about court vision? Mooney was just unbelievable. He was getting looks from places like Duke and Virginia and Maryland. Unfortunately, he just didn't have the grades. But man, just a great, unbelievable point guard. There were not many people that you could say were better point guards than Mooney."

Wi-Hi head coach Butch Waller remembers players coming to him after practice with busted lips and dislocated fingers, because Williams would throw hard, nifty and precise passes that would fool defenses and his own teammates, if they weren't paying attention. "I told them, 'You better damn well look.' He was unbelievable."

"That kid came out of the womb with a basketball," Waller said. "The ball was part of his anatomy. He was a different dude. He could've played in the NBA."

ACKNOWLEDGEMENTS

I first need to thank my wife, Rachel, for supporting me, pushing me and putting up with me throughout the research, writing and editing of this book. It was a labor of love and required many long nights, several road trips and countless hours of work, all while we were planning – then rescheduling – our wedding during a global pandemic. She was the first set of eyes for many of these pages, was a diligent deliverer of coffee, and demanded I stand up and take a lap around our apartment after I had been sitting at my desk for too long. Rachel, thank you. I love you so much.

After my freshman year of college, when I first expressed an interest in pursuing journalism as a career, my Dad was the first person who told me to go for it. He encouraged me to start a website, instilled a strong work ethic in me and inspired me to aim high. Thank you, Dad, and Missy, for everything, and thanks for letting me use your guest room as a second home base while I worked on this. I love you guys – and Mom and Kurt, Sara, Aaliyah and Cam, Josh and Kate, Grandma and Grandpop, Mom-Mom and Pop, and Pat, Linda and Julia – so much. Without the unyielding backing of my family, this book wouldn't have been possible. My family has supported me the whole way, through every blog post, every job change, every freelance gig and throughout the work on this book.

That family also includes the fellas: Connor, Ben, Ryan, Kyle and Thorne. Thanks for being there since Day One.

Cia North was the first person who ever gave me real confidence as a writer. She was my English and creative writing teacher for each of my four years at Colonel Richardson High School. Over the last decade, she became one of my closest friends. She was a great sounding board for me as I worked on this book, and the voice of reason as Rachel and I planned two weddings. Cia, your presence in my life has been invaluable. Thank you, for everything.

Josh Weber invited me to the first basketball game I ever saw at Wi-Hi, back in 2012. I blew up his phone during the months that I worked on this book, asking him questions, picking his brain, or getting him to read something. This book is better because he was always available to talk about basketball, and because he's a great friend. My enthusiasm for Bayside Conference basketball grew because of Josh, his father Bill, and late nights inside the Waller Dome with them.

In the spring of 2015, I got a call from a Virginia number that I didn't recognize. It was Ted Shockley, and he wanted me to meet him at Dave White's Pittsville Dinette for a job interview. The dinette didn't take credit cards though, so we went to the Denny's in Salisbury, had burgers, and Ted offered me a job as a general assignment reporter at the Salisbury Daily Times. Ted was my boss, but he has become a truly awesome friend. Ted, thanks for the burger, the job, proof-reading some pages of this book, your help and friendship over the years.

I need to thank everyone who took time out of their lives to talk with me or help me with this book, whether it was an interview, finding a photo or phone number, or reading something for me: Keve Aluma, Greg Bozman, Bubby Brown, Vic Burns, Brian Butler, Paul Butler, David Byrd, A.B., Andre Collins, Tom Corsey, Hanee Camper, Dan Dobronz, David Dodson, Bill Duck, Todd Dudek, Derrick Fooks, Kelley Gibson, Will Graves, Shelton Hawkins, Bradley Hudson, David Insley, Tia Jackson, Kate Jenkins, Clarence Johnson, Brenda Jones, Doug King, Jamaal King Jr., Jeff Levan, Eddie Miller, Howard Megdal, Alice and Merrill Morgan, Justin Odendhal, Kareem Otey, Steve Parham, Jeff Pearlman, Ben Pensenga, Brad Plutschak, Nick Purnell, James Simmons, Shawn Tucker, Anky Tull, Bill Weber, Richard Woolfolk, Butch Waller, Mike Young and Shawn Yonker. Apologies if I missed anyone.

Special thanks go to Jon Nelson and Brian Reese, who swiftly copy-edited these pages with detail. This book wouldn't have been published without y'all's help.

And thank you to the librarians at Stephen Decatur, Colonel Richardson, Mardela and Cambridge-South Dorchester high schools. And also to the staff at the Talbot Historical Society, and the sports information departments at Maryland, Texas, Colgate, Loyola Maryland, George Washington, UConn, Radford, VCU, James Madison, UT-Chattanooga, Maryland Eastern Shore and Salisbury University.

Also, thank you to WUNC and Elizabeth Baier for allowing me to take time away from work to chip away at this.

SOURCES

"6-1 Guard Brooks Signs With U of L Men's Basketball." Louisville Athletics. April 9, 1999.
https://bit.ly/3CLItmC.

Abraham, Scott. "Friends and Colleagues Remember Late Snow Hill AD Allen Miller." WBOC.com.
Sept. 15, 2010. https://bit.ly/3jORdQz.

Allison, Troy. "The Miracle." *Democratic Messenger*, July 7, 1906.

Assael, Shaun."Three Hoops Nomads Collided At Baylor In A Tragedy That Scarred College Sports."
ESPN.com. July 10, 2012.
https://www.espn.com/espn/magazine/archives/news/story?page=magazine-20031027-article3.

The Baltimore Sun/Evening Sun. Baltimore, Maryland. 1936-2005.

Barnes, Jill. "WBL all-star game survives first test." *The News (Patterson, N.J)*, March 16, 1979.

Barnes, Jill. "State's 1st Pro Women's Basketball Game a Thriller." *The News (Patterson, N.J)*, Dec. 18, 1978.

Berman, Mark. "Former Radford basketball standout Tyrone Travis dies at 49." *The Roanoke Times*, Jan. 4, 2021.

Boling, Dave. "Floyd not Sky-high on UI." *The Spokesman-Review (Spokane, Washington)*, Nov. 24, 1987.

Brown, Angela K. "Dennehy, Dotson friendship had strengthened."
The Associated Press, El Paso Times, July 2, 2003.

"Braves Trip Ocean City Quint, 52-45." *Cumberland Sunday Times*, March 18, 1951.

Capitelli, Lisa. "Decatur's 1970 basketball state champions recognized." *OC Today*, Feb. 7, 2020.

"Co. 'C' Outclasses Seaford Quintet." *Daily Banner*, Nov. 18, 1922.

"Coach Dismissed, 11 Pupils Picket." *Courier-Post*, April 1, 1967.

Cox, Karen L. *No Common Ground: Confederate Monuments and the Ongoing Fight for Racial Justice*.
The University of North Carolina Press. 2021.

The Daily Times/Salisbury Times/Delmarva Daily Times. Salisbury, Maryland. 1923-2022.

Denlinger, Ken. "Lefty Driesell Is Back Doing What He Does Best." *The Los Angeles Times*, Feb. 5, 1989.

Denman, Elliott. "Red Bank's Newest Pro Athlete Is 'Gem' of a Lady." *Asbury Park Press*, Feb. 5, 1979.

Detweiler, Eric. "Where Are They Now? Brian Butler." GW Athletics. Oct. 15, 2020. https://bit.ly/3CJxkTl.

Dimitry, Steve. "Women's Professional Basketball Leagues." Steve Dimitry's Research. https://bit.ly/3AHeDhB.

Dodson, David. "Snow Hill Basketball 2008 1A State Championship Game." YouTube. 1:36.53.
https://www.youtube.com/watch?v=k42vc6GxPrc.

"Dotson's hometown coming to grips with murder charge." *The Associated Press, ESPN.com*, July 23, 2003.

"Dotson: 'I didn't confess to anything'." ESPN.com. July 22, 2003.
http://static.espn.go.com/ncb/news/2003/0721/1583840.html.

"Dotson sentenced to 35 years in Dennehy murder case." *The Associated Press, USA Today*, June 15, 2005.

Erman, Jeff. "Former Terps guard on national title, transfer, historic shot." Inside MD Sports. July 7, 2020.
https://bit.ly/3jIvb1y.

Evans, Jayda. "Catching up with Tia Jackson." *The Seattle Times*, June 28, 2011.

"Ex-Sonic helps calm the Storm." *The Spokesman-Review (Spokane, Washington)*, June 17, 2003.

"Faces In The Crowd." *Sports Illustrated*, April 9, 1984.

Farrell, Roger. "Women Vie For Hoop$." *Daily Record (Morristown, N.J.)*, Nov. 8, 1978.

Farber, Michael. "Gems lose in opener." *The Record (Hackensack, N.J.)*, Dec. 18, 1978.

Ferranti, Seth. "The greatest who never made it." HoopsHype.com. Sept. 3, 2005. https://bit.ly/2UbvNUW.

Fowler, Scott. "No fans? No problem. 'Big Pat' is back, making Charlotte Hornets games feel like home."
The Charlotte Observer, Jan. 15, 2021.

"Gems snap skid at six." *The Herald-News (Passiac, N.J.)*, Feb. 5, 1979.

"Gems win shootout, 163-161." *The Herald-News (Passiac, N.J.)*, April 1, 1979.

"Girls Six-on-Six Basketball in Iowa." Iowa Pathways.
https://www.iowapbs.org/iowapathways/mypath/girls-six-six-basketball-iowa

Gross, Jane. "First-Place Stars Go Second Class." *The New York Times*, Dec. 24, 1979.

Grundy, Pamela, and Susan Shackelford. *Shattering The Glass*. The New Press. 2005.

Hartman, Sid. "Jottings." *Star Tribune (Minneapolis, Minnesota)*, Aug. 3, 1993.

Herbert, Dick. "The Sports Observer." *News and Observer*, Dec. 22, 1958.

Himmelsbach, Adam. "Thomas longs to escape shadow of player's death."
The Free-Lance Star (Fredericksburg, Virginia), Dec. 30, 2007.

Holland, Earl. "Who's The Boz? With Greg Bozman Sr." *The Sports Refuge Podcast*, March 24, 2021.
https://ihr.fm/3ADHDql

"J. Edward Walter Park." Dorchester Recreation.

https://www.dorchesterrecreation.org/Parks%20and%20Facilities/JEdwardWalterPark.pdf.

Johnson, Dave. "Chambers Sets Tone For JMU." *The Daily Press (Newport News, Virginia)*, Feb. 27, 1992.

"Jonestown." Harriet Tubman Underground Railroad Byway.
https://harriettubmanbyway.org/jonestown/.

"Kansas 82, Colgate 68." UPI. March 17, 1995.
https://www.upi.com/Archives/1995/03/17/Kansas-82-Colgate-68/5421795416400/

Kelley, Steve. "Getting on Tia Time." *The Seattle Times*, Nov. 9, 2007.

Kelly, Michael. "Siena men's basketball senior Camper 'everything that's right about college athletics'."
The Daily Gazette (Albany County, N.Y.), March 6, 2021.

Kester-McCabe, Dana. "Delmarva's World War II Prisoner Of War Camps." Delmarva Almanac. https://bit.ly/3fVdueo.

Kondelis, Pat, director. *Disgraced*. Bat Bridge Entertainment; Showtime Networks, 2017.
1 hr., 42 min. https://amzn.to/3fSDF59.

LaDuca, Patty. "'The Blaze' keeps Gems from cold." *The Herald-News (Passiac, N.J.)*, Dec. 18, 1980.

"Lambert announces retirement." D3Hoops.com. Oct. 7, 1999. https://www.d3hoops.com/notables/1999/10/19991007e5xyp9.

Linder, Jeff. "1992-93 Iowa women's basketball: A fairy-tale season." *The Gazette (Cedar Rapids, Iowa)*, Jan. 28, 2018.

"Local Coaching Legend, Barb McCool Loses Fight With Cancer." WBOC.com. Oct. 23, 2009.
https://bit.ly/3yH5zbR

Lumpkin, Taylor. "Students, alumni celebrate new Mardela gym that honors late coach." WMDT.com. Jan. 8, 2019.
https://bit.ly/3lW5zRN

Lyttle, Steve. "After leading Virginia Tech in scoring and rebounding, Keve Aluma enjoys 'being taken seriously'." *The Virginian Pilot*, Nov. 8, 2021.

Town of Mardela Springs. https://mardelasprings.org/history/.

McNamara, John. *The Capital of Basketball*. Georgetown University Press. 2019.

"Meet the Coaches of the Kara Era: Tia Jackson." Duke Athletics. Nov. 5, 2020. https://bit.ly/3fWx1Lg

Metcalfe, Jeff. "Mercury picks pair off Final Four team." *The Arizona Republic*, April 29, 1997.

Miles, Norma, and Robin Chandler-Miles. *Images of America: Pocomoke City*. Arcadia Publishing. 2008.

Miles, Travon. "'Shop Talk 2'- Bayside Championship Edition." WMDT.com. Feb. 26, 2020.
https://www.wmdt.com/2020/02/shop-talk-2-bayside-championship-edition/

Miller, Jeff. "Town stunned by accused in player's disappearance." *Dallas Morning News*, July 2, 2003.

"Millersville Athletics Remembers Richard DeHart." Millersville Athletics. Jan. 26, 2015.
   https://millersvilleathletics.com/news/2015/1/26/MBB_0125153849.aspx

Moran, Nancy, and Derek Wallbank. "Paul Sarbanes, U.S. Senator Who Co-Wrote Anti-Fraud Law, Dies at 87."
   Bloomberg. Dec. 7, 2020. https://bloom.bg/3xHajNk.

Montgomery, Dave, and Danny Robbins. "DOTSON DREAMED OF BEING THE STAR."
   Fort Worth Star-Telegram, Aug. 18, 2003.

Moton High School Alumni. https://motonhighschoolalumni.org/.

"MOTON BASKETBALL 1953-54." Easton High School Hall of Fame. eastonhighschoolhof.com/history-item/moton-basketball-1953-54/.

"Mouring Ready To Take Over When Needed." *The Hartford Courant*, March 16, 2000.

Noble, Edward M. *History of Caroline County, Maryland, from its beginning*. J. W. Stowell Printing Co. 1920.

O'Connor, John. "Fletcher Arritt, Fork Union's unassuming and ultra-successful hoops coach, dies at 79."
   Richmond Times-Dispatch, June 17, 2021.

O'Day, Joe. "Pioneers Shock N.Y. Stars in OT." *New York Daily News*, Nov. 18, 1979.

O'Rourke, Sean. "Mouring Always Had A Lot Of Game." *The Middletown Press*, Dec. 26, 2020.

Parker, Gretchen. "Maryland hometown of Baylor basketball player becomes media circus." *The Associated Press*, July 1, 2003.

Paterno, Vincent. "Gems' Tatterson jumps to Stars." *Morning News (Patterson, N.J.)*, Oct. 11, 1979.

Pilz, Morgan. "Worcester High School memorialized." *OC Today*, Feb. 21, 2019.

WBOC. Pocomoke High School. "Pocomoke High School Mike Roberts 1991." YouTube. 4:14.
   https://www.youtube.com/watch?v=f-qcbNYwydY

"Pocomoke Native Patrick "Big Pat" Doughty Tells About His Journey to Becoming an NBA Announcer."
   Delmarva Life. Feb. 10, 2016. https://bit.ly/3fYtig9.

Porter, Karra. *Mad Seasons*. University of Nebraska Press. 2006.

Pluto, Terry. *Loose Balls: The Short, Wild Life of the American Basketball Association.* Simon and Schuster. 1990.

Pred21. "1993 NBA Draft." YouTube. 2:00:01. https://www.youtube.com/watch?v=_H6-FuXUfNo.

Robertson, Jimmy. "Finding His Future." Hokie Sports. Nov. 23, 2020.
 https://hokiesports.com/news/2020/11/23/mens-basketball-finding-his-future.aspx.

Rhodes, Jason. *Images of America: Somerset County.* Arcadia Publishing. 2012.

Robbins, Danny. "Bliss planned cover-up." *Fort Worth Star-Telegram*, Aug. 16, 2003.

Ryan, Dave. "C-SDHS names 2016 Hall of Fame players." *The Dorchester Banner*, Aug. 4, 2016.

"Salisbury names Gladding women's basketball coach." *The Morning News (Wilmington, Delaware)*, April 4, 1985.

Sadur, Julian. "From Pocomoke to the NBA." WMDT.com. Jan. 17, 2016.
 https://www.wmdt.com/2016/01/from-pocomoke-to-the-nba/

Sanchez, Mark W. "Chilling audio of disgraced hoops coach trying to smear murdered player."
 The New York Post, March 28, 2017. https://bit.ly/3xEddSV.

Schramm, Earl. "Good Prospects on Duke Freshman Squad." *News and Observer*, Jan. 19, 1957.

Simmonds, John. "Warriors Pin Chances on Nate, Barry." *Oakland Tribune.* March 24, 1970.

Smith, Hendrick. "Martial Law Is Imposed In Cambridge, Md., Riots." *The New York Times*, July 13, 1963.

"Snow Hill High School Basketball Team Wins." *Democratic Messenger*, April 21, 1917.

"Snow Hill Girls Win the Basket Ball League Cup." *Democratic Messenger*, May 20, 1916.

"Snow Hillers Trim Pocomoke." *Democratic Messenger*, May 26, 1917.

Soper, Shawn. "Decatur's 1970 Title Team To Be Honored." *The Dispatch (Ocean City, Maryland)*, Jan. 30, 2020.

Soper, Shawn. "Local Legend To Restore Berlin Basketball." *The Dispatch (Ocean City, Maryland)*, Oct. 25, 2018.

The Star Democrat. Easton, Maryland. 1954-2019.

"Stars Re-Sign Miss Gwyn, Acquire Another Center." *The New York Times*, Oct. 10, 1979.

"Stephen Decatur High School Retires Local Legend's Jersey." WBOC.com. Sept. 24, 2008. https://bit.ly/3lXPxql.

Stump, Brice. "Wi-High's coach Butch Waller continues to do it the right way." *The Salisbury Independent*, Feb. 19, 2021.

"SPORTS PEOPLE; Skip Wise Surrenders." *The New York Times*, Nov. 23, 1983.

Sports Reference LLC. Basketball-Reference.com - Basketball Statistics and History.
https://www.basketball-reference.com/.

"Talbot Historical Society Project Rewind: Time to Play Ball." TalbotSpy.com. Jan. 24, 2020.
https://bit.ly/2XdZFRy.

"Thousands Mourn Snow Hill Teacher, Coach." *The Dispatch (Ocean City, Maryland)*, Sept. 16, 2010.

Trecker, Jerry. "Mouring Gives It Best Shot." *The Hartford Courant*, June 10, 2003.

Wallace, Carol. "So you want to be a Star!" *New York Daily News*, Feb. 24, 1980.

The Washington Post. Washington, D.C. 1978-2014.

"Warriors Discover A 'Nugget.'" *The San Francisco Examiner*, Sept. 19, 1970.

Whiteside, Larry. "Sonics burn frigid Celtics." *The Boston Globe*, March 3, 1975.

Wilco, Daniel. "What we know about the first college basketball game ever played." NCAA.com. Jan. 11, 2019.
https://bit.ly/2UaFMJY.

Wise, Mike. "College Basketball; Death and Deception." *The New York Times*, Aug. 28, 2003.

Wise, Mike. "Showtime documentary 'Disgraced' resurfaces story of murdered player at Baylor." The Undefeated.
March 31, 2017. https://bit.ly/3AAJs7s.

Zapcic, Bill. "Tatterson's a Real Gem." *The Daily Register*, Feb. 4, 1979.

ABOUT THE AUTHOR

Mitchell Northam grew up on the Eastern Shore in Federalsburg and graduated from Colonel Richardson High School, Wor-Wic Community College, and Salisbury University. His work has been featured at WUNC, the Atlanta Journal-Constitution, SB Nation, NCAA.com, the Orlando Sentinel, the Associated Press, The Next, Sports Illustrated, InsideMDSports, Pittsburgh Sports Now, and the Delmarva Daily Times. He is a member of the U.S. Basketball Writers Association and a voter in the AP Top 25 Poll for women's college basketball. He lives in North Carolina with his wife Rachel and their cat, Clementine.

This is his first book. You can follow him on Twitter, @primetimeMitch.

COVER ART (AND CREDIT)
BACK, TOP, LEFT TO RIGHT: Talvin Skinner (Maryland Eastern Shore Athletics), Nick Purnell (Mitchell Northam), Kim Horsey (UT Chattanooga Athletics).
FRONT, TOP, LEFT TO RIGHT: Tia Jackson and Barbara McCool (Mardela yearbooks), Butch Waller (Mitchell Northam), Sherron Mills (VCU Athletics).
FRONT, BOTTOM, LEFT TO RIGHT: Levi Fontaine (Maryland Eastern Shore Athletics), Merrill Morgan (Colonel Richardson yearbooks), Kelley Gibson (Maryland Athletics).
Author Photo by Shelton Hawkins.

ABOUT THE BOOK

From Kent County down to Pocomoke City, the Eastern Shore of Maryland has a deep history of successful coaches, talented players and championship-winning teams. Explore nearly a century's worth of games and seasons as the region has fought for respect on the hardwood. Dive deep into teams like the 1952 tourist town boys from Ocean City and the great squads of Moton High School, and players like Stephen Decatur's Keve Aluma, an All-ACC selection at Virginia Tech. Using extensive research and dozens of original interviews, Shore native and sportswriter Mitchell Northam chronicles the Women's Professional Basketball League days of Gail Tatterson Gladding, the rise and fall of Carlton Dotson, and the careers of basketball lifers like Butch Waller, David Byrd and Tia Jackson.

The Hall of Fame Boulevard exhibit was constructed at the Wicomico Youth & Civic Center by Shelton Hawkins, Devon Beck, Andrew Davis and others ahead of the 2021 Governor's Challenge, which was canceled due to COVID-19. Photo by Mitchell Northam.

www.ingramcontent.com/pod-product-compliance
Lightning Source LLC
Chambersburg PA
CBHW050849160426
43194CB00011B/2087